Arista Warrior

Gary A. Donahue

Beijing · Cambridge · Farnham · Köln · Sebastopol · Tokyo

Arista Warrior

by Gary A. Donahue

Copyright © 2013 Gary Donahue. All rights reserved.

Printed in the United States of America.

Published by O'Reilly Media, Inc., 1005 Gravenstein Highway North, Sebastopol, CA 95472.

O'Reilly books may be purchased for educational, business, or sales promotional use. Online editions are also available for most titles (*http://my.safaribooksonline.com*). For more information, contact our corporate/institutional sales department: 800-998-9938 or *corporate@oreilly.com*.

Editors: Mike Loukides and Meghan Blanchette	**Proofreader:** Kiel Van Horn
Production Editor: Kristen Borg	**Indexer:** Angela Howard
Copyeditor: Absolute Services, Inc.	**Cover Designer:** Karen Montgomery
	Interior Designer: David Futato
	Illustrator: Robert Romano

October 2012:   First Edition

Revision History for the First Edition:

2012-10-03   First release

See *http://oreilly.com/catalog/errata.csp?isbn=9781449314538* for release details.

ISBN: 978-1-449-31453-8

[LSI]

For my mother
Joyce A. Grier
November 18, 1931 – July 20, 2012
http://www.gad.net/mother
We all miss you.

Table of Contents

Preface

The examples used in this book are taken from my own experiences, as well as from the experiences of those with or for whom I have had the pleasure of working. Of course, for obvious legal and honorable reasons, the exact details and any information that might reveal the identities of the other parties involved have been changed.

Who Should Read This Book

This book is not an Arista manual. I will not go into the details of every permutation of every command, nor will I go into painful detail of default timers, or counters, or priorities, or any of that boring stuff. The purpose of this book is to get you up and running with an Arista switch, or even a data center full of them. What's more, this book aims to explain Arista-specific features in great detail; however, it may not go into such detail on other topics such as explaining VLANs, routers, and how to configure NTP, since I've covered those topics at length in *Network Warrior*. I will go into detail if a topic is being introduced here that wasn't covered in *Network Warrior*, such as Multiple Spanning Tree (MST), or VRRP. Where possible, I have concentrated on what makes Arista switches great. In short, if you want to learn about networking, pick up *Network Warrior*. If you want to know why Arista is stealing market share from all the other networking equipment vendors, buy this book.

This book is intended for use by anyone familiar with networking, likely from a Cisco environment, who is interested in learning more about Arista switches. Anyone with a CCNA or equivalent (or greater) knowledge should benefit from this book, but the person who will get the most from this book is the entrenched admin, engineer, or architect who has been tasked with building an Arista network. My goal in writing *Arista Warrior* is to explain complex ideas in an easy-to-understand manner. I've taught a few classes on Arista switches, and I see trepidation and fear of the unknown in students when the class begins. By the end of the class, I have students asking when Arista will go public, and if I can get them Arista T-shirts (I don't know, and I can't, but thanks for your emails!). I hope you will find this book similarly informative.

As I wrote in *Network Warrior*, I have noticed over the years that people in the computer, networking, and telecom industries are often misinformed about the basics of these disciplines. I believe that in many cases, this is the result of poor teaching or the use of reference material that does not convey complex concepts well. With this book, I hope to show people how easy some of these concepts are. Of course, as I like to say, "It's easy when you know how," so I have tried very hard to help anyone who picks up my book understand the ideas contained herein.

Let's be brutally honest, most technology books suck. What drew me to O'Reilly in the first place is that almost all of them don't. From the feedback I've received over the years since first writing *Network Warrior*, it has become clear to me that many of my readers agree. I hope that this book is as easy to read as my previous works.

My goal, as always, is to make your job easier. Where applicable, I will share details of how I've made horrible mistakes in order to help you avoid them. Sure, I could pretend that I've never made any such mistakes, but anyone who knows me will happily tell you how untrue that would be. Besides, stories make technical books more fun, so dig in, read on, and enjoy watching me fail.

This book is similar in style to *Network Warrior*, with the obvious exception that there is no (well, very little, really) Cisco content. In some cases I include examples that might seem excessive, such as showing the output from a command's help option. My assumption is that people don't have Arista switches sitting around that they can play with. This is a bit different than the Cisco world, where you can pick up an old switch on the Internet for little money. Arista is a relatively new company, and finding used Arista switches will probably be tough. Hopefully, by including more of what you'd see in an actual Arista switch, this book will help those curious about them.

Lastly, I'd like to explain why I wrote this book. I don't work for Arista, I don't sell Arista gear, and Arista has not paid me to write this book. Some time ago, a client had me do a sort of bake-off between major networking equipment vendors. We brought in all the big names, all of whom said something to the effect of, "We're usually up against Arista in this space!" Because every one of the other vendors inadvertently recommended Arista, we contacted them, got some test gear, and went out to visit their California office.

I've been in IT for almost 30 years, and I've been doing networking for 25. I'm jaded, I'm grouchy, and I distrust everything I read. I've seen countless new ideas reveal themselves as a simple rehashing of something we did with mainframes. I've seen countless IT companies come and go, and I've been disappointed by more pieces of crappy hardware with crappy operating systems than most people can name. I've been given job offers by the biggest names in the business, and turned them all down. Why? Because big names mean nothing to me aside from the possibility of another notch added to my resume.

Nothing impresses me, nothing surprises me, and nothing gets past me. But when I walked out of Arista after three days of meeting with everyone from the guys who write the code to the CEO and founders themselves, I was impressed. Not only impressed, but excited! I'm not easily sold, but I walked out of there a believer, and in the short years since that first introduction, nothing has caused me to change my perception of Arista and their excellent equipment.

When I started writing, there were no Arista books out there. I felt that I could write one that people would enjoy, while doing justice to the Arista way of doing things. As you read this book, I hope that you'll get a feel for what that way is.

Though I'm obviously a fan, these devices are not perfect. I'll show you where I've found issues, and where there might be *gotchas*. That's the benefit of me not being paid by Arista—I'll tell it like it is. To be honest though, in my experience, Arista would tell you the very same things, which is what first impressed me about them. That's why I wrote this book. It's easy for me to write when I believe in the subject matter.

Enough blather—let's get to it!

Conventions Used in This Book

The following typographical conventions are used in this book:

Italic

> Used for new terms where they are defined, for emphasis, and for URLs

`Constant width`

> Used for commands, output from devices as it is seen on the screen, and samples of Request for Comments (RFC) documents reproduced in the text

`Constant width italic`

> Used to indicate arguments within commands for which you should supply values

`Constant width bold`

> Used for commands to be entered by the user and to highlight sections of output from a device that have been referenced in the text or are significant in some way

> Indicates a tip, suggestion, or general note

Indicates a warning or caution

Using Code Examples

This book is here to help you get your job done. In general, you may use the code in this book in your programs and documentation. You do not need to contact us for permission unless you're reproducing a significant portion of the code. For example, writing a program that uses several chunks of code from this book does not require permission. Selling or distributing a CD-ROM of examples from O'Reilly books does require permission. Answering a question by citing this book and quoting example code does not require permission. Incorporating a significant amount of example code from this book into your product's documentation does require permission.

We appreciate, but do not require, attribution. An attribution usually includes the title, author, publisher, and ISBN. For example: "*Arista Warrior* by Gary A. Donahue. Copyright 2013 Gary A. Donahue, 978-1-449-31453-8."

If you feel your use of code examples falls outside fair use or the permission given above, feel free to contact us at *permissions@oreilly.com*.

Safari® Books Online

Safari Books Online (*www.safaribooksonline.com*) is an on-demand digital library that delivers expert content in both book and video form from the world's leading authors in technology and business.

Technology professionals, software developers, web designers, and business and creative professionals use Safari Books Online as their primary resource for research, problem solving, learning, and certification training.

Safari Books Online offers a range of product mixes and pricing programs for organizations, government agencies, and individuals. Subscribers have access to thousands of books, training videos, and prepublication manuscripts in one fully searchable database from publishers like O'Reilly Media, Prentice Hall Professional, Addison-Wesley Professional, Microsoft Press, Sams, Que, Peachpit Press, Focal Press, Cisco Press, John Wiley & Sons, Syngress, Morgan Kaufmann, IBM Redbooks, Packt, Adobe Press, FT Press, Apress, Manning, New Riders, McGraw-Hill, Jones & Bartlett, Course Technology, and dozens more. For more information about Safari Books Online, please visit us online.

How to Contact Us

Please address comments and questions concerning this book to the publisher:

O'Reilly Media, Inc.
1005 Gravenstein Highway North
Sebastopol, CA 95472
800-998-9938 (in the United States or Canada)
707-829-0515 (international or local)
707-829-0104 (fax)

We have a web page for this book, where we list errata, examples, and any additional information. You can access this page at *http://oreil.ly/arista-warrior*.

To comment or ask technical questions about this book, send email to *bookques tions@oreilly.com*.

For more information about our books, courses, conferences, and news, see our website at *http://www.oreilly.com*.

Find us on Facebook: *http://facebook.com/oreilly*

Follow us on Twitter: *http://twitter.com/oreillymedia*

Watch us on YouTube: *http://www.youtube.com/oreillymedia*

Acknowledgments

Writing a book is hard work—far harder than I ever imagined. Though I spent countless hours alone in front of a keyboard, I could not have accomplished the task without the help of many others.

I would like to thank my lovely wife, Lauren, for being patient, loving, and supportive. Thank you for helping me achieve another goal in my life.

I would like to thank Meghan and Colleen for trying to understand that when I was writing, I couldn't play video games, go geocaching, or do other fun things. Thanks also for sitting with me for endless hours in Starbucks while I wrote. I hope I've helped instill in you a sense of perseverance by completing this book. If not, you can be sure that I'll use it as an example for the rest of your lives. I love you both "bigger than Cozy" bunches.

I would like to thank my mother, because she's my mom and because she never gave up on me, always believed in me, and always helped me even when she shouldn't have. We miss you.

I would like to thank my father for being tough on me when he needed to be, for teaching me how to think logically, and for making me appreciate the beauty in the details. I have fond memories of the two of us sitting in front of my RadioShack Model III computer while we entered basic programs from a magazine. I am where I am today largely because of your influence, direction, and teachings. You made me the man I am today. Thank you, Papa. I miss you.

This book would not have been possible without the significant help from the following people at Arista Networks: Mark Berly, Andre Pech, Dave Twinam, Brad Danitz, Nick Giampa, Doug Gourlay, and Kevin McCabe. I'd also like to personally thank Jayshree Ullal, CEO of Arista, for allowing me access to some of the Arista equipment used for examples in this book. This book would simply not have been possible without all of your time and generosity.

A special word of thanks is needed for Mark Berly. I met with Mark many times, and probably emailed him 30 times a day for six months. It takes a special kind of person to tolerate me in the first place, but putting up with my nonstop questions takes someone who is either as nuts as I am, or who really loves the subject at hand, or both. Thank you for taking the time to answer my many hundreds of questions. This book would have sucked without your many helpful insights.

I would like to thank Craig Gleason for his considerable help with VMware and for putting up with my many ridiculous questions on the subject. The sections containing VMware references would not have been possible without your help and enthusiasm.

I would like to especially thank Glenn Bradley with his help designing and implementing my secret underground bunker. An entire chapter of this book would literally have not been possible without your help. You also get special recognition for finding an error in the 2nd edition of *Network Warrior* that made it through two editions, two technical editors, countless edits, and five years of public scrutiny. Not bad. Not bad at all.

I'd like to thank Bill Turner for always delivering what I needed without asking too many questions. May your cowboy changes never cause an outage.

Once again, I would like to thank Michael Heuberger, Helge Brummer, Doug Kemp, and the rest of the team in North Carolina for allowing me the chance to annoy and entertain them all on a daily basis. Oh, and Jimmy Lovelace, too; just because I know he'll love to see his name here.

I would like to thank my editors, Mike Loukides for initially approving the project, and Meghan (with an h!) Blanchette, for dealing with my quirks on an almost daily basis.

I would like to thank all the wonderful people at O'Reilly. Writing this book was a great experience, due in large part to the people I worked with at O'Reilly. This is my third project with O'Reilly, and it just never stops being great.

I would like to thank my good friend, John Tocado, who hopefully by now already knows why. Thank you.

I still wish to thank everyone else who has given me encouragement. Living and working with a writer must, at times, be maddening. Under the burden of deadlines, I've no doubt been cranky, annoying, and frustrating, for which I apologize.

My main drive for the last few months has been the completion of this book. All other responsibilities, with the exception of health, family, and work, took a backseat to my goal. Realizing this book's publication is a dream come true for me. You may have dreams yourself, for which I can offer only this one bit of advice: Work toward your goals and you will realize them. It really is that simple.

Remember the tree, for the mighty oak is simply a nut that stood its ground.

A Quick Note About Versions

When I started writing this book, EOS version 4.8.3 was the state-of-the art release from Arista. As I continued writing over the course of about a year, new versions of code came out. As a result, there are a variety of code revisions used in this book ranging from 4.8.3 to 4.10, which was released after the first draft of the book was finished.

While I would have loved to have gone back and updated all the examples to reflect the latest code, I simply ran out of time. Where there were significant changes or new features added, I made sure to use the latest code. In some cases, part of the chapter shows examples from one rev, while another part shows a different rev. I apologize in advance if this confuses anyone, but I really don't think there should be any issues because the tech reviewers were great about pointing out where I needed to update my examples.

In my defense, the Arista team works so hard on releasing killer new versions of code that I had a hard enough time keeping up with new features, most of which I'm happy to say were included in this book. Hopefully, when I get to write *Arista Warrior* 2nd edition, I'll get the opportunity to go through the entire book and update every example to the latest rev of EOS.

A Quick Note About Code Examples

In many of the examples involving code, I've had to slightly alter the output in order to make it fit within the margins of this book. I've taken great pains to not alter the meaningful output, but rather to only alter the format. For example, in the output of show top, the output includes lines that say something to the effect of:

```
last five minutes: 18.1%, last five seconds 3.1%.
```

In order to make the example fit, I might alter this to read:

```
last five mis: 18%, last five secs 3%.
```

Any changes I've made will in no way alter the point of the output, but the output may look slightly different than what you may see on your screen if you run the same command. In some cases, such as the output of tcpdump, I've simply changed the point in which the line wraps from, say, 80 columns to 70. Again, this should only have the effect of possibly making the output look different than what you would see when using a terminal emulator without such restrictions.

## CHAPTER 1

Why Arista?

If you're reading this book, you've got an interest in Arista products for any number of reasons. My goal is for you to understand why Arista is here, why they should be taken seriously, and why their switches are selling like crazy. So let's get started by explaining how it all began.

A Brief History of Arista

Arista Networks is a successful networking equipment company that's only been around since 2005. It takes something special to succeed in an industry dominated by well-entrenched companies, many of which have been on top for decades. Certainly a good product is needed, but that product and everything it takes to produce it comes from people. The people are what make Arista great. Please indulge me while I give you a quick tour of some of the key players at Arista, because having met many of them, I firmly believe that these people infect everyone around them with the same attitudes, excitement, and belief in what they're doing.

Key Players

There are three people responsible for the creation of Arista Networks: Andy Bechtolsheim, David Cheriton, and Ken Duda. Allow me to explain who these people are, so that you might get an idea of what sort of company Arista is.

Andy Bechtolsheim

Andy Bechtolsheim co-founded a company called Sun Microsystems in 1982. You may have heard of them. In 1995, he left Sun to found a company called Granite Systems. This new company made its mark by developing (then) state-of-the art high-speed network switches. In 1995, Cisco acquired Granite Systems for a cool $220 million. With the sale, Andy became Vice President and General Manager of the Gigabit Systems

Business Unit, where he stayed until 2003. He left Cisco in December of that year to found Kealia, Inc., with a Stanford professor named David Cheriton. Kealia was later acquired by Sun Microsystems, where Andy returned to the role of Senior Vice President and Chief Architect. In 2005, Andy co-founded Arastra, which later changed its name to Arista Networks.

Andy has an M.S. in Computer Engineering from Carnegie Mellon University, and a Ph.D. from Stanford University.

Andy Bechtolsheim is a multibillionaire Silicon Valley visionary. He has either designed or had a hand in the creation of some of the most significant computing and networking devices of the past 30 years. Andy and David Cheriton were the two initial investors in Google. Each of their $100,000 investments are now worth, well, let's just say they made their money back and then some.

David Cheriton

David Cheriton is a Stanford University computer science professor who has an amazing knack for spotting and investing in successful startups. David co-founded Granite Systems with Andy Bechtolsheim, and the two have started other successful companies including the aforementioned Kealia. David served as a technical advisor for Cisco for seven years, and was the Chief Architect for the ASICs used in the Catalyst 4000s and 4500s. He has also served as a technical advisor for companies such as Sun, VMware, and Google. David is one of the original founders of Arastra, later renamed Arista Networks. He is now the Chief Scientist for Arista.

David has multiple inventions and patents to his name, has a Ph.D. in Computer Science from the University of Waterloo, and has been at Stanford since 1981.

Given the track record of Andy and David, and the fact that these two men funded the new company without any other investors, it would seem that Arista is destined for greatness, but the story doesn't stop there.

Ken Duda

Ken Duda is a founder, Chief Technology Officer, and Senior Vice President of Software Engineering at Arista. Prior to founding Arastra (now Arista), Ken was CTO of There.com, where he designed a real-time 3-D distributed system that scaled to thousands of simultaneous users. I have no idea what that means, but it sure sounds cool.

Ken was the first employee of Granite Systems, and while working at Cisco, led the development of the Catalyst 4000 product line.

Ken has three simultaneous engineering degrees from MIT, and a Ph.D. in Computer Science from Stanford University.

Much of what you will read in this book about EOS is a result of Ken Duda's vision. I met Ken while visiting Arista (along with many of the other people mentioned in this chapter), and within minutes, I realized that he was living the dream. Well, to be fair, maybe it was my dream, but what I saw was a seriously smart guy, who knew *the right way to do it*, and who had the freedom to do just that. I may be a hack writer now, but I went to school for programming (COBOL on punch cards, thank you very much), and loved being a programmer (we weren't called developers back then). I gave up programming because I got tired of having to fix other people's crappy code. I wanted to write amazing new systems, but companies weren't looking for that—they wanted grunts to fix their crappy code.

Ken not only gets to write the kind of code he likes, but he gets to design an entire networking equipment operating system from the ground up. When I was there, I drilled him with questions. Wouldn't that delay delivery? Wouldn't investors complain? Didn't you ever get rushed into finishing something early to be first to market? As he answered my questions, it all started to become clear to me. There were no crazy investors demanding artificial deadlines. These guys had decided to do it the right way, and not to deviate from that course. I also realized that everyone at Arista felt the same way. It was my meeting with Ken Duda that started the idea in my mind to write this book. Someone had to tell the world that companies like this could thrive, because in my almost 30 years in this industry, I can tell you that Arista is the first company I've seen that *does it the right way*.

Jayshree Ullal

The three founders certainly set the direction for Arista as a whole, but Jayshree keeps the place running. Jayshree Ullal is the President and CEO of Arista Networks. She was Senior Vice President at Cisco, where she was responsible for Data Center Switching and Services, including the Cisco Nexus 7000, the Catalyst 4500, and the Catalyst 6500 product lines. She was responsible for $10 billion in revenue, and reported directly to John Chambers, CEO of Cisco.

Jayshree has a B.S. in electrical engineering from San Francisco State University, and an M.S. in engineering management from Santa Clara University.

Jayshree was named one of the "50 Most Powerful People" in 2005 by *Network World Magazine*, and one of the "Top Ten Executives" at VMWorld in 2011. She has garnered many awards, including one of the 20 "Women to Watch in 2001" by *Newsweek* magazine.

I can hear you now saying, "blah blah blah, I could read this on Wikipedia." But consider this: Arista is a company peopled by mad scientists who just happen to work in legitimate jobs doing good work. Jayshree keeps them all in line, and keeps the business not only humming, but also prospering. Having managed teams and departments of both developers and engineers, I know what a challenge it can be. She makes it look easy.

All of these people are powerful forces in the networking and IT worlds, and all of them manage to make time to meet with prospective customers and even speak during classes held onsite at Arista. I've been in both situations, and have seen this for myself.

I'm a successful, self-employed consultant who moonlights as a writer for no other reason than I like to write. I haven't wanted to work for anyone but myself for years, maybe even decades; I've been to Arista's headquarters in California multiple times, and each time I left, I felt like I should have gone back and begged for a job. There's something special happening there, and these people are all at the heart of it.

You can read more about Arista and the management team at Arista's website (*http://www.aristanetworks.com/en/company/corporate-profile*).

The Needs of a Data Center

So what's the big deal about data centers? Why do they need special switches anyway? Can't we just use the same switches we use in the office? Hell, can't we just go to Staples and buy some Linksys or Netgears, or D-Links or something?

Believe it or not, I've had this very conversation on more than one occasion with executives looking to save some money on their data center builds. While it may be obvious to me, I quickly learned that it's not apparent to everyone why data centers are unique.

Data centers are usually designed for critical systems that require high availability. That means redundant power, efficient cooling, secure access, and a pile of other things, but most of all, it means no single points of failure.

Every device in a data center should have dual power supplies, and each one of those power supplies should be fed from discrete power feeds. All devices in a data center should have front-to-back airflow, or ideally, airflow that can be configured front to back or back to front. All devices in a data center should support the means to upgrade, replace, or shut down any single chassis at any time without interruption to the often-extreme Service Level Agreements (SLAs). In-Service Software Upgrades (ISSU) should also be available, but this can be circumvented by properly distributing load to allow meeting the prior requirement. Data center devices should offer robust hardware, even NEBS compliance where required, and robust software to match.

While data center switches should be able to deliver all of those features, they should also not be loaded down with features that are not desired in the data center. Examples of superfluous features might include Power Over Ethernet, backplane stacking, VoIP Gateway features, Wireless LAN Controller functions, and other generally office-specific features.

Note that this last paragraph greatly depends on what's being housed in the data center. If the data center is designed to house all the IT equipment for a large office, then PoE and WAN Controllers might be desirable. Really though, in a proper data center, those functions should be housed in proper dual power supply devices dedicated to the desired tasks.

While stacked switches seem like a great way to lower management points and increase port density, you may find that switches that support such features often don't have the fabric speed or feature set to adequately support a data center environment. I've made a lot of money swapping out closet switches for Cisco Nexus and Arista 7000 switches in data centers. Data centers are always more resilient when using real data center equipment. If you don't pay to put them in from the start, you'll pay even more to swap them in later.

Data Center Networking

VMware really shook up the data center world with the introduction of Vmotion. With Vmotion, virtual machines can be migrated from one physical box to another, without changing IP addresses and without bringing the server offline. I have to admit, that's pretty cool.

The problem is that in order to accomplish this, the source and destination servers must reside in the same VLANs. That usually means having VLANs spanning across physical locations, which is just about the polar opposite of what we've spent the last 20 years trying to move away from!

In the past few years, a pile of technologies have surfaced to try to address this issue, from the open standard TRILL, to 802.1aq (Shortest Path Bridging), to Cisco's OTV, and even VXLAN. They all have their benefits, and they all have their (often severe) drawbacks. During that time, some standards have developed around something called Data Center Bridging, which aims to (among other things) make the Vmotion issue a little bit easier to cope with. Features such as priority-based flow control, Fiber Channel over Ethernet (FCoE), and others are also a consideration with data center bridging. Though there is no widely accepted standard as of mid-2012, data center switches should support, or have the ability to support, at least a subset of these technologies. If your executive comes in and says that you need to support some new whizbang data center technology because he read about it in *CIO magazine* on the john that morning, having a data center full of closet switches will mean a rough conversation about how he bought the wrong gear.

The Case for Low Latency

Low latency may seem like a solution in need of a problem if you're used to dealing with email and web servers, but in some fields, microseconds mean millions: millions of dollars, that is.

I talk about trading floors later on in this book, and some of Arista's biggest customers use Arista switches in order to execute trades faster than their competitors. But think about other environments where microseconds translate into tangible benefits. Environments such as computer animation studios that may spend 80 to 90 hours rendering a single frame for a blockbuster movie, or scientific compute farms that might involve tens of thousands of compute cores. If the network is the bottleneck within those massive computer arrays, the overall performance is affected. And imagine the impact that an oversubscribed network might have on such farms. I've never had the pleasure of working in such environments, but I can imagine that dropping packets would be frowned upon.

Sure, those systems require some serious networking, but you might be surprised how much latency can affect more common applications. iSCSI doesn't tolerate dropped packets well, nor does it tolerate a lot of buffering. Heck, even NAS, which can tolerate dropped packets, is often used for systems and applications that do not tolerate latency well. Couple that with the way that most NAS are designed (many hosts to one filer), and things like buffering become a huge issue. Not only have I seen closet switches fail miserably in such environments, I've seen many data center class switches fail too.

Network-Based Storage

The NAS protocol was developed in the early 1980s as a means for university students to share porn between systems. OK, I totally made that up, but I'd be willing to bet that it was one of the first widespread uses of the technology. NAS really was developed in the early 1980s though, and although it's come a long way, it was not designed to be a solution for low-latency, high-throughput storage. NAS was designed to be used over IP, and often uses TCP for reliability. Compared with more low-level solutions such as FibreChannel, NAS is slow and inefficient.

Still, NAS is comparatively inexpensive, doesn't require special hardware on the server side, and many vendors offer specialized NAS solutions aimed at centralizing storage needs for scores, if not hundreds of servers. NAS is a reality in the modern data center, and the networks that NAS rides on must be robust, offer low latency, and whenever possible, not drop packets. Even with non-blocking 10 Gb architectures, it can be easy to oversubscribe the 10 Gbps links to the NAS devices if many servers make simultaneous 10 Gbps reads or writes.

Arista Delivers

So how does Arista deal with the requirements outlined in this chapter? Here's a short list to whet your appetite. Each one of these topics is covered in detail within this book, so here I'll just supply a list with a brief explanation of each feature and a reference to the chapter in which the topic is covered in more detail.

Hardware

Arista switches all have dual power supplies, hot swappable and reversible airflow fans, completely non-blocking fabrics (even the eight-slot chassis switches!), and merchant silicon. In almost every case, they are physically smaller, weigh less, consume less power, and often cost less than comparable switches from other manufacturers; although as you'll come to learn, there really are no other switches that compare. See Chapter 5 for details on the Arista product offerings. Sure they may make great hardware, but the real difference is in the operating systems.

EOS

The Extensible Operating System (EOS) offers an industry standard CLI while offering the power, flexibility, and expandability of Linux. Man, what a mouthful of marketing buzzwords that is. Let's cut the BS and tell it like it is: EOS is Linux, with a Cisco-like CLI. Actually, even that barely tells the whole story. Arista switches run Linux. They don't run some stripped down version of Linux that's been altered beyond recognition—they run Linux. Some other vendors say that their OS is based on Linux, and I guess it is, but on an Arista switch, you can drop down into the *bash* shell and kill processes if you're so inclined. Hell, you can even spawn another CLI session from bash, write scripts that contain CLI commands, send email from CLI, pipe bash commands through CLI, and a host of other exciting things, all because the switch runs Linux and because the programmers care about one thing above all else: doing things the right way.

Arista hardware is amazing, but EOS makes these devices profoundly different than any other vendor's offerings.

Bash

OK, so I blew the surprise with my EOS fan-boy ravings, but yes, you can issue the bash command from CLI and enter the world of Linux. It's not a Linux simulator either – it's bash, in Linux. You can even execute the `sudo shutdown -r now` command if you want, and you know you want to. All your other favorite Linux commands are there too: `ps`, `top`, `grep`, `more`, `less`, `vi`, `cat`, `tar`, `gunzip`, and `python` just to name a few. But not `perl`. Unless you want to add it, in which case you can, because it's Linux.

The fact that these switches run Linux is such a big deal that I recommend learning Linux to my clients when they're considering Arista switches. Of course the beauty of EOS is that you don't have to know Linux thanks to the CLI, but trust me when I say you'll be able to get much more out of your Arista switches with some good Linux experience.

SysDB

SysDB is one of the main features that makes EOS and Arista switches great. Simply put, SysDB is a database on the switch that holds all of the critical counters, status, and state information necessary for processes to run. The processes read and write this information to and/or from SysDB instead of storing it locally. If another process needs the information, it gets it from SysDB. Thus, processes never need to talk to each other; they communicate through SysDB. This dramatically lowers the possibility of one process negatively affecting another. Additionally, if a process dies, it can restart quickly without having to reinitialize all values, since it can read them all from SysDB. See Chapter 10 for more information on SysDB.

MLAG

Multichassis Link Aggregation (MLAG) allows port-channels to exist to multiple switches at the same time. Similar to Cisco's VPC, Arista's MLAG is easier to configure and, in my experience, less likely to induce colorful profanity from me during use. Of course your mileage may vary. See Chapter 12 for more detail about MLAG.

VARP

Virtual ARP (VARP) is an amazingly simple idea that allows multiple switches to respond to ARP requests for the same IP. That might sounds like a bad idea, but delve into Chapter 14 to see why it's a pretty cool feature.

LANZ

Data center switches sometimes suffer from a problem known as *microbursting*, wherein the buffers become overrun and drop packets. The problem is that these microbursts happen often at microsecond intervals, so the switches never report them. These problems can be horrific to diagnose, and even worse to try and explain to executives. That is, unless you have an Arista switch with latency analyzer (LANZ). Check out Chapter 20 to see LANZ in action.

VM Tracer

VM Tracer allows an Arista switch to have visibility into the VMware virtual machines connected to it. It also allows the switch to dynamically create and delete VLANs when they are created on the ESX host, thus rendering you, the network admin, completely obsolete. Well, not really obsolete; I mean, someone has to configure VM Tracer, right? To see the truth about the feature that you may never tell the server guys about, check out Chapter 22.

ZTP

Zero Touch Provisioning (ZTP) allows your Arista switch to not only load its configuration from the network, but also from its operating system. What's more, it can download scripts that tell it to do both of those things and more, all without human interaction. To see it in action, take a look at Chapter 25.

Email

Did you know that Arista switches could be configured to send emails? Not only can they send emails, but they can do it from bash, from EOS, and from within scripts. Any command can be piped directly to your inbox on a properly configured Arista switch. Check out Chapter 19 to see how.

Event Scheduler

Yeah, email is cool, but with an Arista switch, you can schedule a job that will email the status of an interface to you every five minutes. Hell, you could configure your Arista switch to email a message with the subject of "I love Arista switches!" to John Chambers every hour if you'd like, but I don't recommend it. Seriously, don't do that. But check out Chapter 23 to see how; you know, for research.

TCP Dump

You can run *tcpdump* from bash or EOS, and it captures every packet on an interface that is destined for, or sourced, from the CPU of the switch. You could probably pipe the output to email, but I wouldn't recommend that either. See Chapter 24 for details on how to use *tcpdump*.

Event Handler

Event handler lets you configure triggers on your switch that will execute a command when activated. You could trigger an email to your phone every time the switch boots, or you could configure the switch to send you the output of show log last 2 minutes to your email when a specified interface goes up or down. Take a look at Chapter 26 for details.

Event Monitor

Event Monitor records every add, change, and/or deletion of ARP, MAC, and route entries on your switch to a database. You can access the database to produce reports, which can come in very handy when you need to find out what happened, say, yesterday at 6 p.m. when some server you don't care about stopped working. Imagine having a view into what happened on the switch in the past. Now you don't have to imagine! Go read Chapter 27 to see how to make the most of this unique feature.

Extending EOS

Did I mention that Arista switches run Linux? Just like a Linux machine, you can add additional packages that have been written for EOS. These extensions are easy to install, manage, and remove, and in Chapter 28, I'll show you how to do just that.

CloudVision

CloudVision is a feature set that allows for centralized monitoring and management of your network. Currently, this lets you configure your switch (or group of switches) from an instant messenger (IM) client running XMPP, but there will be features available in future releases as well. Configure 100 switches with an IM? Yeah, I'll show you how to do that in Chapter 29.

As you can see, Arista switches can do some pretty interesting things that aren't available on any other switches. Features aside, the OS is written so well and with such attention to detail that even without all the cool features, I think you'll find Arista switches to be a cut above the other vendors' offerings. But enough hype, let's dig in and learn the inner workings of Arista's switches.

## CHAPTER 2

Buffers

When you start talking to vendors about data center switches, you'll start to hear and read about buffers. Some of the vendors have knockdown, drag out fights about these buffers, and often engage in all sorts of half-truths and deceptions to make you believe that their solution is the best. So what is the truth? As with most things, it's not always black and white.

To start, we need to look at the way a switch is built. That starts with the switch fabric.

 The term fabric is used because on large scales, the interconnecting lines look like the weave of fabric. And all this time I thought there was some cool scientific reason.

Imagine a matrix where every port on the switch has a connection for input (ingress) and another for output (egress). If we put all the ingress ports on the left, and all the output ports on top, then interconnect them all, it would look like the drawing in Figure 2-1. In order to make the examples easy to understand, I've constructed a simple, though thoroughly unlikely, three-port switch. The ports are numbered ethernet1, ethernet2, and ethernet3, which are abbreviated e1, e2, and e3.

Looking at the drawing, remember that e1 on the left and e1 on the top are *the same port*. This is very important to understand before moving forward. Remember that modern switch ports are generally full duplex. The drawing simply shows the *ins* on the left and the *outs* on the top. Got it? Good. Let's continue.

First, the fabric allows more than one conversation to occur at a time, provided the ports in each conversation are discrete from the ports in the other conversations. I know, gibberish, right? Bear with me, and all will become clear.

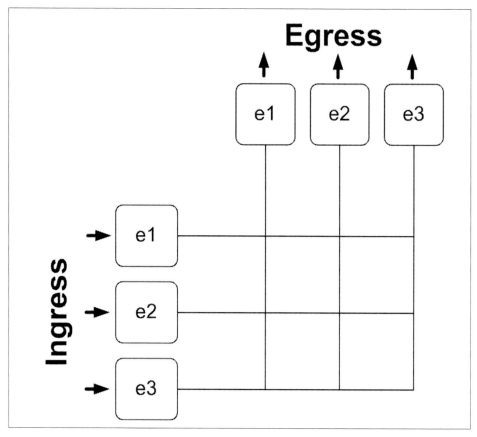

Figure 2-1. Simple switch fabric of a three-port switch

Remember that full duplex means transmit and receive can happen at the same time between two hosts (or ports, in our case). In order to help solidify how the fabric drawing works, take a look at Figure 2-2, where I've drawn up how a full-duplex conversation would look between ports e1 and e2.

Look at how e1's input goes to the point on the fabric where it can traverse to e2's output. Now look at how the same thing is happening so that e2's input can switch to e1's output. This is what a full-duplex conversation between two ports on a switch looks like on the fabric. By the way, you should be honored, because I detest those little line jumpers and haven't used one in probably 10 years. I have a feeling that this chapter is going to irritate my drawing sensibilities, but I'll endure, because I've got deadlines to meet and after staring at the drawings for two hours, I couldn't come up with a better way to illustrate my point.

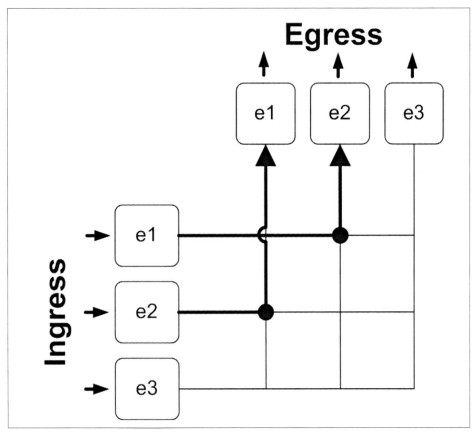

Figure 2-2. Full duplex on a switch fabric

Now that we know what a single port-to-port full duplex conversation looks like, let's consider a more complex scenario. Imagine if you will, that while ports e1 and e2 are happily chattering back and forth without a care in the world, some jackass on e3 wants to talk to e2. Since Ethernet running in full duplex does not listen for traffic before transmitting, e3 just blurts out what he needs to say. Imagine you are having a conversation with your girlfriend on the phone when your kid brother picks up the phone and plays death metal at full volume into the phone. It's like that, but without the heavy distortion, long hair, and tattoos.

Assuming for a moment that the conversation is always on between e1 and e2, when e3 sends its message to e1, what happens? In our simple switch, e3 will detect a collision and drop the packet. Wait a minute, a collision? I thought full-duplex networks didn't have collisions! Full-duplex conversations should not have collisions, but in this case, e3 tried to talk to e2 and e2 was busy. That's a collision. Figure 2-3 shows our collision in action. The kid brother is transmitting on e3, but e2's output port is occupied, so the death metal is dropped. If only it were that simple in real life.

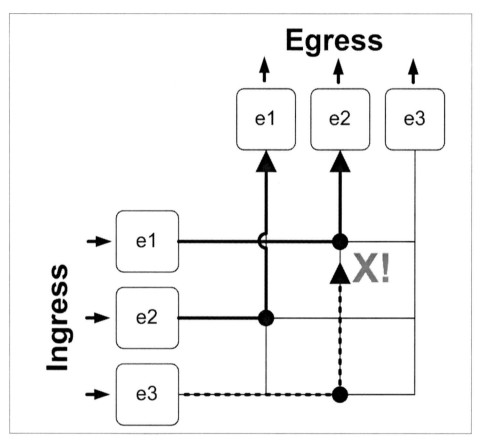

Figure 2-3. Switch fabric collision

If you think that this sounds ridiculous and doesn't happen in the real world, you're almost right. The reason it doesn't seem to happen in the real world, though, is largely because Ethernet conversations are rarely always on, and because of buffers.

In Figure 2-4, I've added input buffers to our simple switch. Now, when port e3 tries to transmit, the switch can detect the collision and buffer the packets until the output port on e2 becomes available. The buffers are like little answering machines for Ethernet packets. Now, when you hang up with your girlfriend, the death metal can be politely delivered in all its loud glory since the output port (you) is available. God bless technology.

This is cool and all, but these input buffers are not without their limitations. Just as an answering machine tape (anyone remember those?) or your voicemail inbox can get full, so too can these buffers. When the buffers get full, packets get dropped. Whether the first packets in the buffer get dropped in favor of buffering the newest packets, or the newest packets get dropped in favor of the older packets is up to the guy who wrote the code.

So if the buffers can get full, thus dropping packets, the solution is to put in bigger buffers, right? Well, yes and no. The first issue is that buffers add latency. Sending packets over the wire is fast. Storing packets into a location in memory, then referencing them and sending them takes time. Memory is also slow, although the memory used in these buffers is much faster than, say computer RAM. It's more like the L2 cache in your CPU, which is fast, but the fact remains that buffering increases latency. Increased latency is usually better than dropped packets, right? As usual, it depends.

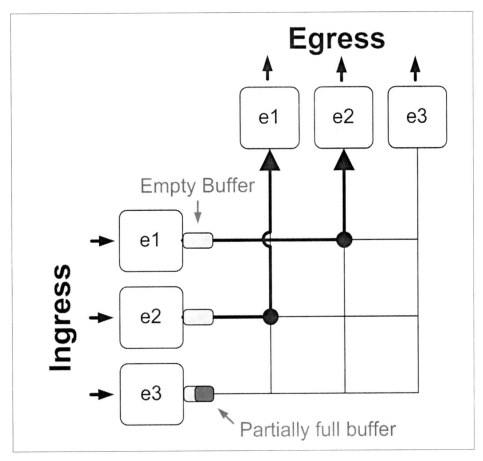

Figure 2-4. Switch fabric with input buffers

Dropped packets might be OK for something like FTP that will retransmit lost packets, but for a UDP-RTP stream like VoIP, increased latency and dropped packets can be disastrous. And what about environments like Wall Street, where microseconds of latency can mean a missed sale opportunity costing millions of dollars? Dropped packets mean retransmissions, which means waiting, but bigger buffers still means waiting—they just mean waiting less. In these cases, bigger buffers aren't always the answer.

In the example I've shown, I started with the assumption that the full-duplex traffic to and from e1 and e2 is always on. This is almost never the case. In reality, Ethernet traffic tends to be very bursty, especially when there are many hosts talking to one device. Consider scenarios like email servers, or even better, NAS towers.

NAS traffic can be unpredictable when looking at network traffic. If you've got 100 servers talking to a single NAS tower, on a single IP address, then the traffic to and from the NAS tower can spike in sudden, drastic ways. This can be a problem in many ways, but one of the most insidious is the *microburst*.

A microburst is a burst that doesn't show up on reporting graphs. Most sampling is done using five-minute averages. If a monitoring system polls the switch every five minutes, then subtracts the number of bytes (or bits, or packets) from the number reported during the last poll, then the resulting graph will only show an average of each five minute interval. Since pictures are worth 1,380 words (adjusted for inflation), let's take a look at what I mean.

In Figure 2-5, I've taken an imaginary set of readings from a network interface. Once, every minute, the switch interface was polled, and the number of bits per second was determined. That number was recorded with a timestamp. If you look at the data, you'll see that once every 6 to 10 minutes or so, the traffic spikes 50 times its normal value. These numbers are pretty small, but the point I'm trying to make is how the reporting tools might reveal this information.

The graph on the top shows each poll, from each minute, and includes a trend line. Note that the trend line is at about 20,000 bits per second on this graph.

Now take a careful look at the bottom graph. In this graph, the data looks very different because instead of including every one-minute poll, I've changed the polling to once every five minutes. In this graph, the data seems much more stable, and doesn't appear to show any sharp spikes. More importantly, though, the trend line seems to be up at around 120,000 bits per second.

This is typical of data being skewed because of the sample rate, and it can be a real problem when the perception doesn't meet reality. The reality is closer to the top graph, but the perception is usually closer to the bottom graph. Even the top graph might be

Time	1 min bps	Time	5 min bps
10:00	2,000	10:05	112,000
10:01	2,000	10:11	134,000
10:02	103,000	10:17	102,000
10:03	2,000	10:23	119,000
10:04	2,000	10:29	112,001
10:05	1,000		
10:06	3,000		
10:07	2,000		
10:08	120,000		
10:09	2,000		
10:10	3,000		
10:11	4,000		
10:12	2,000		
10:13	2,000		
10:14	3,000		
10:15	90,000		
10:16	2,000		
10:17	3,000		
10:18	1,000		
10:19	2,000		
10:20	2,000		
10:21	110,000		
10:22	1,000		
10:23	3,000		
10:24	2,000		
10:25	1,000		
10:26	2,000		
10:27	4,000		
10:28	100,001		
10:29	3,000		
10:30	2,000		

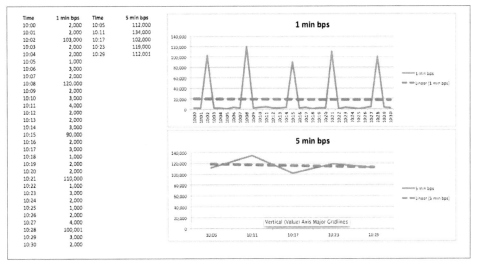

Figure 2-5. Microbursts and averages

wrong, though! Switches operate at the microsecond or even nanosecond level. So what happens when a 10-gigabit interface has 15 gigabits of traffic destined to it, all within a single second or less? Wait, how can a 10-gigabit interface have more than 10-gigabits being sent to it?

Remember the fabric drawing in Figure 2-3? Let's look at that on a larger scale. As referenced earlier, imagine a network with 100 servers talking to a single NAS tower on a single IP address. What happens if, say, 10 of those servers push 5 gigabits per second of traffic to the NAS tower at the same instance in time? The switch port connecting to the NAS switch will send out 10 gigabits per second (since that is the max), and 40 gigabits per second of traffic will be queued.

Network switches are designed to forward packets (frames, to be pedantic) at the highest rate possible. Few devices outside of the networking world can actually send and receive data at the rates the networking devices are capable of sending. In the case of NAS towers, the disks add latency, the processing adds latency, and the OS of the device simply may not be able to deliver a sustained 10 gigabits per second data stream. So what happens when our switch has a metric butt-load of traffic to deliver, and the NAS tower can't accept it fast enough?

If the switch delivers the packets to the output port, but the attached device can't receive them, the packets will again be buffered, but this time as an output queue. Figure 2-6 shows our three-port switch with output buffers added.

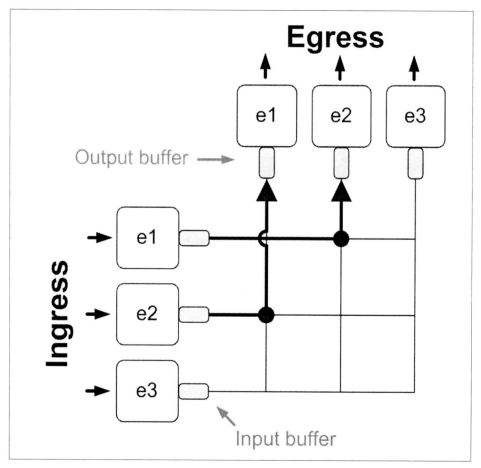

Figure 2-6. Switch fabric with output buffers

As you might imagine, the task of figuring out when traffic can and cannot be sent to and from interfaces can be a complicated affair. It was simple when the interface was either available or not, but with the addition of buffers on both sides, things get more complicated. And this is an extreme simplification. Consider the idea that different flows might have different priorities, and the whole affair becomes even more complicated.

The process of determining when, and if, traffic may be sent to an interface is called *arbitration*. Arbitration is usually managed by an ASIC within the switch, and generally cannot be configured by the end user. Still, when shopping for switches, some of the techniques used in arbitration will come up, and understanding them will help you decide what to buy. Now that we understand why input and output buffers exist, let's take a look at some terms and some of the ways in which traffic is arbitrated within the switch fabric.

FIFO

First In/First Out buffers are those that deliver the oldest packets from the buffer first. When you drive into a tunnel, and the traffic in the tunnel is slow, assuming no change in the traffic patterns within the tunnel, the cars will leave the tunnel in the same order in which they entered: the first car into the tunnel will also be the first car out of the tunnel.

Blocking

Blocking is the term used when traffic cannot be sent, usually due to oversubscription. A non-blocking switch is one in which there is no oversubscription, and where each port is capable of receiving and delivering wire-rate traffic to and from another interface in the switch. If there are 48 10-gigabit interfaces, and the switch has a fabric speed of 480 Gbps (full duplex), then the switch can be said to be non-blocking. Some vendors will be less than honest about these numbers. For example, stating that a 48-port 10-Gb switch has a 480 Gbps backplane does not necessarily indicate that the switch is non-blocking, since traffic can flow in two directions in a full duplex environment. 480 Gbps might mean that only 24 ports can send at 10 Gbps while the other 24 receive at 10 Gbps. This would be 2:1 oversubscription to most people, but when the spec sheet says simple 480 Gbps, people assume. Clever marketing and the omission of details like this are more common than you might think.

Head-of-Line (HOL) Blocking

Packets may (and usually are) destined for a variety of interfaces, not just one. Consider the possibility that with the FIFO output queue on one interface, packets will buffer on the FIFO input buffer side. If the output queue cannot clear quickly enough, then the input buffer will start to fill, and none of those packets will be switched, even though they may be destined for other interfaces. This single packet, sitting at the head of the line, is preventing all the packets behind it from being switched. This is shown in Figure 2-7. Using the car analogy, imagine that there is a possible left turn directly outside the end of the tunnel. It's rarely used, but when someone sits there, patiently waiting for a break in oncoming traffic, everyone in the tunnel has to wait for this car to move before they can exit the tunnel.

 If you're reading this in a country that drives on the left side of the road, then please apply the following regular expression to my car analogies as you read: s/left/right/g. Thanks.

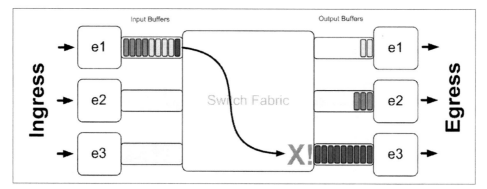

Figure 2-7. Head-of-line blocking

Virtual Output Queuing

Virtual output queuing (VOQ) is one of the common methods deployed by switch vendors to help eliminate the HOL blocking problem (shown in Figure 2-8). If there were a buffer for each output interface, positioned at the input buffer side of the fabric, and replicated on every interface, then HOL blocking would be practically eliminated.

Now, since there is a virtual output queue for every interface on the input side of the fabric, should the output queue become full, the packets destined for the full output queue will sit in its own virtual output queue, while the virtual output queues for all of the other interfaces will be unaffected. In our *left turn at the end of the tunnel* example, imagine an additional *left turn only* lane being installed. While the one car waits to turn left, the cars behind it can simply pass because the waiting car is no longer blocking traffic.

Allocating a single virtual output queue for each possible output queue would quickly become unscalable, especially on large switches. Instead, each input queue may have a smaller set of VOQs, which can be dynamically allocated as needed. The idea is that eight flows is probably more than enough for all but the most demanding of environments.

Arista often employs very deep buffers on its switches. The Arista 7048T switch has 48 1-Gbps interfaces and a huge buffer pool of 768 MB. The buffer pool is allocated dynamically, but let's say that one of the interfaces has been allocated 24 MB of buffer space. A 1-gigabit interface would take about 0.19 seconds to send a 24-megabyte file.

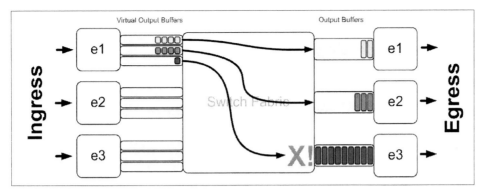

Figure 2-8. Virtual output queuing

The serialization delay is the amount of time it takes to forward bits out of an interface. A 1 gigabit per second interface can send 1 billion bits per second. One billion bits per second equates to roughly 125 megabytes per second. Therefore, a 24 megabyte buffer is capable of holding 0.19 seconds of gigabit traffic. For fun, the same buffer would hold only −.019 seconds of traffic at 10 megabits.

Arista advertises the 7048 as having 768 MB of packet memory, and that all ports can buffer 50 ms of traffic simultaneously (*http://www.aristanetworks.com/en/products/7048*). Fifty ms is 1/20th of a second, or 0.20 seconds. Sorry if I seem redundant. I just like to prove to myself that my math is right, even if I did commit the cardinal sin of ignoring powers of two.

If you start reading up on buffers elsewhere, you are likely to encounter dire warnings about excessively large buffers, and something colorfully referred to as *buffer bloat*. Buffer bloat describes the idea that hardware vendors have increasingly included more and more buffers in an attempt to outperform competitors. While buffer bloat may be a real concern in the home Internet environment, it is likely not a concern in the data center.

Consider what happens when you stream a movie from your favorite streaming source (let's call them Stream-Co). The servers might have 10 Gbps interfaces, which are connected with 10 Gbps switches, and since they're a big provider, they may even have 10 Gbps Internet feeds. The Internet is interconnected with pretty fast gear these days, so let's say, just for fun, that all the connections from Stream-Co to your ISP network are 10 Gbps. Yeah baby—fast is good! Now, your cable Internet provider switches your stream in 10 glorious gigabits per second, until it gets to the device that connects to your cable modem. Let's say that you've got a nice connection, and you can download 50 megabits per second. Can you see the problem?

The kickin' 10 Gbps data flow from Stream-Co has screamed across the country (or even the world) until it gets right to your virtual doorstep, at which point the speed goes from 10 Gbps to 50 Mbps. The difference in speed is not 10:1 like it is in a data center switch, but rather 200:1!

Now let's play a bit and assume that the cable distribution device has 24 MB buffers like our Arista 7048T does. Remember, that 24 MB at 1 Gbps is 20 ms. Well, that same 24 MB at 50 Mbps is 4 seconds! Buffering for 20 ms is not a big deal, but buffering for 4 seconds will confuse the TCP windowing system, and your performance may be less than optimal, to say the least. Additionally, although 24 MB is 4 seconds at 50 Mbps, remember that it's only 0.019 seconds at 10 Gbps. In other words, this buffer would take less than 1/10th of a second to fill, but 4 seconds to empty.

Think about this, too: propagation delay (the time it takes for packets to travel over distance) from New York to California might be 100 ms over multiple providers. Let's add that much on top for computational delay (the amount of time it takes for servers, switches, and routers to process packets), which gives us 200 ms. That's one-fifth of a second, which is a pretty long time in our infinitely connected high-speed world. Imagine that your service provider is getting packets in 200 ms, but is buffering multiple seconds of your traffic. To quote some guy I met on the beach in California, that's not cool, man.

My point with this talk of buffer bloat is to consider all the information before coming to rash conclusions. You may hear vendors pontificate about how big buffers are bad. Big buffers within the data center make a lot more sense than big buffers for cable modem distribution switches.

## CHAPTER 3

Merchant Silicon

If you've shopped for data center switches with any of the major networking equipment vendors recently, you've likely heard the term *merchant silicon* thrown around. There's a lot of back and forth between the major players about custom silicon versus merchant silicon, and which one is better. Let's take a look at the details, and see if one really is better than the other.

The Debate

To start with, let's define our terms:

Custom silicon
> Custom silicon is a term used to described chips, usually ASICs (Application Specific Integrated Circuits), that are custom designed, and usually built, by the company selling the switches in which they are used. Another term I might use would be *in house* when describing such chips. As an example, Cisco Nexus 7000 switches use Cisco-designed proprietary ASICs.

Merchant silicon
> Merchant silicon is a term used to described chips, usually ASICs, that are designed and made by an entity other than the company selling the switches in which they are used. I might be tempted to say such switches use *off-the-shelf* ASICs, though that might imply that I could buy these chips from a retail store. I've looked, and Wal-Mart doesn't carry them. As an example, Arista's 7050S-64 switches use Broadcom's Trident+ ASIC.

So that seems pretty cut and dry, but which one is better? That all depends on what you mean by *better*. Let's take a look at the benefits and drawbacks of each. First, the benefits and drawbacks of custom silicon:

Benefits of custom silicon

- Can be designed to integrate perfectly with a custom operating system
- Can be designed to support proprietary features
- Can be purpose built
- Can provide a significant competitive advantage due to the previous bullet points

Drawbacks of custom silicon

- Requires expensive on-staff expertise
- Requires expensive fabrication facilities
- Often slow to market
- Return on investment can be slow
- Long ROI can lead to longer product lifecycles

Now let's take a look at the benefits and drawbacks of merchant silicon:

Benefits of merchant silicon

- Easy to design around with well-supported APIs
- ASIC vendors are motivated to make stable, successful, and fast products
- Fast to market
- ASIC vendor does one thing: make ASICs
- No overhead involved (no expensive ASIC designers to staff, or expensive manufacturing facilities to build and maintain, etc.)
- Easy to implement, newer ASICs

Drawbacks of merchant silicon

- No custom or proprietary hardware features are possible (the chips may support proprietary features, but anyone that uses these chips has access to them)
- No inherent competitive advantage; any vendor can use same ASIC, although the implementation may be better with one vendor over another

Arista and Merchant Silicon

Arista uses merchant silicon exclusively for all of the reasons listed, but what about the drawbacks? The two drawbacks I listed for merchant silicon seem pretty severe to me, especially the one about there being no competitive advantage. I mean, isn't that why people buy one brand of switch over another, for the competitive advantages?

When I say there's no competitive advantage, I mean that there is no competitive advantage to using that ASIC compared to another vendor using that ASIC. There are a couple of things to take into consideration with that statement. Let's take a look at the Arista 7050S-64 as an example. It uses the Broadcom Trident+ ASIC to deliver 64 ports of 10 Gbps non-blocking goodness in a 1 rack unit box. Many other vendors, as of May 2012, offer similar switches that use the Broadcom Trident+. Arista's advantage in this space is that they have very efficient, modular, and portable hardware designs, and when a newer ASIC such as the Trident+ comes out, they can incorporate it into new products quickly. Other vendors might very well have the same ability, so this advantage might be small or fleeting, but it exists nonetheless. Remember, too, that how a vendor implements an ASIC can have a tremendous advantage. This is one of the areas where Arista shines.

Another issue is the idea that no proprietary features are possible, and that's true, so far as the ASIC hardware is concerned. Arista overcomes this limitation by differentiating themselves with their Extensible Operating System (EOS). Much of this book is dedicated to the features of EOS, so I won't go into them here, but suffice to say, EOS gives a significant competitive advantage to Arista that, so far as I've seen, can't be matched by any other vendor, at least not yet.

Proprietary features can be a good thing, but they can limit the ability to expand a network using different vendors and, in some cases, cause designs to be so tightly integrated into a single vendor as to cause severe limitations in the future. This limitation, commonly called *vendor lock*, can be a real problem when it comes time to upgrade the network.

Perhaps the most compelling argument for the success of merchant silicon–based switches is that some of the biggest proponents of custom silicon have released merchant silicon switches. Cisco's Nexus 3000 switches all use Broadcom Trident ASICs. And why wouldn't they? If the Trident ASIC is an advantage for Arista, and anyone can buy them from Broadcom, then Cisco has every right to build the best switch they can, using the same hardware. It's up to you to decide if Cisco's NX-OS is a better choice than Arista's EOS.

Arista Product ASICs

EOS offers the ability to show what ASIC is installed in your switch. To see the ASIC in use, use the show platform ? command. Here's the output from a 7124SX:

```
Arista-7124#sho platform ?
  fm4000  fm4000 chip
```

Here's the output from a 7050S-64:

```
Arista-7050#sho platform ?
  trident  Trident chip
```

The choices offered by each switch are different, depending on the ASIC installed. Here are the options for the 7124SX:

```
Arista-7124#sho platform fm4000 ?
  bali1                           bali1 switch
  interface                       Show interface-specific info
  mac-address-table               hardware MAC address table
  mac-flush-request-status        Show internal MAC flushing status
  mirror-groups                   Show internal mirror session info
```

And here are the options presented on a 7050S-64:

```
Arista-7050#sho platform trident ?
  counters            Trident debug counters
  interface           Show internal interface state
  mac-address-table   Show hardware MAC address table
  mmu                 Trident MMU information
  mroutes             Show internal multicast routes
  routes              Show internal routes
  tcam                Trident TCAM information
```

If you can get your hands on an Arista switch, I encourage you to dig around in these commands, because there is some really useful information in there. Table 3-1 is a list of the ASIC types for each Arista switch, as of May 2012.

Table 3-1. ASICs found in Arista switches

Switch Model	ASIC
DCS-7048-T	Petra
DCS-7048T-A	Petra
DCS-7050Q-16	Trident
DCS-7050S-52	Trident
DCS-7050S-64	Trident
DCS-7050T-52	Trident
DCS-7050T-64	Trident
DCS-7120T-4S	FM4000
DCS-7124FX	FM4000
DCS-7124S	FM4000
DCS-7124SX	FM4000
DCS-7148-4S	FM4000
DCS-7148SX	FM4000
DCS-7504	Petra
DCS-7508	Petra

Certain ASICs provide certain features. For example, the LANZ feature is only available on Arista 712X switches due to the FM4000 ASICs they incorporate. Since the 7050S-64 does not use the FM4000 ASIC, the switch does not support LANZ.

 As I was performing the final edits for this book, EOS version 4.10 was released. This version includes a feature called LANZ-Lite, which provides a similar feature on the 7500 and 7048T switches, although I should note that it does not work quite the same way due to the different ASICs involved.

In your day-to-day network operation duties, do you care what ASICs are in your switches? Probably not. Still, it pays to know what you're talking about when the vendors come a-courting.

It's also important to consider what sort of power we're talking about here. Consider this: the Arista 7050S-64 supports 64 10 Gbps non-blocking Ethernet ports in a 1 rack unit (RU) switch, using one ASIC. The admittedly aging Cisco 6509 supports only 28 10 Gbps non-blocking Ethernet ports, and that's in a full 15RUs, consuming much more power and producing much more heat. It also uses a lot more than one ASIC to do it, which is one of the reasons that these big switches consume more power and generate more heat. The 6509 is capable of many more enterprise features and is almost infinitely more expandable than the Arista 7050S-64, so it's not a strictly apples-to-apples comparison. Unless all you need is non-blocking 10 Gbps port density, in which case the Arista 1RU switch wins handily.

The Cisco 6509 is a great switch, and I'm not knocking it here. It is, however, a great example of the long product cycle induced by the custom silicon mindset. Though it supports high-density 10 Gbps blades, with only 40 Gbps available in each slot (using Sup 720s), those blades are highly oversubscribed. It's been around for a long time though.

There is one more potential benefit to merchant silicon, and that is the possible future of Software Defined Networks (SDN). Think of SDN as a cluster of switches, all controlled by a single software brain that is running outside of the physical switches. With such a design, the switches become nothing more than ASICs in a box that receive instructions from the master controller. In such an environment, the switch's operating system would be much simpler, and the hardware would need to be commoditized so that any vendor's switch could be added to the master controller with ease. Merchant silicon–based switches lend themselves to this type of design paradigm, whereas a custom silicon solution would likely only support a master controller from that switch's vendor.

This is a bit of an oversimplification of the idea behind SDN, but it does seem to excite the executives that hear about it. We're a few years away from this application in my opinion. Currently, SDN-type features are being used for things like security and monitoring.

Will SDN become a widespread reality? I don't know. I think the idea has merit, but as of mid-2012, I'm not making purchasing decisions based on it. That viewpoint may change in the next few years.

So, which is better: custom silicon, or merchant silicon? As far as Arista is concerned, merchant silicon is the path they've chosen. I can't tell you which is better, because I've seen great products from both camps. I will tell you that I really like what I'm seeing as a result of the competition caused by vendors moving to merchant silicon. Take EOS, for example. I think it's the best networking operating system I've ever seen. If that came to be as a result of using merchant silicon, then I'm a fan.

## CHAPTER 4

Fabric Speed

One of the things you'll hear over and over from switch vendors is how fast their switch is, or how fast the fabric is, or how much backplane capacity it has. But what does all that mean?

 This book is not intended to explain every possible detail of switch fabrics, but rather to help you understand what the term *fabric speed* means in a general sense. Entire books could be written on this topic, but my goal here is to help you understand the confusing and often misleading numbers that many vendors include in their switch specification sheets.

In a top-of-rack switch, the fabric is the interconnections between all the interfaces. The term *backplane* in this case is pretty much synonymous with *fabric* (though probably inaccurate). On a chassis switch, the terms can be thought of a bit differently.

On a chassis switch, each module may have a fabric, and interfaces within a module may switch between each other while staying local to the blade. When a packet sourced on one blade must travel to another blade, though, the packet needs a path between the blades. The connections between the blades are often called the backplane, although really, that term is more about the hardware connecting the modules to each other. Semantics aside, what you need to know is that there is a master fabric connecting all these modules together in a chassis switch.

In modern chassis switches, like the Arista 7500 and Cisco Nexus 7000, the backplane fabric resides in hot swappable modules in the back of the chassis. In older switches, like the Cisco 6509, they used to consume slots in the front of the switch (at the expense of other useful modules). Later, Cisco incorporated the fabric modules into the supervisors so that more slots could be used in the front for interfaces.

There are many ways in which modules can connect to the backplane fabric. There may be ASICs on the modules that allow packets to flow intramodule without intervention from the fabric modules. Or, the fabric modules may interconnect every port in every module. How the modules are constructed, and how they connect to the backplane, both determine how fast the backplane fabric is. Really, though, many vendors play games with numbers and try to hide what's really going on. Let's take a look at why.

Let's look at our simple three-port 10 Gbps switch, shown in Figure 4-1. In this switch, the fabric is simple, and non-blocking. *Non-blocking* means that each port is capable of sending and receiving traffic at wire speed (the maximum speed of the interface) to and from any other port. A non-blocking switch is capable of doing this on all ports at once. Remember, on these fabric drawings, that the ingress is on the left and the egress is on the top. That means that when you see interface e1 in two places that it's the same interface. It exists in two places to show how packets come in and leave through the fabric.

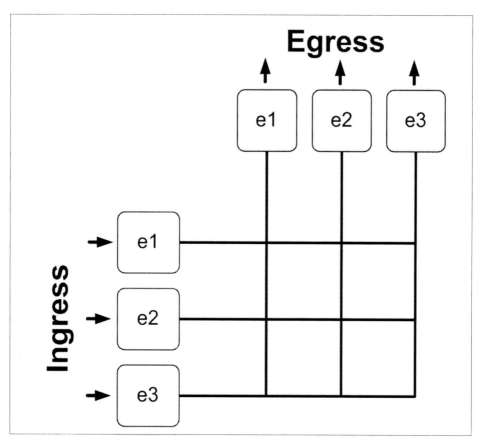

Figure 4-1. Simple three-port switch fabric

Now imagine that our simple switch used ASICs to control the flow of packets between ports. There is one ASIC on the ingress, and one on the egress. The kicker here, though, is that each ASIC is only capable of forwarding 10 Gbps at a time. This design is shown in Figure 4-2.

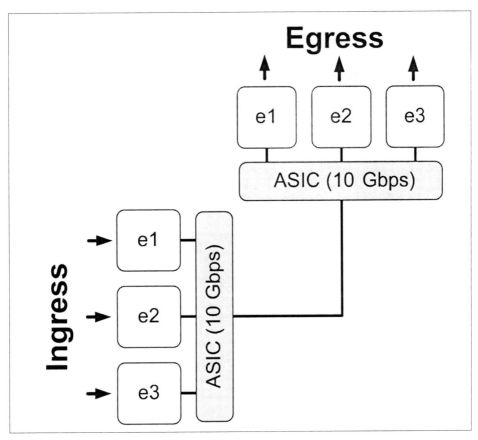

Figure 4-2. Simple three-port switch fabric with ASICs

All of a sudden, with the addition of the 10 Gbps ASICs, our switch has lost our non-blocking status (assuming each port is 10 Gbps). Though each interface forwards bits to its connected device at 10 Gbps, should more than two ports be used at the same time, their maximum combined transmit and receive can only be 10 Gbps. Think that sounds bad? Well, it is, assuming you need a non-blocking switch. The truth is, very few networks require real non-blocking architectures. Most eight-port gigabit switches found in the home are blocking architectures just like this. But how often do you really need to push 100% bandwidth through every port in your small office/home office (SOHO) switch? Probably never. And guess what? Building switches this way is inexpensive, which is a plus in the SOHO switch market.

Let's look at a bigger switch. In Figure 4-3, I've built an eight-port 10 Gbps switch. This switch is non-blocking, as evidenced by the fact that each interface has a possible full-speed connection to any other interface.

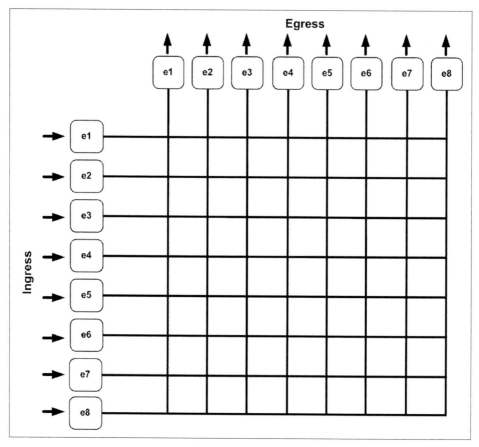

Figure 4-3. An eight-port 10 Gbps non-blocking switch

How might this switch look if we used oversubscription to lower costs? If we used the same 10 Gbps ASICs, each controlling four 10 Gbps interfaces, it might look like the drawing in Figure 4-4.

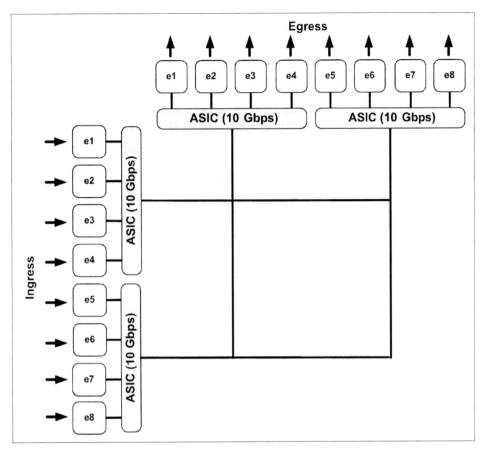

Figure 4-4. An oversubscribed eight-port 10 Gbps switch

If you think stuff like this couldn't happen in a modern switch, think again. The Netgear SOHO GS108T switch advertises that it has "eight 10/100/1000 Mbps ports, capable of powering 2000 Mbps of data throughput." Even the big iron is commonly oversubscribed. The Cisco Nexus N7K-M132XP-12L module, shown in Figure 4-5, sports 32 10 Gbps ports, but each group of four ports only supports an aggregate bandwidth of 10 Gbps. This is illustrated by the fact that one out of each of the four ports can be placed into dedicated mode, in which that port is guaranteed the full 10 Gbps. When put in this mode, the three other ports attached to the ASIC are disabled.

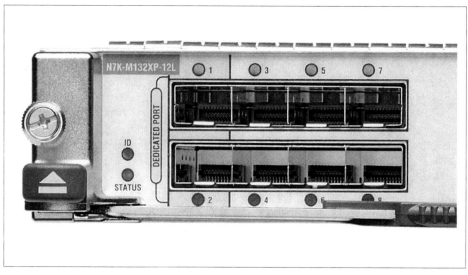

Figure 4-5. Cisco M7K-M132XP-12L module with dedicated pots highlighted

This is not a knock on Netgear or Cisco. In fact, in this case I applaud them for being up front about the product's capabilities, and in the case of the Cisco blade, providing the ability to dedicate ports. On a server connection, I'm perfectly OK oversubscribing a 10 Gbps port because most servers are incapable of sending 10 Gbps anyway. On an inter-switch link, though, I'd like to be able to dedicate a 10 Gbps port. My point is that this oversubscription is very common, even in high-dollar data center switches.

What if we could get a single super-ASIC that could control all of the ports? Such a switch might look like the one I've drawn in Figure 4-6. In this switch, each port still has full 10 Gbps connectivity to any other port on the switch, but there is no oversubscription. This is accomplished by having what I'll call a next-generation ASIC that can handle the high bandwidth requirements of a non-blocking 10 Gbps switch.

Some switch vendors take a different approach and cascade ASICs. Take a look at Figure 4-7. Here, there are 16 ports, divided into two modules. Each of the four ports is controlled by a single 10 Gbps ASIC. Each of those ASICs connects to a 40 Gbps ASIC that manages interconnectivity between all the modules. This works, but it doesn't scale well. I've seen this type of solution in 1RU or 2RU switches with only a couple of expansion modules. Note that the backplane speed cannot be improved with such a design, as it is purposely built for this scale.

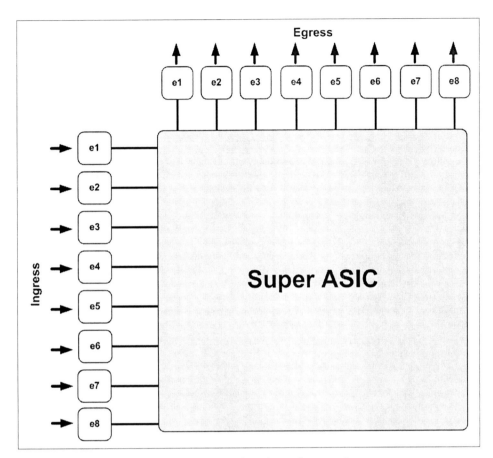

Figure 4-6. Non-blocking eight-port ASIC-based 10 Gbps switch

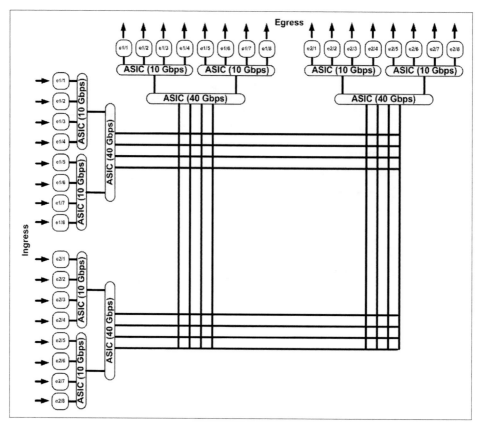

Figure 4-7. Cascaded ASICs

This type of switch will get you 10 Gbps connectivity, but at a lower aggregate through-put, which equates to oversubscription. Fine for an office switch, and for some datacenter switches, but for high-end networking, I'd like to see a non-blocking eight-port 10 Gbps switch. That would look something like the switch depicted in Figure 4-8.

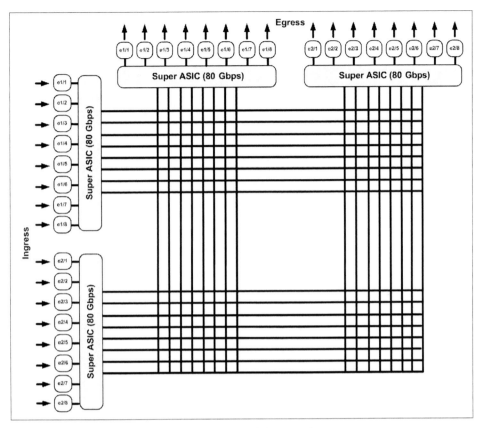

Figure 4-8. Non-blocking 16-port 10 Gbps modular switch

This is better, but it's still not scalable because we can't add any connections to the core fabric. So what if we used even bigger, better ASICs to mesh all of our modules together? In Figure 4-9, ASICs perform the intermodule connectivity. In this model, assuming the hardware was designed for it, we could theoretically add more modules, provided the ASICs in the center could support the aggregate bandwidth.

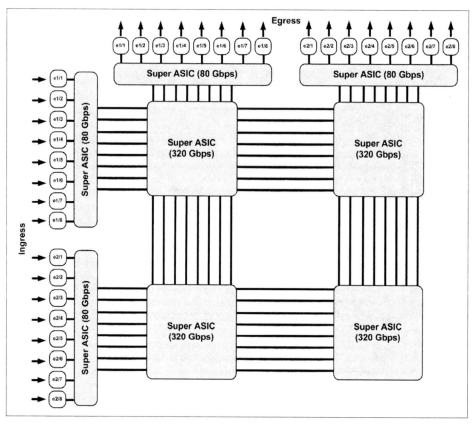

Figure 4-9. Non-blocking ASIC-based 16-port modular switch

When it really comes down to it, how the backplane functions rarely matters. What matters is whether or not the switch is truly non-blocking. If that's done with 1 ASIC or 12, does it really matter? Probably not to those of use who are designing and building networks, but to the guys that write the code, it can make their lives easier or harder.

Arista switches incorporate a few different designs, depending on the design requirements of the switch. The Arista 7050S-64 uses a single Broadcom Trident+ ASIC to switch 64 non-blocking 10 Gbps ports. To put that in perspective, that's more non-blocking port density than a Cisco 6509 loaded with the latest supervisors and seven 8-port 10 Gbps modules. There are a lot of ASICs in a fully loaded 6509.

That's not to say that the single ASIC approach is always the right solution. The Arista 7500 chassis 48-port 10 Gbps non-blocking modules has one ASIC per every eight ports (six per module). Each module has a total of 1.25 Tb access to the backplane fabric (648 Gbps TX and 648 Gbps RX), which translates to the possibility of each slot supporting multiple 40 Gbps and even 100 Gbps interfaces, all of which would be non-blocking.

## CHAPTER 5

Arista Products

The Arista product portfolio can seem a little confusing at first because many of the switches look similar, but once you dig in you'll realize why each model exists, and how you might use it in your own networks.

Remember, Arista switches are purpose built for the data center. You probably wouldn't buy an Arista switch for a VoIP deployment that requires PoE. Though you could certainly use an Arista switch in your enterprise office environment, they don't make a PoE model, the switches aren't stackable, and Arista doesn't really chase the office-switch market. These switches are made for data centers, and have features required for such deployments.

Every Arista switch has dual (or more) power supplies, hot swappable fans with front-to-back (or reverse) airflow, and a myriad of other features required for highly available data center environments. Let's start with an overview of data center–specific features common to all Arista switches.

Power

All Arista switches support multiple, redundant power supplies as well as multiple fans, all of which are hot swappable. All of the top-of-rack switches have the fans and power supplies on the back of the switch, whereas the chassis-based switches have the power connectors on the front. An Arista 7050S-64 switch with the power supplies and fans removed is shown in Figure 5-1.

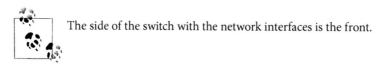 The side of the switch with the network interfaces is the front.

I was pleasantly surprised when I unpacked my first Arista switch to see that the power cables supplied included C13-C14 connectors. These connectors are commonly used in data centers that employ large power distribution units (PDUs) within racks. Normally, I end up with a box of unused power cables that get replaced with the C13-C14 variety. Arista once again shows that these switches are purpose built for the data center.

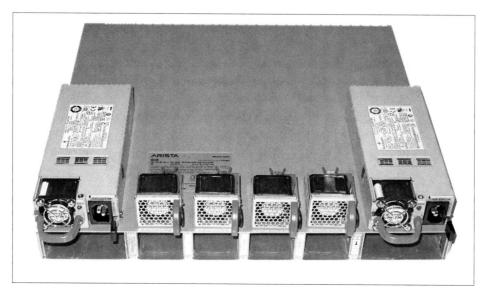

Figure 5-1. Arista 7050S-64 switch with the power supplies and fans removed

Airflow

Airflow is configurable in all Arista switches through the use of color-coded power supplies and fans. All red-handled power supplies and fans pull air from the front (interface side) of the switch back through to the back. All blue-handled power supplies and fans pull air from the back (power side) of the switch to the front. Two switches, each with different airflow options installed, are shown in Figure 5-2.

Figure 5-2. Color-coded fan modules indicating airflow direction

Optics

Arista optics are often less expensive than other vendors. In fact, I've seen Arista win bids based on the price of their optics alone. Even if the Arista switch was more expensive than the competitor's, the price of the Arista optics resulted in the bottom line being less than the competitor's quote.

The price is nice, but a low price is useless if the item doesn't work. I'm happy to say that in my experience, they work as well as any other vendor's optics (if not better!)

 Be warned that vendors are disallowing the use of other vendor's optics. A Cisco Small Form-Factor Pluggable Transceiver (SFP) will not work in an Arista switch, nor will an HP SFP work in a Cisco switch. I despise this game, because it's a way to force me into buying the same company's optics when another's may be less expensive, or even work better. Sadly, many of the big vendors do it, so I can't single out any one of them. I find the practice repugnant since the SFP interface is supposed to be an open standard designed for vendor interoperability (search for the terms *sfp multi source agreement* to read the original multivendor agreement on the SFP standard).

If you've done any data center networking in the past few years, then you're no doubt familiar with the SFP+, an example of which is shown in Figure 5-3.

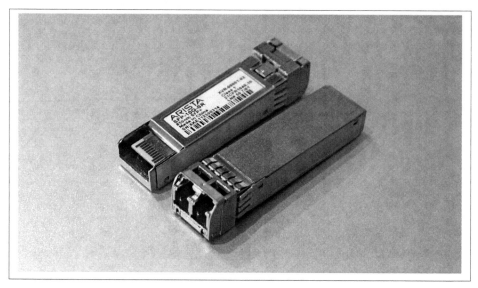

Figure 5-3. Arista SFP-10G-SR optics

The SFP+ is the evolution of the old GBIC standard optic. The GBIC was limited to 1 Gbps, whereas the SFP+ supports 10 Gbps. The XenPak supported 10 Gbps, but it is huge. With SFP+ optics, it is possible to fit 48 (or more) 10 Gbps interfaces within a single rack unit of space.

 Andy Bechtolstein, founder of Arista, was one of the principal people responsible for the development and subsequent acceptance of the GBIC standard.

Also available are 40 Gbps QSFP+ modules, which are a slightly wider form factor than the SFP+. Both the QSFP+ and the SFP+ support twinax cables that allow for short-reach connectivity at a much lower cost than traditional optics.

EOS

One of the best features of all Arista switches (in my humble opinion), is the fact that they all run the same EOS code images. I did an install that had four different models of Arista switches. I needed to get them all on the same rev of code. I downloaded EOS version 4.8.1, put it on a USB thumb drive, walked to each switch and copied the code onto flash. There is no need to figure out what hardware you have prior to downloading.

There is no need for long, complicated file names. There are no release trains, no versions for different feature sets, and generally just no pain when it comes to EOS. Every switch runs the same binary image. Simple is good, and Arista gets that. Spend some time upgrading Arista switches and you'll detest upgrading on any other switch.

Arista switches are currently divided into two types of hardware layout—one rack unit top-of-rack switches, and multirack unit chassis-based switches. There are multiple types within each type, so let's take a look.

 Information regarding the current stable of Arista products can be found online at Arista's website (*http://www.aristanetworks.com/en/ products*). The information contained within this chapter is accurate at the time of final editing. Technologies change quickly, so contact your Arista sales representative for the most current information available.

For a quick comparison of all the current Arista switches, the *Arista Product Quick Reference Guide* (*http://www.aristanetworks.com/media/system/pdf/AristaProduct QuickReferenceGuide.pdf*) is an invaluable tool.

Top-of-Rack Switches

I'm sorting these switches a little bit differently than Arista does on their website, because this order makes more sense to me. I'm the writer, and I win (unless my editor overrides me), so please indulge me while I take you through the Arista top-of-rack switches, starting with the 1 Gbps models.

I'd like to add a quick word about these switches before starting. After working with Cisco Nexus 5000s and 5500s for years, unpacking my first Arista top-of-rack switch revealed a pleasant surprise. They're small! The form factor of these switches is substantially smaller than the Cisco Nexus switches. They're easier to mount, they have a more traditional face that mounts flush with other switches, and the rack mount kits are simple, logical, and easy to install. They are data center class switches in a form factor almost as small as office switches. They produce less heat and consume less power too, which is a nice selling point when talking to executives, especially when corporate *green initiatives* are in play.

One-Gigabit Switches

As of this writing, Arista only makes one gigabit copper switch, which is the 7048T-A (Figure 5-4).

Arista 7048T-A

The 7048T-A switch, like all Arista switches, is designed with data center traffic in mind. To that end, it contains very deep buffers (see the chapter on buffers for more information), which are capable of storing 20 ms of 1 Gbps traffic per port. This deep buffering is invaluable in the data center where connectivity between 1 Gbps devices and 10 Gbps devices is common.

Figure 5-4. Arista 7048T-A (image courtesy of Arista Networks)

I use these switches anywhere I need 1 Gbps copper connections. Although it is possible to support 1 Gbps copper with copper SFPs in a 10 Gbps interface, 10 Gbps interfaces are expensive, as are the SFPs required to use them. If you have a lot of gigabit copper, this is the switch to use.

The 7048T-A has 48 1 Gbps copper interfaces, 4 10 Gbps/1 Gbps SFP+ interfaces, one management interface, a usable USB port, and a console port. This switch utilizes four hot swappable fans and two hot swappable power supplies. As with all Arista switches, airflow is reversible by replacing the fans and power supplies.

Ten-Gigabit Switches: 7100 Series

The 7100 series of switches are described by Arista as *ultra low-latency* switches. With features not found in any other switch, even within Arista's own product offerings, these switches are game changers for many networks. Let's take a look at them to see why.

Arista 7124SX

When I was first introduced to Arista, I was running a bake-off between multiple data center switch vendors, all of which you've no doubt heard of. At the time, I had never heard of Arista and, believe it or not, the other vendors led us to them. After three different vendors said something to the effect of, "Wow, usually we're up against Arista in this space," we gave them a call. To help with our vendor comparison, Arista arranged for us to have a pair of switches to put in our lab for a 30-day evaluation. The switch they chose to give us was the 7124SX, as shown in Figure 5-5.

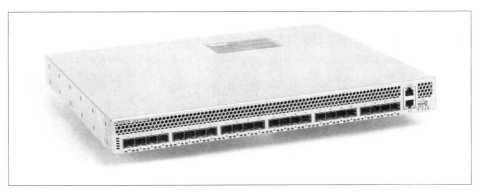

Figure 5-5. Arista 7124SX (image courtesy of Arista Networks)

Arista chose to let us borrow this switch because it showcases all of the features that make Arista switches great. It has a 0.5 μs latency port to port. That's not milliseconds, it's microseconds. For those of you who like to think of such things, light travels one mile (1.6 km) in 5.4 microseconds (in a vacuum). This switch could forward almost 10 packets in that time! One half microsecond is equivalent to 500 nanoseconds, or 0.0005 milliseconds!

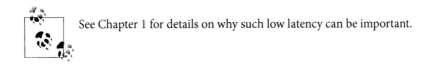 See Chapter 1 for details on why such low latency can be important.

This switch runs EOS, like every other Arista switch, but also supports LANZ due to the ASIC employed. It sports a non-blocking 480 Gbps backplane, which ensures a non-blocking backplane at wire rate regardless of packet size. In short, this switch kicks ass, all while only consuming 120 watts of power. This switch will forward 360 million packets per second using L2/L3.

This switch has 24 SFP+ 10 Gbps/1 Gbps ports, one management port, one USB port, and one console port.

7148SX

The Arista 7148SX switch is similar to the 7124SX, but with 48 10 Gbps interfaces. Since it has more ports, it has an increased backplane that supports 960 Gbps. The downside of having more ports in this architecture is that the port-to-port latency jumps up to between 0.6 and 1.2 microseconds due to the fact that it uses a multichip architecture. If the traffic stays on one ASIC, the latency is the same as the older 7124S (predecessor to the 7124SX). That may not sound like a big deal, but in ultra low-latency environments like Wall Street, that 0.5 microsecond could cost millions. This switch was the first 48 port non-blocking 10 Gbps top-of-rack 1RU switch on the market, and is shown in Figure 5-6.

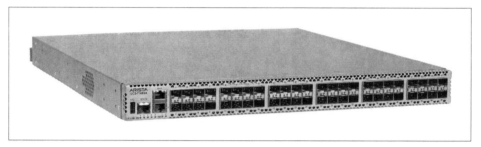

Figure 5-6. Arista 7148SX (image courtesy of Arista Networks)

This switch consumes more power at 600 watts, which is to be expected given the higher port count and additional ASICs used to drive all the ports. This switch will forward 720 million packets per second over L2/L3.

Though this switch has some impressive numbers, I prefer the 24-port 7124SX for low-latency applications, and the 7050S-64 for high port density 10 Gbps applications, since it has the potential for 40 Gbps uplinks while still sporting 48 10 Gbps interfaces.

Arista 7124FX

The Arista 7124FX switch is something new for 2012. This device is referred to as an *application switch* because it includes a *Field Programmable Gate Array* (FPGA) with eight dedicated 10 Gbps SFP+ ports. An FPGA is like an ASIC, but where an ASIC is hard coded at the factory, an FPGA is programmable by the end user. The 7124FX switch is shown in Figure 5-7.

What's so great about having an FPGA in a network switch? Imagine your company is doing Wall Street trades. Imagine that something comes up for sale, and whoever buys it first will make a million dollars in future profits. If your company could receive that offer then process and commit to the sale before your competitors, then your company would make a cool million.

In the world of Wall Street, milliseconds can mean billions of dollars. Normally, packets get delivered to the switch and are then forwarded to the server, where they ride up the protocol stack to the application that executes the trade. The commit message then has to go back down the stack and then be sent over the wire to the switch, where it is forwarded to the destination interface and sent on its way. Let's say, for the sake of argument, that the process takes 1 millisecond.

Figure 5-7. Arista 7124FX application switch (image courtesy of Arista Networks)

Now, imagine that we could run that trading process in an ASIC instead of on a server. And imagine if that ASIC resided directly on the network switch. Computational delay might be lowered by an order of magnitude or more. Additionally, we wouldn't have to worry about switch-to-server latency, switch forwarding delay, or serialization delay on both interfaces. Sure, we're talking about infinitesimal increments of time, but cutting off microseconds means you increase your chances of acting on a trade before your competitors do.

Now, imagine 1,000 such transactions per day, and you can see why a switch like this would be a game changer for those who can take advantage of its abilities. And on top of all that, this switch retains the blazing fast sub-500 nanosecond (ns) performance of its 7124SX brother.

Ten-Gigabit Switches: 7050 Series

The 7050 series is my personal favorite of the top-of-rack Arista switches. With extreme port density, 40 Gbps connectivity, and the option of 10 Gbps copper connections, these switches have a lot to offer. The main drawback of these switches compared to, say, the 7124SX, is that the latency is a bit higher, and they don't support the LANZ feature.

Arista 7050 series switches have some cool features such as an optional 50 GB solid-state drive (SSD) option for onboard storage of logs, packet captures, PXEboot images, or anything else you can dream up. Let's a take a look at each model a bit closer.

7050S-52

The Arista 7050S-52, shown in Figure 5-8, sports 52 10 Gbps SFP+ interfaces, one management interface, one console interface, and a usable USB port.

Fifty-two 10 Gbps interfaces in a 1RU switch is cool in and of itself, but these 52 interfaces are completely non-blocking. The switch backplane is 1.04 Tb per second! Port-to-port latency is between 800 to 1,150 nanoseconds, and the switch consumes only 103 watts of power.

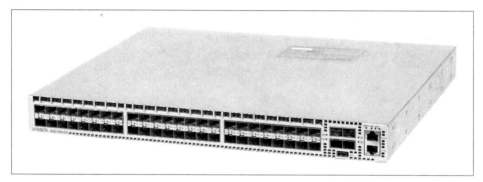

Figure 5-8. Arista 7050S-52 (image courtesy of Arista Networks)

7050T-52

The 7050 52-port 10 Gbps switch also comes in a copper model. The 7050T-52, shown in Figure 5-9, sports 48 copper 10 Gbps interfaces, and four SFP+ 10 Gbps interfaces. If you've got the copper infrastructure in place to support 10 Gbps over twisted pair, the 7050T-52 could be a great solution that allows an upgrade to 10 Gbps without rewiring.

Figure 5-9. Arista 7050T-52 (image courtesy of Arista Networks)

Even if you're building a data center from scratch, consider the idea of using 10 Gbps copper within the racks. For each link using fiber, you'll need an SFP+ on either end. Even with Arista's great SFP+ pricing, you're talking a minimum of US$500 per link. If you could fill up 48 ports with 10 Gbps fiber, you're looking at $24,000 in optics alone, and that's for each switch! Even if you pay $100 per run for Cat-6A copper cables, the savings in optics alone could pay for your networking gear when spread out over an entire data center.

Another advantage of the copper interface is that it supports 100 Mbps, 1 Gbps, and 10 Gbps speeds, whereas the SFP+ ports only support 1 Gbps and 10 Gbps—and even then, only with different optics.

The 7050T-52 typically consumes about 347 watts of power, and has a port-to-port latency of 3.0 to 3.3 microseconds.

7050S-64

As cool as the 7050S-52 is, the 7050S-64 is even cooler! If you think 52 10 Gbps non-blocking interfaces in a 1RU switch is impressive, how about 64?

The Arista 7050S-64 switch, shown in Figure 5-10, contains the normal complement of management, console, and USB interfaces, along with 48 10 Gbps SFP+ interfaces, and four QSFP+ 40 Gbps interfaces.

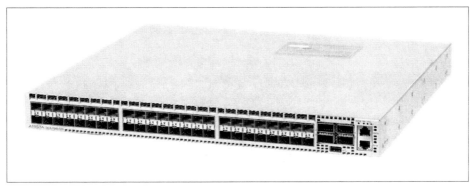

Figure 5-10. Arista 7050S-64 (image courtesy of Arista Networks)

QSFP+ interfaces are 40 Gbps, but the way they work is by bonding four 10 Gbps interfaces together with a *Serializer/Deserializer* (SERDES) chip. Consider it, in principle, to be a super-fast ether channel, although the technology is not the same. It's more like multilink PPP, but let's not get hung up on details now.

Because the QSFP+ is actually four bonded 10 Gbps interfaces, those four interfaces can be split out. With the proper splitter cable, each 40 Gbps interface can be configured as four 10 Gbps interfaces. Hence, there are 64 10 Gbps interfaces in a single 1RU switch.

By default, the interfaces are 10 Gbps, and look like this in the CLI:

```
8X-R2-NAS1#sho int status | begin Et47
Et47              connected    1      full   10G 10GBASE-SR
Et48              connected    1      full   10G 10GBASE-SR
Et49/1            notconnect   1      full   10G Not Present
Et49/2            notconnect   1      full   10G Not Present
Et49/3            notconnect   1      full   10G Not Present
Et49/4            notconnect   1      full   10G Not Present
Et50/1            notconnect   1      full   10G Not Present
Et50/2            notconnect   1      full   10G Not Present
Et50/3            notconnect   1      full   10G Not Present
Et50/4            notconnect   1      full   10G Not Present
[--- output truncated ---]
```

Port-to-port latency on the 7050S-64 switch is 800 to 1,150 nanoseconds with SFP+ interfaces, and 950 to 1,350 nanoseconds with QSFP+ interfaces. The 7050S-64 switch consumes around 125 watts of power.

7050T-64

Just as the 7050S-52 comes in a copper interface version, so too does the 64-port version. The 7050T-64, shown in Figure 5-11, contains 48 copper 10 Gbps interfaces, but like the 7050S-64, also contains four 40 Gbps QSFP+ ports that can be split out to four 10 Gbps interfaces each.

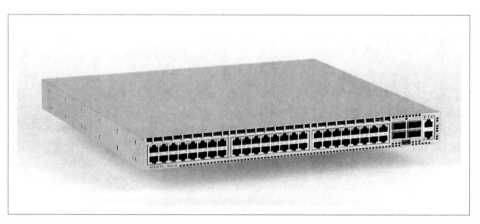

Figure 5-11. Arista 7050T-64 (image courtesy of Arista Networks)

The 7050T-64 typically consumes about 372 watts of power, and has a port-to-port latency of 3.0 to 3.3 microseconds.

7050Q-16

The 7050Q-16 switch, pictured in Figure 5-12, is similar to the 7050S-64 in that it has 64 10 Gbps interfaces available, but this switch is designed where QSFP+ density is needed. With 16 QSFP+ interfaces and 8 SFP+ interfaces, you might ask why this switch only has 64 10 Gbps interfaces. Since Arista doesn't fool around with oversubscription like some other switch vendors, the last two QSFP+ ports are switchable.

Figure 5-12. Arista 7050Q-16 (image courtesy of Arista Networks)

Ports 15 and 16 can either be a single 40 Gbps QSFP+, or four 10 Gbps SFP+, right on the box. Though the QSFP+ ports can still be split out using splitter cables, it's nice to have the option of using existing cables if you have them. Note that if you do use the SFP+ ports, the last two QSFP+ ports become unavailable.

Chassis Switches

The Arista 7500 chassis-based switches are designed for high density, high performance applications. With current modules offering 192 or 384 wire-speed non-blocking 10 Gbps SFP+ interfaces, these switches have raised the bar in chassis-based switches.

Arista 7500 Series

There are two models in the Arista 7500 line: the four-slot 7504, and the eight-slot 7508. Each switch offers 648 Gbps bandwidth per linecard slot, which can also be written as 1.25 Tb, full duplex. Switch vendors often throw around these numbers in an effort to either impress or confuse buyers. When I was researching chassis switches for a client, it was maddening trying to get the truth out of some vendors. With Arista, they're always up front about the switch's capabilities.

Arista 7500 switches have hot swappable supervisors, shown in Figure 5-13. These switches support 2.3 GB of packet buffering per module, 4.5 microsecond port-to-port latency (64-byte frame; up to 14 microseconds for 9000 byte jumbo frames), and are designed to support 40 Gbps and 100 Gbps deployments.

Figure 5-13. Arista 7500 Supervisor (image courtesy of Arista Networks)

In my research, these chassis switches performed better than other vendor's similar options. At the time of my tests (mid-2011), there were no other vendors who delivered true non-blocking 48-port, 10 Gbps modules in a chassis switch with an "industry standard" CLI. My work with Arista, along with my research into these switches, so impressed me that I decided to write this book. They're that good.

Both models have four (2+2) hot swappable power supplies, two (N+1) hot swappable supervisors, hot swappable N+1 fabric cards, hot swappable N+1 fan modules, and data center reversible airflow.

Being chassis switches, these models have some major differences than their top-of-rack counterparts. First, they have dual, removable supervisor modules. These modules include a console port, a management port, a USB port, a color LCD display screen, and some buttons to help navigate the menus on the small screens.

All modules, be they supervisors or linecards, have large handles on the sides that also provide some cable management. A module, partially removed from a 7508 chassis, is shown in Figure 5-14.

The supervisors both have color screens that show status information, an example of which is shown in Figure 5-15, and by default, the Arista logo. One of the cool features of the 7500s is that you can load your company logo onto the switch so that the little screens display your own branding. Executives selling data center colocation space eat that stuff up because it really makes the data center look sharp, assuming of course that your company logo doesn't suck.

Let's take a look at each model in the 7500 line, so you can see the details for yourself.

Figure 5-14. Arista 7508 switch with one module partially removed (image courtesy of Arista Networks)

Figure 5-15. Arista 7508 supervisor with status screen shown (image courtesy of Arista Networks)

7504

The 7504, shown in Figure 5-16, is the four-slot version of the Arista 7500 product line. This 7RU chassis supports four modules and two supervisors. Power connections are on the front, but the hot swappable power supplies are removed from the back. Additional modules on the back include hot swappable fans and fabric modules.

Figure 5-16. Arista 7504 (image courtesy of Arista Networks)

The 7504 modular chassis switch supports high density 10 Gbps deployments in a small size. Given its 7RU size, six of them could be mounted in a single 42RU cabinet; although, if you needed that much density, you'd probably be looking at the 7508 instead.

The 7504 supports two supervisors, each with a console, management, and USB interface; 192 possible wire speed 10 Gbps interfaces; 4.5 microsecond latency (with 64 byte packets); 2+2 grid redundant power; N+1 supervisor; fan and fabric redundancy; 18 GB of packet buffers; and 384 virtual output queues.

7508

The Arista 7508 switch, shown in Figure 5-17, is the eight-slot version of the 7500 product line. The specs are the same as the 7504, with the following difference: the 7508 can support 384 wire speed 10 Gbps interfaces. The fan modules are separate from the fabric on the 7508, whereas they are combined on the 7504. It's also bigger and, as we all know, bigger is better.

Figure 5-17. Arista 7508 (image courtesy of Arista Networks)

## CHAPTER 6

Introduction to EOS

The operating system for Arista switches is called the Extensible Operating System, or EOS for short. Arista describes EOS as "...the interface between the switch and the software that controls the switch and manages the network." This is sort of like Apple's OS X operating system, in that what you see is actually a Unix shell—Unix is doing all the heavy lifting behind the scenes. Arista switches run Unix natively, but to make them easier for nonprogrammers to understand, EOS makes them look more like traditional (Cisco) networking devices.

The word *extensible* means "capable of being extended." EOS was designed from the ground up to allow third-party development of add-ons. This is a first in the networking world, and is a big departure from traditional proprietary operating systems. This extensibility is shown in detail in Chapters 11, 28, and 29.

Arista is a big believer in open standards, and there are no proprietary protocols found in EOS. Even features such as MLAG and VARP, both Arista developments, use behaviors found in existing open-standard protocols, the details of which we will see later in Chapters 12 and 14.

Perhaps even more impressively, Arista allows the user to access the underlying Linux operating system and to even write Python scripts that can control the switch. This is a significant difference from other vendors who advertise that their switches run a derivative of Linux. While those switches may be based on Linux, you can't get to it, and all the power of Linux remains just out of your grasp, while you struggle with a new operating system that's mostly like the one you've grown accustomed to.

On an Arista switch, the switch is running Linux. In fact, the switch is actually a Linux server with custom hardware that has a lot of interfaces. I'll show you just how true that is in this book.

Some customers have even built their own interface to the switches, bypassing EOS altogether. Arista offers APIs for programmers toward this end, and even hosts a website where customers can share their ideas or scripts with other users. This website, entitled *EOS Central*, can be found at *http://eos.aristanetworks.com/* (registration is required).

SysDB

Arista switches have, at their heart, a database called SysDB. This database contains the state information and settings for the switch, organized in such a way that every module can access it with ease. What's more, Arista allows developers to access SysDB so that they can create add-ons.

Traditional networking hardware uses a monolithic software architecture. This means that there is a pretty significant risk of a bug in one section of code affecting or even bringing down the entire device. Furthermore, updating one section of code can be difficult because there may be repercussions in other areas unforeseen by the developer.

Arista's EOS is more modular. Not only does EOS separate the networking state from the processing, but drivers, processes, management, and even security patches run in user address space, not in the kernel. This means that any process can be restarted without affecting the state of the network that it controls. This also means that any module can be upgraded without affecting traffic flow. Modules can be added with ease, and faults are isolated to their individual user spaces. Should one process crash, it cannot affect the rest of the system. Should the process crash or lock up, the EOS process manager (ProcMgr) can restart it without affecting other modules, and without affecting the networking state. Since SysDB is just a database, and contains no application code, it is extremely reliable.

Since EOS is so modular, the drivers for the ASICs are merely modules. Because of this, EOS is the same for every switch Arista makes. There are no release trains, no hardware-specific downloads, and no hours wasted trying to find the right code. If you want EOS 4.7.7, you download the code named *EOS-4.7.7.swi*. If you have a 384-port 7508 chassis switch or a 24-port 7124 fixed-configuration switch, the software image is the same.

You can see this in action, though indirectly. When you first log in to an Arista switch, the first thing you might do is issue the show run command. Since even your CLI session is a process with its own user space, the first time you issue the show run command, the process must mount the SysDB database. That takes a second or two, and you may notice the lag. After you get the output delivered, if you execute the show run command again, it delivers the output much faster because SysDB is already mounted. If you disconnect and then connect again, you'll spawn a new CLI process, which must then mount SysDB once more.

In fact, if you're impatient enough when first logging in and if you bang on the Enter key, you might be treated to the following message:

```
Arista-7124SX login: admin
waiting for mounts to complete ...ok
Arista-7124SX>
```

Technically, this message may appear without banging on the Enter key, but I've never been patient enough for that to happen. What can I say? I'm a happy key masher.

> I've been informed that this message is actually being removed from future releases since it plays havoc with scripts.

Using EOS

If you've used a Cisco switch running IOS, you can use an Arista switch. As soon as you log into an Arista switch, you'll recognize the look and feel—it's very similar to Cisco's IOS. The important distinction is that it is not IOS—the internals have been completely written from scratch—only the command-line interface (CLI) is similar.

> There is a joke in the industry that Arista does Cisco better than Cisco does. What they mean by this quip is that probably 90% of what you're used to seeing on Cisco IOS is the same on Arista EOS—it's just written better. Of course "better" is a subjective term, but consider this: if you've ever had to learn NX-OS after spending years on IOS, I can all but guarantee that migrating to EOS will be easier.

One of the things that frustrated me when I hooked up my first Arista switch was the fact that, by default, telnet is not enabled. In its default configuration, SSH is the only means allowed to remotely access EOS. Certainly console access is allowed, and telnet can be enabled, but in this time of PCI, Sarbanes-Oxley, and countless other security-centric requirements, keeping telnet disabled is a good idea.

For my examples, I'm connecting through the console (through a console server). Logging into EOS is as simple as it is with IOS:

```
Arista-1 login: admin
Last login: Wed Sep 28 14:40:14 on ttyS0

Arista-1>
```

With only simple login authentication configured I am dropped into *EXEC* mode, which should look pretty familiar. At this point I can access *Privileged EXEC* mode with the enable command:

```
Arista-1>enable
Arista-1#
```

The prompt has changed as I'd expect it to, and I now have the power. At this point, I'll add my own username because I like to be accountable for my actions. Actually, that's a lie. I'm so lazy that I like to have the same username and password on every device I've ever configured so that I don't have to remember them. OK, so that's not true either, but I figured I'd configure a username just to show how the process of configuration works in EOS.

Again, this is just like IOS. I'll configure from the terminal using the `config terminal` command, then configure my username, then exit:

```
Arista-1#conf t
Arista-1(config)#
```

At this point, I am in *global configuration* mode:

```
Arista-1(config)#username GAD secret ILikePie
Arista-1(config)#exit
Arista-1#exit

Arista-1 login:
Arista-1 login: GAD
Password: ILikePie
Arista-1>en
Arista-1#
```

See? Just like IOS, even down to the behavior of truncated commands being accepted, so long as they are not ambiguous. For example, while in configuration mode, entering just `ro` will not work because the CLI interpreter cannot figure out if I mean `route-map` or `router`:

```
Arista-1(config)#ro
% Ambiguous command
```

I can, however, find out what commands are available in one of two ways. First, I can hit question mark. This will give me a list of available commands that match what I've entered so far:

```
Arista-1(config)#ro?
route-map  router
```

I can also hit the Tab key, at which point the switch will respond with the longest match based on what I've typed so far:

```
Arista-1(config)#ro<TAB>
Arista-1(config)#route
```

Note that I did not type the word `route`; the switch inserted that via *autocompletion* when I hit Tab. At this point I decided that it's the `router` command I was looking for, so I added the `r`, and then hit question mark. The switch then recognized that `router` is a command, and listed the possible associated keywords:

```
Arista-1(config)#router ?
  bgp   Border Gateway Protocol
  ospf  Open Shortest Path First (OSPF)
```

I chose one of these protocols, after which the switch put me into protocol specific mode, and altered the command line to show where I was:

```
Arista-1(config)#router ospf 100
Arista-1(config-router-ospf)#
```

As with IOS, typing exit (or its nonambiguous abbreviation) got me out of the current level and popped me back up one level:

```
Arista-1(config-router-ospf)#ex
Arista-1(config)#
```

 You don't need to type exit. If you want to work in another mode, you can just type in the command and EOS will switch modes for you, assuming it can figure out the proper mode.

By typing end, or Control-Z, I was able to exit configuration mode entirely:

```
Arista-1(config-router-ospf)#end
Arista-1#
```

At this point I'd like to add that the EOS CLI recognizes some Emacs control characters. I am constantly amazed that even networking guys with decades of experience are unaware of these simple CLI key combinations. The following Control key combinations will have the effects listed:

Control-A
  Moves the cursor to the beginning of line

Control-E
  Moves the cursor to the end of line

Control-B
  Moves the cursor back one character (same as left arrow)

Control-F
  Moves the cursor forward one character (same as right arrow)

Esc-B
  Moves the cursor back one word

Esc-F
  Moves the cursor forward one word

Like IOS, entering the interface command, followed by the interface name, will put you into interface configuration mode. Interface configuration mode is similar to IOS, but more robust.

 Interfaces on Arista switches are all Ethernet, and are not named in accordance with their speed or type. All Ethernet interfaces on a fixed configuration switch have the name ethernet *interface#* (the space is optional). Ethernet interfaces on modular switches have the name, ethernet *slot#/interface#*. For example, the first interface on an Arista 7124 is ethernet1, or e1 for short. The first interface in slot number one of an Arista 7508 modular switch is ethernet 1/1 or e1/1.

Here, I've entered the interface configuration mode for ethernet 1:

```
Arista-1#conf t
Arista-1(config)#int e1
Arista-1(config-if-Et1)#
```

 There is no need to enter the command config terminal (conf t) in EOS. Old habits die hard, however, and I've been typing that since 1989. Simply typing conf works just as well.

One of the cool enhancements to EOS is that it has no interface range command like there is in IOS. To configure multiple interfaces at one time, simply enter them separated by either a hyphen (for a range) or a comma (for a list). Here I've entered configuration mode for the interfaces e1, e2, e3, and e10. I've included the first three as a range:

```
Arista-1(config)#int e1-3, e10
Arista-1(config-if-Et1-3,10)#
```

Check out the command prompt. It doesn't show just "range," but rather shows what interfaces are being configured. I love this feature, because I can never remember what I typed a few short seconds ago. Be warned, though, that it can be a bit unwieldy with long lists of interfaces, since they will all show up in the command prompt:

```
Arista-1(config)#int e1,3,5,7,9,11,13,15,17,19
Arista-1(config-if-Et1,3,5,7,9,11,13,15,17,19)#
Arista-1(config-if-Et1,3,5,7,9,11,13,15,17,19)#description Odd Ports
```

Another nice feature of EOS is that I don't have to exit configuration mode to run exec mode commands. I just run them, and EOS figures it all out. There is no do command necessary with EOS:

```
Arista-1(config-if-Et1,3,5,7,9,11,13,15,17,19)#sho run | include Odd
   description Odd Ports
   description Odd Ports
```

```
description Odd Ports
description Odd Ports
description Odd Ports
description Odd Ports
description Odd Ports
description Odd Ports
description Odd Ports
description Odd Ports
```

Technically, any mode can run commands from any parent mode. If you enter commands from a different mode at the same level (interface- and protocol-specific mode, for example), then the mode will switch accordingly. You cannot, however, execute child mode commands from a parent mode. For example, you cannot execute interface-specific commands from within the global configuration mode.

Just like IOS, I was able to pipe the output of show run to include, which only outputs what I wanted to see. This behavior is similar to the grep command in Unix. There are a bunch of options for piping in EOS, which you can see by entering | ? (vertical bar, question mark) after any show command:

```
Arista-1#sho run | ?
  LINE       Filter command pipeline
  append     Append redirected output to URL
  begin      Begin with the line that matches
  exclude    Exclude lines that match
  include    Include lines that match
  no-more    Disable pagination for this command
  nz         Include only non-zero counters
  redirect   Redirect output to URL
  tee        Copy output to URL
```

Though include is similar to grep, it differs in a significant way. This distinction is important when stacking pipes. The command sho int | inc Ethernet will output the following:

```
Arista#sho int | inc Ethernet
Ethernet1 is down, line protocol is down (notconnect)
  Hardware is Ethernet, address is 001c.7308.80af (bia 001c.7308.80af)
Ethernet2 is down, line protocol is down (notconnect)
  Hardware is Ethernet, address is 001c.7308.80b0 (bia 001c.7308.80b0)
Ethernet3 is down, line protocol is down (notconnect)
  Hardware is Ethernet, address is 001c.7308.80b1 (bia 001c.7308.80b1)
Ethernet4 is down, line protocol is down (notconnect)
  Hardware is Ethernet, address is 001c.7308.80b2 (bia 001c.7308.80b2)
Ethernet5 is administratively down, line protocol is down (disabled)
  Hardware is Ethernet, address is 001c.7308.80b3 (bia 001c.7308.80b3)
[--- output truncated ---]
```

Now let's say that I wanted to further filter that output, and only include the lines that include the word *Hardware*. My inclination would be to add another pipe with another include, like this: sho int | inc Ethernet | inc Hardware. The problem is, this doesn't work:

```
Arista#sho int | inc Ethernet | inc Hardware
Arista#
```

If I change my includes to greps, then it works as I desire:

```
Arista#sho int | grep Ethernet | grep Hardware
  Hardware is Ethernet, address is 001c.7308.80af (bia 001c.7308.80af)
  Hardware is Ethernet, address is 001c.7308.80b0 (bia 001c.7308.80b0)
  Hardware is Ethernet, address is 001c.7308.80b1 (bia 001c.7308.80b1)
  Hardware is Ethernet, address is 001c.7308.80b2 (bia 001c.7308.80b2)
  Hardware is Ethernet, address is 001c.7308.80b3 (bia 001c.7308.80b3)
  Hardware is Ethernet, address is 001c.7308.80b4 (bia 001c.7308.80b4)
  Hardware is Ethernet, address is 001c.7308.80b5 (bia 001c.7308.80b5)
```

So why does this happen? While include is part of the command-line interpreter, grep is a Unix command. Piping is a Unix function, so EOS behaves more like Unix when stacking pipes the way I have.

> Remember, Arista switches aren't similar to Linux devices, they *are* Linux devices. If what you're doing isn't working the way you'd expect it to, try thinking in terms of a Linux OS. More often than not, you'll find your answer in the way Linux works.

EOS runs a flavor of Linux, and many of the command behaviors reflect that ancestry. For example, unlike IOS, by default there is no pagination enabled in EOS when using the console. Therefore, when you execute the show run command, the output will scroll by until the entire running configuration has been displayed. To paginate on the fly, pipe your output to more. Just like using more in Unix, this will pause the output after the screen length (-1) has been met, at which point the prompt --more-- will be shown. At this point, user input is required to continue. Hitting Enter or Return will result in the advancement of a single line, while hitting the spacebar will show another page. Hitting the letter q (or Q) or entering Control-C will break the output and return you to the command prompt:

```
Arista-1#sho run | more
! device: Arista-1 (DCS-7124S, EOS-4.7.3-EFT1)
!
! boot system flash:/EOS-4.7.3-EFT.swi
!
no aaa root
!
username GAD secret 5 $1$S4ddK.QkzZdxfffJ$2yi.y.tqweS/9l.1
!
logging console debugging
```

```
!
hostname Arista-1
!
spanning-tree mode mstp
no spanning-tree vlan 4094
!
--More--
```

Speaking of show running-config, there's a cool feature in EOS that will include all of the commands, even the defaults that aren't usually shown. This is done by including the all keyword, and can be done even when showing parts of the config such as an interface. Let me show you what I mean. Here's the output from the command show run int e24:

```
Arista#sho run int e24
interface Ethernet24
   switchport access vlan 901
   switchport mode trunk
```

And here's the output of the show run all int e24 command, truncated for brevity. All of the commands you see here are active; they're just defaults, so they're not usually shown:

```
Arista#sho run all int e24
interface Ethernet24
   no description
   no shutdown
   default load-interval
   logging event link-status use-global
   no dcbx mode
   no mac-address
   no link-debounce
   no flowcontrol send
   no flowcontrol receive
   no speed
   switchport access vlan 901
   switchport trunk native vlan 1
   switchport trunk allowed vlan 1-4094
   switchport mode trunk
   switchport mac address learning
   no switchport private-vlan mapping
   switchport
   snmp trap link-status
   no channel-group
   lacp rate normal
   lacp port-priority 32768
   lldp transmit
   lldp receive
   no priority-flow-control
   no priority-flow-control priority 0
   no priority-flow-control priority 1
[-- output truncated --]
```

Another cool function you can invoke while piping is the nz command. This will output only lines that have values of nonzero. Let's look at an example. Here we have the output from the command show interface Ethernet 23:

```
Arista-1#sho int e23
Ethernet23 is up, line protocol is up (connected)
  Hardware is Ethernet, address is 001c.7308.fa60 (bia 001c.7308.fa60)
  MTU 9212 bytes, BW 10000000 Kbit
  Full-duplex, 10Gb/s, auto negotiation: off
  Last clearing of "show interface" counters never
  5 minutes input rate 764 bps (0.0% with framing), 1 packets/sec
  5 minutes output rate 579 bps (0.0% with framing), 1 packets/sec
     76946 packets input, 6948712 bytes
     Received 0 broadcasts, 4818 multicast
     0 runts, 0 giants
     0 input errors, 0 CRC, 0 alignment, 0 symbol
     0 PAUSE input
     44504 packets output, 5239033 bytes
     Sent 2 broadcasts, 8423 multicast
     0 output errors, 0 collisions
     0 late collision, 0 deferred
     0 PAUSE output
```

The lines in bold within the output all show values of zero. Chances are, we don't care about this information, so why not display the same output without those lines? As here:

```
Arista-1#sho int e23 | nz
Ethernet23 is up, line protocol is up (connected)
  Hardware is Ethernet, address is 001c.7308.fa60 (bia 001c.7308.fa60)
  MTU 9212 bytes, BW 10000000 Kbit
  Full-duplex, 10Gb/s, auto negotiation: off
  Last clearing of "show interface" counters never
  5 minutes input rate 774 bps (0.0% with framing), 1 packets/sec
  5 minutes output rate 577 bps (0.0% with framing), 1 packets/sec
     76956 packets input, 6949720 bytes
     Received 0 broadcasts, 4820 multicast
     44508 packets output, 5239461 bytes
     Sent 2 broadcasts, 8423 multicast
```

This output was taken a few seconds later, so some of the values have changed, but notice that the lines that were all zero before are no longer included.

This can be especially useful for commands like show interface counters, where by default there could be pages of all zero counters:

```
Arista-1#sho int count
Port      InOctets     InUcastPkts      InMcastPkts      InBcastPkts
Et1        962378                0            6216                0
Et2             0                0               0                0
Et3             0                0               0                0
Et4             0                0               0                0
Et5             0                0               0                0
Et6             0                0               0                0
```

```
Et7            0              0              0              0
Et8            0              0              0              0
Et9            0              0              0              0
[--- output truncated ---]
```

Here's the same command piped through nz:

```
Arista-1#sho int count | nz
Port      InOctets    InUcastPkts      InMcastPkts      InBcastPkts
Et1         964901           0             6233              0
Et19       6628804           0            45236              0
Et20       6629197           0            45237              0
Et23       6991534       72572             4848              0
Et24      30532241       74169             8711           4844
Po1       37523065      146741            13554           4844
Po12        964645           0             6230              0

Port      OutOctets   OutUcastPkts     OutMcastPkts     OutBcastPkts
Et1         767462           0             4827              0
Et1         460815           0             2413              0
Et20        434283           0             2413              0
Et23       5271088       36301             8475              2
Et24      24998928      188576             4845              0
Po1       30269272      224877            13315              2
Po12        766888           0             4823              0
```

Every line that contains all zero counters has been removed, and only the useful information remains.

When I first started using Arista switches, I had been using Cisco Nexus switches for years, and the lack of the | last output modifier bugged me when using commands like show log. Then I sat and thought about what I knew about EOS and had a crazy idea. Remember earlier in this chapter where I showed how we could pipe to the Unix grep command? It struck me that grep was not listed as one of the options when piping:

```
SW1(config)#sho run | ?
   LINE       Filter command pipeline
   append     Append redirected output to URL
   begin      Begin with the line that matches
   exclude    Exclude lines that match
   include    Include lines that match
   no-more    Disable pagination for this command
   nz         Include only non-zero counters
   redirect   Redirect output to URL
   tee        Copy output to URL
```

I reasoned that if I could pipe to one Unix command, I would likely be able to pipe to others. The Unix command that would serve me here is tail, so I cast caution to the wind and went for it with all the vigor of a sleep-deprived nerd hell-bent on discovery.

Here's the output of the show log command piped through more:

```
Arista#sho log | more
Syslog logging: enabled
    Buffer logging: level debugging
    Console logging: level errors
    Trap logging: level informational
    Sequence numbers: disabled
    Syslog facility: local4
    Hostname format: Hostname only
```

Facility	Severity	Effective Severity
aaa	debugging	debugging
acl	debugging	debugging
agent	debugging	debugging
bgp	debugging	debugging
clear	debugging	debugging
envmon	debugging	debugging
eth	debugging	debugging
extension	debugging	debugging
focalpoint	debugging	debugging
fru	debugging	debugging
fwk	debugging	debugging
hardware	debugging	debugging
igmpsnooping	debugging	debugging

```
--More—
```

With bated breath, I entered my wicked conglomeration of EOS and Unix commands:

```
Arista#sho log | tail
May 18 18:12:04 Arista Fru: %FRU-6-FAN_INSERTED: Fan tray 4 has been
inserted
May 18 18:12:04 Arista Fru: %FRU-6-FAN_INSERTED: Fan tray 5 has been
inserted
May 18 18:12:09 Arista Ebra: %LINEPROTO-5-UPDOWN: Line protocol on
Interface Ethernet11, changed state to up
May 18 18:12:09 Arista Ebra: %LINEPROTO-5-UPDOWN: Line protocol on
Interface Ethernet10, changed state to up
May 18 18:12:11 Arista Lldp: %LLDP-5-NEIGHBOR_NEW: LLDP neighbor with
chassisId 001c.7308.80ae and portId "Ethernet11" added on interface
Ethernet10
May 18 18:12:11 Arista Lldp: %LLDP-5-NEIGHBOR_NEW: LLDP neighbor with
chassisId 001c.7308.80ae and portId "Ethernet10" added on interface
Ethernet11
May 18 18:14:01 Arista SuperServer: %SYS-5-SYSTEM_RESTARTED: System
restarted
May 18 18:20:40 Arista Cli: %SYS-5-CONFIG_I: Configured from console
by admin on con0 (0.0.0.0)
May 19 13:41:56 Arista Fru: %FRU-6-TRANSCEIVER_REMOVED: The
transceiver for interface Ethernet24 has been removed
May 19 13:42:08 Arista Fru: %FRU-6-TRANSCEIVER_INSERTED: A
transceiver for interface Ethernet24 has been inserted.
manufacturer: Arista Networks model: SFP-1G-SX part number
SFP-1G-SX rev 0002 serial number XCW1036QH081
```

Holy crap! It worked! Such was my enthusiasm that my wife came into my home office at 2 a.m. and told me to go to bed, or at least keep it down. I suppose I should be lucky to have a wife, being a guy who finds the ability to mix EOS and Unix commands exciting.

As previously discussed, Unix pipes can even be stacked:

```
Arista#sho log | tail | grep FAN
May 18 18:12:04 Arista Fru: %FRU-6-FAN_INSERTED:
Fan tray 4 has been inserted
May 18 18:12:04 Arista Fru: %FRU-6-FAN_INSERTED:
Fan tray 5 has been inserted
```

Why stop at two? Now that my wife had left me to my late night spell casting, I ventured down the rabbit hole. How about adding some redirection?

```
Arista#sho log | tail | grep FAN > /mount/flash/GAD.txt
```

Because tail is a Unix command, we must specify the full path to get to the flash drive. You'll see what happens if you don't in Chapter 9.

Now, my *GAD.txt* file is stored on the flash drive, and can be seen with the dir command from EOS:

```
Arista#dir
Directory of flash:/

        -rwx    225217184    Apr 16 05:38  EOS-4.8.1.swi
        -rwx    245827739    Apr 16 11:19  EOS-4.9.1.swi
        -rwx    248665992    May 12 22:36  EOS-4.9.3.swi
        -rwx          127    May 17 02:16  GAD
        -rwx          156    May 21 20:40  GAD.txt
        -rwx          137    May 18 18:20  boot-config
        drwx         4096    May 18 18:11  debug
        drwx         4096    May 18 18:11  persist
        drwx         4096    May 17 02:27  schedule
        -rwx         1351    May 18 18:20  startup-config
        -rwx            0    May 14 23:46  zerotouch-config
```

## CHAPTER 7

Upgrading EOS

Upgrading EOS is a simple process. In a nutshell, get the software image onto the switch, configure the switch to see the new image, and then reboot the switch. Let's start by taking a look at the current version of EOS on our 7124S switch by using the show version command:

```
Arista#sho ver
Arista DCS-7124S-F
Hardware version:     06.02
Serial number:        JSH10170315
System MAC address:   001c.7308.80ae

Software image version: 4.7.8
Architecture:           i386
Internal build version: 4.7.8-535760.EOS478
Internal build ID:      530a4112-b24f-40ef-bbe2-8c4b139a797d

Uptime:                 4 days, 20 hours and 4 minutes
Total memory:           2042400 kB
Free memory:            891220 kB
```

We can see from this output that our switch is running EOS version 4.7.8.

Check out the model number in the first line of output, which reads DCS-7124S-F. The -F indicates that this switch shipped with front-to-rear airflow fans. If the model number had a -R appended to it, the fans would be rear-to-front. Cool, huh? Well I think it is, but then, little things like this excite me.

If we felt like poking around further where we don't belong (and who doesn't?), then we could use the show version detail command, which will regale us with page upon page of process names and their requisite versions:

```
Arista#sho version detail
Arista DCS-7124S-F
Hardware version:     06.02
Deviations:           D0000213, D0000203
Serial number:        JSH10170315
System MAC address:   001c.7308.80ae

Software image version: 4.7.8
Architecture:           i386
Internal build version: 4.7.8-535760.EOS478
Internal build ID:      530a4112-b24f-40ef-bbe2-8c4b139a797d

Uptime:               4 days, 20 hours and 6 minutes
Total memory:         2042400 kB
Free memory:          890972 kB

Installed software packages:


Package            Version        Release
----------------------------------------------
Aaa                1.0.0          535760.EOS478
Aboot-utils        2.0.5          535760.EOS478
Acl                1.0.0          535760.EOS478
Adt7462            1.0.1          535760.EOS478
Altera             1.0.1          535760.EOS478

[-- pages of output removed to keep my editor from hurting me --]

xz                 4.999.9        0.2.beta.20091007git.fc12
xz-libs            4.999.9        0.2.beta.20091007git.fc12
xz-lzma-compat     4.999.9        0.2.beta.20091007git.fc12
yum                3.2.27         2.fc12
yum-metadata-parser 1.1.2         14.fc12
zile               2.3.9          2.fc12
zip                2.31           8.fc12
zlib               1.2.3          23.fc12

Component  Version
---------- ----------------------------------------
Aboot      Aboot-norcal1-1.9.2-140514.2006.eswierk
scd        0x13
```

 See the line in bold (as well as many others) in the previous output that ends with *.fc12*? That indicates that the package on that line was built on Fedora Core 12.

Interesting information if you're Arista TAC (Technical Assistance Center), but probably overkill for us. Our goal in this chapter is to upgrade this switch from EOS version 4.7.8 to version 4.8.1. So let's get started.

The first thing we'll do is take a look at what devices there are available to us on the Arista 7124S using the dir ? command:

```
Arista#dir ?
  all-filesystems  List files on all filesystems
  extension:       Directory or file name
  file:            Directory or file name
  flash:           Directory or file name
  system:          Directory or file name
  /all             List all files, including hidden files
  /recursive       List files recursively
  <cr>
```

Arista switches all contain useful USB ports. Figure 7-1 shows the USB port on a 7124S switch, located to the far left of the device. After years of using switches from other vendors that contained USB ports that were unavailable, being able to slap a thumb drive in and actually make use of it came as a pleasant surprise.

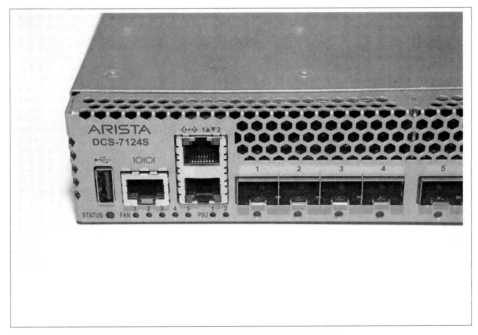

Figure 7-1. Arista 7124S switch console and USB ports

Upon insertion of a USB drive, the dir ? command yields different results:

```
Arista#dir ?
  all-filesystems  List files on all filesystems
  extension:       Directory or file name
  file:            Directory or file name
  flash:           Directory or file name
  system:          Directory or file name
  usb1:            Directory or file name
  /all             List all files, including hidden files
  /recursive       List files recursively
  <cr>
```

Now we see the *usb1:* device, which was not there previously.

Executing the `dir` command by itself will default to the current directory, which is in *flash/*:

```
Arista#dir
Directory of flash:/

        -rwx    222153243        Dec 22  2011  EOS-4.7.8.swi
        -rwx           24        Dec 22  2011  boot-config
        drwx         4096        Apr 10 23:20  debug
        -rwx            0        May  7  2008  fullrecover
        drwx         4096        Apr 10 23:20  persist
        -rwx         2674        Apr 10 23:13  startup-config
        -rwx            0        Apr 10 23:20  zerotouch-config

 1862512640 bytes total (1418162176 bytes free)
```

As we can see, there is an existing EOS image in this directory, entitled *EOS-4.7.8.swi*. This image corresponds to the version shown earlier with the `show version` command. References to the image file may also be found in the running configuration. We will use the command found here to upgrade the system in this chapter:

```
Arista#sho run | inc boot
! boot system flash:EOS-4.7.8.swi
```

The sharp-eyed among you may have noticed that the command is commented out. This is due to there not actually being a `boot system` command configured. This command, as shown, is generated by the switch for reasons that will become apparent later in this chapter.

Let's take a look at what's on the new USB drive that's been inserted. We can do this by specifying the *usb1:* device discovered previously:

```
Arista#dir usb1:
Directory of usb1:/

        -rwx    221921815        Sep 21  2011  EOS-4.7.7.swi
        -rwx    225217184        Oct 26  2011  EOS-4.8.1.swi

 4001914880 bytes total (3553292288 bytes free)
```

It looks like we've got two EOS images to choose from. Since 4.8.1 is what we're currently after, let's move it to the system flash. To do this, we'll use the copy *source destination* command. Arista allows a variety of source and destinations when copying. To see them all, issue the copy ? command:

```
Arista#copy ?
  boot-extensions       Copy boot extensions configuration
  extension:            Source file path
  file:                 Source file path
  flash:                Source file path
  ftp:                  Source file path
  http:                 Source file path
  https:                Source file path
  installed-extensions  Copy installed extensions status
  running-config        Copy from current system configuration
  scp:                  Source file path
  startup-config        Copy from startup configuration
  system:               Source file path
  tftp:                 Source file path
  usb1:                 Source file path
```

In this case, since we're using a USB drive, the source will be usb:*filename*, and the destination will be flash:. If we were to source the file from a TFTP server, then the source would be tftp:.

```
Arista#copy usb1:EOS-4.8.1.swi flash:
Arista#
```

On this rev of code, there is no pretty progress indicator. Luckily, the system copies pretty quickly, and this image is only about 225 MB, so there isn't much time to panic. Still, if pressing enter and not getting a response makes you panic, then be prepared to grit your teeth for a few seconds while the copy ensues. Once the copy is done, we can verify that it resides in its new home in the *flash:/* directory.

```
Arista#dir
Directory of flash:/

        -rwx   222153243    Dec 22  2011   EOS-4.7.8.swi
        -rwx   225217184    Apr 15 19:48   EOS-4.8.1.swi
        -rwx          24    Dec 22  2011   boot-config
        drwx        4096    Apr 10 23:20   debug
        -rwx           0    May 7   2008   fullrecover
        drwx        4096    Apr 10 23:20   persist
        -rwx        2674    Apr 10 23:13   startup-config
        -rwx           0    Apr 10 23:20   zerotouch-config

1862512640 bytes total (1192943616 bytes free)
```

Now that we have our EOS image safely on board, we can configure the system to use it. But what happens if we don't? With two images on flash, and the system not configured to use either, which one will it choose? For fun, I rebooted the system, during which I saw the following messages:

```
Arista#reload
Proceed with reload? [confirm]

Broadcast message from root@ArisStopping sshd: [  OK  ]
SysRq : Remount R/O
Restarting system


Aboot 1.9.2-140514.2006.eswierk


Press Control-C now to enter Aboot shell
Booting flash:EOS-4.7.8.swi
Starting new kernel
[-- output removed --]
```

EOS will not simply boot the first image it finds on flash. The reason for this will become apparent in another paragraph or two, so hang in there. For now, let's go ahead and configure the system to boot from the new image. As with other vendors, the command to do this is the boot system command:

```
Arista(config)#boot system ?
   file:   Software image URL
   flash:  Software image URL
   usb1:   Software image URL
```

Did you notice that the *usb1:* file system is included in the output? We could configure the switch to boot from an image on the USB drive if we so desired. Almost anything we can do with normal flash, we can also do with USB, provided that there is a drive in the USB slot. For now, though, let's go ahead and configure the switch to boot from its new image in flash:

```
Arista(config)#boot system flash:EOS-4.8.1.swi
```

EOS supports tab completion, so instead of copying and pasting the entire filename, try using the Tab key. Luckily, Arista keeps all the image names short and tidy, which is another pleasant surprise after decades of other vendors' lengthy filenames.

Now that we've got the new image primed and ready to go, let's reboot the switch:

```
Arista(config)#reload
Proceed with reload? [confirm]
```

Hold on a minute! We didn't save the configuration, so why didn't the system prompt us to save it before rebooting? The boot system command doesn't really make changes to the running config. Instead, it writes to a file on *system:/* called *boot-config*.

```
Arista(config)#dir
Directory of flash:/

        -rwx   222153243        Dec 22  2011   EOS-4.7.8.swi
        -rwx   225217184        Apr 15 12:48   EOS-4.8.1.swi
        -rwx          25        Apr 15 20:03   boot-config
        drwx        4096        Apr 15 20:11   debug
        -rwx           0         May 7  2008   fullrecover
        drwx        4096        Apr 15 20:10   persist
        -rwx        2676        Apr 15 19:55   startup-config
        -rwx           0        Apr 10 23:20   zerotouch-config

   1862512640 bytes total (1189879808 bytes free)
```

As you see, *boot-config* is the filename used for a process called *Aboot*. Aboot is the boot-loader for the switch (which is really a Linux system, remember). Aboot will be covered in more detail later in the book. For now, understand that without the boot-loader's configuration file, our switch will not boot. I took the liberty of deleting this file to prove my point. With both image files present, and no *boot-config* file found, the switch flounders shortly after initialization:

```
Arista(config)#reload
System configuration has been modified. Save? [yes/no/cancel/diff]:
Invalid response
System configuration has been modified. Save? [yes/no/cancel/diff]:y
Proceed with reload? [confirm]

Broadcast meStopping sshd: [  OK  ]
[  575.544430] SysRq : Remount R/O
Restarting system


Aboot 1.9.2-140514.2006.eswierk


Press Control-C now to enter Aboot shell
No SWI specified in /mnt/flash/boot-config
Welcome to Aboot.
Aboot#
```

That's it; the switch is dead in the water. What's worse, if you've ever been near a modern switch from most any vendor when it boots, you'll know that all the fans go to full power upon power up, and then slow down to an acceptable level after boot up. With no EOS image to load, the switch spins its fans at full speed. It's annoying, and no one likes it, especially my wife who came down to yell at me about all the noise while I was writing this chapter. But I digress...

Aboot will be covered in another chapter, but for now, let's get our noisy switch back online before my wife kills me:

```
Aboot# boot mnt/flash/EOS-4.8.1.swi
```

This will boot the switch from the proper image, but after deleting the *boot-config* file, we will need to put it back. To further reinforce that the *boot-config* file is where the magic happens, take a look at the output from the show boot command after the switch boots:

```
Arista#sho boot
Software image: (not set)
Console speed: (not set)
Aboot password (encrypted): (not set)
```

But what about the *running-config*? Didn't the switch figure out where we booted from? Not really. Remember, we told Aboot what image to boot from, but that only applied for this instance. The boot mnt/flash/EOS-4.8.1.swi Aboot command did not update the *boot-config* file, it just booted the system. As a result, the *running-config* contains no reference to a boot image, because the *running-config* gets that information from the *boot-config* file. The proper way to fix this is with the boot system command:

```
Arista#boot system flash:/EOS-4.8.1.swi
```

The output from show boot looks much better now, and the system will boot normally, just as long as we keep our paws off of the *boot-config* file:

```
Arista(config)#sho boot
Software image: flash:/EOS-4.8.1.swi
Console speed: (not set)
Aboot password (encrypted): (not set)
```

From this point on, the switch will load the specified image on reload. Without the diversion for showing you how the switch reacts to not having a *boot-config* file, the process was very simple: get the code on the system, update the *boot-config* file with the boot system command, and reload.

If you're running MLAG, check out Chapter 12 for details about upgrading using MLAG ISSU, which allows for a switch pair to be upgraded with minimal packet loss and no STP reconvergence!

## CHAPTER 8

LLDP

Link Layer Discovery Protocol (LLDP) is the open source answer to Cisco's proprietary Cisco Discovery Protocol (CDP). LLDP is specified in IEEE 802.1AB and is similar to CDP in many ways. Let's take a look at LLDP in action, and see what you may need to do to make it work with other vendors' devices.

My Arista 7124S switch is connected to a Cisco 3750. The connection is between G1/0/52 on the 3750 and e24 on the Arista. When I turn up the port, I get the following message on the Arista console:

```
Apr 10 23:21:35 Arista Lldp: %LLDP-5-NEIGHBOR_NEW: LLDP neighbor with
chassisId 001c.b084.cfb4 and portId "[ Arista e24 ]" added on
interface Ethernet24
```

Without configuring anything, the Arista switch has discovered the Cisco switch, even though the Arista switch is not running CDP. Let's dig in and see what Arista sees:

```
Arista#sho lldp
LLDP transmit interval      : 30 seconds
LLDP transmit holdtime      : 120 seconds
LLDP reinitialization delay : 2 seconds

Enabled optional TLVs:
  Port Description
  System Name
  System Description
  System Capabilities
  Management Address (best)
  IEEE802.1 Port VLAN ID
  IEEE802.3 Link Aggregation
  IEEE802.3 Maximum Frame Size

Port      Tx Enabled  Rx Enabled
Et1       Yes         Yes
Et2       Yes         Yes
```

Et3	Yes	Yes
Et4	Yes	Yes
Et5	Yes	Yes
Et6	Yes	Yes
Et7	Yes	Yes
Et8	Yes	Yes
Et9	Yes	Yes
Et10	Yes	Yes
Et11	Yes	Yes
Et12	Yes	Yes
Et13	Yes	Yes
Et14	Yes	Yes
Et15	Yes	Yes
Et16	Yes	Yes
Et17	Yes	Yes
Et18	Yes	Yes
Et19	Yes	Yes
Et20	Yes	Yes
Et21	Yes	Yes
Et22	Yes	Yes
Et23	Yes	Yes
Et24	Yes	Yes

That's pretty boring. I'd rather see what switches are connected where, so I'll use the show lldp neighbors command. This should seem pretty familiar to anyone who has used CDP on a Cisco switch:

```
Arista#sho lldp neighbors
Last table change time   : 0:00:06 ago
Number of table inserts  : 3
Number of table deletes  : 0
Number of table drops    : 0
Number of table age-outs : 0

Port      Neighbor Device ID       Neighbor Port ID     TTL
Et10      Arista                   Ethernet11           120
Et11      Arista                   Ethernet10           120
Et24      SW-3750.cisco.com        [ Arista e24 ]       120
```

Now that's more like it! Ports e10 and e11 are connected to each other, which is why the hostname is Arista. Why do I have the switch connected to itself? Because I like to force equipment to do unusual things in order to try and get them to fail in spectacular ways. On port e24, the Neighbor Device ID is shown as *SW-3750.cisco.com*, which is a conglomeration of the hostname and the default domain name on the 3750. If you've never changed the domains on your Cisco switches, expect them all to show up as *host name*.cisco.com. I detest defaults when my OCD kicks in, so I went straight to my 3750 and changed the domain to gad.net:

```
SW-3750(config)#ip domain name gad.net
```

Shortly thereafter, the change showed up on my Arista switch:

```
Arista#sho lldp neighbors
Last table change time   : 0:00:33 ago
Number of table inserts  : 3
Number of table deletes  : 0
Number of table drops    : 0
Number of table age-outs : 0


Port    Neighbor Device ID      Neighbor Port ID      TTL
Et10    Arista                  Ethernet11            120
Et11    Arista                  Ethernet10            120
Et24    SW-3750.gad.net         [ Arista e24 ]        120
```

Unfortunately, the Cisco switch is not so open-minded, at least by default. Here's the output of the command show cdp neighbors on the 3750:

```
SW-3750#sho cdp neighbors
Capability Codes: R - Router, T - Trans Bridge, B- Source Route Bridge
                  S - Switch, H - Host, I - IGMP, r - Repeater, P - Phone

Device ID          Local Intrfce Holdtme  Capability Platform  Port ID
R1-PBX             Gig 1/0/10    144        R S I     2811      Fas 0/0
R1-PBX             Gig 1/0/11    135        R S I     2811      Fas 0/1
TS-1               Gig 1/0/39    122          R       2611      Eth 0/1
SEP0019AA96D096    Gig 1/0/42    126         H P      IP Phone  Port 1
Cisco-WAP-N        Gig 1/0/1     120         T I      AIR-AP125 Gig 0
SEP04FE7F689D33    Gig 1/0/2     125         H P      IP Phone  Port 1
SEP000DBC50FCD1    Gig 1/0/4     147         H P      IP Phone  Port 1
SEP00124362C4D2    Gig 1/0/42    147         H P      IP Phone  Port 1
```

While there are all sorts of interesting devices like WAPs and IP-Phones listed, there is no mention of the Arista switch. And although the Arista switch will listen to and understand the CDP advertisements, the 3750 doesn't see the LLDP advertisements being sent by Arista. Luckily, we can change that with the Cisco command lldp run:

```
SW-3750(config)#lldp run
```

While this won't let us see the Arista switch with the show cdp neighbor command, we can now see it with the show lldp neighbor command:

```
SW-3750#sho lldp neighbors

Capability codes:
    (R) Router, (B) Bridge, (T) Telephone, (C) DOCSIS Cable Device
    (W) WLAN Access Point, (P) Repeater, (S) Station, (O) Other

Device ID          Local Intf Hold-time  Capability  Port ID
SEP04FE7F689D33    Gi1/0/2    180         B,T         04FE7F689D33:P1
Office Switch      Gi1/0/42   120         B           g1
Arista             Gi1/0/52   120         B           Ethernet24

Total entries displayed: 3
```

Not only can we see the Arista switch on port G1/0/52, but we can also see some other devices that we heretofore could not see. The device named *Office Switch* is a Netgear eight-port 1 Gb switch that I didn't even know supported LLDP. What a pleasant surprise! I also found it interesting that the IP-Phone with the device-ID of *SEP04FE7F689D33* supports CDP and LLDP simultaneously.

As with CDP on a Cisco switch, detail information may be shown. Using the show lldp neighbors detail command will output a pile of useful information, but it's displayed a bit differently than the similar Cisco command. Where Cisco sorts this information by device discovered, Arista sorts it by interface, and shows every interface on the switch. I've removed some of the output, including one of the Arista-connected interfaces, in the interest of brevity:

```
Arista(config)# sho lldp neighbors detail
Interface Ethernet1 detected 0 LLDP neighbors:

Interface Ethernet2 detected 0 LLDP neighbors:

Interface Ethernet3 detected 0 LLDP neighbors:
[-- output removed --]

Interface Ethernet9 detected 0 LLDP neighbors:

Interface Ethernet10 detected 1 LLDP neighbors:

  Neighbor 001c.7308.80ae/Ethernet11, age 26 seconds
  Discovered 0:38:09 ago; Last changed 0:22:55 ago
    - Chassis ID type: MAC address (4)
      Chassis ID     : 001c.7308.80ae
    - Port ID type: Interface name (5)
      Port ID      : "Ethernet11"
    - Time To Live: 120 seconds
    - System Name: "Arista"
    - System Description: "Arista Networks EOS version 4.7.8 running
on an Arista Networks DCS-7124S"
    - System Capabilities : Bridge, Router
      Enabled Capabilities: Bridge
    - Management Address Subtype: Ethernet (6)
      Management Address      : 001c.7308.80ae
      Interface Number Subtype  : Unknown (1)
      Interface Number        : 0
      OID String            :
    - IEEE802.1 Port VLAN ID: 0
    - IEEE802.1/IEEE802.3 Link Aggregation
      Link Aggregation Status: Capable, Disabled (0x01)
      Port ID              : 0
    - IEEE802.3 Maximum Frame Size: 9236 bytes

[-- output removed --]

Interface Ethernet23 detected 0 LLDP neighbors:
```

```
Interface Ethernet24 detected 1 LLDP neighbors:

  Neighbor 001c.b084.cfb4/[ Arista e24 ], age 3 seconds
  Discovered 0:37:44 ago; Last changed 0:18:08 ago
    - Chassis ID type: MAC address (4)
      Chassis ID      : 001c.b804.cfb4
    - Port ID type: Interface alias (1)
      Port ID        : "[ Arista e24 ]"
    - Time To Live: 120 seconds
    - Port Description: "GigabitEthernet1/0/52"
    - System Name: "SW-3750.gad.net"
    - System Description: "Cisco IOS Software,
      C3750 Software (C3750-ADVIPSERVICESK9-M),
      Version 12.2(37)SE, RELEASE SOFTWARE (fc2)
Copyright (c) 1986-2007 by Cisco Systems, Inc.
Compiled Thu 10-May-07 16:31 by antonino"
    - System Capabilities : Bridge, Router
      Enabled Capabilities: None
    - Management Address Subtype: IPv4 (1)
      Management Address      : 192.168.1.4
      Interface Number Subtype : ifIndex (2)
      Interface Number        : 52
      OID String             :
    - IEEE802.1 Port VLAN ID: 901
    - IEEE802.3 MAC/PHY Configuration/Status
      Auto-negotiation       : Not Supported
      Advertised Capabilities: 10BASE-T (full-duplex)
      Operational MAU Type   : 1000BASE-SX (full-duplex) (26)
```

You can filter the output by specifying an interface, both with and without detail. Here is an example without detail:

```
Arista(config)#sho lldp neighbors ethernet 24
Last table change time  : 0:23:47 ago
Number of table inserts : 3
Number of table deletes : 0
Number of table drops   : 0
Number of table age-outs : 0

Port    Neighbor Device ID        Neighbor Port ID        TTL
Et24    SW-3750.gad.net           [ Arista e24 ]          120
```

That's it for now. Using LLDP will become second nature after a short time using Arista gear.

## CHAPTER 9

Bash

Arista switches are really Linux servers optimized and programmed to be network switches. By this point in the book, that should not be a surprise, but what may be surprising is the depth to which you, the administrator, may gain access to the system.

 If you really don't like the idea of junior engineers having access to bash, you can limit their access to bash using AAA.

To access bash, type the command bash from the enable prompt:

```
Arista-1#bash

Arista Networks EOS shell

[GAD@Arista-1 ~]$
```

At this point, I am within a bash shell on the switch. The prompt, by default, will be [*username@hostname directory*]$. In the previous example, I logged in to the switch with my username (GAD), as configured in the EOS CLI. I have not created a username in Unix; the switch took care of that for me.

At this point, I have just about all the control that I would have as a user in Linux. I am not a *superuser*, and my home directory is empty:

```
[GAD@Arista-1 ~]$ ls
[GAD@Arista-1 ~]$
```

I can navigate around the filesystem, just like I can on a Linux server:

```
[GAD@Arista-1 ~]$ cd /
[GAD@Arista-1 /]$ cd /usr/
[GAD@Arista-1 usr]$ ls
bin  etc  games  include  kerberos  lib  libexec  local  sbin  share
src  tmp
```

If you're at all familiar with Linux, then you'll be right at home in this bash shell:

```
[GAD@Arista-1 usr]$ ls -alh
total 0
drwxr-xr-x 13 root root  203 Oct 11 05:56 .
drwxr-xr-x 29 root root  220 Oct 27 20:41 ..
dr-xr-xr-x  2 root root  13K Oct 11 05:57 bin
drwxr-xr-x  2 root root    3 Aug 25  2009 etc
drwxr-xr-x  2 root root    3 Aug 25  2009 games
drwxr-xr-x  3 root root   53 Oct 11 05:56 include
drwxr-xr-x  3 root root   28 Oct 11 05:56 kerberos
dr-xr-xr-x 28 root root  35K Oct 11 05:57 lib
drwxr-xr-x  5 root root  377 Oct 11 05:56 libexec
drwxr-xr-x 11 root root  127 Oct 11 05:56 local
dr-xr-xr-x  2 root root 2.4K Oct 11 05:57 sbin
drwxr-xr-x 57 root root  896 Oct 11 05:57 share
drwxr-xr-x  4 root root   43 Oct 11 05:56 src
lrwxrwxrwx  1 root root   10 Oct 11 16:49 tmp -> ../var/tmp
```

To prove the point that an Arista switch is a Linux server with specialized interface hardware, I'll show the network interfaces from bash:

```
[GAD@Arista-1 usr]$ ifconfig -a
cpu       Link encap:Ethernet  HWaddr 00:1C:73:08:FA:49
          UP BROADCAST RUNNING MULTICAST  MTU:9216  Metric:1
          RX packets:18 errors:0 dropped:0 overruns:0 frame:0
          TX packets:0 errors:0 dropped:0 overruns:0 carrier:0
          collisions:0 txqueuelen:1000
          RX bytes:1080 (1.0 KiB)  TX bytes:0 (0.0 b)

et1       Link encap:Ethernet  HWaddr 00:1C:73:08:FA:49
          UP BROADCAST RUNNING MULTICAST  MTU:9212  Metric:1
          RX packets:33944 errors:0 dropped:0 overruns:0 frame:0
          TX packets:62802 errors:0 dropped:0 overruns:0 carrier:0
          collisions:0 txqueuelen:1000
          RX bytes:4209056 (4.0 MiB)  TX bytes:9981736 (9.5 MiB)

et2       Link encap:Ethernet  HWaddr 00:1C:73:08:FA:49
          UP BROADCAST MULTICAST  MTU:9212  Metric:1
          RX packets:0 errors:0 dropped:0 overruns:0 frame:0
          TX packets:0 errors:0 dropped:0 overruns:0 carrier:0
          collisions:0 txqueuelen:1000
          RX bytes:0 (0.0 b)  TX bytes:0 (0.0 b)
[-- output truncated --]
```

Heck, even vmstat works:

```
[GAD@Arista-1 usr]$ vmstat 5 5
procs ----------memory---------- -swap- --io- --system-- -----cpu-----
 r  b   swpd   free   buff  cache   si so bi bo   in   cs us sy id wa st
 0  0      0 754368 104220 752528    0  0  0  0   16   10  8  1 91  0  0
 0  0      0 754376 104220 752548    0  0  0  0 1037 1266  8  1 91  0  0
 1  0      0 754376 104220 752548    0  0  0  0 1025 1238  7  1 91  0  0
 0  0      0 754376 104220 752548    0  0  0  0 1073 1359  8  1 91  0  0
 0  0      0 754376 104220 752548    0  0  0  0 1040 1284  7  1 91  0  0
```

I feel it is important to reiterate that all these Linux commands work because the Arista switch is a Linux machine. This is not a bash emulation; this is bash. It is more accurate to think that the CLI on the Arista switch is a switch OS emulation; although to be painfully accurate, that is not right either.

The CLI environment on an Arista switch is a process in Linux. We can see this from bash by executing the command, Cli. Here, I'll spawn a CLI session, execute the CLI command, show clock, and then exit. Exiting a spawned CLI session returns me from whence I came—the bash shell:

```
[GAD@Arista-1 usr]$ Cli
Arista-1>
Arista-1>sho clock
Mon Nov  7 19:20:55 2011
timezone is UTC
Arista-1>exit
[GAD@Arista-1 usr]$
```

The Cli command has some pretty interesting options. Just like most other Linux commands, I can see them by appending --help at the command line:

```
 [GAD@Arista-1 usr]$ Cli --help
Usage: Cli [options]

Options:
  -h, --help              show this help message and exit
  -s SYSNAME, --sysname=SYSNAME
                          system name (default: ar)
  -k SYSDBSOCKNAME, --sysdbsockname=SYSDBSOCKNAME
                          Specify the unix domain socket of the
                          upstream Sysdb process
  -l, --standalone        run in standalone mode (without Sysdb).
                          Implies --disable-aaa
  --pdb                   run under pdb
  -c COMMAND, --command=COMMAND
                          run COMMAND non-interactively; separate
                          multiple commands with carriage returns
  -A, --disable-aaa       Do not communicate with the Aaa agent.  This
                          disables authentication, authorization and
                          accounting of commands executed in this Cli
                          instance.
```

```
-M, --disable-automore
                        Do not apply paging filter for show commands
                        executed in this Cli instance.
-e, --echo              echo commands when running non-interactively
-p PRIVILEGE, --privilege=PRIVILEGE
                        Start the session with this privilege level.
                        Legal values are 0-15 (default: 1)
-i PLUGINS, --plugin=PLUGINS
                        Load this plugin explicitly, and suppress
                        normal plugin search.  May be specified
                        repeatedly.
-I, --no-plugins        suppress any plugins from loading
-G, --disable-guards    Do not guard any commands.
```

One of the more interesting options is the -c *command* or --command=*command* choices. Using these options, I can execute CLI commands from within bash. For example, while in bash, executing Cli -c "sho ver" will spawn a CLI process, execute the CLI command show version, then exit, reporting the output to *stdout*:

```
[GAD@Arista-1 usr]$ Cli -c "sho ver"
Arista DCS-7124S-F
Hardware version:    07.00
Serial number:       JSH10426696
System MAC address:  001c.7308.fa49

Software image version: 4.8.1
Architecture:           i386
Internal build version: 4.8.1-495947.2011eric481Showstopper
Internal build ID:      b15379fb-13e9-4255-819f-e55dde3c3471

Uptime:              1 week, 3 days, 22 hours and 46 minutes
Total memory:        2043424 kB
Free memory:         733244 kB

[GAD@Arista-1 usr]$
```

Because this is Linux, I can pipe other commands too. Here, I'll use grep to only show the line containing the word "image":

```
[GAD@Arista-1 usr]$ Cli -c "sho ver" | grep image
Software image version: 4.8.1
```

For my next trick, I'll redirect the output to a file; but first, I need to be back in my home directory where I have write permissions:

```
[GAD@Arista-1 usr]$ cd ~
[GAD@Arista-1 ~]$
[GAD@Arista-1 ~]$ Cli -c "sho ver" | grep image > GAD.txt
```

I should now have a file in my home directory named *GAD.txt* that contains the output from my command. Let's take a look:

```
[GAD@Arista-1 ~]$ ls
GAD.txt
```

Sure enough, there it is. Using `cat` should work, and it does:

```
[GAD@Arista-1 ~]$ cat GAD.txt
Software image version: 4.8.1
[GAD@Arista-1 ~]$
```

Be careful here though! Writing files to my home directory is great, but I learned the hard way that anything written to the filesystem does not survive a reboot.

 That's worth a more prominent warning. Anything you write to the filesystem will not survive a reboot. There are only a few directory structures that remains untouched by a reboot: */mnt/flash*, */mnt/usb1* (if installed), and the SSD drive if your switch has one. If you want the output of your scripts or commands to be saved after a reboot, you must store them in one of these locations. You have been warned!

Just as I could run a CLI command through the `Cli` command in Linux, I can run bash commands from the `bash` command in CLI. Sure, that may sound like circular logic, but let me show you what I mean.

Remember how I got into bash from CLI? I typed the command `bash`:

```
Arista-1#bash

Arista Networks EOS shell

[GAD@Arista-1 ~]$
```

That's pretty cool, but what if I just need the output of a single command, and don't want to go through the hassle of dropping into bash, executing the command and exiting again? Good news! I can execute bash commands from CLI, without actually dropping to the bash command line. All I have to do is append the Linux command I want to run.

Let's say that I wanted to get the output of the Linux command, `uname -a`. To do this from CLI, all I need to do is issue the command `bash uname -a`. This will return the output from the Unix command to me without ever leaving CLI:

```
Arista-1#bash uname -a
Linux Arista-1 2.6.32.28.Ar-488566.2011fruggeri481 #1 SMP PREEMPT Thu
  Sep 29 02:20:09 EDT 2011 x86_64 x86_64 x86_64 GNU/Linux
Arista-1#
```

Note that any commands you execute will be relative to your home directory. Thus, logged in as GAD, if I ask for my current directory with the Unix `pwd` command, I will get the following results:

```
Arista#bash pwd
/home/GAD
```

This book is loaded with examples where I use bash commands through CLI, or use the bash shell. Once you get the hang of how this works, you'll start to appreciate the power inherent in the design of Arista switches. Once you feel the power, you'll cringe every time you have to use another vendor's switch.

## CHAPTER 10

SysDB

One of the most impressive EOS features that makes it stand out from the competition is SysDB. Simply put, SysDB is a *System Database* on the switch that holds all the state, variables, and any other important information so that processes may access it. Doesn't sound too earth-shattering, does it? Read on.

Traditionally, switches (and every other networking device out there) were built using *monolithic code*. Naturally, when I read the word *monolithic*, I think of apes dancing around the monolith in Stanley Kubrik's masterpiece, *2001*. That's actually not a bad analogy, aside from the whole "spark of humanity" thing.

Networking devices have been around for decades now, and many of them are very mature products, running very mature code. Executives like to use the word *mature* to describe something that's been around long enough to have all of the bugs worked out. Developers don't always agree with the usage of this word.

The problem is that some of this code has been around for decades too. In keeping with our monolithic analogy, imagine a switch that was first brought to market in, say, the year 2001. Now imagine that this switch is still in production 12 years later, and the software is up to around version 13, only instead of calling it version 13, let's call it something else, say, version 215. You know, because the number 13 is bad luck in many cultures, especially those that worship monolithic code.

Anyway, imagine that the initial software written for the switch consumed about 10 MB of disk space. Now imagine that every year, for the next 12 years, more and more features were added to that code. Imagine that the switch became so full of features that after those 12 years, the code grew to consume 100 MB of disk space.

Technology advances at a frightening pace. Features expected as standard offerings today might not have been conceivable 12 years before. New hardware becomes more complex, which requires more complex code, all of which is added on to the original code base. If the original coders didn't anticipate 12 years of growth, then they may not have made the original code easily expandable. Maybe, in the past 12 years, memory architectures changed. If you're as old as I am, you might remember a time when 640 K was more memory than a computer would ever need. Today, my Mac Pro currently has 24 GB of RAM. Things change. I can't imagine running a DOS machine today. As of July 2012, Windows XP was all the rage 12 years ago. Would you want a switch based on Windows XP?

That's not all, though. Even if the code was written well, and all those years of added routines were also written well, the fact remains that it's a single giant chunk of code that gets shoveled into memory. If you load an image that supports Spanning Tree Protocol (STP), but you don't need STP, the STP process is still in memory, sitting there, consuming space. Not only would that process consume space, but what would happen if that one piece of code crashed? With that code only a routine in the giant pile of monolithic code, the entire switch would crash. Bummer.

So there must be a better way, right? Sure there is! Linux changed everything in the server world, and it's doing so in the networking world as well. With Linux, the switch runs a kernel and a process manager. The process manager manages each process (hence the clever name) and restarts them if they crash. With this model, should STP crash, it wouldn't take the rest of the switch down with it. Or would it?

To properly protect a Linux system from misbehaving processes, each process should be written to use its own *user virtual address space*. Without getting into a server architecture discussion, understand that this type of memory is protected space that is only addressable by the process that owns it. If written using this model, then should STP crash, only STP is affected; the rest of the switch continues to run unaffected.

There are two problems with this paradigm. First, many vendors don't properly utilize user virtual address space, so one misbehaving process often affects other processes. Second, if STP crashes, your network will reconverge when STP comes back online. This is because the STP lost all of its known network topology, timer values, and such when it crashed, so it must start as if the switch was just booted. Arista has solved both problems.

Arista code is well written, and follows strict rules regarding user virtual address space. If the STP process crashes, no other process will be affected. More impressively, though, all state information for all processes is stored in the central database called *SysDB*. If that doesn't seem impressive, consider this: on an Arista switch, STP runs and stores all its state information in SysDB. When any process starts, the first thing it does is go to SysDB to retrieve state information. If it finds a state, it uses it. If not, it initializes. Let's take that to the next logical conclusion.

When a switch is booted, STP loads, checks SysDB (just booted, no state found), determines its state (through convergence, etc.), and then writes that state to SysDB. For some reason, STP crashes. Because STP is isolated, no other processes are affected. When STP crashes, the process manager restarts STP. STP loads, after which it immediately checks SysDB, where it finds state information. STP loads that information, and no convergence is necessary.

Don't believe me? Let's have a look. First, I'll add a timestamp to my command prompt. By issuing the `prompt %H[%D{%T}]%p` command, the prompt will change to *hostname[HH:MM:SS]command-mode*:

```
SW1(config)#prompt %H[%D{%T}]%p
SW1[21:54:22](config)#
```

Sure, that's a busy prompt, but it will help to illustrate how quickly the next few events take place.

> What I'm about to do is something that you shouldn't do in a production environment. Though the impact will be negligible (that's the point of this example), the complexities of a production environment should never be taken for granted.

I've built a simple network between two switches, as shown in Figure 10-1. There are two switches, SW1 and SW2. SW1 is an Arista switch, and SW2 is a terrific example of a monolithic code switch from another vendor. The network has a loop built into it, and SW1 is the root of Spanning-Tree MST instance 1. The interface g1/0/16 is blocking on the non-Arista switch.

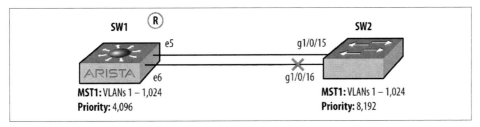

Figure 10-1. Simple network built for abusing EOS processes

With this network humming along nicely, and STP performing as it should, we'll go in and attempt to destroy it by killing STP on the Arista switch.

There are a number of ways to kill a process in an Arista switch. First, the hard way, which involves dropping to bash, finding the process number and killing it with the –9 (*sigterm*) flag:

```
SW1[22:27:49]#bash

Arista Networks EOS shell
```

The process names all begin with capital letters, so remember that when searching for the process:

```
[admin@SW1 ~]$ ps -ef | grep Stp
root      1512  1505  0 10:13 ?        00:00:05 StpTopology    -d -i
root     12713 12712  0 22:26 ?        00:00:00 Stp            -d -i
admin    12760 12739  0 22:27 pts/2    00:00:00 grep --color=auto Stp
```

Now that we know where the process is, we can kill it. Remember, only root can kill processes, so you'll need to use sudo:

```
[admin@SW1 ~]$ sudo kill -9 12713
```

The process manager sees the untimely death of the STP process so quickly that I couldn't capture output with it missing:

```
[admin@SW1 ~]$ ps -ef | grep Stp
root      1512  1505  0 10:13 ?        00:00:05 StpTopology    -d -i
root     12777 12776  0 22:28 ?        00:00:00 Stp            -d -i
admin    12824 12739  0 22:30 pts/2    00:00:00 grep --color=auto Stp
```

Of course, we could also just use the much friendlier killall command:

```
[admin@SW1 ~]$ sudo killall -9 Stp
```

That actually lets us kill STP with one command that can be called from within the CLI, so that helps to make my example flow better. Back in CLI, I can use the bash command along with the desired command. Watch the timestamps as I show the status of MST1, kill STP, then show the status of MST1 again:

```
SW1[22:35:33]#sho spanning-tree mst 1
##### MST1      vlans mapped:    1-1024
Bridge          address 001c.7308.80ae  priority     4097 (4096 sysid 1)
Root            this switch for MST1

Interface       Role        State      Cost      Prio.Nbr Type
--------------- ----------  ---------- --------- -------- ------------
Et5             designated forwarding 20000      128.5    P2p
Et6             designated forwarding 20000      128.6    P2p

SW1[22:35:34]#bash sudo killall -9 Stp
SW1[22:35:35]#sho spanning-tree mst 1
##### MST1      vlans mapped:    1-1024
Bridge          address 001c.7308.80ae  priority     4097 (4096 sysid 1)
Root            this switch for MST1

Interface       Role        State      Cost      Prio.Nbr Type
--------------- ----------  ---------- --------- -------- ------------
Et5             designated forwarding 20000      128.5    P2p
Et6             designated forwarding 20000      128.6    P2p
```

Within a second of killing the STP process, the process manager restarted it, and thanks to SysDB, STP never missed a beat. When the STP process started, it immediately requested the current state of the network from SysDB. Since there was a state found there, it simply used that instead of needing to start from an unknown network topology. Since this all happened well within the window of STP timers, the network didn't reconverge, and the other switch didn't even realize there was a problem.

I should warn you; be careful when killing processes. If you're a bit overzealous, you'll likely annoy the process manager, which may scold you with the following message:

```
SW1[22:42:19]#Jul  1 22:35:36 SW1 ProcMgr-worker:
%PROCMGR-3-PROCESS_DELAYRESTART: 'Stp' (PID=12994) restarted too often!
Delaying restart for 120.0 (HH:MM:SS)
(until 2012-07-01 22:44:19.942820)
```

That's one more reason not to play with this stuff in a production environment! Here's what the other switch in my test network reported during my two minutes in the penalty box:

```
SW2#
Jul  1 18:31:43: %SW_MATM-4-MACFLAP_NOTIF: Host 001c.7308.80ae in
vlan 100 is flapping between port Gi1/0/15 and port Gi1/0/16
SW2#
Jul  1 18:31:58: %SW_MATM-4-MACFLAP_NOTIF: Host 001c.7308.80ae in
vlan 100 is flapping between port Gi1/0/15 and port Gi1/0/16
```

 That's worth another warning. Don't kill processes in a production switch unless you really know what you're doing, or Arista Support tells you to, or you're looking to get fired anyway.

As a quick aside, if you start playing around with process killing, you'll likely discover the agent command. With this command, you can kill any process without resorting to bash commands. To kill the STP process, the following command would have the same effect as the bash sudo killall -9 Stp command we used earlier:

```
VM-SW3#agent stp terminate
Stp was terminated
```

Be warned though, if you issue the agent *process-name* shutdown command in configuration mode, the process will not come back! I can't tell you how many times I've used the agent Stp shutdown command instead of the agent Stp terminate command, and then spent a half hour trying to figure out why STP wasn't working. Luckily, agent *process-name* shutdown commands appear in the *running-config*, so when I finally get to the show running-config stage of my panicked troubleshooting, I'm gently reminded that I'm an idiot.

We've seen what happens when STP get's killed, which illustrates the power and benefit of SysDB, but what happens if SysDB itself dies a horrible, unnatural death? Let's find out!

```
SW1#bash sudo killall -9 Sysdb
SW1#Jun 30 17:36:47 SW1 Fru: %FWK-3-SOCKET_CLOSE_REMOTE: Connection
to Sysdb (pid:28194) at tbl://sysdb/ closed by peer (EOF)
Jun 30 17:36:47 SW1 Fru: %FWK-3-SELOR_PEER_CLOSED: Peer closed
socket connection. (tbl://sysdb/-in)(Sysdb (pid:28194))

Jun 30 17:36:47 SW1 Fru: %FWK-3-SELOR_EXIT: Process exiting.
Jun 30 17:36:47 SW1 Launcher: %FWK-3-SOCKET_CLOSE_REMOTE: Connection
to Sysdb (pid:28194) at tbl://sysdb/ closed by peer (EOF)

[--- Lots of processes screaming about SysDB dying removed ---]

Jun 30 17:36:47 SW1 PhyAeluros: %FWK-3-SELOR_PEER_CLOSED: Peer
closed socket connection. (tbl://sysdb/-in)(Sysdb (pid:28194))
Jun 30 17:36:47 SW1 PhyAeluros: %FWK-3-SELOR_EXIT: Process exiting.
Connection to Sysdb (pid:28194) at tbl://sysdb/ closed by peer (EOF)
Exiting because NboAttrLog connection has closed.

SW1 login:
```

In a nutshell, after killing the process at the heart of the entire switch, it recovered gracefully. To be fair, *gracefully* means that all the processes needed to reinitialize, and the end result was the same as rebooting the switch, but consider this: on my Arista 7124SX, it takes 1 minute and 45 seconds from the point where I enter the reload now command to the point where I get a login prompt (it takes longer if I pull the power since the hardware needs to initialize). If I kill SysDB, I get a login prompt after 15 seconds.

Let's have some fun and use that to our advantage. Since the *running-config* resides in SysDB, and SysDB is reinitialized when it's killed, I'm going to load a completely new configuration on the switch without rebooting. Ever been frustrated by needing to reboot in order to load a completely new configuration? This isn't a total cure, but it sure beats rebooting.

First, I'll save the current *startup-config* to a file named *OLD-Config*:

```
SW1#copy startup-config OLD-Config
```

Next, I'll remove the current *startup-config* with the write erase command:

```
SW1#write erase
```

I've written a simple configuration file that has nothing except the defaults and a changed hostname, just to show that the new configuration actually gets loaded. The new hostname will be *GAD*. The file name for this configuration is *GAD-Config*:

```
SW1#copy GAD-Config startup-config
```

At this point, my switch is running according to the configuration loaded in the *running-config*, but when it boots, it will load the code in *startup-config*, which has my new hostname installed. Remember, if I were to reboot the switch, it would take almost two minutes. Instead, I'll kill SysDB and watch what happens:

```
SW1#bash sudo killall -9 Sysdb
SW1#Jun 30 18:01:25 SW1 Fru: %FWK-3-SOCKET_CLOSE_REMOTE: Connection
to Sysdb (pid:2359) at tbl://sysdb/ closed by peer (EOF)
Jun 30 18:01:25 SW1 Launcher: %FWK-3-SOCKET_CLOSE_REMOTE: Connection
 to Sysdb (pid:2359) at tbl://sysdb/ closed by peer (EOF)
Jun 30 18:01:25 SW1 Fru: %FWK-3-SELOR_PEER_CLOSED: Peer closed socket
connection. (tbl://sysdb/-in)(Sysdb (pid:2359))

[--- Processes whining about SysDB removed ---]

Jun 30 18:01:25 SW1 PhyAeluros: %FWK-3-SELOR_PEER_CLOSED: Peer closed
socket connection. (tbl://sysdb/-in)(Sysdb (pid:2359))
Jun 30 18:01:25 SW1 PhyAeluros: %FWK-3-SELOR_EXIT: Process exiting.

SW1 login:
```

 Another way to accomplish this, which is probably a lot cleaner, is to use the `service ProcMgr restart` command, which will have the same result, but allow the system to perform a graceful restart. My goal in this chapter was to show how EOS handles a catastrophic failure, and graceful restarts are boring, so I decided to kill SysDB with reckless abandon instead.

Notice that the hostname hasn't changed? This is due to the fact that the hostname shown at this stage is actually the Linux hostname. Once I log in, the CLI process will report the newly configured EOS hostname:

```
SW1 login: admin
Last login: Sat Jun 30 21:47:12 on ttyS0
GAD>
```

And just like that, in 15 seconds flat, I've reloaded my Arista switch with a new configuration. Try that with a monolithic code–based switch from another vendor! To be completely fair, the time until all interfaces are up, all protocols settle, and things like MLAG stabilize will depend on the switch platform and the configuration.

 If you decide to play around with killing SysDB, be warned that as stated, it has the same effect as rebooting the switch. That means that unsaved changes to the *running-config* will be lost. Since killing SysDB isn't *really* graceful, there's no warning about unsaved changes. But if you're doing things like killing SysDB, then you must know what you're doing, right?

SysDB is the heart of Arista's EOS, and as I've hopefully shown in this chapter, the resiliency of SysDB along with the power of Linux makes for an amazingly robust switch operating system that almost can't be killed. Now if you'll excuse me, I have to go try and piece together the *running-config* I lost from that last example.

## CHAPTER 11

Python

In this chapter, I'll show you how Python was used to create much of what you see when using the CLI, and then I'll show you how to mess with it. Think about that for a minute; not only is EOS designed from the ground up to be extensible, but Arista has also given us the ability to alter the way in which the switch behaves. As far as I'm aware, this is unprecedented in the realm of networking devices. Sure, other devices are based on Linux, but you can't get to it, and you certainly can't change anything outside of the typical user-configurable options.

When I visited Arista for the first time, I asked Ken Duda (Founder, Chief Technology Officer, and Senior Vice President of Software Engineering) if they worried about end users rendering their switches inoperable by messing with stuff they didn't understand. His answer, and I'm paraphrasing here, was that Arista believed in the open source concept so strongly that they encouraged users to make new and exciting solutions based on their products. When I asked what would happen if I managed to Python my switch into a useless pile of network-crushing slag, I was told that Arista would try to help, but that since I had fundamentally altered the intended function of the switch, that my support would be on a best effort case. Again, I'm paraphrasing; I don't think the word *slag* was ever uttered during that conversation.

I've been in the IT industry for roughly 385 years (since 1984). In all that time, I've learned appropriate bitterness and derision for new ideas that are just recycled failures from the era of mainframes. Arista not only does things differently, they act differently. The ability to ruin my switch would be a support nightmare for any other company. Arista embraces the possibilities that for every clod like me who can't code Python to save his life, there might be someone out there with new ideas that could make an Arista switch into something wonderful that was previously unimaginable. To that end, I'm going to show you how to mess with the CLI.

The entire EOS experience can be viewed, managed, and even changed from the bash shell. Let's look at an extremely simple example of what I mean.

 If you're afraid of *vi*, or you don't know Python, or Unix gives you chills, then you shouldn't do any of this. Yes, you can muck things up beyond recognition, and yes, Arista will attempt to help you if you do, but your support will be best efforts when you alter the fundamental way your switch works. You can cause a lot of damage messing with these files. This example is meant to show the power and extensible nature of EOS. Mess with it at your own risk.

Within bash, we can find the Python scripts used by EOS for every CLI command. They are located in */usr/lib/python2.6/site-packages/CliPlugin/* on version 4.8.1.

Within this directory are hundreds of files, but for this example, I'll edit the output of the show version command to include the line "GAD Rocks!" Why? Because I'm a bored nerd with a keyboard, that's why.

From within the bash shell, we'll need to change to the proper directory:

```
[GAD@Arista-1 ~]$ cd /usr/lib/python2.6/site-packages/CliPlugin/
[GAD@Arista-1 CliPlugin]$
```

 File locations differ between versions. Later versions use different versions of Python based on where it resides in the Fedora distribution on which EOS is built. EOS versions 4.9 and 4.10 use Python 2.7, for example.

There are too many files to sift through, but I recommend you poke around and see what's available for your troublemaking, er, development pleasure. To limit what we're looking for, I'll use the command `ls -al *Cli*py`:

```
[GAD@Arista-1 CliPlugin]$ ls -al *Cli*py
-rw-r--r-- 1 root root  55478 Jun  9 12:44 AaaCli.py
-rw-r--r-- 1 root root  57944 Jun 10 16:36 AclCli.py
-rw-r--r-- 1 root root  12387 Jun 10 16:36 AclCliRules.py
-rw-r--r-- 1 root root  22636 Jun  9 12:52 AgentCli.py
-rw-r--r-- 1 root root   6923 Jun  9 12:41 AliasIntfCli.py
-rw-r--r-- 1 root root   7671 Jun 10 16:38 BackupIntfCli.py
-rw-r--r-- 1 root root   5696 Jun 10 16:56 BeaconLedCli.py
-rw-r--r-- 1 root root   5994 Jun  9 12:52 BootCli.py
-rw-r--r-- 1 root root  30684 Jun 10 16:27 BridgingCli.py
-rw-r--r-- 1 root root   3731 Jun  9 12:37 CliCli.py
```

```
-rw-r--r-- 1 root root     834 Jun  9 12:37 CliError.py
-rw-r--r-- 1 root root    7795 Jun  9 12:52 ClockCli.py
-rw-r--r-- 1 root root   11040 Jun 10 17:11 DcbxCli.py
[--- output truncated ---]
```

Look around and it should become obvious what commands are controlled by which scripts. For my ludicrous project, I'm looking for the script that controls the output of the show version command. With a little bit of searching, I discovered the file *Version Cli.py*:

```
-rw-r--r-- 1 root root    6188 Sep 28 19:01 VersionCli.py
```

Since I have pathetically dated programming skills and I'm not afraid to use them, I dug right in and edited that file:

```
[GAD@Arista-1 CliPlugin]$ sudo vi VersionCli.py
```

 As with most implementations of Linux, you should not become root. Use of the sudo command will become second nature. If you really, *really* want to be running around like you own the place, you can feel like root by using the sudo bash command. But don't. It's not good for you.

This rewarded me with a *vi* session with the *VersionCli.py* file open:

```
# Copyright (c) 2006-2010 Arista Networks, Inc.  All rights reserved.
# Arista Networks, Inc. Confidential and Proprietary.

import Tac, CliParser, BasicCli, os, Tracing, EosVersion, Ethernet

__defaultTraceHandle__ = Tracing.Handle( 'VersionCli' )
t0 = Tracing.trace0

#---------------------------------------------------------------------
# The "show version [detail]" command.
#---------------------------------------------------------------------
tokenVersion = CliParser.KeywordRule(
    'version',
    helpdesc='Show switch version information' )

tokenDetail = CliParser.KeywordRule(
    'detail',
    helpdesc='Show additional version information',
    name='detail' )

def showVersion( mode, detail=None ):
"VersionCli.py" 156L, 6188C
```

Knowing enough to be dangerous, I scrolled down a bit, looking for the beginning of the showVersion definition (seen at the bottom of the previous screen):

```
tokenDetail = CliParser.KeywordRule(
   'detail',
   helpdesc='Show additional version information',
   name='detail' )

def showVersion( mode, detail=None ):
   vi = EosVersion.VersionInfo( mode.sysdbRoot )
   # Print information about the switch hardware

   print "Arista %s" % ( vi.modelNameExtended() )
   print "Hardware version:    %s" %( vi.hardwareRev() )
   if detail:
      deviations = vi.deviations()
      if deviations:
         print "Deviations:            %s" %( ", ".join( deviations ) )
   print "Serial number:      %s" %( vi.serialNum() )
   entityMib = mode.sysdbRoot[ 'hardware' ][ 'entmib' ]
   print "System MAC address:  %s" \
         %Ethernet.convertMacAddrCanonicalToDisplay(
entityMib.systemMacAddr )
   print ""

   # Print information about the running software image.
   print "Software image version: %s" % vi.version()
```

I inject a nice chunk of Python statement to print GAD Rocks!, which looks like this:

```
def showVersion( mode, detail=None ):
   vi = EosVersion.VersionInfo( mode.sysdbRoot )
   # Print information about the switch hardware

   # Added by GAD 9-28-11
   print ""
   print "GAD Rocks!"
   ptint ""

   print "Arista %s" % ( vi.modelNameExtended() )
   print "Hardware version:    %s" %( vi.hardwareRev() )
   if detail:
      deviations = vi.deviations()
      if deviations:
         print "Deviations:            %s" %( ", ".join( deviations ) )
   print "Serial number:      %s" %( vi.serialNum() )
   entityMib = mode.sysdbRoot[ 'hardware' ][ 'entmib' ]
```

I saved my changes, exited *vi*, and moved to test my brilliant creation. To do so, I launched another session of CLI from the command line with the Cli Unix command.

 Remember how I wrote that even the CLI environment is a process that runs in its own user space? The Cli command lets us launch a new CLI process from Unix. Pretty cool, huh?

When I saw this mess, I knew that I'd done something wrong:

```
[GAD@Arista-1 CliPlugin]$ Cli
Error loading plugin 'VersionCli'
================ Exception raised in 'Cli [interac          ' (PID 18604;
PPID 18283) ================
Local variables by frame (innermost frame last):

  File "/usr/lib/python2.6/site-packages/Plugins.py", line 173,
in _loadPluginAttrs
                dirName = 'CliPlugin'
             moduleName = 'CliPlugin.VersionCli'
                   name = 'VersionCli'
             pluginList = [('AaaCli', <function Plugin at 0x986fca4>,
 (), ()), ('AclCli', <function Plugin at 0x9ad99cc>, (), ()),
('AclCliRules', None, (), ()), ('AgentCli', <function Plugin at
0x9ae3534>, (), ()), ('AliasIntfCli', <function Plugin at 0x9ae364c>,
(), ()), ('BackupIntfCli', <function Plugin at 0x9b01dbc>, (), ()),
('Banner', <function Plugin at 0x9afc064>, (), ()), ('BeaconLedCli',
<function Plugin at 0x9afc33c>, (), ()), ('BootCli', None, (), ()),
('BridgingCli', <function Plugin at 0x9b0e17c>, (), ()), ('CliCli',
None, (),
[--- output truncated ---]
```

Sure enough, here's what I entered, with the mistake in bold:

```
# Added by GAD 9-28-11
print ""
print "GAD Rocks!"
ptint ""
```

Apparently ptint isn't a command in Python. Who knew? After fixing my syntax error and making ptint into print, I tried again:

```
[GAD@Arista-1 CliPlugin]$ Cli
Arista-1>
```

Much better. Now let's see what the output of show version looks like:

```
Arista-1>sho ver

GAD Rocks!

Arista DCS-7124S-F
Hardware version:      07.00
Serial number:         JSH10426696
System MAC address:    001c.7308.fa49

Software image version: 4.7.7
Architecture:           i386
Internal build version: 4.7.7-470791.EOS477release
Internal build ID:      91635ce6-88e9-4d07-abe0-3412ea936472
```

```
Uptime:                 9 minutes
Total memory:           2043420 kB
Free memory:            803864 kB
```

Success! How cool is that? Sure it's a useless modification, but what if your company demanded something like "Property of GAD Technology – Unauthorized use is prohibited" at the end of every command's output? You could do that with EOS. What if you wanted to display bytes per second instead of bits per second on some command output? (EOS is actually so cool that it converts the displayed values between bps, Kbps, Mbps, and Gbps, on the fly in show interface commands.) Or better yet, you wanted to create a new command that did something wonderful. All of those ideas and more are possible with EOS.

 If you're running EOS version 4.9 or later, you may need to issue the bash command sudo killall FastClid-server to make your changes appear in CLI. This is due to the new *FastCLId-server* process that makes the CLI load faster by preloading all of the CLI plug-ins.

There's one more step that needs to be done, or our change will not stay after a reboot. The files we messed with are in a temporary filesystem that is created and mounted at boot time. That means that they are created every time, so our changes will not "stick" after booting.

To rectify this, first copy your altered script to the */mnt/flash* directory. This directory is persistent between reboots, so it's a safe place to store altered code:

```
[GAD@Arista-1 CliPlugin]$ cp VersionCli.py /mnt/flash/VersionCliNEW.py
```

Now for the tricky part: the EOS developers have gone to great lengths to make EOS customizable. To that end, when EOS starts, it looks for a script in */mnt/flash* called rc.eos. This script allows you to make changes to EOS before it loads. We'll use it to copy our new script and overwrite the existing one that was just created at boot time:

```
[GAD@Arista-1 CliPlugin]$ cd /mnt/flash
[GAD@Arista-1 flash]$ vi rc.eos
```

In my case, I had to create *rc.eos*, after which I added the following:

```
#!/bin/sh

# Includes the file /etc/swi-version
. /etc/swi-version

if [ $SWI_VERSION == 4.7.7 ]; then
    # Version is same as original - proced with copy
    echo SWI version match copying modified parser files
    cp /mnt/flash/VersionCliNEW.py \
```

```
             /usr/lib/python2.6/site-packages/CliPlugin/VersionCli.py
    else
        # Version is different - do not overwrite script
        echo WARNING: SWI version has changed to $SWI_VERSION
    fi
```

This script can be tested by running it through `sudo`:

```
[GAD@Arista-1 flash]$ sudo ./rc.eos
SWI version match copying modified parser files
```

On newer EOS revisions (4.9 and later), the smoother way to accomplish this is with `event-handler`. `event-handler` is covered in detail in Chapter 26, but for now, here are the commands that will solve this issue.

First, instead of making the script reside in *rc.eos*, create the bash script elsewhere. I've created one named *Load-GAD-CLI* in */mnt/flash*. I then issue the following commands to create an event handler:

```
Arista(config)#event-handler Boot-CLI
Arista(config-handler-Boot-CLI)#trigger onBoot
Arista(config-handler-Boot-CLI)#action bash sudo /mnt/flash/Load-GAD-CLI
Arista(config-handler-Boot-CLI)#exit
```

This will run my script much later in the boot process, which can be a bit cleaner than using *rc.eos*, since that loads very early in the boot process. This technique only works on EOS 4.9 and later, and naturally, since the script shown was written for 4.7.7, I'd need an updated script as well.

At this point, my change persisted after rebooting and I proceeded to add *Python Operating System developer* to my resume.

 One final note is in order. When upgrading EOS, you should check any changes you have made. If the core Fedora distribution changed, then the Python version (and related directory structure) will change. Additionally, libraries used by the original Python script may have changed, and the original script you altered may have changed.

At this point you should be able to see that EOS is very similar to Cisco's IOS so far as look and feel are concerned. You should also understand that underneath the surface, EOS is considerably more open and powerful than IOS could ever hope to be. Once you grow accustomed to the power and flexibility of EOS, using anything else becomes an exercise in frustration.

## CHAPTER 12

MLAG

Multichassis Link Aggregation (MLAG), is the Arista term for linking a port-channel to multiple switches instead of just one. The technology accomplishes the same basic goal as Cisco's Virtual Port Channel (vPC); although, in my experience, MLAG is simpler to configure and less likely to fail in colorful, job-threatening ways.

MLAG Overview

The term LAG is an abbreviation for *Link Aggregation*, which is a non-Cisco way of describing the bonding of multiple physical links into a single logical link. In Cisco parlance, this technology is called *Etherchannel*. Different vendors use different terms for similar solutions, but the term LAG has become a cross-vendor acceptable way of describing the idea.

A LAG connects multiple physical links on the same switch. MLAG is designed to allow two or more links on multiple switches into a single logical link. Why would you want to do this? Let's take a look.

With a traditional network design, interconnecting three switches results in a loop. Loops are bad, so Spanning Tree Protocol (STP) blocks the interface on the link farthest from the root. An example of this is shown in Figure 12-1.

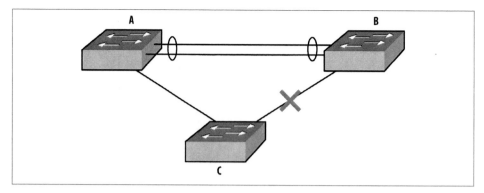

Figure 12-1. Traditional STP-blocked network loop

In this scenario, there is a LAG connecting switch A to switch B. Switch C connects to both A and B switches, forming a loop. STP has blocked the interface on switch C that leads to switch B in order to break said loop. This design will allow for failover if the link between switches A and C were to fail, but the failover can take 30 seconds or more (substantially less if rapid STP is used). Not only that, but only one half of the available bandwidth too and from switch C is available for use. Wouldn't it be cool if we could use that extra link? Even better, if we used LAG technology, then a single link failure wouldn't incur an outage because the second link would already be active.

With MLAG, two Arista switches fool the third switch (or any other dot1Q-capable device) into thinking that it is talking with a single device. In other words, two Arista switches appear to be one Arista switch to dot1Q. This is shown in Figure 12-2.

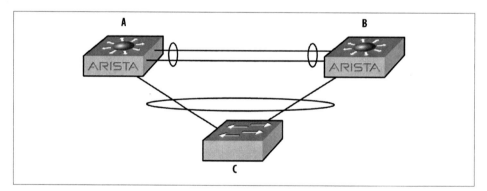

Figure 12-2. Simple MLAG design

With MLAG active, switch C sees a 20 Gbps logical interface, to a single device, even though it is connected to two devices. Arista accomplishes this feat by advertising the same device ID from both switch A and switch B. In order to do this, switch A and switch B must communicate over the A–B switch link, which must be configured with a VLAN that acts as a *peer-link*.

MLAG is configured within something called an *MLAG Domain*. The MLAG Domain ID identifies the switch to another switch that will share MLAGs. Multiple MLAG domains must be used when interconnecting MLAGs between MLAG pairs. I'll explain that one in a bit. For now, let's build an MLAG pair.

Configuring MLAG

The first thing we need to do is make sure that both MLAG peers are on the same (as in identical) revision of code. Will it work if the switches have different code? Probably, but I've seen some funkiness when the versions didn't match. Arista writes great code, but any protocol like this is happier when the code revisions match.

 As this chapter was being edited, EOS version 4.9.3 was released. EOS 4.9.3 introduced the feature called MLAG ISSU, which allows switches within an MLAG pair to run different versions of code. This allows you to upgrade each switch within an MLAG pair without ever bringing the attached MLAGs down.

Before configuring MLAG, check to make sure that the control plane allows the MLAG traffic on each switch. This should be enabled by default. The way to see if it is, is to show the access list entitled *default-control-plane-acl*:

```
Arista-1#sho ip access-lists
IP Access List default-control-plane-acl [readonly]
        10 permit icmp any any
        20 permit ip any any tracked
        30 permit ospf any any
        40 permit tcp any any eq ssh telnet www snmp bgp https
        50 permit udp any any eq bootps bootpc snmp
        60 permit tcp any any eq mlag ttl eq 255
        70 permit udp any any eq mlag ttl eq 255
        80 permit vrrp any any
        90 permit ahp any any
        100 permit pim any any
        110 permit igmp any any
        120 permit tcp any any range 5900 5910
```

If there is a different ACL for the control plane, then we would need to make sure that the two bold lines are included in the ACL filtering the control plane.

Let's build a simple MLAG setup using the network shown in Figure 12-3.

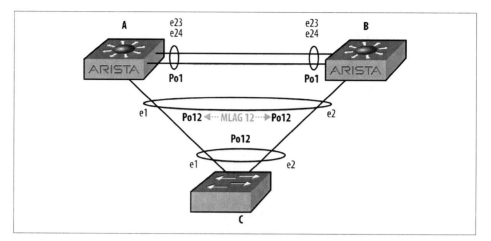

Figure 12-3. MLAG network detail

We'll need to create a peer-link over which the two switches can communicate. This link can be a single link, but for redundancy, it should always be a port-channel containing a minimum of two physical links. In this example, there are two 24-port switches, so let's use the last two interfaces, e23 and e24:

```
Arista-1(config)#int e23-24
Arista-1(config-if-Et23-24)#channel-group 1 mode active
```

Next, we configure the port-channel to be a trunk:

```
Arista-1(config-if-Et23-24)#int po 1
Arista-1(config-if-Po1)#switchport mode trunk
```

If you're used to Cisco switches, you'll notice that the switch did not bark at us about trunk encapsulation. Here's what would happen on a Cisco switch:

```
Cisco-1(config)#int f1/0/7
Cisco-1(config-if)#switchport mode trunk
Command rejected: An interface whose trunk encapsulation is "Auto"
can not be configured to "trunk" mode.
```

Arista does not negotiate trunk encapsulation, because it only supports dot1q trunks. Cisco switches also support ISL, which is a Cisco proprietary protocol. But enough of my attention deficit issues; let's continue.

With the port-channel configured as a trunk, we need to create a VLAN that will be used only for MLAG peer-to-peer communication. The Arista examples use VLAN 4094, so let's keep that tradition alive:

```
Arista-1(config)#vlan 4094
Arista-1(config-vlan-4094)#trunk group MLAG-Peer
```

The trunk group *MLAG-Peer* command creates a *trunk group*, which is a cool way of assigning VLANs to trunks. We now need to assign the same group to the peer-link:

```
Arista-1(config-vlan-4094)#int po 1
Arista-1(config-if-Po1)#switchport trunk group MLAG-Peer
```

Now, VLAN 4094 will only be included on trunks that are also assigned to the MLAG-Peer trunk group. By doing this, when we create a new trunk, by default VLAN 4094 will *not* be included. This keeps the MLAG peer-link traffic on this link, and only on this link (unless you add the MLAG-Peer trunk group to another trunk, but don't do that).

The trunk group names for the peer VLAN should be configured to be the same on both switches. The configuration for VLANs and VLAN trunk groups must be identical in order to successfully establish an MLAG association between two switches.

Now that we know this VLAN is limited to the peer-link, we can disable spanning-tree on the VLAN:

```
Arista-1(config)#no spanning-tree vlan 4094
```

Note that this is a global command, and not an interface command. It will fail with a % Incomplete command message if run from interface configuration mode since it is used to set cost and port priority there.

Since MST is the default spanning tree protocol in use on Arista switches, and MST is not VLAN based, this command will not have the same result that it would if Rapid-PVST were enabled. It is still a best practice to disable spanning tree from the MLAG peer VLAN in case Rapid-PVST is ever enabled.

 Disabling STP is almost always a bad idea. In this case, the MLAG peer-link always needs to be up in order to prevent a split brain scenario. Since the peer-link is using a trunk group, and there's only one VLAN on the link, then a loop should never occur. The only way a loop could possibly occur would be (in this example) for the MLAG-Peer trunk group to be included on other links from the MLAG pair. So don't do that. Ever.

Since MLAG communicates over layer 3, we must assign an IP address to the VLAN on each side:

```
Arista-1(config)#int vlan 4094
Arista-1(config-if-Vl4094)#ip address 10.0.0.1/30
```

Now, MLAG itself must be configured:

```
Arista-1(config)#mlag
Arista-1(config-mlag)#local-interface vlan 4094
Arista-1(config-mlag)#peer-address 10.0.0.2
Arista-1(config-mlag)#peer-link port-channel 1
Arista-1(config-mlag)#domain-id MLAG-1
```

The commands should be relatively obvious. We've assigned the MLAG local interface
to be the VLAN SVI we just created (VLAN 4094); we've told the switch that the peer
for this MLAG domain is at the IP address 10.0.0.2; the peer-link is riding over port-
channel 1; and the MLAG domain ID is MLAG-1.

The domain ID is the means whereby the switch differentiates different MLAG groups.
This will be shown in more detail later in this chapter.

At this point, the status of the peer-link should be up. This can be shown with the
command show mlag:

```
Arista-1(config-if-Po12)#sho mlag
MLAG Configuration:
domain-id           :              MLAG-1
local-interface     :              Vlan4094
peer-address        :              10.0.0.2
peer-link           :        Port-Channel1

MLAG Status:
state               :              Inactive
peer-link status    :                   Up
local-int status    :                   Up
system-id           :    00:00:00:00:00:00

MLAG Ports:
Disabled            :    0
Configured          :    0
Inactive            :    0
Active-partial      :    0
Active-full         :    0
```

The last paragraph that begins with MLAG ports shows all zeroes because we have not
created any MLAGs yet. Let's go ahead and create a simple MLAG.

In this example, I've set up two Arista switches (Arista-1 and Arista-2) connected to a
single Cisco 3750. The two Arista switches will be forming an MLAG peer, while the
Cisco switch will view the link as a regular port-channel.

The Cisco switch is configured as follows:

```
interface Port-channel12
  switchport trunk encapsulation dot1q
  switchport mode trunk

interface GigabitEthernet1/0/1
  switchport trunk encapsulation dot1q
  switchport mode trunk
```

```
channel-group 12 mode active
!
interface GigabitEthernet1/0/2
 switchport trunk encapsulation dot1q
 switchport mode trunk
 channel-group 12 mode active
```

This forms a simple port-channel (Po12) that is comprised of the physical links, G1/0/1 and G1/0/2. All ports are 1 gigabit. The port-channel will use the dot1Q protocol due to the mode active keywords in the channel-group commands.

To minimize page flipping, let's look at the network again. The network is shown in Figure 12-4.

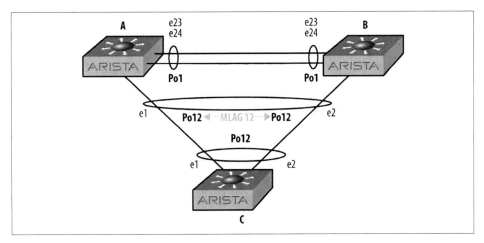

Figure 12-4. The MLAG network once more

At this point, the configuration for MLAG is very simple. On Arista-1, we'll use port e1, and assign it to port-channel 12.

 It may be confusing to see that all three switches are using port-channel 12. Note that they do NOT need to be the same. I strongly urge you to keep them the same, at least on the MLAG peers. I've worked on installations where the MLAG peers shared an MLAG using different port-channel interfaces, and it was a nightmare to debug during an outage. Keep it simple, and you'll keep your job.

Logically, Figure 12-5 shows how switch C sees the network with MLAG enabled on switches A and B. At this point, switch C has no idea that switches A and B are two different devices, at least so far as LACP (Link Aggregation Control Protocol) is concerned.

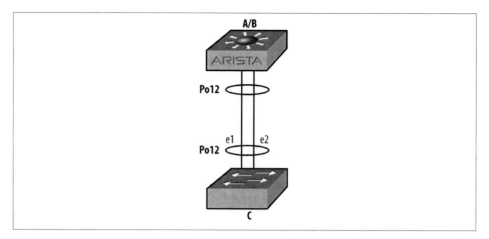

Figure 12-5. How switch C sees the network with MLAG enabled

We are using mode active on the Arista switches in order to use LACP. Wherever possible, you should use LACP in active mode for the greatest resiliency:

```
Arista-1(config)#int e1
Arista-1(config-if-Et1)#channel-group 12 mode active
```

Now that the interface Po12 exists, we'll assign it to mlag 12:

```
Arista-1(config-if-Et1)#int po 12
Arista-1(config-if-Po12)#mlag 12
```

 I can't stress this enough: please make your MLAG numbers correspond to the port-channel numbers to which they are assigned. They don't have to match, but your life will be a living hell while you try to debug mismatched MLAGs in an outage with the CEO yelling at you while you type. Not that that's ever happened to me.

Now we need to do the same steps on Arista-2. The only difference is that on this switch I'm using the e2 interface:

```
Arista-2(config)#int e2
Arista-2(config-if-Et2)#channel-group 12 mode active
```

Now we can configure the port-channel interface:

```
Arista-2(config-if-Et2)#int po 12
Arista-2(config-if-Po12)#mlag 12
```

At this point, the MLAG should be up, but in our case, it's not. As with every networking problem, we'll start at the physical layer and work our way up. After seeing an orange link light on the G1/0/2 Cisco interface, I checked the interface on both sides of the link. Here is the Arista side:

```
Arista-2(config-if-Po12)#sho int po 12
Port-Channel12 is down, line protocol is lowerlayerdown (notconnect)
  Hardware is Port-Channel, address is 001c.7301.0f19
  MTU 9212 bytes
  Full-duplex, 0b/s
  Active members in this channel: 0
  Last clearing of "show interface" counters never
  5 minutes input rate 0 bps (- with framing), 0 packets/sec
  5 minutes output rate 0 bps (- with framing), 0 packets/sec
     0 packets input, 0 bytes
     Received 0 broadcasts, 0 multicast
     0 input errors
     0 packets output, 0 bytes
     Sent 0 broadcasts, 0 multicast
     0 output errors
```

Hmm…that doesn't look good. Let's see what the Cisco side says:

```
Cisco-1#sho int g1/0/2
  GigabitEthernet1/0/2 is up, line protocol is down (suspended)
  Hardware is Gigabit Ethernet, address is 000f.9080.4982
(bia 000f.9080.4982)
  MTU 9000 bytes, BW 1000000 Kbit, DLY 10 usec,
     reliability 255/255, txload 1/255, rxload 1/255
  Encapsulation ARPA, loopback not set
  Keepalive not set
  Full-duplex, 1000Mb/s, link type is auto, media type is
10/100/1000BaseTX SFP
  input flow-control is off, output flow-control is unsupported
  ARP type: ARPA, ARP Timeout 04:00:00
  Last input 00:00:01, output 00:00:01, output hang never
  Last clearing of "show interface" counters never
  Input queue: 0/75/0/0 (size/max/drops/flushes); Total output drops:0
  Queueing strategy: fifo
  Output queue: 0/40 (size/max)
  5 minute input rate 0 bits/sec, 0 packets/sec
  5 minute output rate 0 bits/sec, 0 packets/sec
     1521 packets input, 200736 bytes, 0 no buffer
     Received 1521 broadcasts (1521 multicasts)
     0 runts, 0 giants, 0 throttles
     0 input errors, 0 CRC, 0 frame, 0 overrun, 0 ignored
     0 watchdog, 1521 multicast, 0 pause input
     0 input packets with dribble condition detected
     1090 packets output, 132480 bytes, 0 underruns
     0 output errors, 0 collisions, 0 interface resets
     0 babbles, 0 late collision, 0 deferred
     0 lost carrier, 0 no carrier, 0 PAUSE output
     0 output buffer failures, 0 output buffers swapped out
```

Ah! The Cisco side has suspended one of the links. Why?

Apparently some idiot forgot to configure the peer-link VLAN on Arista-2. Because there were two switches advertising two different device IDs within the same LACP bundle, the Cisco switch suspended one of them. This condition is called *split brain*, and is what I like to call *bad*. Luckily, the Cisco switch is smart enough to notice. Here's what the Cisco switch saw with MLAG broken. First, interface G1/0/1:

```
Cisco-1#sho int g1/0/1 etherchannel | begin Dev ID
Port      Flags   Priority  Dev ID        Age    key    Key
Gi1/0/1   SA      32768     001c.7308.fa49 1s     0x0    0xC

Age of the port in the current state: 0d:00h:06m:24s
```

And next, interface G1/0/2, the other interface within the port-channel 12 bundle:

```
Cisco-1#sho int g1/0/2 etherchannel | begin Dev ID
Port      Flags   Priority  Dev ID        Age    key    Key
Gi1/0/2   SA      32768     001c.7301.0f17 14s    0x0    0xC

Age of the port in the current state: 0d:00h:05m:48s
```

Look carefully at the device IDs. They're different (001c.7308.fa49 versus 001c.7301.0f17). As far as the Cisco switch is concerned, there are two different devices trying to form a single port-channel (which there are), and that's not allowed. Hence, the Cisco switch suspended one of them as being invalid.

Once I fixed the VLAN issue, the following popped up on Arista-1:

```
Sep 27 19:58:41 Arista-1 Lag+LacpAgent: %LACP-4-PARTNER_CHURN: LACP
Partner Churn Detected on Ethernet1

Sep 27 19:58:56 Arista-1 Mlag: %MLAG-4-INTF_INACTIVE_PEER: Interface
Port-Channel12 is link down on the MLAG peer. MLAG 12 is inactive.

Sep 27 19:58:56 Arista-1 Ebra: %LINEPROTO-5-UPDOWN: Line protocol on
Interface Port-Channel12, changed state to up

Sep 27 19:59:14 Arista-1 Mlag: %MLAG-6-INTF_ACTIVE: Local interface
Port-Channel12 and peer interface Port-Channel12 are link up.  MLAG
12 is active.
```

Once the MLAG became active, the Cisco switch was duped into believing that the two devices were really one. How? They both have the same device ID now. Here is the output of the same two commands we used earlier, showing the device IDs properly in sync. First for interface G1/0/1:

```
Cisco-1#sho int g1/0/1 etherchannel | begin Dev ID
Port      Flags   Priority  Dev ID        Age    key    Key
Gi1/0/1   SA      32768     021c.7301.0f17 3s     0x0    0xC

Age of the port in the current state: 0d:00h:08m:33s
```

And then for interface G1/0/2:

```
Cisco-1#sho int g1/0/2 etherchannel | begin Dev ID
Port      Flags  Priority Dev ID           Age   key   Key
Gi1/0/2   SA     32768    021c.7301.0f17   9s    0x0   0xC

Age of the port in the current state: 0d:00h:08m:18s
```

With the MLAG working, the Arista-1 switch shows a proper status:

```
Arista-1#sho mlag
MLAG Configuration:
domain-id          :             MLAG-1
local-interface    :             Vlan4094
peer-address       :             10.0.0.2
peer-link          :         Port-Channel1

MLAG Status:
state              :             Active
peer-link status   :                Up
local-int status   :                Up
system-id          :  02:1c:73:01:0f:17

MLAG Ports:
Disabled           :  0
Configured         :  0
Inactive           :  0
Active-partial     :  0
Active-full        :  1
```

Notice that the system ID matches the device ID that we saw on the Cisco switch.

To see the status of individual MLAG interfaces, use the show mlag interfaces command:

```
Arista-1#sho mlag interfaces
                                                       local/remote
    mlag    desc            state     local   remote      status
    ---------------------------------------------------------------
      12             active-full    Po12    Po12       up/up
```

Here is the output of the other switch with three configured MLAGs, of which only one is active:

```
Arista-2#sho mlag interfaces
                                                       local/remote
    mlag    desc            state     local   remote      status
    ---------------------------------------------------------------
       5              configured    Po5      -         down/-
      12             active-full    Po12    Po12       up/up
      34              configured    Po34     -         down/-
```

If MLAG is active, but the peer's link (not the peer-link!) is down for whatever reason, then the status of the MLAG will be Active-partial:

```
Arista-1#sho mlag
MLAG Configuration:
domain-id          :          MLAG-1
local-interface    :          Vlan4094
peer-address       :          10.0.0.2
peer-link          :      Port-Channel1

MLAG Status:
state              :          Active
peer-link status   :          Down
local-int status   :     LowerLayerDown
system-id          :  02:1c:73:01:0f:17

MLAG Ports:
Disabled           :    0
Configured         :    0
Inactive           :    0
Active-partial     :    1
Active-full        :    0
```

To get some detail regarding the state of MLAG in general, use the show mlag detail command:

```
Arista-1#sho mlag detail
MLAG Configuration:
domain-id          :          MLAG-1
local-interface    :          Vlan4094
peer-address       :          10.0.0.2
peer-link          :      Port-Channel1

MLAG Status:
state              :          Active
peer-link status   :          Down
local-int status   :     LowerLayerDown
system-id          :  02:1c:73:01:0f:17

MLAG Ports:
Disabled           :    0
Configured         :    0
Inactive           :    0
Active-partial     :    1
Active-full        :    0

MLAG Detailed Status:
State                     :          primary
State changes             :                8
Last state change time    :      0:00:07 ago
primary-priority          :            32767
Peer primary-priority     :               20
Peer MAC address          :  00:1c:73:01:0f:17
Reload delay              :      300 seconds
Peer ports errdisabled    :            False
Heartbeat interval        :          2000 ms
```

```
Heartbeat timeout                  :              5000 ms
Last heartbeat timeout             :       17:43:48 ago
Heartbeat timeouts since reboot :                    1
Peer monotonic clock offset        :    80.151683 seconds
Agent should be running            :                 True
P2p mount state changes            :                    4
Failover                           :                 True
Secondary from failover            :               False
```

After rebooting the Arista-2 switch, the ports within MLAG pairs are set to *ErrDisabled* for 300 seconds. This allows all of the upper level protocols to stabilize before traffic is forwarded over the links. Additionally, ports don't always come up in the order in which we might expect. For example, the peer-link should always come up first in order for MLAG to work properly, but I always configure the peer-link to be the last ports on the switch. If the switch were to initialize ports in the order in which they are shown in the configuration, then the peer-link would come up last. The delay is applied to all non-peer-link ports to prevent that from happening.

This interval is configurable with the `reload-delay` command within MLAG configuration, although care should be taken when altering this value as network instability may result when the delay is too short.

 The time it takes for a switch to finish booting varies based on the number of ports in the switch and the complexity of the config. For example, a 7508 with 384 ports will take a bit longer to come up than a 7124 with only 24 ports. The 300 second time was chosen as a conservative value for a typical 1RU switch. If you're using chassis switches with hundreds of ports, the value may need to be higher.

Remember that the other link in the MLAG pair (e1 on Arista-1 in this example) is up and forwarding traffic. So long as your devices are dual homed to both switches using MLAG, they should stay online while one of the switches in the MLAG pair reboots:

```
Arista-2(config)#mlag configuration
Arista-2(config-mlag)#reload-delay ?
  <0-3600>  Seconds
```

Here is the status of Arista-2's e2 interface after a reload:

```
Arista-2#sho int e2
Ethernet2 is down, line protocol is down (errdisabled)
  Hardware is Ethernet, address is 001c.7301.0f19 (bia 001c.7301.0f19)
  MTU 9212 bytes
  Auto-duplex, Auto-speed, auto negotiation: off
  Last clearing of "show interface" counters never
  5 minutes input rate 0 bps (- with framing), 0 packets/sec
  5 minutes output rate 0 bps (- with framing), 0 packets/sec
     0 packets input, 0 bytes
```

```
Received 0 broadcasts, 0 multicast
0 runts, 0 giants
0 input errors, 0 CRC, 0 alignment, 0 symbol
0 PAUSE input
0 packets output, 0 bytes
Sent 0 broadcasts, 0 multicast
0 output errors, 0 collisions
0 late collision, 0 deferred
0 PAUSE output
```

While in this state, MLAG can see the peer switch, and even acknowledges that the other half of its MLAG interface is up. That doesn't keep me from wondering why my MLAGs are all down after rebooting a switch. When it comes to MLAGs, I'm stubbornly stupid for about two minutes, after which I remember to look and see how much time I have left:

```
Arista-2#sho mlag detail
MLAG Configuration:
domain-id        :            MLAG-1
local-interface  :            Vlan4094
peer-address     :            10.0.0.1
peer-link        :        Port-Channel1

MLAG Status:
state            :            Active
peer-link status :              Up
local-int status :              Up
system-id        : 02:1c:73:01:0f:17

MLAG Ports:
Disabled         :   0
Configured       :   0
Inactive         :   0
Active-partial   :   1
Active-full      :   0
```

Newer versions of EOS have more robust output for the show mlag detail command. Here's an example from version 4.9.3 where you can see what the reload timer is, and how much longer you have to wait (both in bold in this example). This output also shows that the ports are ErrDisabled in the next line. The other switch in the MLAG pair will display Peer ports errdisabled = True in this condition:

```
SW3#sho mlag detail
MLAG Configuration:
domain-id          :            MLAG-1
local-interface    :            Vlan4094
peer-address       :            10.0.0.2
peer-link          :        Port-Channel1

MLAG Status:
state              :            Inactive
negotiation status :            Connecting
```

```
peer-link status       :            Down
local-int status       :      LowerLayerDown
system-id              :    00:00:00:00:00:00

MLAG Ports:
Disabled               :            2
Configured             :            0
Inactive               :            0
Active-partial         :            0
Active-full            :            0

MLAG Detailed Status:
State                            :            inactive
State changes                    :            1
Last state change time           :            0:00:27 ago
primary-priority                 :            32767
Peer primary-priority            :            0
Peer MAC address                 :    00:00:00:00:00:00
Reload delay                     :            300 seconds
Reload delay time left           :            273 seconds
Ports errdisabled                :            True
Lacp standby                     :            False
Heartbeat interval               :            2000 ms
Heartbeat timeout                :            5000 ms
Last heartbeat timeout           :            never
Heartbeat timeouts since reboot  :            0
Peer monotonic clock offset      :            unknown
Agent should be running          :            True
P2p mount state changes          :            0
Failover                         :            False
Secondary from failover          :            False
```

After 300 seconds, the interface comes back up automatically, and the MLAG becomes active. Here is the status for the physical interface on Arista-2:

```
Arista-2#sho int e2
Ethernet2 is up, line protocol is up (connected)
  Hardware is Ethernet, address is 001c.7301.0f19 (bia 001c.7301.0f19)
  MTU 9212 bytes, BW 1000000 Kbit
  Full-duplex, 1Gb/s, auto negotiation: on
  Last clearing of "show interface" counters never
  5 minutes input rate 103 bps (0.0% with framing), 0 packets/sec
  5 minutes output rate 280 bps (0.0% with framing), 0 packets/sec
     14 packets input, 4113 bytes
     Received 0 broadcasts, 14 multicast
     0 runts, 0 giants
     0 input errors, 0 CRC, 0 alignment, 0 symbol
     0 PAUSE input
     84 packets output, 11060 bytes
     Sent 0 broadcasts, 7 multicast
     0 output errors, 0 collisions
     0 late collision, 0 deferred
     0 PAUSE output
```

Here is the MLAG status on Arista-2 after 300 seconds has passed:

```
Arista-2#sho mlag
MLAG Configuration:
domain-id          :              MLAG-1
local-interface    :             Vlan4094
peer-address       :             10.0.0.1
peer-link          :          Port-Channel1

MLAG Status:
state              :              Active
peer-link status   :                Up
local-int status   :                Up
system-id          :  02:1c:73:01:0f:17

MLAG Ports:
Disabled           :  0
Configured         :  0
Inactive           :  0
Active-partial     :  0
Active-full        :  1
```

I've been promising that I'd explain when to use multiple MLAG IDs all through this chapter, so I think it's time to deliver.

If you need to connect one MLAG pair to another MLAG pair, each pair should have its own MLAG domain ID. Let's take a look. The network layout for what we're discussing is shown in Figure 12-6.

The two switches on the left (1 and 2) are an MLAG pair, and the two switches on the right (3 and 4) are an MLAG pair. In order to connect them together as shown, each pair should have its own MLAG Domain ID. Why? Let's think about that for a minute. If 1, 3, and 4 were all configured in the same domain, then things might get pretty confusing for the switches.

What you'll find if you build this though, is that it will work if they all have the same MLAG domain. So why require an MLAG domain at all? My guess would be that between the MLAG domains and the use of IP addresses in the MLAG peer-link, future versions of EOS might support MLAG between multiple (as in more than two) switches. Although I have no proof of this, I would recommend making all of your MLAG peer-links have unique IP networks and MLAG domains, especially in environments where multiple MLAG domains can reach each other. Sure, the trunk group feature helps to isolate the MLAG IP addresses, but I always like to err on the side of possibility.

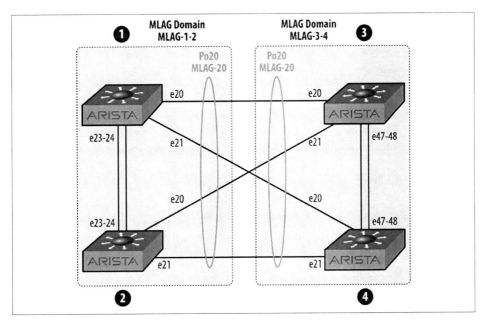

Figure 12-6. Multiple MLAG domain ID example

MLAG ISSU

MLAG ISSU (In-Service Software Upgrade) is a feature enabled on EOS version 4.9.3 and later. With MLAG ISSU, you can upgrade an MLAG switch pair with minimal (sub-second) packet loss and no STP reconvergence. Without MLAG ISSU, or if you upgrade while ignoring the switch's dire warnings regarding the state of MLAG ISSU, you'll likely have one or more network topology changes that will result in one or more STP reconvergence events, and no one wants that.

The Arista documentation on MLAG ISSU indicates that the following steps need to be followed in this order to properly upgrade an MLAG ISSU switch pair:

1. Verify primary/secondary state of MLAG on each switch using the `show mlag de tail` command, or to be brief, the `show mlag det | grep State` (with a capital "S") command.
2. Ensure configuration consistencies.
3. Resolve ISSU warnings (from the output of reload).
4. Upgrade MLAG secondary switch.
5. Monitor MLAG status using `show mlag detail`.

6. Confirm MLAG secondary status.

7. Upgrade MLAG primary peer switch.

8. Confirm overall MLAG status.

 When upgrading 7500 peers with dual supervisors, you'll need to upgrade the standby supervisors on both switches, then upgrade the active supervisor on the MLAG secondary, and finally the last remaining supervisor.

By having switches running MLAG ISSU code, the switches will know if they can be upgraded without causing an outage. If they cannot, then the switch will give you a warning when rebooting. Here's an example of such a warning on a switch running 4.9.3:

```
SW4(config)#reload
If you are performing an upgrade, and the Release Notes for the new
version of EOS indicate that MLAG is not backwards-compatible with the
currently installed version (4.9.3), the upgrade will result in packet
loss.

The following MLAGs are not in Active mode. Traffic to or from these
ports will be lost during the upgrade process:
                                                        local/remote
    mlag        desc            state      local  remote    status
  --------- ----------- --------------- ----------- --------- -----------
       10                  active-partial   Po10       -        up/-
       20                  active-partial   Po20       -        up/-
       26                  active-partial   Po26       -        up/-

Stp is not restartable. Topology changes will occur during the upgrade
process.


Proceed with reload? [confirm]
```

 Using the `reload now` command will cause the switch to bypass these warnings, so don't use the `reload now` command when doing an MLAG ISSU upgrade.

Here's a list of common ISSU warnings and the way to resolve them.

Compatibility check

The version you're upgrading to might not be compatible with the version you're on. But then again, it might! Read the release note to make sure that it is.

Active-partial MLAG warning

The MLAG shown is not active on the other switch in the MLAG pair. If it should be, then bring it up. If not, you can ignore this message (often seen if the requirements have changed but the old config is still in place).

STP is not restartable

Usually waiting 30 to 120 seconds will reward you with this warning resolving itself. To see the status of STP restartability (I totally made that word up), use the show spanning tree bridge detail command:

```
Arista-10#sho spanning-tree bridge detail | inc agent

Stp agent is restartable
```

Reload delay too low

Remember the reload delay we talked about earlier in this chapter? Well, if the switch thinks that that it's too low (lower than the default of 300 seconds for top-of-rack switches and 600 seconds for modular switches), it will bark at you with this warning.

Peer has errdisabled *interfaces*

This is usually an indication that you're impatient and haven't waited long enough for the peer to reboot. Remember, the peer's MLAG-enabled interfaces will stay in an errdisabled state for the duration of the reload delay after booting, assuming the other switch is up, and if you're on a switch that shows this warning, that's a good assumption.

The biggest step you should take before considering an MLAG ISSU upgrade is to carefully read the release notes and TOI (Transfer of Information) documents found on the Arista support site. They can be found alongside the EOS binary images. Don't be afraid to call or email your Arista sales engineer or open a TAC case either. Some shops don't do upgrades often enough to remain sharp on the syntax and gotchas, and these folks love to help.

Remember, not all versions of EOS support MLAG ISSU, only 4.9.3 and later. Also, there will likely be versions where you won't be able to upgrade to using ISSU. For example, if and when EOS gets to version 38.3.2, I doubt you'll be able to upgrade using MLAG ISSU from 4.9.3, but hey, those Arista developers are pretty sharp, so you never know.

## CHAPTER 13

Spanning Tree Protocol

Spanning tree protocol (STP) is very important in layer-2 networks, and its impact should be clearly understood when designing or even troubleshooting a network. If you've been around Cisco gear for the majority of your networking life, you've probably used Per-VLAN Spanning Tree (PVST) or Rapid-PVST (RPVST). In this chapter, I'm going to primarily cover a form of STP that is becoming more common in large data centers: Multiple Spanning Tree (MST).

Data center networks have very different requirements than enterprise networks do. For example, few of the enterprise networking professionals I meet know that many switches have spanning tree limitations. I worked for a client that had Cisco 3750s in the core of a small data center. Things seemed to work alright until they added the 257th VLAN, and that's when they learned that Cisco 3750s only support STP up to 256 VLANs. Bummer.

I was brought in to help solve the problem, and after my recommendation of, "Buy data center class chassis switches" was ignored, I looked for other options. That's when I learned about MST.

Arista switches can run a variety of STP types. You can change the type using the `spanning-tree mode` *mode-type* command:

```
SW1(config)#spanning-tree mode ?
  mstp        Multiple spanning tree protocol
  none        Disable spanning tree
  rapid-pvst  Per VLAN rapid spanning tree protocol
  rstp        Rapid spanning tree protocol
```

Since I've covered spanning tree and rapid-PVST in *Network Warrior*, I'm going to focus mostly on MST in this chapter. Buckle up, because if you've never used MST, you're in for a fun ride.

MST

MST is a version of STP that is much simpler than PVST, yet I rarely see it implemented. I think a big part of that is due to the fact that there is very little documentation out there, and what is available, well, let's just say that reading ancient Sumerian would be easier.

MST appears to be very difficult, but it doesn't need to be. Like anything technical, if you make it too complicated it will be difficult to understand, so keep it simple and you'll do fine. MST can be simpler to configure, easier to manage, often makes more sense (when deployed simply), and uses less CPU cycles than PVST. When I discovered that Arista switches were configured with MST as the default, it was love at first sight. Hey, I never said I wasn't a nerd.

MST is based on Rapid Spanning Tree Protocol (RSTP), which is a great thing because it offers some great backwards compatibility as we'll see later in this chapter. If you're thinking, *well, isn't PVST multiple spanning trees?*, you're right, but MST works differently. The problem with PVST is that there's a spanning tree instance running for every VLAN. On an enterprise network comprised of 20 or 30 (or even 100) VLANs, that's not a big deal. In a data center, where there may easily be hundreds of VLANs, things start to get problematic.

First, each spanning tree instance requires CPU and memory resources, and unless you're a fan of the old *even VLANs on the left and odd VLANs on the right*, then all the VLANs will likely have the same topology anyway. Let's say you are a fan of splitting your VLANs up between two core switches (I am not), then you've got two topologies (assuming all trunks allow all VLANs, of course). Why have potentially hundreds of spanning tree instances running when there are only two topologies?

 I have never been a fan of splitting up STP topologies with odd/even VLANs. It makes troubleshooting harder, and simply isn't needed in most modern networks. Fifteen years ago, when switches were slow, I could see needing to distribute the load, but in a modern network, I'll take simplicity every time. Besides, with MLAG, VARP, and other cool features available in Arista switches, there's no need for any of this manual load-balancing nonsense any more.

MST allows you to have one spanning tree instance for all your VLANs. Or, if you're still hell bent on balancing which switch is the root based on some arbitrary pattern such as even/odd, you can split your VLANs up into *instances*, each with its own root. Oh, and MST is a standards-based protocol. There are no proprietary things to worry about, and it works with any vendor's switch that supports it.

There are some vendor-interaction complexities with MST, as we'll see later in this chapter, but rest assured, MST is still an open standard.

The MST documentation goes into painful detail about MST, the CST, the IST, the MSTI, the CIST, and who knows what else. I'll explain all this to you, and show you why it doesn't need to be all that difficult. Naturally, I'll do this in a way that makes sense to me, and seems to make sense to people I teach. My goal is not to get you certified; my goal is to make you understand.

Let's start with a simple scenario to see how MST works. In Figure 13-1, there are two switches: SW1 and SW2. These two switches are connected together with two links.

Figure 13-1. Two switches connected with two links

Of course, such a topology is a problem because it creates a loop, and loops are bad. Spanning tree, in its default state on Arista switches, shuts down one of the links, as shown in Figure 13-2. For details about which link gets blocked, I recommend the excellent chapter on Spanning Tree in *Network Warrior* (can that guy write or what?). For now, suffice to say that the blocked port is the interface farthest from the root bridge. In my little network, SW2 won the battle for root bridge status (everything is set to defaults for now) so the e48 interface on SW1 ended up blocking.

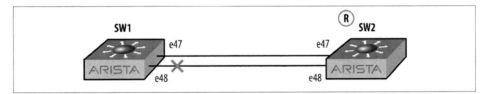

Figure 13-2. STP saving the day by breaking the loop

This simple network shouldn't be a surprise to anyone who has ever used spanning tree, but the difference is that out of the box, Arista switches use MST, so let's take a look at what the switches report.

The command to show STP information is the same as it is in IOS: show spanning-tree. Here's the output for SW1:

```
SW1#sho spanning-tree
MST0
  Spanning tree enabled protocol mstp
  Root ID    Priority    32768
             Address     001c.7317.4a8e
             Cost        0 (Ext) 2000 (Int)
             Port        47 (Ethernet47)
             Hello Time  2.000 sec Max Age 20 sec Forward Delay 15 sec

  Bridge ID  Priority    32768  (priority 32768 sys-id-ext 0)
             Address     001c.7317.5da2
             Hello Time  2.000 sec Max Age 20 sec Forward Delay 15 sec


Interface         Role       State      Cost      Prio.Nbr Type
---------------- ---------- ---------- --------- -------- ------------
Et47              root       forwarding 2000      128.47   P2p
Et48              alternate  discarding 2000      128.48   P2p
```

This output shows the information we'd need when looking at STP, including the root
bridge's information, which includes the root bridge's priority (the default is 32,768),
the root bridge's MAC address, this bridge's priority, this switch's MAC address, and the
status of every interface that has received Bridge Protocol Data Units (BPDUs). This
output clearly shows that interface Et47 is the root port, and that interface Et48 is the
alternate root port, which is blocking (discarding).

Here's the output for SW2:

```
SW2#sho spanning-tree
MST0
  Spanning tree enabled protocol mstp
  Root ID    Priority    32768
             Address     001c.7317.4a8e
             This bridge is the root

  Bridge ID  Priority    32768  (priority 32768 sys-id-ext 0)
             Address     001c.7317.4a8e
             Hello Time  2.000 sec Max Age 20 sec Forward Delay 15 sec


Interface         Role       State      Cost      Prio.Nbr Type
---------------- ---------- ---------- --------- -------- ------------
Et47              designated forwarding 2000      128.47   P2p
Et48              designated forwarding 2000      128.48   P2p
```

This switch shows that it is the root and the bridge information for itself. The ports on this switch are both designated since it's the root bridge.

The thing to notice is the first line of output on both switches. On this line, they each say *MST0*.

MST0 is the default *instance* in MST. I'll cover instances in a minute, but the thing to remember now is that MST0 is always on, it's always active, and every interface forwards MST0 BPDUs. You cannot disable MST0. That will become important later on in this chapter, but for now, understand that because MST0 is always on, if you connect two switches running MST together like I have, then MST will run and behave as you'd expect.

To that end, I'd like to make SW1 the root bridge because I can't sleep knowing that a higher numbered switch (SW2 versus SW1) is in charge. There are a couple of ways to do this, the simplest being the `spanning-tree root primary` command:

```
SW1(config)#spanning-tree root primary
```

This has the almost immediate effect of making SW1 the root. Here's the proof that the STP bridge priority is now 8,192:

```
SW1(config)#sho spanning-tree
MST0
  Spanning tree enabled protocol mstp
  Root ID    Priority    8192
             Address     001c.7317.5da2
             This bridge is the root

  Bridge ID  Priority    8192  (priority 8192 sys-id-ext 0)
             Address     001c.7317.5da2
             Hello Time  2.000 sec Max Age 20 sec Forward Delay 15 sec

Interface         Role        State       Cost       Prio.Nbr Type
---------------- ---------- ---------- ---------- -------- -----------
Et47              designated forwarding 2000       128.47   P2p
Et48              designated forwarding 2000       128.48   P2p
```

I say *almost immediate* because MST is *fast*. I've done mass switch migrations to MST and was amazed that after changing over 200 switches, we never once noticed an outage or disruption of service. Like RSTP, MST has much tighter timers than traditional spanning tree. This speed is one of the things that I like about MST, and it is one of the reasons that I recommend its use.

Another way to change the priority is with the `spanning-tree priority` *priority-value* command. Here I'll goose the priority up a notch to 4,096:

```
SW1(config)#spanning-tree priority 4096
SW1(config)#sho spanning-tree
MST0
  Spanning tree enabled protocol mstp
  Root ID    Priority    4096
             Address     001c.7317.5da2
             This bridge is the root

  Bridge ID  Priority    4096  (priority 4096 sys-id-ext 0)
             Address     001c.7317.5da2
             Hello Time  2.000 sec Max Age 20 sec Forward Delay 15 sec

Interface        Role       State        Cost      Prio.Nbr Type
---------------- ---------- ------------ --------- -------- -----------
Et47             designated forwarding  2000       128.47   P2p
Et48             designated forwarding  2000       128.48   P2p
```

Note that the `spanning-tree priority` command only works on MST0, which will make more sense in a bit.

One of the things that is not terribly obvious is that MST does not care about VLANs in its default state. Whenever I explain MST to someone, this is one of the hardest things for them to wrap their heads around, likely because we've all used PVST for years, if not decades.

Remember when I wrote that MST0 is active on all interfaces at all times? It does so because MST, in its basic form, has no concept of VLANs. So long as MST0 can see another bridge (or BPDUs from that bridge to be precise), there's a link to that bridge, and MST will act accordingly.

One of the other things special about MST0 is that it will interact with a switch that's running RPVST. How can it do this if it doesn't comprehend VLANs? That depends on the vendor, but in a nutshell, the switches will interoperate because MST is based on RSTP.

On a Cisco switch, MST0 sends identical BPDUs out every VLAN on every interface. How is that not RPVST? The difference is that it sends the *same* BPDU out every VLAN (that of MST0), not VLAN-specific BPDUs. This is a very important distinction to understand, because it can bite you if you're not careful. With the Cisco model, if you configure MST0 with a priority of 4,096, then it will likely become the root bridge on every VLAN on an attached PVST switch.

I worked in a network that had STP problems due to old switches that didn't support more than 256 STP-active VLANs. To counter this, they turned STP off on new VLANs. When we migrated to MST, the core (which should be migrated first) went from only advertising BPDUs on 256 VLANs to advertising BPDUs on all 400 VLANs! The CPU on the core went down because it didn't have to process 400 different BPDUs on 400 VLANs, but the attached switches' CPUs went through the roof because they suddenly had 400 VLANs worth of BPDUs to deal with. The attached switches, which were still running PVST, had no idea about MST yet, so they had to process almost twice as many BPDUs as before, and since STP is a CPU-based process, their CPU utilization skyrocketed. Once we migrated them to MST, they settled down nicely.

Arista switches, at least up to EOS version 4.9.3.2, only send MST0 BPDUs on the default VLAN (VLAN1 by default). Since I had first used MST on Cisco switches, and had grown accustomed to the way they sent BPDUs on every VLAN, I was convinced that I had found a bug when my Arista switches didn't behave the same way. When I talked to Arista about it, they pointed out that there is nothing in the RFCs that specifies BPDUs for MST0 being sent out every VLAN. In fact, since Cisco's PVST doesn't adhere to the original standards, I could argue that Arista is doing it right while Cisco has added their own additional feature, as they often do.

So what does this all mean for you in the real world? Let's take a look. I've built a small lab with three switches (SW1, SW2, and SW3), as shown in Figure 13-3. SW1 has a priority of 8,192, SW2 has a priority of 32,768 (the default), and SW3 (the one in the middle of the drawing) has a priority of 4,096. There are two VLANs configured that span all three switches: VLAN 100 and VLAN 200. The links between the switches are trunks with all VLANs permitted.

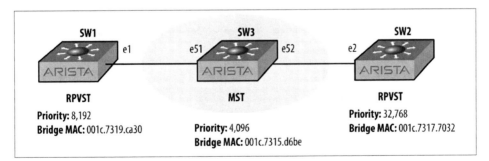

Figure 13-3. RPVST Split by MST using Arista Switches

If all three of these switches were running Rapid PVST, then SW3 would be the root for all VLANs. With MST thrown in the middle, things change a bit, and unless you're careful, the results may surprise you.

First, let's take a quick look at SW3 in the middle:

```
SW3#sho spanning-tree
MST0
  Spanning tree enabled protocol mstp
  Root ID    Priority    4096
             Address     001c.7315.d6be
             This bridge is the root

  Bridge ID  Priority    4096  (priority 4096 sys-id-ext 0)
             Address     001c.7315.d6be
             Hello Time  2.000 sec  Max Age 20 sec  Forward Delay 15 sec

Interface        Role       State      Cost      Prio.Nbr Type
---------------- ---------- ---------- --------- -------- ------------
Et51             designated forwarding 2000      128.51   P2p Boundary
Et52             designated forwarding 2000      128.52   P2p Boundary
```

Looks simple enough. This bridge is the root, and other than it having a priority of 4,096, it appears as if the switch is pretty much in a default configuration. Now let's take a look at SW1, which is running RPVST:

```
SW1#sho spanning-tree
VL1
  Spanning tree enabled protocol rapid-pvst
  Root ID    Priority    4096
             Address     001c.7315.d6be
             Cost        2000 (Ext) 0 (Int)
             Port        1 (Ethernet1)
             Hello Time  2.000 sec  Max Age 20 sec  Forward Delay 15 sec

  Bridge ID  Priority    8193  (priority 8192 sys-id-ext 1)
             Address     001c.7319.ca30
             Hello Time  2.000 sec  Max Age 20 sec  Forward Delay 15 sec

Interface        Role       State      Cost      Prio.Nbr Type
---------------- ---------- ---------- --------- -------- ------------
Et1              root       forwarding 2000      128.1    P2p

VL100
  Spanning tree enabled protocol rapid-pvst
  Root ID    Priority    8292
             Address     001c.7319.ca30
             This bridge is the root

  Bridge ID  Priority    8292  (priority 8192 sys-id-ext 100)
             Address     001c.7319.ca30
             Hello Time  2.000 sec  Max Age 20 sec  Forward Delay 15 sec
```

```
Interface        Role       State      Cost      Prio.Nbr Type
---------------- ---------- ---------- --------- -------- ------------
Et1              designated forwarding 2000       128.1    P2p

VL200
  Spanning tree enabled protocol rapid-pvst
  Root ID    Priority    8392
             Address     001c.7319.ca30
             This bridge is the root

  Bridge ID  Priority     8392  (priority 8192 sys-id-ext 200)
             Address      001c.7319.ca30
             Hello Time   2.000 sec Max Age 20 sec Forward Delay 15 sec

Interface        Role       State      Cost      Prio.Nbr Type
---------------- ---------- ---------- --------- -------- ------------
Et1              designated forwarding 2000       128.1    P2p
```

Certainly, the output of the show spanning tree command is different due to this switch running RPVST instead of MST, but look at the VLANs and their respective root bridges. VLAN1 (the default VLAN) shows that SW3 is the root, while all the other VLANs show themselves to be the root. This is due to the fact that MST does not send out BPDUs on every VLAN, only the default VLAN (VLAN1 in this example).

Now let's look at SW2. Can you guess what it will show?

```
SW2#sho spanning-tree
VL1
  Spanning tree enabled protocol rapid-pvst
  Root ID    Priority    4096
             Address     001c.7315.d6be
             Cost        2000 (Ext) 0 (Int)
             Port        2 (Ethernet2)
             Hello Time  2.000 sec Max Age 20 sec Forward Delay 15 sec

  Bridge ID  Priority    32769  (priority 32768 sys-id-ext 1)
             Address     001c.7317.7032
             Hello Time  2.000 sec Max Age 20 sec Forward Delay 15 sec

Interface        Role       State      Cost      Prio.Nbr Type
---------------- ---------- ---------- --------- -------- ------------
Et2              root       forwarding 2000       128.2    P2p

VL100
  Spanning tree enabled protocol rapid-pvst
  Root ID    Priority    8292
             Address     001c.7319.ca30
             Cost        2000 (Ext) 0 (Int)
             Port        2 (Ethernet2)
             Hello Time  2.000 sec Max Age 20 sec Forward Delay 15 sec
```

```
  Bridge ID  Priority    32868  (priority 32768 sys-id-ext 100)
             Address     001c.7317.7032
             Hello Time  2.000 sec Max Age 20 sec Forward Delay 15 sec

Interface         Role       State     Cost      Prio.Nbr Type
---------------- ---------- ---------- --------- -------- ------------
Et2               root       forwarding 2000      128.2    P2p

VL200
  Spanning tree enabled protocol rapid-pvst
  Root ID    Priority    8392
             Address     001c.7319.ca30
             Cost        2000 (Ext) 0 (Int)
             Port        2 (Ethernet2)
             Hello Time  2.000 sec Max Age 20 sec Forward Delay 15 sec

  Bridge ID  Priority    32968  (priority 32768 sys-id-ext 200)
             Address     001c.7317.7032
             Hello Time  2.000 sec Max Age 20 sec Forward Delay 15 sec

Interface         Role       State     Cost      Prio.Nbr Type
---------------- ---------- ---------- --------- -------- ------------
Et2               root       forwarding 2000      128.2    P2p
```

SW2 (the rightmost switch in Figure 13-3) shows that, again, SW3 is the root for VLAN1, but SW1 is the root for all the remaining VLANs! It's almost like RPVST BPDUs were tunneled through MST or something. In a way, that's not far from the truth.

SW3 is the root on VLAN1 for the same reason that SW1 saw SW3 as the root. Since MST operates on the default VLAN, this makes perfect sense.

RPVST uses a multicast MAC address (01:80:C2:00:00:00) to send BPDUs, and sends BPDUs on all VLANs. Switches not configured for multicast flood these packets out all ports on the respective VLAN, so when SW1 sends out its BPDUs, SW3 forwards them, but doesn't process them because MST does not listen for BPDUs on VLANs other than the default. The BPDUs from SW1 are then received by SW2, which processes them due to it running RPVST.

This behavior is different than what you would see with a Cisco switch in the middle. With a Cisco switch running MST in the middle (configured with the same priority of 4,096), the Cisco switch would become the root bridge for all VLANs. This is due to the fact that Cisco enhanced the MST protocol to have this effect.

Watch out! If you've designed a network with a Cisco switch in the core running MST, and you've got PVST switches attached to it, replacing that Cisco core switch with an Arista switch will likely change the STP root bridge on most of the VLANs in your network. If you don't have a root bridge configured for your VLANs in this scenario, they will negotiate one, and it may not be the one that you would otherwise prefer.

Additionally, with an Arista switch in the core running MST, if you add switches to it that are running PVST, they will either become the root for the nondefault VLANs, or they will negotiate with other PVST switches on your network *through* the MST core.

OK, so MST0 works as expected, and it's simple, and we know how to change the root bridge. We've seen how it behaves with RPVST attached, which is interesting, but for many environments, that's good enough. Let's dig in a bit and see how a more complicated scenario might look.

MST0 is only the tip of the iceberg when it comes to MST. Though MST is not a PVST in the sense that BPDUs are not sent out every VLAN, it has the ability to separate groups of VLANs into separate spanning trees. How is that different than PVST? Imagine that you have 400 VLANs active on your network. With PVST, you would have 400 spanning tree instances, each with its own root bridge, and each one sending out BPDUs aplenty.

With MST, BPDUs are only ever sent over VLAN1 (by default), but VLANs can be grouped into MST *instances*. For example, you could put VLAN 100 into MST1, 200 into MST2, 300 into MST3, and 400 to 499 into MST4.

With your VLANs grouped like this, you could still do some manual splitting by making one core switch the root for MST1 and MST3, while another switch could be the root for MST2 and MST4. As I wrote earlier, I'm not a fan of this type of manual balancing, but I do like to have options, and my customers' desires often override my recommendations anyway.

To keep things simple, I'll use the network in Figure 13-4 for the next examples. This network has only three VLANs, VLAN 100, 200, and 300, all of which are active on all switches and trunked on all links. Note that these are the same switches I used earlier, and I've just changed the connections to form a loop while also configuring all three switches for MST.

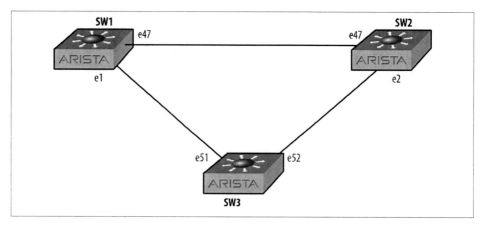

Figure 13-4. Simple MST network

To start things off, I'm going to create a new MST instance. Many of the commands for MST are done in the spanning-tree mst configuration mode. Like many other such modes, changes do not take effect until you exit the mode:

```
SW1(config)#spanning-tree mst configuration
SW1(config-mst)#
```

In order to add a new MST instance, use the command instance, followed by the *instance number*, and then the VLANs to be included in the instance. To place VLAN 100 into MST instance 1, I'll use the instance 1 vlan 100 command. Note that VLANs can be listed individually, separated by commas, or listed as ranges:

```
SW1(config-mst)#instance 1 vlans 100
```

Now, I'll put VLANs 200 and 300 into MST instance 2:

```
SW1(config-mst)#instance 2 vlans 200,300
```

Once I exit, spanning tree will be configured, and I should see three instances in MST instead of one:

```
SW1(config-mst)#exit
SW1(config)#exit
SW1#sho spanning-tree
MST0
  Spanning tree enabled protocol mstp
  Root ID    Priority    4096
             Address     001c.7315.d6be
             Cost        2000 (Ext) 0 (Int)
             Port        1 (Ethernet1)
             Hello Time  2.000 sec Max Age 20 sec Forward Delay 15 sec
```

```
Bridge ID  Priority     8192  (priority 8192 sys-id-ext 0)
           Address      001c.7319.ca30
           Hello Time   2.000 sec Max Age 20 sec Forward Delay 15 sec

Interface        Role       State       Cost       Prio.Nbr  Type
---------------- ---------- ----------- ---------- --------- -----------
Et1              root       forwarding  2000       128.1     P2p Boundary
Et47             alternate  discarding  2000       128.47    P2p Boundary

MST1
  Spanning tree enabled protocol mstp
  Root ID    Priority    32769
             Address     001c.7319.ca30
             This bridge is the root

  Bridge ID  Priority    32769  (priority 32768 sys-id-ext 1)
             Address     001c.7319.ca30
             Hello Time  2.000 sec Max Age 20 sec Forward Delay 15 sec

Interface        Role       State       Cost       Prio.Nbr  Type
---------------- ---------- ----------- ---------- --------- -----------
Et1              master     forwarding  2000       128.1     P2p Boundary
Et47             alternate  discarding  2000       128.47    P2p Boundary

MST2
  Spanning tree enabled protocol mstp
  Root ID    Priority    32770
             Address     001c.7319.ca30
             This bridge is the root

  Bridge ID  Priority    32770  (priority 32768 sys-id-ext 2)
             Address     001c.7319.ca30
             Hello Time  2.000 sec Max Age 20 sec Forward Delay 15 sec

Interface        Role       State       Cost       Prio.Nbr  Type
---------------- ---------- ----------- ---------- --------- -----------
Et1              master     forwarding  2000       128.1     P2p Boundary
Et47             alternate  discarding  2000       128.47    P2p Boundary
```

MST0 still sees SW3 as the root from my earlier example, but all the other VLANs show SW1 to be the root. This is because the other VLANs are in different MST regions on this switch than they are on the other two. This is where MST confuses people, so hang on and let's examine what's really happening. To make things a bit clearer, Figure 13-5 shows a visual representation of what's going on.

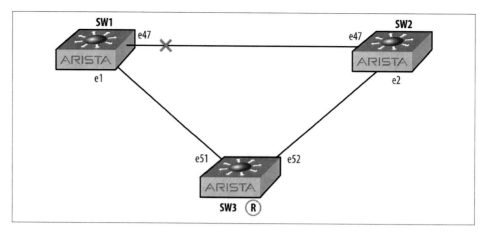

Figure 13-5. MST network with blocked port

First, MST0 continues to function the way it always has. MST1 and MST2 are new regions, but they only exist on SW1. So what happens to these VLANs on switches SW2 and SW3? Let's take a look. Here's SW2:

```
SW2#sho spanning-tree
MST0
  Spanning tree enabled protocol mstp
    Root ID    Priority    4096
               Address     001c.7315.d6be
               Cost        0 (Ext) 2000 (Int)
               Port        2 (Ethernet2)
               Hello Time  2.000 sec Max Age 20 sec Forward Delay 15 sec

    Bridge ID  Priority    32768  (priority 32768 sys-id-ext 0)
               Address     001c.7317.7032
               Hello Time  2.000 sec Max Age 20 sec Forward Delay 15 sec


Interface        Role       State      Cost      Prio.Nbr Type
---------------- ---------- ---------- --------- -------- ------------
Et2              root       forwarding 2000        128.2  P2p
Et47             designated forwarding 2000        128.47 P2p Boundary
```

And here's the same output from SW3:

```
SW3#sho spanning-tree
MST0
  Spanning tree enabled protocol mstp
    Root ID    Priority    4096
               Address     001c.7315.d6be
               This bridge is the root

    Bridge ID  Priority    4096  (priority 4096 sys-id-ext 0)
               Address     001c.7315.d6be
               Hello Time  2.000 sec Max Age 20 sec Forward Delay 15 sec
```

Interface	Role	State	Cost	Prio.Nbr	Type
Et51	designated	forwarding	2000	128.51	P2p Boundary
Et52	designated	forwarding	2000	128.52	P2p

So they both see SW3 as the root, just like SW1 did, but they only show MST0. So why are the new MST instances that only exist on SW1 blocking port Et47?

The key to this, and many of the complexities than can result when using MST, lies in the fact that these interfaces are what MST calls *boundary* ports. A boundary port is one that connects to something other than the instance for which that port is configured. Look at the last two lines from SW3's output, shown previously. Interface Et51 shows a port type of *P2p Boundary*, while Et52 shows a port type of *P2p*. Look again at the drawing in Figure 13-5, and remember that only SW1 is configured for MST instances 1 and 2 at this point. Port Et51 on SW3 is connected to SW1, which is configured differently than SW3, while Et52 is connected to SW2, which still has the same configuration. Technically, there's more to it than the configurations being different, but we'll get to that in a minute. For now, understand that the switch sees the connected device as different, and therefore outside of this switch's MST configuration.

There are a few common scenarios that will result in boundary ports. First, when a switch configured with spanning tree protocol other than MST is attached, the port will be put into a boundary state. Look at the example where I put an MST switch in the middle of two RPVST switches in Figure 13-3 and you'll see two boundary ports. These ports are a result of MST being connected to RPVST switches.

To make the network a bit more logical, I'm going to configure SW1 to be the root for all of our new MST instances (but not MST0). This is done in global configuration mode with the spanning-tree mst *instance-number* priority *priority-value* command. You can also specify the word root instead of priority *priority-value*:

```
SW1(config)#spanning-tree mst 1 priority 8192
SW1(config)#spanning-tree mst 2 priority 8192
```

Another reason that ports will be configured as boundary ports is when MST is running on both switches, but the instances don't match. When attached switches are in the same MST instance, they form a *region*. To be painfully accurate, the switches need to have matching regions, with matching VLAN-to-region mapping, and the same configuration names. This leads me to one of the main points of confusion (and misconfiguration) I've seen in the field when using MST. Let me show you what I mean, since it's easier to see firsthand. I'll now configure SW2 to have the same MST–VLAN mappings, but I'll add a *configuration name*, which will force the switches to be in different regions, even though they have the same instance numbers.

```
SW2(config)#spanning-tree mst configuration
SW2(config-mst)#instance 1 vlan 100
SW2(config-mst)#instance 2 vlan 200,300
SW2(config-mst)#name Switch2
SW2(config-mst)#exit
```

Here's how SW2 sees its world with regard to spanning tree:

```
SW2#sho spanning-tree
MST0
  Spanning tree enabled protocol mstp
  Root ID    Priority    4096
             Address     001c.7315.d6be
             Cost        2000 (Ext) 0 (Int)
             Port        2 (Ethernet2)
             Hello Time  2.000 sec Max Age 20 sec Forward Delay 15 sec

  Bridge ID  Priority    32768  (priority 32768 sys-id-ext 0)
             Address     001c.7317.7032
             Hello Time  2.000 sec Max Age 20 sec Forward Delay 15 sec

Interface        Role       State      Cost      Prio.Nbr Type
---------------- ---------- ---------- --------- -------- ------------
Et2              root       forwarding 2000        128.2  P2p Boundary
Et47             alternate  discarding 2000        128.47 P2p Boundary

MST1
  Spanning tree enabled protocol mstp
  Root ID    Priority    32769
             Address     001c.7317.7032
             This bridge is the root

  Bridge ID  Priority    32769  (priority 32768 sys-id-ext 1)
             Address     001c.7317.7032
             Hello Time  2.000 sec Max Age 20 sec Forward Delay 15 sec

Interface        Role       State      Cost      Prio.Nbr Type
---------------- ---------- ---------- --------- -------- ------------
Et2              master     forwarding 2000        128.2  P2p Boundary
Et47             alternate  discarding 2000        128.47 P2p Boundary

MST2
  Spanning tree enabled protocol mstp
  Root ID    Priority    32770
             Address     001c.7317.7032
             This bridge is the root

  Bridge ID  Priority    32770  (priority 32768 sys-id-ext 2)
             Address     001c.7317.7032
             Hello Time  2.000 sec Max Age 20 sec Forward Delay 15 sec
```

```
Interface        Role       State       Cost      Prio.Nbr Type
---------------- ---------- ---------- --------- -------- ------------
Et2              master     forwarding 2000       128.2    P2p Boundary
Et47             alternate  discarding 2000       128.47   P2p Boundary
```

To recap, SW1 and SW2 are now both configured for MST0, 1, and 2, but SW1 and SW2 both see themselves as the root bridge for MST1 and MST2. If there's one thing that seems to confuse people about MST, it's this type of configuration. At a quick glance, SW2 is configured the same way as SW1, and when looking at the output of show spanning-tree, it looks like they're configured properly because they show MST0, 1, and 2. The key here is in the last two lines in each instance's output. Here's the output from the show spanning-tree mst1 command on SW2:

```
SW2#sho spanning-tree mst 1
##### MST1     vlans mapped:    100
Bridge         address 001c.7317.7032  priority   32769 (32768 sysid 1)
Root           this switch for MST1

Interface        Role       State       Cost      Prio.Nbr Type
---------------- ---------- ---------- --------- -------- ------------
Et2              master     forwarding 2000       128.2    P2p Boundary
Et47             alternate  discarding 2000       128.47   P2p Boundary
```

Note the last two lines, especially the line showing the status of interface Et47, which is the link to SW1. The type is *P2p Boundary*, which indicates that while this switch is configured to be in MST *instance* 1 (which it is), it is not in the same *region* as SW1. Given the current configuration of SW1 and SW2, there are two easy ways to resolve this: add the configuration name to SW1, or remove it from SW2. Let's remove it from SW2, because I'm a firm believer in making configurations as simple as possible:

```
SW2(config)#spanning-tree mst configuration
SW2(config-mst)#no name
SW2(config-mst)#exit
```

Now let's see what the output of show spanning-tree mst 1 looks like:

```
SW2#sho spanning-tree mst 1
##### MST1     vlans mapped:    100
Bridge         address 001c.7317.7032  priority   32769 (32768 sysid 1)
Root           address 001c.7319.ca30  priority    8193 (8192 sysid 1)

Interface        Role       State       Cost      Prio.Nbr Type
---------------- ---------- ---------- --------- -------- ------------
Et2              alternate  discarding 2000       128.2    P2p Boundary
Et47             root       forwarding 2000       128.47   P2p
```

The status of interface Et47 has gone from *alternate* to *root*, from *discarding* to *forwarding*, and the type is now *P2p*, and no longer *P2p Boundary*. This is what an MST instance should look like when paired with a switch in the same region.

Now that we took care of interface Et47, what's up with Et2? Remember, Et2 is connected to SW3, and we haven't configured that switch with MST1 or MST2 yet. Because SW2 *is* configured for MST1, it sees that interface as active in the *instance*. Because the attached switch on that interface is not configured to be in this instance (and also name and VLAN map), the switch considers it to be in a different *region,* and thus, the port is in a *P2p Boundary* state. Let's go ahead and put SW3 into the same MST configuration, and all of our ports should become state *P2p.*

First, here's the output of show spanning-tree on SW3:

```
SW3#sho spanning-tree
MST0
  Spanning tree enabled protocol mstp
  Root ID    Priority    4096
             Address     001c.7315.d6be
             This bridge is the root

  Bridge ID  Priority     4096  (priority 4096 sys-id-ext 0)
             Address     001c.7315.d6be
             Hello Time  2.000 sec Max Age 20 sec Forward Delay 15 sec

Interface        Role       State      Cost     Prio.Nbr Type
---------------- ---------- ---------- -------- -------- --------------------
Et51             designated forwarding 2000      128.51  P2p Boundary
Et52             designated forwarding 2000      128.52  P2p Boundary
```

So, SW3 is the root for MST0 and has no other configuration yet. It sees both its ports as *P2p Boundary* ports because there are switches attached with different instance VLAN maps. Let's change that by getting SW3 in line with the other two:

```
SW3(config)#spanning-tree mst configuration
SW3(config-mst)#instance 1 vlan 100
SW3(config-mst)#instance 2 vlan 200,300
SW3(config-mst)#exit
```

Let's see how that's affected the spanning tree. Here's the output of show spanning-tree on SW3 after these changes:

```
SW3#sho spanning-tree
MST0
  Spanning tree enabled protocol mstp
  Root ID    Priority    4096
             Address     001c.7315.d6be
             This bridge is the root

  Bridge ID  Priority     4096  (priority 4096 sys-id-ext 0)
             Address     001c.7315.d6be
             Hello Time  2.000 sec Max Age 20 sec Forward Delay 15 sec
```

```
Interface         Role        State      Cost      Prio.Nbr Type
---------------- ---------- ---------- --------- -------- ------------
Et51             designated forwarding 2000      128.51   P2p
Et52             designated forwarding 2000      128.52   P2p


MST1
  Spanning tree enabled protocol mstp
  Root ID    Priority    8193
             Address     001c.7319.ca30
             Cost        2000
             Port        51 (Ethernet51)
             Hello Time  0.000 sec Max Age  0 sec Forward Delay  0 sec

  Bridge ID  Priority    32769  (priority 32768 sys-id-ext 1)
             Address     001c.7315.d6be
             Hello Time  2.000 sec Max Age 20 sec Forward Delay 15 sec

Interface         Role        State      Cost      Prio.Nbr Type
---------------- ---------- ---------- --------- -------- ------------
Et51             root        forwarding 2000      128.51   P2p
Et52             designated forwarding 2000      128.52   P2p


MST2
  Spanning tree enabled protocol mstp
  Root ID    Priority    8194
             Address     001c.7319.ca30
             Cost        2000
             Port        51 (Ethernet51)
             Hello Time  0.000 sec Max Age  0 sec Forward Delay  0 sec

  Bridge ID  Priority    32770  (priority 32768 sys-id-ext 2)
             Address     001c.7315.d6be
             Hello Time  2.000 sec Max Age 20 sec Forward Delay 15 sec

Interface         Role        State      Cost      Prio.Nbr Type
---------------- ---------- ---------- --------- -------- ------------
Et51             root        forwarding 2000      128.51   P2p
Et52             designated forwarding 2000      128.52   P2p
```

Huzzah! SW3 is still the root for MST0, but it sees SW1 as the root for MST1 and MST2. All ports are in a *P2p* state, and there are no boundary ports in any instances. Let's take a look at MST1, first on SW1 and then on SW2:

```
SW1#sho spanning-tree mst 1
##### MST1    vlans mapped:    100
Bridge        address 001c.7319.ca30  priority     8193 (8192 sysid 1)
Root          this switch for MST1

Interface         Role        State      Cost      Prio.Nbr Type
---------------- ---------- ---------- --------- -------- ------------
Et1              designated forwarding 2000      128.1    P2p
Et47             designated forwarding 2000      128.47   P2p
```

No boundary ports anymore!

Here's the output from SW2:

```
SW2#sho spanning-tree mst 1
##### MST1    vlans mapped:    100
Bridge        address 001c.7317.7032  priority   32769 (32768 sysid 1)
Root          address 001c.7319.ca30  priority    8193 (8192 sysid 1)


Interface      Role       State       Cost    Prio.Nbr Type
-------------- ---------- ----------- -------- -------- ------------
Et2            alternate  discarding  2000     128.2    P2p
Et47           root       forwarding  2000     128.47   P2p
```

And again, this switch has no more boundary ports. This is the way MST should look when all your switches are configured to be in the same region.

 Remember that just because you see the correct MST instance on your switch, don't automatically assume that it's in the same region. If you see *P2p Boundary* ports in your instances, you might have a misconfigured switch. In order for switches to be in the same region, they must have matching instance VLAN maps, the same configuration name, and the same configuration revision number.

MST Terminology

Let me take a moment and describe how all these instances and regions interact. To help us along, let's define some terms. I've already used most of these terms in the chapter, so most of this should be apparent by now:

Instance
A group of VLANs mapped into a single spanning tree. Instance numbers can be within the range of 1 to 4,096. There can be as many as 16 instances configured on a switch.

MSTI
The technical term for any MST instance other than instance 0.

Region
A region is one or more switches (technically, bridges) connected together that are configured with the same VLAN instance maps, the same configuration name, and the same configuration revision (all of these are configured within the spanning-tree mst configuration mode).

CST
The Common Spanning Tree is what we've seen as MST instance 0 (MST0). The CST is the means whereby regions are interconnected.

IST

    Internal Spanning Tree is used on Instance 0 (MST0, or the CST) for the inter-instance spanning tree. Consider it to be the spanning tree that connects all the regions together.

CIST

    The Common and Internal Spanning Tree is comprised of all regions, along with the CST (MST0).

It took me a long time to get this all straight, likely because I've spent too much of my life thinking about girls and not enough time studying, but I've come up with some comparisons that work for me and seem to help other people as well.

To put all of this stuff into perspective, take a look at Figure 13-6. In this drawing, the large oval represents the *CIST*, as it contains everything within it. Within the CIST, there are three smaller circles. These circles each represent an MST *region*. The final configuration from my example earlier in this chapter resulted in a single region. Before there was a single region, there were multiple regions due to the mismatched instance VLAN maps and the temporarily entered configuration name. Where regions connect with other regions, they do so at CIST boundary ports, which we saw in the earlier example.

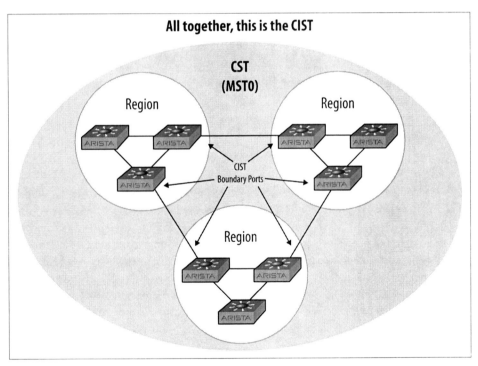

Figure 13-6. Multiple MST regions interconnected with MST0

If you're familiar with BGP, each region is sort of like a BGP confederation, in that the region behaves like a single bridge in relation to other regions. Since each region has its own root, the topology within the region is distinct from the topology outside of the region. The topology between regions is distinct from the topology within regions. I like to call each of the regions a *super switch* when teaching people who are not familiar with BGP, which is completely inaccurate, but it gets the point across. The way the CST (MST0) sees the regions shown in Figure 13-6 is represented in Figure 13-7.

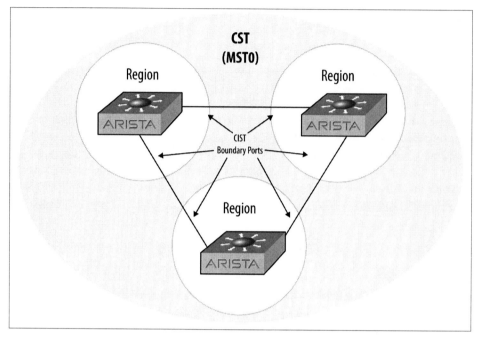

Figure 13-7. Regions as seen by the CST (MST0)

As I warned earlier, it's easy to get switches configured into their own region without realizing it. When I design an MST-based network, I like to make each instance into its own region where possible, because this makes it easier for junior engineers to visualize what's going on. Since the regions aren't really identified in the output of the spanning tree commands, I like to separate them using instances. Now, this may not be possible in your network, especially if you're a fan of balancing even/odd VLANs between core switches. Still, so long as the instance VLAN mapping remains consistent, and the configuration names and revisions match, then getting your regions mapped should be relatively straightforward. That said, here's some advice that will help when using MST:

- As Einstein said, make it as simple as possible, but no simpler. The more complicated you make your MST design, the harder it will be to understand.

- There aren't really benefits to running multiple regions unless you have a very complicated network. Where I have physically disparate networks in the same building, I'll put them into different instance numbers, so that if they ever do get connected, they will form boundary ports and won't just extend the region.

- One of the ways I like to use regions is when layer-2 networks span physical buildings. I have a client that has VLANs spanning four buildings. By limiting the interbuilding connectivity, and making each building its own region, then the building itself becomes a *super switch*, and any improper new links will only affect the CST topology, and not the topology within the building.

- If your network is small, consider a single MST instance with a single region. Though you shouldn't keep everything in MST0, placing all your switches and all your VLANs into MST1 isn't necessarily a bad thing.

Why Pruning VLANs Can Be Bad

This little tip is one of those things that people seem to learn the hard way. Let's see if I can help you avoid the pain and misery that can occur when you inadvertently split VLANs with MST. Don't ask me how I know about the pain and suffering. You'll just have to take my word on that part.

In Figure 13-8, I've drawn a simple network that looks a lot like the one I've used previously in this chapter. In this network, there are three switches and two VLANs. PC-A, connected to SW2, is on VLAN 300, as is PC-B, which is on SW3. The links between the switches are trunks, but the link between SW2 and SW3 does not have VLAN 300 allowed.

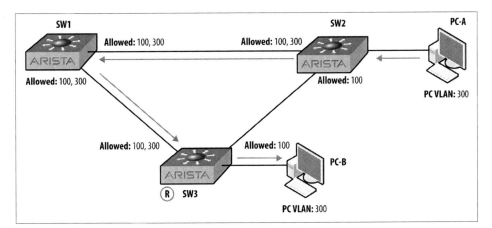

Figure 13-8. Pruned trunks in a PVSTP network

The point of this lesson is to remember that MST does not care about VLANs, only instances. In this network, with PVST, VLAN 300 has no loop, but VLAN 100 does, so only VLAN 100 has a blocked port. That's OK, because there is an alternate path, and all traffic can flow on all VLANs.

Figure 13-9 shows the same network with MST running on all switches. In this example, all switches are configured properly in MST1, and they are all in the same region. Since MST doesn't care about VLANs and only loops within regions, the link between SW1 and SW2 will be blocked, which will cause PC-A to no longer have a path to PC-B. We have a special term for this in networking: it's called *bad*.

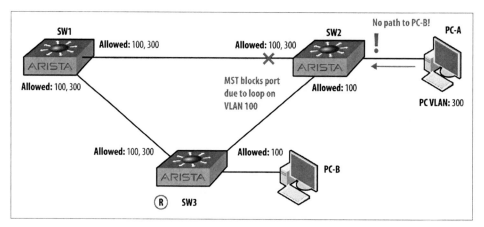

Figure 13-9. Simple, broken network thanks to my trunk-pruning ineptitude

There are a couple of ways to prevent this from happening. If all of these switches truly belong in the same region, then you could stop pruning VLAN 300 from the SW2–SW3 link. Pruning can be a great way to limit traffic on links, but in this network, I doubt that VLAN 300 really needed to be pruned in the first place. That's of little comfort, though, when it worked before you converted to MST and now it doesn't. It turns out that some executives are really sensitive about things like this.

Another way to resolve this problem is to put VLAN 100 in one MST instance, and VLAN 300 in another. Then, the VLAN 100 instance would block the SW1–SW2 link as shown, but the VLAN 300 instance would have no ports blocked, since that instance would not see a loop. Watch out for overly complex instance VLAN maps though, since making things complicated leads to switches in different regions when you're not careful about matching MST configurations.

Spanning Tree and MLAG

When MLAG is configured, one of the switches in the MLAG cluster will become the primary switch. The MLAG primary switch will do all of the STP processing, and changes to the secondary will have no effect. There is a pretty big caveat to that statement though, and that is that changes made to the secondary MLAG switch's STP configuration will be *accepted* to the *running-config*, but they will not take effect unless, that is, the primary MLAG switch relinquishes its role as primary, at which point, all the commands entered on the secondary (now primary) switch will suddenly become active. What's worse, you may not see this coming. Allow me to demonstrate.

I have two switches, SW1 and SW2, configured as an MLAG pair. I have STP configured, and SW1 is the root, but it won because of a priority tie. SW2 is also the MLAG primary switch. I'll be working on SW1, so here's proof that it's the MLAG secondary switch:

```
SW1(config)#sho mlag det | grep state
state                         :              Active
State                         :           secondary
State changes                 :                   1
Last state change time        :         1:01:44 ago
P2p mount state changes       :                   1
```

Now, I'll go into SW1 and start mucking with STP. I want to make the priority lower to force it to be the root:

```
SW1(config)#spanning-tree mst 1 root primary
```

When I make this change, nothing happens. Frustrated because my change has no effect, I decide to hardcode the priority:

```
SW1(config)#spanning-tree mst 1 priority 8192
```

Again, nothing happens. Beyond frustrated, I issue the show spanning-tree mst 1 command to see what's up:

```
SW1(config)#sho spanning-tree mst 1
MST1
  Spanning tree enabled protocol mstp
  Root ID    Priority    32769
             Address     021c.7313.35ec
             This bridge is the root

  Bridge ID  Priority    32769  (priority 32768 sys-id-ext 1)
             Address     021c.7313.35ec
             Hello Time  2.000 sec Max Age 20 sec Forward Delay 15 sec

Interface       Role       State      Cost      Prio.Nbr Type
--------------- ---------- ---------- --------- -------- -----------
Et20            designated forwarding 2000      128.220  P2p
Et21            designated forwarding 2000      128.221  P2p
```

```
PEt20              designated forwarding 2000      128.20   P2p
PEt21              designated forwarding 2000      128.21   P2p
PPo10              designated forwarding 1999      128.101  P2p
Po10               designated forwarding 2000      128.102  P2p
```

If I hardcoded the priority to 8,192, why isn't it showing my change? Disgusted and impatient, I rebooted the other switch, because that was so much easier than reading the documentation. Imagine though, that instead of me rebooting a switch in a lab that these switches are in production, and after my changes didn't work, I gave up and walked away. You know, because that's what happens in real data centers. Anyway, for whatever reason, at this point, SW2 (the primary MLAG switch) reboots. As soon as it goes down, I get the normal MLAG message on SW1's console:

```
SW1(config)#
May 22 15:34:05 SW1 Mlag: %FWK-3-SOCKET_CLOSE_REMOTE: Connection
to Mlag (pid:2328) at tbt://20.20.20.2:4432/ closed by peer (EOF)
May 22 15:34:05 SW1 Mlag: %FWK-3-SELOR_PEER_CLOSED: Peer closed
socket connection. (tbt://20.20.20.2:4432/-in)(Mlag (pid:2328))
```

All of a sudden and without any real warning, SW1 is the root bridge for MST1 with a priority of 8,192:

```
SW1(config)#sho spanning-tree mst1
MST1
  Spanning tree enabled protocol mstp
  Root ID    Priority    8193
             Address     021c.7313.35ec
             This bridge is the root

  Bridge ID  Priority    8193  (priority 8192 sys-id-ext 1)
             Address     021c.7313.35ec
             Hello Time  2.000 sec Max Age 20 sec Forward Delay 15 sec

Interface        Role       State       Cost       Prio.Nbr Type
---------------- ---------- ----------- ---------- -------- -----------
Et20             designated discarding 2000        128.20   P2p
Et21             designated discarding 2000        128.21   P2p
Po10             designated discarding 1999        128.102  P2p
```

This happened because this switch is now the MLAG primary, as evidenced by the output of show mlag detail | grep state:

```
SW1(config)#sho mlag det | grep state
state                 :         Active
State                 :                  primary
State changes         :                      3
Last state change time :        0:19:54 ago
P2p mount state changes :                     3
```

The fact that this happens like this is not really a problem; it is functioning by design. The problem is that when configuring STP on the secondary MLAG switch, there are no warnings that your changes are being saved, and no warnings that any changes made will take effect when and if this switch becomes the primary. Be very careful about making changes to STP when configuring the MLAG secondary switch.

This behavior was recorded on switches running EOS 4.9.3.2. When I told Arista about it, they agreed that there should be some sort of warning, so I wouldn't be surprised if this gets safer in a future release.

One last note, because this comes up a lot: no, you should not disable STP if you're using MLAG (or any vendor's MLAG technology). Ask any networking consultant if he's heard of a spanning tree event being caused by someone bringing in a home office switch and connecting it where it didn't belong. I know I've seen that more than once. Hell, I had a client who refused to run more than two Ethernet runs to each cube, insisting that should anyone need more ports, they could just bring in a switch from home. This is an outage waiting to happen, and STP is the last line of defense against the loop-inducing server guy who needs 14 ports on his desk. Do yourself a favor and outlaw switches on (or under) desks. And keep STP running, because when you outlaw desktop switches, only outlaws will have desktop switches…or something.

## CHAPTER 14

First Hop Redundancy

First hop redundancy is the ability for one or more devices to share the same IP address in order to provide multidevice resiliency in default gateway scenarios (though they can be nondefault gateways, too). Usually, this involves one device owning the IP address while other devices stand by, ready to assume control of the address should the owner fail. This is not always the case, however, as we'll see.

Cisco's proprietary Hot Standby Router Protocol (HSRP) is probably what most Cisco shops are using to accomplish this, but outside of the Cisco world the Virtual Router Redundancy Protocol (VRRP) is the standard. This is likely due to the fact that it is an open source protocol, and therefore supported by multiple vendors. Arista's EOS supports VRRP, but also introduces an interesting new feature called Layer-3 Anycast Gateway, or Virtual Address Resolution Protocol (VARP). In this chapter, we'll take a look at both VRRP and VARP, including configuration examples and reasons why you might choose one solution over the other.

VRRP

If all you've ever used is Cisco's HSRP, then don't worry, because VRRP is pretty much the same thing. In fact, it's so similar that Cisco complained vigorously when the RFC for VRRP was announced. VRRP is defined in RFCs 2338, 3768, and 5798, while Cisco's HSRP is defined in RFC 2281. The RFC for HSRP states that:

> 2 **Conditions of Use**
>
> US Patent number 5,473,599 [2], assigned to Cisco Systems, Inc. may
> be applicable to HSRP. If an implementation requires the use of any
> claims of patent no. 5,473,599, Cisco will license such claims on
> reasonable, nondiscriminatory terms for use in practicing the
> standard. More specifically, such license will be available for a
> one-time, paid up fee.

Cisco complained to the Internet Engineering Task Force (IETF) with the following:

> In Cisco's assessment, the VRRP proposal does not represent any significantly different functionality from that available with HSRP and also implementation of *draft-ietf-vrrp-spec-06.txt* would likely infringe on Cisco's patent #5,473,599. When Cisco originally learned of the VRRP proposal, the Hot Standby Router Protocol was then promptly offered for standardization with the understanding that, if approved, licenses for HSRP would be made available on reasonable, nondiscriminatory terms for implementation of the protocol.

The full text of Cisco's response to the VRRP RFC is available online (*http://www.ietf.org/ietf-ftp/IPR/VRRP-CISCO*). My point in this little legal tangent is that VRRP is *very* similar to HSRP, so it's nothing to be afraid of. But surely, there must be differences, or Cisco would be suing every vendor that uses VRRP. Let's take a look at how to configure VRRP, and we'll see how things differ as we go. I'll be making comparisons to Cisco's HSRP, since most of the people I've taught Arista topics to come from a Cisco background.

First, we need to get some terms straight. In VRRP, a *virtual router* is one or more devices configured as a sort of cluster, wherein one of the devices is the *master router*, and the rest are *backup routers*. This is a bit different than HSRP, in that HSRP can have only one active router, and one standby router. Any other devices configured in the same HSRP group are in a listening state. When an HSRP event occurs that causes both the active and backup routers to fail, a new election takes place among the listening routers.

With VRRP, multiple routers may be configured to be in the virtual router, and they'll all be backup routers if not elected as the master.

 The term router is used accurately, even though we're talking about switches in this book, since VRRP can only be configured on an L3 interface.

A VRRP virtual router is defined by "A virtual router identifier (VRID) and a set of IP addresses" according to RFC 2338. In other words, in order for routers to become part of a virtual router, they must agree on the VRID and IP addresses. The VRID is the group number (just like HSRP), and the IP addresses are the VIPs to be shared.

 A quick note about Arista's implementation of VRRP is in order. In many vendors' implementations, the configured IP address of the interface can be used as the VIP. According to the RFC, this is an option, and it looks like Arista did not opt to include this option, at least up to EOS version 4.9.3.2.

Basic Configuration

So let's get started by looking at a simple network, as shown in Figure 14-1. There are two switches, both connected to VLAN 99. Each switch has a Switch Virtual Interface (SVI) configured and IP routing enabled. The server will be configured to use these switches as its default gateway.

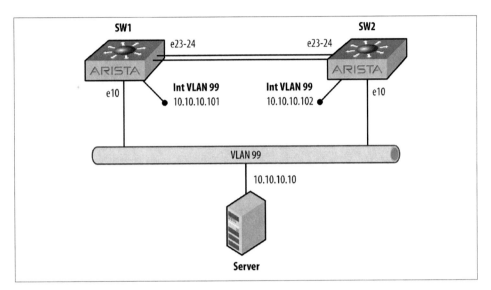

Figure 14-1. A simple network in need of VRRP

Let's start with the existing configuration of SW1:

```
SW1(config)#sho run int vlan 99
interface Vlan99
   ip address 10.10.10.101/24
```

And here's SW2:

```
SW2(config)#sho run int vlan 99
interface Vlan99
   ip address 10.10.10.102/24
```

It would be difficult to get much simpler than that! So let's add the simplest of VRRP configs. Naturally, we'll need to get into interface configuration mode:

```
SW1(config)#int vlan 99
SW1(config-if-Vl99)#
```

In its simplest form, VRRP just needs a virtual router group number, and a group IP address:

```
SW1(config-if-Vl99)#vrrp 99 ip 10.10.10.100
```

The group number can be any number inclusive of 1 to 255. According to the Arista configuration guide (section 3.1.1), *Two virtual routers cannot be assigned the same VRID, even when they are on different VLANs. A virtual router's scope is restricted to a single LAN.* This can seem misleading, but I think the RFC has the answer:

> However, there is no restriction against reusing a VRID with a different address mapping on different LANs. The scope of each virtual router is restricted to a single LAN.

In short, you can have the same group number on multiple interfaces, but you cannot have the same group number/IP address combination on two interfaces, which makes perfect sense, since you can't really have the same IP network on two interfaces anyway.

At this point, VRRP is active, and the status can be viewed with the show vrrp command:

```
SW1(config-if-Vl99)#sho vrrp
Vlan99 - Group 99
  State is Master
  Virtual IP address is 10.10.10.100
  Virtual MAC address is 0000.5e00.0163
  Advertisement interval is 1.000s
  Preemption is enabled
  Preemption delay is 0.000s
  Preemption reload delay is 0.000s
  Priority is 100
  Master Router is 10.10.10.101 (local), priority is 100
  Master Advertisement interval is 1.000s
  Master Down interval is 3.609s
```

Since this is all it takes to get a virtual router configured, many people prefer to add the IP address last if they will be altering any of the default values. If you've got devices out there looking for this IP address, it just became available, and when we go in and muck with the default values, the status of the new IP may change. Speaking of defaults, let's take a look at them from the previous output. Without configuring anything, the switch has become the master. That makes sense, since there are no other switches participating yet. Note that the *advertisement interval* is one second, and that *preemption* is enabled. By comparison, HSRP sends *hello packets* every three seconds, which raises another important difference between the two protocols.

With HSRP, both the active and standby routers send hello packets, while any routers configured to listen just, well, listen. With VRRP, only the active router sends out advertisements; the backup routers all just listen.

Preemption is enabled by default with VRRP, which I think is great because, honestly, I can't remember the last time I configured HSRP without preemption enabled. Still, if you'd like to disable preemption, you can do so with the no vrrp *group-number* preempt command:

```
SW1(config-if-Vl99)#no vrrp 99 preempt
```

Preemption can also be delayed with a couple of interesting options shown by using the question mark after the delay keyword:

```
SW1(config-if-Vl99)#vrrp 99 preempt delay ?
  minimum  Specifies the minimum delay period in seconds that causes
           the local router to postpone taking over the active role.
           The range is from 0 to 3600 seconds (1 hour). The default
           is 0 second (no delay).

  reload   Specifies the preemption delay, in seconds, after a reload
           only. This delay period applies only to the first
           interface-up event after the router has reloaded.
  <cr>
```

In order to set the minimum delay for 30 seconds and the reload delay for 60 seconds, you can combine both into the following single command:

```
SW1(config-if-Vl99)#vrrp 99 preempt delay minimum 30 reload 60
```

The VRRP master router sends out advertisements every one second by default. To change it, use the vrrp *group-number* timers advertise *seconds* command. Here, I've changed the default to 10 seconds:

```
SW1(config-if-Vl99)#vrrp 99 timers advertise 10
```

Now that I've messed with all the defaults, let's take a look at the output of show vrrp again:

```
SW1(config-if-Vl99)#sho vrrp
Vlan99 - Group 99
  State is Master
  Virtual IP address is 10.10.10.100
  Virtual MAC address is 0000.5e00.0163
  Advertisement interval is 10.000s
  Preemption is disabled
  Preemption delay is 30.000s
  Preemption reload delay is 60.000s
  Priority is 100
  Master Router is 10.10.10.101 (local), priority is 100
  Master Advertisement interval is 10.000s
  Master Down interval is 30.609s
```

OK, that was fun, but let's put all those values back to their defaults so we can move on:

```
SW2(config-if-Vl99)#vrrp 99 preempt
SW2(config-if-Vl99)#default vrrp 99 timers advertise
SW1(config-if-Vl99)#default vrrp 99 preempt delay
```

Let's make sure that everything is back to normal:

```
SW1(config-if-Vl99)#sho vrrp
Vlan99 - Group 99
  State is Master
  Virtual IP address is 10.10.10.100
  Virtual MAC address is 0000.5e00.0163
```

```
Advertisement interval is 1.000s
Preemption is enabled
Preemption delay is 0.000s
Preemption reload delay is 0.000s
Priority is 100
Master Router is 10.10.10.101 (local), priority is 100
Master Advertisement interval is 1.000s
Master Down interval is 3.609s  Master Advertisement interval is 1.000s
Master Down interval is 3.609s
```

Now let's see what happens when we add SW2 to the mix with all the defaults left alone:

```
SW2(config)#int vlan 99
SW2(config-if-Vl99)#vrrp 99 ip 10.10.10.100
```

Let's see what SW2 thinks about our new VRRP config:

```
SW2(config-if-Vl99)#sho vrrp
Vlan99 - Group 99
State is Backup
Virtual IP address is 10.10.10.100
Virtual MAC address is 0000.5e00.0163
Advertisement interval is 1.000s
Preemption is enabled
Preemption delay is 0.000s
Preemption reload delay is 0.000s
Priority is 100
Master Router is 10.10.10.101, priority is 100
Master Advertisement interval is 1.000s
Master Down interval is 3.609s
```

Looks good, and everything has the same default values. The new VRRP-enabled network is shown in Figure 14-2.

So what made SW2 decide to become the backup router? It became the backup because a master already existed and that master had the same priority as SW2. Here's what the RFC says on the subject:

```
The protocol should ensure after Master election that no state
transition is triggered by any Backup router of equal or lower
preference as long as the Master continues to function properly.
```

If I were to pull off all the configurations and configure SW2 first, it would become the master, and when I configured SW1, then SW1 would become the backup. This can be different behavior than that exhibited by HSRP. If two routers are both configured in the same group, on the same VLAN, with the same VIP, they will negotiate who will become the master, and a new master may be chosen (depending on the version of code; this behavior has changed over time).

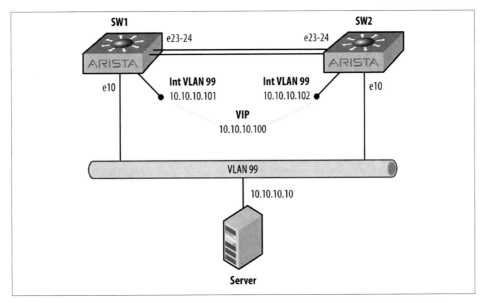

Figure 14-2. VRRP enabled on our simple network

I like to have a little more control over which switch becomes the master router, so I'll assign a priority to the VRRP group. Since SW2 is currently the backup, let's configure it with a higher priority and see what happens. The default priority is 100. The priority value can be any integer in the range of 1 to 254, so let's make SW2 have a priority of 105:

```
SW2(config-if-Vl99)#vrrp 99 priority 105
```

Higher priorities are better in VRRP. Well, who's to say what *better* really means? I suppose that I could say that higher priorities are more desirable, but that makes me think that the master routers should be prettier. Instead, I'll write that the router with the highest priority will become the master router, and leave it at that. Also, a priority of 255 indicates that the interface IP is the VIP, which is why doing so will force the router to become the master. Only you can't do that in EOS, so never mind.

The switch quickly becomes the master since it has a higher priority than SW1:

```
SW2(config-if-Vl99)#sho vrrp
Vlan99 - Group 99
  State is Master
  Virtual IP address is 10.10.10.100
  Virtual MAC address is 0000.5e00.0163
  Advertisement interval is 1.000s
```

```
Preemption is enabled
Preemption delay is 0.000s
Preemption reload delay is 0.000s
Priority is 105
Master Router is 10.10.10.102 (local), priority is 105
Master Advertisement interval is 1.000s
Master Down interval is 3.590s
```

So now that we've got SW2 set with a higher priority, let's see how preemption works. I'll just shut down the SVI for VLAN 99 on SW2:

```
SW2(config-if-Vl99)#shut
```

In short order, SW1 becomes the master router:

```
SW1#sho vrrp
Vlan99 - Group 99
  State is Master
  Virtual IP address is 10.10.10.100
  Virtual MAC address is 0000.5e00.0163
  Advertisement interval is 1.000s
  Preemption is enabled
  Preemption delay is 0.000s
  Preemption reload delay is 0.000s
  Priority is 100
  Master Router is 10.10.10.101 (local), priority is 100
  Master Advertisement interval is 1.000s
  Master Down interval is 3.609s
```

Remember when we added SW2, it became the backup because SW1 was already the master, and the priorities were the same? This time, when SW2 starts advertising itself as a master with a priority of 105, it should immediately take over master duty:

```
SW2(config-if-Vl99)#no shut
```

SW1 gives up its role as master since a better master is available:

```
SW1#sho vrrp
Vlan99 - Group 99
  State is Backup
  Virtual IP address is 10.10.10.100
  Virtual MAC address is 0000.5e00.0163
  Advertisement interval is 1.000s
  Preemption is enabled
  Preemption delay is 0.000s
  Preemption reload delay is 0.000s
  Priority is 100
  Master Router is 10.10.10.102, priority is 105
  Master Advertisement interval is 1.000s
  Master Down interval is 3.609s
```

Technically, the router preempted when we first changed the priority, but I just wanted to show that failing the new master and then bringing it back online would force another preemption.

Most VRRP implementations I've used allow the VRRP VIP to be the same as the physical interface's IP address on the master router. In fact, the RFC specifically mentions that using the physical IP address of a router will automatically make it the master. As of EOS 4.9.3.2, the ability to use the physical interface's IP address as the VIP is not supported, and will result in an error:

```
SW1(config-if-Vl99)#vrrp 99 ip 10.10.10.101
% Address 10.10.10.101 is already assigned to interface Vlan99
```

One of the cool features of VRRP that I rarely see used is the ability to serve multiple IP addresses within the group:

```
SW2(config-if-Vl99)#vrrp 99 ip 10.10.10.99 secondary
SW2(config-if-Vl99)#vrrp 99 ip 10.10.10.98 secondary
```

And here's the result:

```
SW2(config-if-Vl99)#sho vrrp
Vlan99 - Group 99
  State is Master
  Virtual IP address is 10.10.10.100
    Secondary Virtual IP address is 10.10.10.98
    Secondary Virtual IP address is 10.10.10.99
  Virtual MAC address is 0000.5e00.0163
  Advertisement interval is 1.000s
  Preemption is enabled
  Preemption delay is 0.000s
  Preemption reload delay is 0.000s
  Priority is 105
  Master Router is 10.10.10.102 (local), priority is 105
  Master Advertisement interval is 1.000s
  Master Down interval is 3.590s
```

Of course, any such configuration should be done on all routers within the group. Another allowable configuration involves multiple groups within the same interface, with each group providing different VIPs. I'll configure VRRP group 66 on both switches, serving the IP address 10.10.10.66. Here's SW1:

```
SW1(config-if-Vl99)#vrrp 66 ip 10.10.10.66
SW1(config-if-Vl99)#vrrp 66 priority 105
```

And here's SW2:

```
SW2(config-if-Vl99)#vrrp 66 ip 10.10.10.66
```

While I've configured SW2 to have a higher priority in the VRRP 99 group, I configured VRRP group 66 to have the higher priority on SW1. Remember, this is all within the same VLAN (99). Let's see what the status looks like on SW1 now:

```
SW1(config-if-Vl99)#sho vrrp
Vlan99 - Group 66
  State is Master
  Virtual IP address is 10.10.10.66
  Virtual MAC address is 0000.5e00.0142
```

```
    Advertisement interval is 1.000s
    Preemption is enabled
    Preemption delay is 0.000s
    Preemption reload delay is 0.000s
    Priority is 105
    Master Router is 10.10.10.101 (local), priority is 105
    Master Advertisement interval is 1.000s
    Master Down interval is 3.590s

  Vlan99 - Group 99
    State is Backup
    Virtual IP address is 10.10.10.100
      Secondary Virtual IP address is 10.10.10.98
      Secondary Virtual IP address is 10.10.10.99
    Virtual MAC address is 0000.5e00.0163
    Advertisement interval is 1.000s
    Preemption is enabled
    Preemption delay is 0.000s
    Preemption reload delay is 0.000s
    Priority is 100
    Master Router is 10.10.10.102, priority is 105
    Master Advertisement interval is 1.000s
    Master Down interval is 3.609s
```

With this VRRP configuration, the IP address 10.10.10.66 is currently being served by SW1, while the IP addresses 10.10.10.98 to 100 are being served by SW2. In VRRP terms, SW1 is the master router for group 66, and SW2 is the master router for group 99.

 I'm not a big fan of doing this type of balancing, but you could use it to have some of your servers use one router while some of your servers use another, all while being on the same VLAN. I call this sort of design *manual load balancing*, and I don't recommend it because, invariably, someone doesn't keep track of what server is assigned where, then one router gets overwhelmed or some other problem occurs, and then it's your fault. Wherever possible, I try not to make things my fault, unless of course they're good things, in which case I'll absolutely take the blame.

VRRP can be secured using clear text or encrypted passwords by using the vrrp *group-id* authentication command. Options for encryptions include text and ietf-md5. Here's how a plain text password would be configured:

```
    SW1(config-if-Vl99)#vrrp 99 auth text ILikePie
```

When using a clear-text password, the password is clearly visible, which is likely why they call it clear text. It is also the reason why you shouldn't use it:

```
    SW1(config-if-Vl99)#sho vrrp int vlan 99 | grep Auth
      Authentication text, string "ILikePie"
```

If you're going to bother using passwords, then do yourself a favor and encrypt them with the `ietf-md5 key-string` *string* option:

```
SW1(config-if-Vl99)#vrrp 99 auth ietf-md5 key-string ILikePie
```

When using MD5 passwords, the password is not shown in the status output, or in the *running-config*:

```
SW1(config-if-Vl99)#sho vrrp int vlan 99 | grep Auth
  Authentication MD5, key-string
```

The last thing to cover regarding VRRP is the ability to track other interfaces. While I think this has more value on WAN routers where serial links are likely to fail in colorful and interesting ways, the ability to track another interface is always welcome, so let's see how it works. First, we'll start with a baseline VRRP configuration. Here's the configuration for SW2, which is back to having only one group and a priority of 105:

```
SW2(config-if-Vl99)#sho run int vlan 99
interface Vlan99
   ip address 10.10.10.102/24
   vrrp 99 priority 105
   vrrp 99 ip 10.10.10.100
```

Here's the status for this switch:

```
SW2(config)#sho vrrp
Vlan99 - Group 99
  State is Master
  Virtual IP address is 10.10.10.100
  Virtual MAC address is 0000.5e00.0163
  Advertisement interval is 1.000s
  Preemption is enabled
  Preemption delay is 0.000s
  Preemption reload delay is 0.000s
  Priority is 105
  Master Router is 10.10.10.102 (local), priority is 105
  Master Advertisement interval is 1.000s
  Master Down interval is 3.590s
```

The first step in tracking another interface is to create an object to track. Currently, as of EOS version 4.9.3.2, the only objects that can be created are *interface line protocol* objects. I can see that Arista, being the forward thinkers that they are, have left the doors open for all sorts of objects in the future. I imagine that I'd be able to track IP routes, ARP entries, MAC-table entries, and all sorts of wonderful things, but for now, let's ignore my rambling daydreams and focus on the type we have available to us.

To create an object, you must specify an object name. I'm going to call mine GAD, because I'm the damn writer and I like seeing my initials in lights…or something. After specifying the object name, append the object type to be tracked. Judicious use of tab completion and the question mark will show you that this is the only choice to be made, unless you'd like to use your own initials, in which case I say, fine be that way:

```
SW2(config)#track GAD int e10 line-protocol
```

Once the object is created, you can reference it with the vrrp *group-number* track *object-name* interface command. There are two options: *decrement* and *shutdown*. Decrement will lower the priority by the specified amount, and shutdown will disable the VRRP group entirely. For this example, I'll decrement the priority by 10:

```
SW2(config)#int vlan 99
SW2(config-if-Vl99)#vrrp 99 track GAD decrement 10
```

With this track configured, should interface e10 go down, the priority for VRRP group 99 will drop 10 points, from 105 down to 95, which would make it five less than SW1's default priority of 100. Let's shut down interface e10 and see what happens:

```
SW2(config-if-Vl99)#int e10
SW2(config-if-Et10)#shut
```

With that done, let's see what VRRP looks like on SW2:

```
SW2(config-if-Et10)#sho vrrp
Vlan99 - Group 99
  State is Backup
  Virtual IP address is 10.10.10.100
  Virtual MAC address is 0000.5e00.0163
  Advertisement interval is 1.000s
  Preemption is enabled
  Preemption delay is 0.000s
  Preemption reload delay is 0.000s
  Priority is 95
  Master Router is 10.10.10.101, priority is 100
  Master Advertisement interval is 1.000s
  Master Down interval is 3.629s
```

Works as expected! So, for the most part, we're done!

Miscellaneous VRRP Stuff

VRRP has some cool features, as we've seen, but for some reason, I'm tickled by the idea that a VRRP group can be shut down like an interface can. To do so, just use the vrrp *group-id* shut interface command:

```
SW2(config-if-Vl99)#vrrp 99 shut
```

To bring it back up, negate the command:

```
SW2(config-if-Vl99)#no vrrp 99 shut
```

We've already seen the results of the show vrrp command, but with many groups configured, it can get unwieldy. The command can be modified with the interface keyword, which is useful, but for my money the show vrrp brief command is the go-to command in busy environments:

```
SW1#sho vrrp brief
Port        Group Prio Time  Own State   MaIp          GrIp
Vlan99      66    105  3589      Master  10.10.10.101  10.10.10.66
Vlan99      99    100  3609      Backup  10.10.10.102  10.10.10.100
```

With track objects configured, you can see them with the show track command. This can be very useful, especially when you have an object tracked in more than one place:

```
SW2#sho track
Tracked object GAD is up
   Interface Ethernet10 line-protocol
      3 change, last change time was 1:17:30 ago
   Tracked by:
      Vlan99 vrrp instance 99
```

This command also has a brief modifier, but be careful because you have to spell out the word brief, or else the parser thinks you're specifying the name of a track object:

```
SW2#sho track brief
Tracked object GAD is up
```

VARP

Virtual ARP, or *Layer-3 Anycast Gateway*, is a feature that's so simple, I'm amazed that no one has ever thought of it before. Put simply, multiple devices are configured to respond to ARP and GARP requests for a shared virtual IP address using a shared virtual MAC address. Seriously, that's all it does. So what's so great about that?

First, by the very nature of the fact that both switches in a pair respond to ARP requests for the same IP address, that means that some devices will learn the MAC address from one switch, while other devices will learn from the other switch (assuming a pair). That also means that both switches can actively receive packets destined for the IP address. This active–active behavior is something that neither VRRP nor HSRP can replicate. Not only that, but VARP is completely standards-based.

Cisco's Gateway Load Balancing Protocol (GLBP) offers ARP load balancing, which is kind of similar at a high level, but much more complicated to configure and understand, which brings me to the second benefit. VARP takes just two lines of configuration on each switch for a single IP address, and one additional line for each additional IP to be shared. There are no options, no timers, and no additional features to worry about. It just works.

Third, because packets that are received on a VARP address are forwarded to the next hop destination on the same switch on which they were received (assuming IP routing is enabled and properly configured), these packets never need to traverse the interswitch link, thus reducing traffic latency, not to mention load on switches that don't really need to carry the traffic in the first place.

This is accomplished by configuring a virtual MAC address globally on each switch. The switches will respond to ARP requests for each of the IP addresses to be shared with this configured MAC address, regardless of the VLAN or interface on which the request is heard.

Let's take a look at how VARP might be used. First, let's take a look at VRRP in use on a sample network. In Figure 14-3, there are four servers on VLAN 99, all configured to use the VRRP VIP of 10.10.10.100 as their default gateways. When they communicate with the server at 20.20.20.20, the packets all go to the active router, which is SW1, where they are forwarded from the SVI on VLAN 100. Since MLAG forwards packets from the switch on which they were received, all of these packets will be forwarded from SW1's e10 interface to the server at 20.20.20.20.

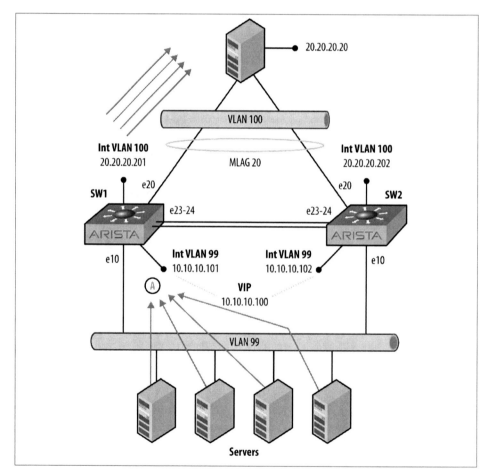

Figure 14-3. Packet flow using VRRP

Now, let's compare that flow with the traffic flow for the same network using VARP. In Figure 14-4, since both switches have responded to the ARP requests for the default gateway of 10.10.10.100, both switches will receive packets from a random sampling of the servers that sent the ARP requests.

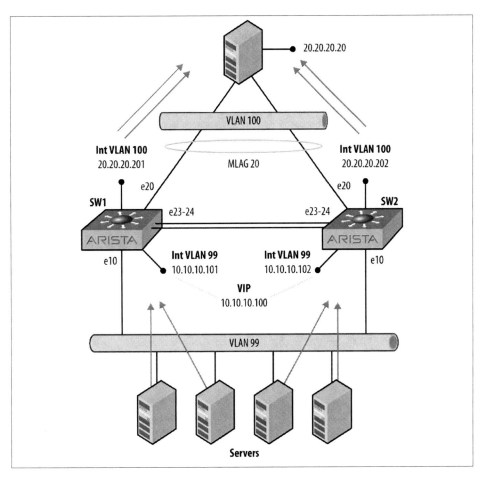

Figure 14-4. A VARP-enabled network

Though Figure 14-4 shows a nice, even distribution of servers, this is due to my neurosis that prevents me from crossing lines in drawings unless absolutely necessary. VARP does not weigh, distribute, or otherwise manage load in any way. The servers just believe whatever ARP response they received first, even if more than one gateway responds (see RFC 1027 if you don't believe me).

Note also that should a packet arrive on a switch other than the active router, then the packet will be forwarded over the peer-link in order to get to the active router, after which it will then be forwarded at layer-3.

Since MLAG forwards packets out the same switch wherever possible, the packets are then distributed over both switches, thus better utilizing the switches, the uplinks, and the network in general.

One thing to remember about VARP is that traffic is *never* sourced from the virtual address. That means that the VIP cannot be used in routing, nor can it be used as a source address for protocols or features that support changing the source interface or address.

Configuring VARP

If you're lucky enough to have a lab full of Arista switches, you should clear all the VRRP stuff that we worked on earlier in this chapter. The configuration for the VLAN 99 SVI on SW1 should look like this to start:

```
SW1(config)#sho run int vlan 99
interface Vlan99
   ip address 10.10.10.101/24
```

And here's SW2's fresh VLAN 99 SVI configuration:

```
SW2(config)#sho run int vlan 99
interface Vlan99
   ip address 10.10.10.102/24
```

The first step is to configure the MAC address that our VIPs will use. This MAC will be used for every VIP we create on every VLAN, so make it count. I've blatantly stolen this MAC address from the Arista article on VARP because I was too lazy to look up the rules for making up MAC addresses.

What can I say? Writing a book involves looking up a lot of things, and I just couldn't bear to look up one…more…damn…thing.

```
SW1(config)#ip virtual-router mac-address 00:1c:73:00:00:99
```

If you don't do this step, then the next step will fail. The next step is to configure a VIP on an interface, and if it fails, don't say I didn't warn you:

```
SW1(config)#int vlan 99
SW1(config-if-Vl99)#ip virtual-router address 10.10.10.100
```

VARP cannot be configured on routed Ethernet interfaces, including the management interfaces. It is only configurable on VLAN interfaces. While the Arista *Configuration Guide* doesn't specifically say that it won't work on Ethernet interfaces, to be fair, it only mentions VLAN interfaces in the VARP section. If you need first hop redundancy on physical interfaces, you'll need to use VRRP.

That's it! The switch is now responding to ARP requests for the VIP 10.10.10.100 with the MAC address we took so much time to research and create. Once these two steps are done, you'll be able to ping the VIP:

```
SW1#ping 10.10.10.100
PING 10.10.10.100 (10.10.10.100) 72(100) bytes of data.
80 bytes from 10.10.10.100: icmp_req=1 ttl=64 time=0.062 ms
80 bytes from 10.10.10.100: icmp_req=2 ttl=64 time=0.014 ms
80 bytes from 10.10.10.100: icmp_req=3 ttl=64 time=0.011 ms
80 bytes from 10.10.10.100: icmp_req=4 ttl=64 time=0.011 ms
80 bytes from 10.10.10.100: icmp_req=5 ttl=64 time=0.011 ms

--- 10.10.10.100 ping statistics ---
5 packets transmitted, 5 received, 0% packet loss, time 0ms
rtt min/avg/max/mdev = 0.011/0.021/0.062/0.020 ma
```

Pinging the VIP only works on EOS versions 4.8.1 and later. If you want to use VARP, you really should use a later version because the inability to ping the VIP will drive you slowly mad. Now you know how I got this way.

We can also ping the VARP address from SW2 now:

```
SW2#ping 10.10.10.100
PING 10.10.10.100 (10.10.10.100) 72(100) bytes of data.
80 bytes from 10.10.10.100: icmp_req=1 ttl=64 time=0.597 ms
80 bytes from 10.10.10.100: icmp_req=2 ttl=64 time=0.159 ms
80 bytes from 10.10.10.100: icmp_req=3 ttl=64 time=0.153 ms
80 bytes from 10.10.10.100: icmp_req=4 ttl=64 time=0.102 ms
80 bytes from 10.10.10.100: icmp_req=5 ttl=64 time=0.153 ms

--- 10.10.10.100 ping statistics ---
5 packets transmitted, 5 received, 0% packet loss, time 2ms
rtt min/avg/max/mdev = 0.102/0.232/0.597/0.184 ms
```

Now we'll configure the virtual router MAC address on SW2. It should be the same as the MAC address configured on SW1:

```
SW2(config)#ip virtual-router mac-address 00:1c:73:00:00:99
```

At this point, you will not be able to ping the VARP address because you've configured the MAC address in VARP but not entered an IP. This will override the other switch's ARP information in the local ARP cache. Let's take a look:

```
SW2(config)#sho arp
Address         Age (min)  Hardware Addr   Interface
10.10.10.5              0  000c.29a4.b705  Vlan99, Port-Channel20
10.10.10.100           0  001c.7300.0099  Vlan99, not learned
10.10.10.101           0  001c.7313.4ce0  Vlan99, Port-Channel1
10.10.10.103           0  001c.7317.5da2  Vlan99, Port-Channel20
20.20.20.1             0  001c.7313.4ce0  Vlan4094, not learned
```

The ARP entry is in the table as is plainly evident here, but ping no longer works:

```
SW2(config)#ping 10.10.10.100
PING 10.10.10.100 (10.10.10.100) 72(100) bytes of data.

--- 10.10.10.100 ping statistics ---
5 packets transmitted, 0 received, 100% packet loss, time 8005ms
```

So let's add the virtual IP to VLAN 99 on SW2:

```
SW2(config)#int vlan 99
SW2(config-if-Vl99)#ip virtual-router address 10.10.10.100
```

And now pinging the VIP works again:

```
SW2(config-if-Vl99)#ping 10.10.10.100
PING 10.10.10.100 (10.10.10.100) 72(100) bytes of data.
80 bytes from 10.10.10.100: icmp_req=1 ttl=64 time=0.061 ms
80 bytes from 10.10.10.100: icmp_req=2 ttl=64 time=0.014 ms
80 bytes from 10.10.10.100: icmp_req=3 ttl=64 time=0.011 ms
80 bytes from 10.10.10.100: icmp_req=4 ttl=64 time=0.012 ms
80 bytes from 10.10.10.100: icmp_req=5 ttl=64 time=0.011 ms

--- 10.10.10.100 ping statistics ---
5 packets transmitted, 5 received, 0% packet loss, time 0ms
rtt min/avg/max/mdev = 0.011/0.021/0.061/0.020 ms
```

Not only is this all we need for VARP to work, that's about all that can be done. I like this feature because it's simple, it works, it takes advantage of the way existing, open protocols work, and it's easy to configure.

By the way, you can add more than one virtual IP address per VLAN. To do so, just add another IP address with the ip virtual-router address *ip-address* interface command. Feel free to add as many as you'd like, up to the limit of 500 per VLAN. I'll just add three so you won't have to flip through 10 pages of code. Besides, my editor would just tell me to take them all out anyway:

```
SW2(config-if-Vl99)#ip virtual-router address 10.10.10.99
SW2(config-if-Vl99)#ip virtual-router address 10.10.10.98
SW2(config-if-Vl99)#ip virtual-router address 10.10.10.97
```

To see the status of your handiwork, use the show ip virtual router command, which will show you the configured MAC address and all VIPs, along with the real IP address and the interfaces on which they're operating:

```
SW2#sho ip virtual-router
IP virtual router is configured with MAC address: 001c.7300.0099
Interface   IP Address        Virtual IP Address   Status    Protocol
Vlan99      10.10.10.102/24   10.10.10.97          up        up
Vlan99      10.10.10.102/24   10.10.10.98          up        up
Vlan99      10.10.10.102/24   10.10.10.99          up        up
Vlan99      10.10.10.102/24   10.10.10.100         up        up
```

 Even though the VIP will respond to pings on the latest versions of EOS, the VIP and configured MAC address do not show up in the ARP table, nor do they show up in Event Monitor. This is, after all, *virtual* ARP.

Note that if you have virtual router configured on some interfaces, the output of show ip virtual-router will include all L3 interfaces, even those without a virtual router address configured. Here's a switch with only one interface configured with a VIP (VLAN 99). The others appear in the output, but show a VIP of 0.0.0.0. The first entry, VLAN 100, has a configured SVI with no IP address at all, which is why the IP address column shows 0.0.0.0 as well. The second line is our original, single VIP on VLAN 99, and the last line shows a VLAN with a configured IP address, but no VIPs configured:

```
Arista(config)#sho ip virtual-router
IP virtual router is configured with MAC address: 00:1c:73:00:00:99
Interface   IP Address       Virtual IP Address
Vlan100     0.0.0.0          0.0.0.0
Vlan99      10.10.10.101     10.10.10.100
Vlan901     192.168.1.180    0.0.0.0
```

If you configure the interfaces with a virtual router address, but don't configure the global virtual router MAC address, your virtual router won't work, even though you might think that it should. Here's what it looks like when starting with no VARP configuration:

```
SW1(config)#int vlan 99
SW1(config-if-Vl99)#ip virtual-router address 10.10.10.100
```

It looks fine, but the status tells you it's not. If you're not used to configuring VARP, this can be confusing. You just configured the virtual router address, and it's telling you that the virtual router is not configured:

```
SW1#sho ip virtual-router
IP virtual router is not configured
```

Once you add the virtual router MAC address, things get better:

```
SW1(config)#ip virtual-router mac-address 00:1c:73:00:00:99
```

And now everything appears as it should:

```
SW1(config)#sho ip virtual-router
IP virtual router is configured with MAC address: 001c.7300.0099
Interface  IP Address        Virtual IP Address   Status     Protocol
Vlan99     10.10.10.101/24   10.10.10.100         up         up
```

VARP is a very cool protocol, and was one of the first things that piqued my interest when visiting Arista the first time. I encourage you to try it out if at all possible, and see how it can be used in your environment. And if you decide it's not for you, you can always use VRRP.

## CHAPTER 15

Routing

Dynamic routing in a data center switch is not something I normally see done outside the core switches in a data center, and even then I prefer to move it out to edge devices and let the switching architecture focus on fast movement of packets at layer-2. Still, customers sometimes demand dynamic routing on their switches, and who am I to deny them (after recommending alternatives in writing)?

I'll warn you up front that there are few (if any) fantastic discoveries awaiting you in this chapter. IP routing is not really a core requirement of data center switching, and the protocols supported all function the way you'd expect them too. IP routing is a pretty mature technology, with most protocols having a maturity measuring in decades. If there's one thing to understand from this chapter, it's that the protocols work the same way they do on any other device that supports them according to the RFCs.

Arista switches support only open routing protocols. In other words, protocols that aren't proprietary and that don't require a certain vendor's equipment, or licensing, or certifications. In short, Arista supports BGP (v2 and v3), OSPF (v2 and v3), PIM-SM, and RIPv2.

 EOS version 4.10 or later is required for OSPFv3 and BGPv4.

I won't be explaining how these protocols work in this chapter. That job has already been done by other books in dizzying detail. Instead, I'm going to show you how to configure your Arista switch to connect to each protocol. I'll be keeping it simple and, to that end, I'll be using the network shown in Figure 15-1 for this chapter.

Dynamic routing requires a layer-3 feature license in order to be supported by Arista TAC (Technical Assistance Center), although static routing is free. That doesn't mean you can't use them; it just means that without the license, you can't get support from Arista TAC for them if you do. Actually, it does mean you can't use them (legally). Plus, you'll feel bad, what with all the shame, self-loathing, and all.

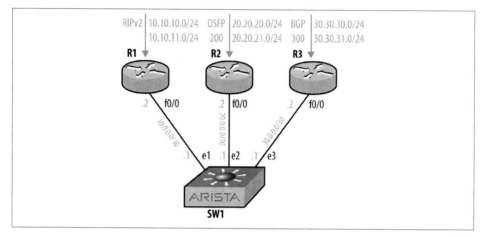

Figure 15-1. Three routers, one switch

Our simple multiprotocol network contains three routers, R1 running RIPv2, R2 running OSPF process 200, and R3 running BGP with the Autonomous System Number (ASN) 300. To start, SW1 will have only IP addresses configured on the three interfaces, e1 through e3. There are no routing protocols configured to start:

```
SW1#sho run int e1-3
interface Ethernet1
   description [ To R1 ]
   speed sfp-1000baset auto 100full
   no switchport
   ip address 10.0.0.1/30
interface Ethernet2
   description [ To R2 ]
   speed sfp-1000baset auto 100full
   no switchport
   ip address 20.0.0.1/30
interface Ethernet3
   description [ To R3 ]
   no switchport
   ip address 30.0.0.1/30
```

The `speed sfp1000baset auto 100full` commands are required because I'm using two Arista copper SFPs connecting to R1 and R2, both of which have only 100 Mbps Ethernet interfaces. See Chapter 31 for more information on this command.

 One hundred Mbps is not supported on the 7050Q, nor is it supported when using 1 Gbps fiber SFPs.

To show the default state of the switch's routing table, here's the output of `show ip route`:

```
SW1#sho ip route
Codes: C - connected, S - static, K - kernel,
       O - OSPF, IA - OSPF inter area, E1 - OSPF external type 1,
       E2 - OSPF external type 2, N1 - OSPF NSSA external type 1,
       N2 - OSPF NSSA external type2, B I - iBGP, B E - eBGP,
       R - RIP, A - Aggregate


 C       10.0.0.0/30 is directly connected, Ethernet1
 C       20.0.0.0/30 is directly connected, Ethernet2
 C       30.0.0.0/30 is directly connected, Ethernet3
```

By default, IP routing is disabled. In this state, trying to configure RIP will result in an error, although the switch will let you continue to configure the protocol:

```
SW1(config)#router rip
! IP routing not enabled
SW1(config-router-rip)#
```

Enabling IP routing is done exactly the way in which you'd expect, with the `ip routing` command:

```
SW1(config)#ip routing
```

Once that's done, we can configure routing protocols without being hassled. Let's start with RIP.

RIP

```
SW1(config)#router rip
SW1(config-router-rip)#
```

As I'm sure you're aware, the routing information protocol (RIP) comes in two flavors, version 1 and version 2. Honestly though, when was the last time you needed RIPv1? The last time I saw it was on the CCIE lab exam, and the only reason it was there was to cause me grief. Apparently Arista agrees, because RIPv1 isn't even an option in EOS. It's RIPv2 or nothing…just the way I like it. Well, not that I would willingly design a network using RIP, but you get the idea. Here is the result of asking for help in RIP configuration mode:

```
SW1(config-router-rip)#?
  comment          Up to 240 characters, comment for this mode
  default          Set a command to its defaults
  default-metric   Set default-metric for RIP
  distance         Define an administrative distance
  exit             Exit from RIP configuration mode
  help             Description of the interactive help system
  network          Configure routing for a network
  no               Negate a command or set its defaults
  redistribute     Redistribute routes in to RIP
  show             Show running system information
  shutdown         Shut down RIP
  timers           Adjust RIP timers
  !                Append to comment
```

One of my favorite Arista features is the ability to add comments to configurations, so I'm going to do that now. There are two ways to do this: with the comment command, which will drop you into a multiline comment mode, or with the *bang* (!) character, which will just add a single line. Using a *bang* will also append your comment to an existing comment:

```
SW1(config-router-rip)#! - RIPv2 link to R1
```

Now I'll add a network statement to enable the e1 interface to send and listen to RIPv2 messages. I like to keep these statements as specific as possible to keep unwanted interfaces from becoming active:

```
SW1(config-router-rip)#network 10.0.0.1/30
```

Every time I play with this, I get burned because I'm not used to it. By default, when configuring a routing protocol, it remains in a *shutdown* state. If you've entered all your network statements and can't figure out why it's not working, do a show active from within protocol configuration mode, or check the *running-config* to see if the routing protocol is shut down:

```
SW1(config-router-rip)#sho active
router rip
  ! - RIPv2 link to R1
  network 10.0.0.1/32
  shutdown
```

At this point, all I need to do to get RIPv2 working is to negate the shutdown command:

```
SW1(config-router-rip)#no shut
```

With that out of the way, the switch now sees the routes being sent by R1:

```
SW1(config-router-rip)#sho ip route
Codes: C - connected, S - static, K - kernel,
       O - OSPF, IA - OSPF inter area, E1 - OSPF external type 1,
       E2 - OSPF external type 2, N1 - OSPF NSSA external type 1,
       N2 - OSPF NSSA external type2, B I - iBGP, B E - eBGP,
       R - RIP, A - Aggregate
```

```
C     10.0.0.0/30 is directly connected, Ethernet1
R     10.10.10.0/24 [120/2] via 10.0.0.2
R     10.10.11.0/24 [120/2] via 10.0.0.2
C     20.0.0.0/30 is directly connected, Ethernet2
C     30.0.0.0/30 is directly connected, Ethernet3
```

RIPv2 uses multicast on the well-known IP address 224.0.0.9. If you'd like to force the use of broadcasts, you can do so on an interface with the `ip rip v2-broadcast` command:

```
SW1(config)#int e1
SW1(config-if-Et1)#ip rip v2-broadcast
```

To see the RIP database, use the `show ip rip database` command:

```
SW1#sho ip rip database
10.10.10.0/255.255.255.0
    [1] via 10.0.0.2, 00:00:25, Ethernet1, active
10.10.11.0/255.255.255.0
    [1] via 10.0.0.2, 00:00:25, Ethernet1, active
```

To see RIP neighbors, use the `show ip rip neighbors` command:

```
SW1#sho ip rip neighbors
RIP Gateway Summary
Address     Last-Heard Bad-Packets Num-Routes  Bad-Routes  Flags
10.0.0.2    00:00:05   0           2            0          ACCEPTED
```

As of EOS 4.9.3.2, there are no provisions to set a manually configured RIPv2 neighbor using unicast.

OSPF

The Open Shortest Path First (OSPF) routing protocol is generally the internal gateway routing protocol of choice when intervendor routing is required. Let's configure our Arista switch to talk to R2 based on the network diagram in Figure 15-1. First, we'll need to enable OSPF and assign a process ID. I'll use the same process ID as used on R2, although this is not a requirement for communication. I'll also add this switch to Area 0 to keep things simple:

```
SW1(config)#router ospf 200
SW1(config-router-ospf)#
```

Unlike RIP, OSPF is not disabled by default, and as soon as the `router ospf` *process-id* command is entered, OSPF is running. I like to manually set my OSPF router IDs so that the highest IP address isn't used:

```
SW1(config-router-ospf)#router-id 1.1.1.1
```

If you've been working with OSPF for a while, you're probably used to using the log-adjacency-changes command. Well, that works here too:

```
SW1(config-router-ospf)#log-adjacency-changes
```

I like comments, so let's go ahead and add one:

```
SW1(config-router-ospf)#! - OSPF process 200 to R2
```

Next I'll add a network command to enable interfaces within the range. Again, I like to keep these commands as tight as possible, so I'll include only the exact IP address of the interface I'd like to add, which is e2 (20.0.0.1):

```
SW1(config-router-ospf)#network 20.0.0.1/32 area 0
```

Within a few seconds, the switch discovers its neighbor and they determine who gets to hold the coveted roll of designated router. With logging enabled, you should see a message similar to this when the neighbor adjacency is formed:

```
Jul  2 18:31:08 SW1 Rib: %OSPF-4-OSPF_ADJACENCY_ESTABLISHED:
NGB 2.2.2.2, interface 20.0.0.1 adjacency established
```

 If you're not seeing these messages even after enabling them, make sure you've got logging set to the console properly. I generally use the logging console informational global command to get just the right amount of logs. Any more than that gets annoying for me, but then, I'm easily annoyed.

The neighbor adjacencies can be seen with the show ip ospf neighbor command:

```
SW1(config-router-ospf)#sho ip ospf nei
Neighbor ID      Pri    State        Dead Time    Address      Interface
2.2.2.2           1     FULL/DR      00:00:36     20.0.0.2     Ethernet2
```

At this point, we should be receiving routes, which of course can be verified with the show ip route command:

```
SW1(config-router-ospf)#sho ip route
Codes: C - connected, S - static, K - kernel,
       O - OSPF, IA - OSPF inter area, E1 - OSPF external type 1,
       E2 - OSPF external type 2, N1 - OSPF NSSA external type 1,
       N2 - OSPF NSSA external type2, B I - iBGP, B E - eBGP,
       R - RIP, A - Aggregate


C      10.0.0.0/30 is directly connected, Ethernet1
R      10.10.10.0/24 [120/2] via 10.0.0.2
R      10.10.11.0/24 [120/2] via 10.0.0.2
C      20.0.0.0/30 is directly connected, Ethernet2
O E2   20.20.20.0/24 [110/10] via 20.0.0.2
O E2   20.20.21.0/24 [110/10] via 20.0.0.2
C      30.0.0.0/30 is directly connected, Ethernet3
```

To see how the OSPF process sees routes (which may be different than what you see in the output of show ip route), use the show ip ospf database command:

```
SW1(config-router-ospf)#sho ip ospf database

            OSPF Router with ID(1.1.1.1) (Process ID 200)

                Router Link States (Area 0.0.0.0)

Link ID        ADV Router      Age       Seq#       Checksum Links
1.1.1.1        1.1.1.1         00:04:01  0x80000008 0x00BF30 1
2.2.2.2        2.2.2.2         00:00:32  0x80000004 0x00EC05 1

                Net Link States (Area 0.0.0.0)

Link ID        ADV Router      Age       Seq#       Checksum
20.0.0.2       2.2.2.2         00:04:02  0x80000001 0x00AE64

                Type-5 AS External Link States

Link ID        ADV Router      Age       Seq#       Checksum Tag
20.20.20.0     2.2.2.2         00:00:21  0x80000001 0x00FC5D 2
20.20.21.0     2.2.2.2         00:00:21  0x80000001 0x00F167 2
```

As you can see, this is all pretty straightforward, and there aren't any surprises. If you're used to Cisco routers, you might miss things like Totally Stubby Areas because these are not found in the standard. Authentication can be used on OSPF interfaces, timers can be adjusted, and costs can be set, just like you'd expect. You cannot run more than one OSPF process, however:

```
SW1(config-router-ospf)#router ospf 100
% More than 1 OSPF instance is not supported
```

BGP

For my Border Gateway Protocol (BGP) example, I'll use a different ASN than the one in use on R3, because this is probably more likely to be seen in the field. I'll configure the Arista switch to be in ASN 1000, while R3 is in ASN 300.

First, we need to enable BGP with the router bgp *asn* command:

```
SW1(config)#router bgp 1000
SW1(config-router-bgp)#
```

You know I need to add a comment:

```
SW1(config-router-bgp)#! - BGP 1000 to R3 (ASN 300)
```

In its simplest form, all we really need to do is configure the neighbor with the proper ASN as configured on that router:

```
SW1(config-router-bgp)#neighbor 30.0.0.2 remote-as 300
```

Indeed, in this simple network, SW1 has received two routes from R3:

```
SW1#sho ip route
Codes: C - connected, S - static, K - kernel,
       O - OSPF, IA - OSPF inter area, E1 - OSPF external type 1,
       E2 - OSPF external type 2, N1 - OSPF NSSA external type 1,
       N2 - OSPF NSSA external type2, B I - iBGP, B E - eBGP,
       R - RIP, A - Aggregate


C       10.0.0.0/30 is directly connected, Ethernet1
R       10.10.10.0/24 [120/2] via 10.0.0.2
R       10.10.11.0/24 [120/2] via 10.0.0.2
C       20.0.0.0/30 is directly connected, Ethernet2
O E2    20.20.20.0/24 [110/10] via 20.0.0.2
O E2    20.20.21.0/24 [110/10] via 20.0.0.2
C       30.0.0.0/30 is directly connected, Ethernet3
B E     30.30.30.0/24 [200/0] via 30.0.0.2
B E     30.30.31.0/24 [200/0] via 30.0.0.2
```

BGP on a data center switch is sort of a mixed bag. On the one hand, it can solve some problems where you need to route, but it's really not suited to be an Internet gateway router running full tables. Take a look at the running BGP configuration after only adding these few commands:

```
SW1(config-router-bgp)#sho active
router bgp 1000
   ! - BGP 1000 to R3 (ASN 300)
   bgp log-neighbor-changes
   neighbor 30.0.0.2 remote-as 300
   neighbor 30.0.0.2 maximum-routes 12000
```

If you expect the switch to be holding 300,000 prefixes, you'll want to change that setting.

So What?

So, by now, you're probably thinking that this is the lamest chapter in the book so far. Don't worry, I struggled with how much routing to actually cover, and decided to keep it very simple. The point is that configuring IP routing is done just about exactly the same as it is on those other companies' switches. So what's the big deal? Let's put what we've done so far in this chapter together with something we've learned in previous chapters, and hopefully you'll see what makes these switches so darn cool.

Remember in the SysDB chapter, we talked about monolithic code and what would happen if the OSPF process died. Well, let's make that happen and see exactly what occurs.

Routing happens from a single process in EOS: the *Rib* process. I'm not sure why each protocol didn't get its own agent, but I'll take advantage of the fact to seriously abuse the switch.

First, I'll set the prompt to show the time again:

```
SW1(config)#prompt %H[%D{%T}]%p
SW1[03:11:30](config)#exit
SW1[03:11:32]#
```

Here's the state of the routing table as it stands after the changes made in this chapter:

```
SW1[03:12:11]#sho ip route | begin Gateway
Gateway of last resort:
 S      0.0.0.0/0 [1/0] via 192.168.1.1

 C      10.0.0.0/30 is directly connected, Ethernet1
 R      10.10.10.0/24 [120/2] via 10.0.0.2
 R      10.10.11.0/24 [120/2] via 10.0.0.2
 C      20.0.0.0/30 is directly connected, Ethernet2
 O E2   20.20.20.0/24 [110/10] via 20.0.0.2
 O E2   20.20.21.0/24 [110/10] via 20.0.0.2
 C      30.0.0.0/30 is directly connected, Ethernet3
 B E    30.30.30.0/24 [200/0] via 30.0.0.2
 B E    30.30.31.0/24 [200/0] via 30.0.0.2
 C      50.50.50.0/24 is directly connected, Vlan101
 C      192.168.1.0/24 is directly connected, Management1
```

And now, I'll kill the Rib process, thereby killing all routing protocols on the switch:

```
SW1[03:15:23]#agent Rib terminate
Rib was terminated
```

The switch doesn't so much as hiccup, and within four seconds, RIP routes appear:

```
SW1[03:15:27]#sho ip route | begin Gateway
Gateway of last resort:
 S      0.0.0.0/0 [1/0] via 192.168.1.1

 C      10.0.0.0/30 is directly connected, Ethernet1
 R      10.10.10.0/24 [120/2] via 10.0.0.2
 R      10.10.11.0/24 [120/2] via 10.0.0.2
 C      20.0.0.0/30 is directly connected, Ethernet2
 S      20.20.20.0/24 [155/0] via 192.168.1.1
 C      30.0.0.0/30 is directly connected, Ethernet3
 C      50.50.50.0/24 is directly connected, Vlan101
 C      192.168.1.0/24 is directly connected, Management1
```

Seven seconds later, the OSPF routes are back:

```
SW1[03:15:34]#sho ip route | begin Gateway
Gateway of last resort:
 S      0.0.0.0/0 [1/0] via 192.168.1.1

 C      10.0.0.0/30 is directly connected, Ethernet1
 R      10.10.10.0/24 [120/2] via 10.0.0.2
 R      10.10.11.0/24 [120/2] via 10.0.0.2
 C      20.0.0.0/30 is directly connected, Ethernet2
 O E2   20.20.20.0/24 [110/10] via 20.0.0.2
```

```
O E2    20.20.21.0/24 [110/10] via 20.0.0.2
C       30.0.0.0/30 is directly connected, Ethernet3
C       50.50.50.0/24 is directly connected, Vlan101
C       192.168.1.0/24 is directly connected, Management1
```

And four seconds after that, the BGP routes are restored:

```
SW1[03:15:38]#sho ip route | begin Gateway
Gateway of last resort:
 S      0.0.0.0/0 [1/0] via 192.168.1.1

 C      10.0.0.0/30 is directly connected, Ethernet1
 R      10.10.10.0/24 [120/2] via 10.0.0.2
 R      10.10.11.0/24 [120/2] via 10.0.0.2
 C      20.0.0.0/30 is directly connected, Ethernet2
 O E2   20.20.20.0/24 [110/10] via 20.0.0.2
 O E2   20.20.21.0/24 [110/10] via 20.0.0.2
 C      30.0.0.0/30 is directly connected, Ethernet3
 B E    30.30.30.0/24 [200/0] via 30.0.0.2
 B E    30.30.31.0/24 [200/0] via 30.0.0.2
 C      50.50.50.0/24 is directly connected, Vlan101
 C      192.168.1.0/24 is directly connected, Management1
```

Now certainly, this isn't exactly an Internet edge router with hundreds of thousands of prefixes, but think about this for a minute: if this switch was running monolithic code, and the OSPF process crashed, the switch would have (at best) rebooted. How long does it take for a switch to reboot? I recently did some failover testing for a client, and timed the following devices:

Arista 7048T:	1m39s
Arista 7124SX:	1m41s
Arista 7050S:	1m42s
Cisco Nexus 5548:	3m19s
Cisco Nexus 7010:	6m23s
Cisco VSS 6509:	12m13s

Even taking the best time of 1 minute 39 seconds, the time saved by the switch taking advantage of agents, the process manager, and SysDB, the routing table was completely restored in 15 seconds as opposed to over a minute. If you compare this to a monolithic system like the VSS 6509, then almost 12 minutes were saved.

Now, I could argue that the Cisco Nexus switches run a Linux-based OS, and they talk about process managers, so maybe they could survive the routing process being killed. Sadly, there's no way I know of to kill a process in NX-OS, so I couldn't try it. I guess we'll never know. Of course, I have seen a bug where a single process caused the box to core (reload) on a Cisco 5010, so I'd have to say that the process manager didn't save me that time.

## CHAPTER 16

Access Lists

At some point, we all need to write an access list. Like most things in EOS, doing so is very similar to doing so in IOS, with some minor changes here and there that we'll cover in this chapter.

There are a variety of different Access-Control List (ACL) types, depending on how and where they are applied. The types include:

Port-based ACL (PACL)
   PACLs are applied to ports.

Router-based ACL (RACL)
   RACLs are applied to SVIs.

MAC-Based ACLs (MACL or MAC ACL)
   MACLs are ACLs that filter based on MAC address.

Control Plane ACL
   ACL used to filter access to the CPU on the switch. This ACL is where you would filter SSH, SNMP, Telnet, and so on to the switch itself.

Let's look at the benefits and limitations of ACLs in EOS. According to the Arista *Configuration Guide* for EOS version 4.9.3.2, the following are features for ACLs:

- Ingress ACLs
- Port ACL applied on layer-2 Ethernet interfaces
- Port ACL on port-channel interfaces. Ports in a port-channel apply the port-channel's ACL
- Filters: IPv4 protocol, source and destination address, TCP and UDP ports, TCP flags, and TTL

- List size: 512 active rules; diminished capacity if rules contain L4 and port range filters

- Broadcast and multicast storm control

The same document also lists the following:

- Egress ACLs
- Filters based on IPv6/MAC

I've never had much of a use for egress ACLs on routers, so on the surface that's not a big deal for me.

 There are some valid uses for egress ACLs on switches, especially cut-through models. Additionally, the ability to deny traffic from leaving an interface when it was sourced from one or more specific source interfaces can be useful on a switch.

I'm sure IPv6 ACLs will be added in the future, so I'm not terribly worried about that either. MAC access lists are supported, and I'll show them later in this chapter. Unless I've confused what they mean by "filters based on MAC," in which case I apologize to everyone involved.

I'm not going to write about how ACLs work since there are many books out there that explain this. Instead, I'm going to concentrate on how Arista ACLs are different than what you may be used to. To that end, let's talk about a pretty significant difference regarding where ACLs can be applied.

One of the first things I like to do on a switch is to lock down what networks can get to it. On a Cisco switch, I'd just whip up a simple ACL and apply it to the VTY (virtual teletype terminal) interface. Naturally, I tried to do that on my Arista switches, and to my surprise, there were no VTY interfaces!

Arista does this sort of access restriction very differently from other vendors. If you want to restrict access to the switch, you don't need an ACL for the (nonexistent) VTY interfaces, or an ACL for SNMP, or an ACL for NTP. Instead, since all of these are really virtual interfaces to the switch's control plane, Arista just puts a single ACL on the control plane itself. In fact, there is a default, read-only ACL present on the switch out of the box that doesn't show up in the *running-config*. To see it, use the command show ip access-lists:

```
SW11#sho ip access-lists
IP Access List default-control-plane-acl [readonly]
        statistics per-entry
        10 permit icmp any any [match 9, 9:43:42 ago]
```

```
        20 permit ip any any tracked [match 6029, 0:00:00 ago]
        30 permit ospf any any
        40 permit tcp any any eq ssh telnet www snmp bgp https
[match 88, 0:04:18 ago]
        50 permit udp any any eq bootps bootpc snmp rip
        60 permit tcp any any eq mlag ttl eq 255
        70 permit udp any any eq mlag ttl eq 255
        80 permit vrrp any any
        90 permit ahp any any
       100 permit pim any any
       110 permit igmp any any [match 3, 2 days, 18:24:42 ago]
       120 permit tcp any any range 5900 5910 [match 8, 1:08:49 ago]
       130 permit tcp any any range 50000 50100
       140 permit udp any any range 51000 51100
```

This is actually a great example to use to show the format of ACLs in EOS, so let's take a look at how it's built in order to understand ACLs.

If all your management traffic gets to the switch through the management interfaces, then you could filter those interfaces, which would have the same end result as filtering the VTY. The difference is that filtering access to the control plane is not interface specific. If you later change your management interface from the physical interface *Ma1* to an SVI, say *int vlan10*, then your physical interface ACLs would need to be moved. Problem is, as of EOS version 4.9.3, ACLs cannot be applied to SVIs!

First, notice that the command is show ip access-lists, and not show access-lists. Arista switches haven't been around for decades, so there are no legacy needs for protocols like IPX, AppleTalk, DECnet, or XNS. There are also no numbered ACLs in EOS. There are IP access lists, and they require names instead of an ancient set of coded number ranges. Hallelujah.

Some of these protocols can be filtered with MAC access lists. See later in this chapter for details.

The name of the default control plane access list is *default-control-plane-acl*. To see only that access list, use the show ip access-lists *ACL-name* command. In a switch with no other ACLs, the output would be the same as the previous example. You can also get a summary of an ACL by adding the summary keyword:

```
SW11#sho ip access-lists default-control-plane-acl summ
IPV4 ACL default-control-plane-acl
        Total rules configured: 14
        Configured on: control-plane
```

Since this is a special-case ACL that's read only, let's go ahead and create a new one that we can mess with. I'll show you how to alter the ACL applied to the control plane later in this chapter.

There are two types of ACLs that can be created: standard and extended. Extended ACLs are the default, and allow the specification of source and destination IP addresses, as well as ports and protocols. Standard ACLs only allow source IPs to be specified.

Basic IP ACLs

To create a standard ACL, use the `ip access-list standard` *ACL-name* configuration mode command. Here, I'll create a standard ACL called *Jerks*:

```
SW11(config)#ip access-list standard Jerks
SW11(config-std-acl-Jerks)#
```

This drops me into ACL configuration mode, which is a wonderfully powerful tool for the creation and maintenance of ACLs. Let's start by adding a comment:

```
SW11(config-std-acl-Jerks)#remark [ People I dislike ]
```

I'm a big believer in comments, and add them wherever I can. So now that we know what this ACL is for, let's add some deny statements. Since this is a standard ACL, I'm only able to deny IP addresses or IP address ranges. There are three ways to do so, and this is one of my most favorite things to show people who are new to Arista.

First, we can use the old fashioned inverse mask. I'll write a line to deny everyone on the 10.10.10.0/24 network:

```
SW11(config-std-acl-Jerks)#deny 10.10.10.0 0.0.0.255
```

That's boring, so let's add another deny entry for everyone on the 11.11.11.0/24 network, but this time I'll use a normal mask:

```
SW11(config-std-acl-Jerks)#deny 11.11.11.0 255.255.255.0
```

Not only that, but I can apply a similar mask just by using CIDR notation:

```
SW11(config-std-acl-Jerks)#deny 12.12.12.0/24
```

At this point, I'm done excluding whole networks worth of jerks, so I'd like to see my handiwork. Since this is EOS, I know I don't need to exit configuration mode to exit show commands, so I'll take advantage of that fact now:

```
SW11(config-std-acl-Jerks)#sho ip access-lists Jerks
```

Well that's a letdown. Where's my ACL? Because we're in ACL configuration mode, the ACL hasn't yet been saved. In order to commit it, I'd need to exit ACL configuration mode. If I want to see what I've created so far, I can use the ACL configuration command, show:

```
SW11(config-std-acl-Jerks)#show
Standard ip Access List Jerks
      10 remark [ People I dislike ]
      20 deny 10.10.10.0/24
      30 deny 11.11.11.0 255.255.255.0
      40 deny 12.12.12.0/24
```

There it is! Take a good look at what you see there, because it's not exactly what I entered. Look at the first deny line (line 20), and see that it shows *deny 10.10.10.0/24*, but what I typed was deny 10.10.10.0 0.0.0.255. The switch took my inverse mask and converted it to a CIDR mask for me. How cool is that?

Do you know anyone who likes inverse masks? I don't. I think they only exist to further the endlessly profitable certification machine. Any company that lets you enter regular masks in ACLs is OK in my book. Hey, this is my book!

Line 30 shows exactly what I typed: deny 11.11.11.0 255.255.255.0. So why wasn't this line converted to a CIDR mask like the other one?

EOS allows you to enter either a CIDR mask or a network mask. According to the documentation, inverse masks aren't even on the list! Since a regular subnet mask is allowed, and that's what I typed, I imagine that EOS is being polite and keeping it the way I typed it. The fact that my switch translated my inverse mask for me is just icing on the cake.

To save the access list, exit ACL configuration mode:

```
SW11(config-std-acl-Jerks)#exit
```

Now the ACL is active:

```
SW11(config)#sho ip access-list Jerks
Standard IP Access List Jerks
      10 remark [ People I dislike ]
      20 deny 10.10.10.0/24
      30 deny 11.11.11.0 255.255.255.0
      40 deny 12.12.12.0/24
```

Oh, but I forgot about all of those jerks over in the 13.13.13.0/24 network, so let me go back in there and add them. But I'd like to make them even higher in the jerk priority than those jerks in the 12.12.12.0/24 network. In order to do so, I'll add the line with a line number of 35:

```
SW11(config)#ip access-list standard Jerks
SW11(config-std-acl-Jerks)#35 deny 13.13.13.0/24
```

And hey, don't all ACLs *deny* by default? They sure do, which means that my little jerk list is pointless because even with all those networks, it will still just deny everyone, so I'll need to add a permit any to the end. I'll use line number 47 to put it on the end of the list:

```
SW11(config-std-acl-Jerks)#47 permit any
```

And now I'll use the show command again to see my handiwork:

```
SW11(config-std-acl-Jerks)#show
Standard ip Access List Jerks
        10 remark [ People I dislike ]
        20 deny 10.10.10.0/24
        30 deny 11.11.11.0 255.255.255.0
        35 deny 13.13.13.0/24
        40 deny 12.12.12.0/24
        47 permit any
```

OK, so my lines are there, but my OCD is taking over and I can't stand the fact that my line numbers are no longer neatly numbered by 10s. Luckily, I have the tools to satisfy my obsession; namely, the resequence command. This command takes an initial number and a step number. If you want to have the first line start at 100, and each line increment by 10, use the following command:

```
SW11(config-std-acl-Jerks)#resequence 100 10
```

Let's take a look. Remember, since we haven't exited, we can mess with this all day long and it doesn't take effect:

```
SW11(config-std-acl-Jerks)#show
Standard ip Access List Jerks
        100 remark [ People I dislike ]
        110 deny 10.10.10.0/24
        120 deny 11.11.11.0 255.255.255.0
        130 deny 13.13.13.0/24
        140 deny 12.12.12.0/24
        150 permit any
```

Nah, that's boring. How about starting with the number 3, and incrementing by threes?

```
SW11(config-std-acl-Jerks)#resequence 3 3
SW11(config-std-acl-Jerks)#show
Standard ip Access List Jerks
        3 remark [ People I dislike ]
        6 deny 10.10.10.0/24
        9 deny 11.11.11.0 255.255.255.0
        12 deny 13.13.13.0/24
        15 deny 12.12.12.0/24
        18 permit any
```

Fun! I could do this all day, but I'll spare you my madness. If you'd like to see what sort of damage you've caused before committing, you can use the show diff command. This will call the Linux diff command and compare the current state of the ACL to the original state. Here's a sample from my current mess:

```
SW11(config-std-acl-Jerks)#show diff
---
+++
@@ -1,6 +1,8 @@
 Standard ip Access List Jerks
-        10 remark [ People I dislike ]
-        20 deny 10.10.10.0/24
-        30 deny 11.11.11.0 255.255.255.0
-        40 deny 12.12.12.0/24
+        3 remark [ People I dislike ]
+        6 deny 10.10.10.0/24
+        9 deny 11.11.11.0 255.255.255.0
+        12 deny 13.13.13.0/24
+        15 deny 12.12.12.0/24
+        18 permit any
```

You could also use the show active command to see the currently active ACL:

```
SW11(config-std-acl-Jerks)#show active
Standard ip Access List Jerks
        10 remark [ People I dislike ]
        20 deny 10.10.10.0/24
        30 deny 11.11.11.0 255.255.255.0
        40 deny 12.12.12.0/24
```

As always, exiting saves the ACL:

```
SW11(config-std-acl-Jerks)#exit
SW11(config)#sho ip access-list Jerks
Standard IP Access List Jerks
        3 remark [ People I dislike ]
        6 deny 10.10.10.0/24
        9 deny 11.11.11.0 255.255.255.0
        12 deny 13.13.13.0/24
        15 deny 12.12.12.0/24
        18 permit any
```

Ooh…I really hate that Bob guy on the 14 network. In fact, his loathsome IP address deserves its own remark:

```
SW11(config-std-acl-Jerks)#16 rem [ Ooh, and I REALLY hate Bob ]
SW11(config-std-acl-Jerks)#17 deny 14.14.14.14/32
```

OCD's got ahold of me again, so I really need to renumber. Notice how my 14.14.14.14/32 entry got converted to host 14.14.14.14:

```
SW11(config-std-acl-Jerks)#resequence 10 10
SW11(config-std-acl-Jerks)#show
Standard ip Access List Jerks
```

```
10 remark [ People I dislike ]
20 deny 10.10.10.0/24
30 deny 11.11.11.0 255.255.255.0
40 deny 13.13.13.0/24
50 deny 12.12.12.0/24
60 remark [ Ooh, and I REALLY hate Bob ]
70 deny host 14.14.14.14
80 permit any
```

To apply the access list to an interface, use the `ip access-group` command, just like you'd expect. You do need to specify that the ACL is being applied inbound, even though outbound is not supported, so I wouldn't be surprised if outbound ACLs will be supported in a future release:

```
SW11(config)#int e1
SW11(config-if-Et1)#ip access-group Jerks in
```

As of EOS version 4.9.3, ACLs can only be assigned to physical interfaces and the control plane. Assigning ACLs to SVIs is not supported.

Advanced IP ACLs

Advanced IP ACLs let you specify a host of options on which to filter, aside from just a source IP address. Let's work with the control plane access list as an example, because this is a pretty common thing to do with a data center switch right out of the box. Here's the *default-control-plane-acl* from a 7050S running 4.8.5. Let's examine every line so we know what we're dealing with. The first line is the `statistics per-entry` line:

```
statistics per-entry
```

The `statistics per-entry` command reports how many times each line was matched, and how long ago the last match was. This command shows up as an unsupported feature on my 7050, but seems to work on my 7124SX just fine. Here's the output from trying to use it on a 7050:

```
SW10(config-acl-GAD)#statistics per-entry
% Unavailable command (not supported on this hardware platform)
```

 The Arista *Configuration Guide* indicates that this command is only supported on the 7100 series of switches.

That's funny, because it's configured in the *default-control-plane-acl*, and seems to work there, too. Look for match entries when you show your ACLs if you have this configured. Here's an example:

```
SW10#sho ip access-list default-control-plane-acl | grep match
    10 permit icmp any any [match 23, 4:49:20 ago]
    20 permit ip any any tracked [match 17481, 0:00:00 ago]
    110 permit igmp any any [match 3, 5 days, 19:09:49 ago]
    120 permit tcp any any range 5900 5910 [match 23, 7:44:21 ago]
```

Next, a favorite of anyone who likes to ping, the `permit icmp any any` line:

```
    10 permit icmp any any
```

This line allows anyone to ping the switch. The destination should usually be any for
the control plane ACL, and you'll see that all of these lines have exactly that configured.

The next line, `permit ip any any tracked`, means "permit any ICMP, UDP, or TCP
packets from existing connections." In other words, packets received in reply to packets
sourced by the switch. If you ping from CLI, the switch sources those ping packets, and
this filter will allow the replies. Other examples might include BGP communications,
OSPF, VRRP, and any other protocol where the switch might advertise or send hellos:

```
    20 permit ip any any tracked
```

The line `permit ospf any any` shouldn't be too difficult to figure out. Let's just say that
it makes OSPF work. Why wouldn't the previous line do that? The previous line will
only permit packets in response to those sent by the switch. If another switch or router
were to send an OSPF hello packet, then line 20 would not match it, while this line would
permit it:

```
    30 permit ospf any any
```

The next line shows `40 permit tcp any any eq ssh telnet www snmp bgp https`,
and is a great example of a way to consolidate ACL lines. On one line, the ACL will
permit any of the following TCP packets: Telnet, HTTP (WWW), SNMP, BGP, and
HTTPS.

```
    40 permit tcp any any eq ssh telnet www snmp bgp https
```

The only real drawback of stacking ports or protocols like this is that matches and logs
(covered later in this chapter) will only trigger once per line. If you need more granularity
and would like to know how many times SNMP is hit on its own, then you'd need to
separate SNMP out onto its own line.

The next line shows a similar stacking of protocols (or their standard ports, to be more
accurate) with the line `permit udp any any eq bootps bootpc snmp rip`. This line
is separate from the previous line because this line is for UDP protocols, while the
previous one was for TCP protocols:

```
    50 permit udp any any eq bootps bootpc snmp rip
```

The next two lines both list MLAG as the protocol. There are two lines because one is
for TCP and one is for UDP. Why not include them in the TCP and UDP lines? Because

in these MLAG-specific lines, Arista has included a Time to Live (TTL) modifier to the line. This modifier will deny MLAG packets if the TTL value is anything other than 255. This helps to keep any devices except for directly attached switches from interfering with MLAG communications:

```
60 permit tcp any any eq mlag ttl eq 255
70 permit udp any any eq mlag ttl eq 255
```

VRRP, configured in line 80, is a protocol (#118), and not part of IP (protocol #4), so it gets its own line:

```
80 permit vrrp any any
```

The next line permits AHP from anywhere to anywhere. AHP stands for Accelerated Hydrogen Peroxide. Oh, wait…wrong Google page. Sorry about that. AHP is the Authentication Header Protocol used with IPSec:

```
90 permit ahp any any
```

PIM is short for Protocol Independent Multicast, which is used in Multicast:

```
100 permit pim any any
```

IGMP is the Internet Group Management Protocol, also used in Multicast:

```
110 permit igmp any any
```

The following three lines are for features available on Arista switches:

```
120 permit tcp any any range 5900 5910
130 permit tcp any any range 50000 50100
140 permit udp any any range 51000 51100
```

Anywhere that a protocol or port name is listed, the corresponding protocol or port number could be used instead. For example, the following two lines are identical; although after the ACL is saved, both lines will show *www*:

```
permit tcp any any eq 80
permit tcp any any eq www
```

The fact that you can stack protocols can make for some weird entries. The following ACL is accepted, though of course only the first line would ever be matched:

```
IP Access List GAD2
        10 permit tcp any any eq www
        20 permit tcp any any eq www www
        30 permit tcp any any eq www www www www
```

To get a list of common protocols or ports, use the question mark when entering ACL entries. Here's the list of protocols in EOS version 4.8.5:

```
Arista(config-acl-GAD2)#permit ?
  ahp      Authentication Header Protocol
  icmp     Internet Control Message Protocol
  igmp     Internet Group Management Protocol (IGMP)
  ip       Any Internet Protocol
```

```
    ospf    OSPF routing protocol
    pim     Protocol Independent Multicast (PIM)
    tcp     Transmission Control Protocol
    udp     User Datagram Protocol
    vrrp    Virtual Router Redundancy Protocol
    <0-255> IP protocol number
```

The list of ports is pretty long, so I'll just show the first few and the last few, starting with a partial list of TCP ports. Note that you can always enter the port number, even if it's not on the list:

```
Arista(config-acl-GAD2)#permit tcp any any eq ?
    bgp         Border Gateway Protocol (179)
    chargen     Character generator (19)
    cmd         Remote Shell/Rsh (514)
    daytime     Daytime (13)
    discard     Discard (9)
    domain      Domain Name Service (53)
    echo        Echo (7)
    exec        Remote Process Execution/Rexec (512)
    finger      Finger (79)
    ftp         File Transfer Protocol (21)
    ftp-data    FTP data connections (20)

[--- output removed ---]

    telnet      Telnet Protocol (23)
    time        Time (37)
    uucp        Unix-to-Unix Copy Program (540)
    whois       Nicname (43)
    www         World Wide Web (HTTP) (80)
    <0-65535>   Port number
```

And here is a partial list of UDP ports:

```
Arista(config-acl-GAD2)#permit udp any any eq ?
    bootpc      Bootstrap Protocol (BOOTP) client (68)
    bootps      Bootstrap Protocol (BOOTP) server (67)
    daytime     Daytime (13)
    discard     Discard (9)
    dnsix       DNSIX security protocol auditing (195)
    domain      Domain Name Service (53)
    echo        Echo (7)
    isakmp      Internet Security Association and Key Management
                Protocol (500)
    mlag        MLAG Protocol (4432)

[--- output removed ---]

    tftp        Trivial File Transfer Protocol (69)
```

```
time          Time (37)
who           Who service, rwho (513)
xdmcp         X Display Manager Control Protocol (177)
<0-65535>     Port number
```

MAC ACLs

MAC ACLs are just like IP ACLs, only with MAC addresses instead of IP addresses, and with no provision for any OSI layers above the layer-3. OK, so those are a lot of differences. Let's take a look at one and all will become clear. MAC ACLs are configured with the mac access-list *acl-name* command:

```
Arista(config)#mac access-list Slackers
Arista(config-mac-acl-Slackers)#
```

This drops you into the same group configuration mode as an IP ACL. No changes are saved until you exit, and you can abort your changes with the abort command. The same resequence, permit, deny, and other commands are available as well:

```
Arista(config-mac-acl-Slackers)#?
  abort          Exit without committing pending changes
  default        Set a command to its defaults
  deny           Specify packets to drop
  exit           Exit from MAC ACL Configuration mode
  help           Description of the interactive help system
  no             Negate a command or set its defaults
  permit         Specify packets to accept
  remark         Specify a comment
  resequence     Resequence the list
  show           Show running system information
  statistics     Count packets that match the list
  <1-4294967295> Sequence Number
```

Let's add the statistics per-entry command, just to show that it works on my 7124SX switch:

```
Arista(config-mac-acl-Slackers)#statistics per-entry
```

Using the permit command, the question mark indicates that we can use either a MAC address in the format hhhh.hhhh.hhhh or the word any:

```
Arista(config-mac-acl-Slackers)#permit ?
  H.H.H  Source MAC address
  any    Any source address
```

You must specify a mask (not an inverse mask):

```
SW1(config-mac-acl-GAD)#permit b88d.123d.0bfc ?
  H.H.H  Source MAC address mask
```

You can specify a source and destination MAC address, or use the word *any* for either. Here, my ACL entry permits from the MAC address *b88d.123d.0bfc* to any destination. To match a single host, I'll use a mask of all 00s:

```
SW1(config-mac-acl-GAD)#permit b88d.123d.0bfc 0000.0000.0000 any
```

Whenever I work with MAC addresses, I get annoyed because systems always show them in one format, and filters always want them in another. EOS will recognize other formats, even though it doesn't show that in the command help:

```
SW1(config-mac-acl-GAD)#permit b8:8d:12:3d:0b:fc 00:00:00:00:00:00 any
```

What's even better (to me, at least), is that no matter what you enter, EOS converts it to the one-byte format. Here, I've configured using one format (the one shown in the command help), and it displays in another:

```
SW1(config)#mac access-list GAD
SW1(config-mac-acl-GAD)#permit b88d.123d.0bfc 0000.0000.0000 any
SW1(config-mac-acl-GAD)#exit
```

And now I'll show my MAC ACL to see how the format has changed:

```
SW1(config)#sho mac access-list GAD
MAC Access List GAD
        10 permit b8:8d:12:3d:0b:fc 00:00:00:00:00:00 any
```

Applying ACLs

Applying ACLs is done the same way that it is done in that other industry standard networking operating system from that other company. You know the one I mean.

To enable an IP ACL on an interface, use the ip access-group *ACL-name* in command in interface configuration mode:

```
SW1(config)#int e1
SW1(config-if-Et1)#ip access-group GAD in
```

Note that as of EOS version 4.9.3.2, there is no option other than in.

To apply a MAC ACL, use the mac access-group *ACL-name* in command:

```
SW1(config)#int e1
SW1(config-if-Et1)#mac access-group GAD in
```

Once again, as of EOS 4.9.3, there is no support for applying ACLs to SVIs.

To apply an ACL to the control plane, first create an ACL. I know, sounds crazy, but remember that you cannot alter the default ACL, so you'll need to create a new one. What I generally do is copy the default into a text editor, then edit it, and save it with a new name in the switch. Here, I've altered the default list by removing SSH and SNMP from line 40, then added the two lines beneath it with more specific rules. I've also added the keyword log to every line. This will send a log message to the switch every time the line is matched. I've logged some of the lines, which is something I recommend. Logs should only record important data, so be judicial in this keyword's use. The log keyword only takes effect when an ACL is applied to the control plane. Here's my modified ACL:

```
ip access-list Control-Plane
  ! !*------------------------------------------------------------*
  ! !! ACL to permit/prohibit access to the switch's control plane !
  ! !! All SSH/SNMP/Telnet/etc. filters go here.                    !
  ! !*------------------------------------------------------------*
  10 permit icmp any any
  20 permit ip any any tracked
  30 permit ospf any any
  40 permit tcp any any eq telnet www bgp https
  50 permit tcp host 10.10.10.0/24 any eq snmp
  60 permit tcp 10.10.10.0/24 any eq ssh log
  70 permit udp any any eq bootps bootpc rip
  80 permit tcp any any eq mlag ttl eq 255
  90 permit udp any any eq mlag ttl eq 255
  100 permit vrrp any any
  110 permit ahp any any
  120 permit pim any any
  130 permit igmp any any
  140 permit tcp any any range 5900 5910
  150 permit tcp any any range 50000 50100
  160 permit udp any any range 51000 51100
```

To apply the new ACL to the control plane, enter `control-plane` configuration mode as follows:

```
SW10(config)#control-plane
SW10(config-cp)#
```

There isn't much you can do here yet, but you can apply an ACL with the `ip access-group` ACL-name in command:

```
SW10(config-cp)#ip access-group Control-Plane in
```

Exit the mode, and your change has been saved. As always, be careful messing with this ACL. If you're doing so on a remote switch, it's pretty easy to lock yourself out if you make a mistake.

As you can see, ACLs are pretty similar to what you're probably used to. I think the differences are welcome and easy to remember.

## CHAPTER 17

Quality of Service

Quality of Service (QoS) on a switch can be a confusing subject, especially if you're used to dealing with things like low-latency queuing on Cisco routers. It doesn't help that a lot of the documentation for QoS on switches isn't great (from any vendor), so I'm going to try my best to explain it here in a way that's easy to understand.

QoS on an Arista (and many other) switches is different than it is on a router because, aside from the obvious fact that switches aren't routers, they operate primarily at layer-2. When dealing with routers, we usually work with either IP precedence or Differentiated Services Code Point (DSCP) fields, both of which reside in the layer-3 headers of packets. Switches operate primarily at layer-2, and while typical Ethernet packets don't include a field for QoS, packets encoded with 802.1Q do. When an Ethernet frame includes the 802.1Q tag, we usually think of it as being VLAN tagged for use in a trunk, but these tags have other uses as well.

The 802.1Q tag is not just a VLAN tag. While I'm not usually a fan of digging into packet formats, it's important to understand the method used for tagging CoS into non-VLAN-tagged frames. The entire 802.1Q tag is four bytes in length, and includes the following four fields:

Tag Protocol Identifier (TPID)
> This 16-bit field contains the value 0v 0x8100 to identify the frame as 802.1Q.

Priority Code Point (PCP)
> A three-bit field used for frame priority. This field contains the values used for Class of Service (CoS).

Canonical Format Indicator (CFI)
> This field is always set to 0 unless you're still using Token Ring, in which case you can enjoy seeing a smug little 1 when you decode the packets.

VLAN Identifier (VID)
    This is the 12-bit field that specifies the VLAN to which this packet is assigned.

There are two fields we care about in this chapter. The CFI and the VID. The CFI contains the CoS values, and the VID contains the VLAN ID.

If you're wondering how we can do QoS on non-VLAN-tagged frames after all this page space has been spent on 802.1Q and VLAN tags, then you're about to be rewarded with the answer. The trick here is that there are two reserved VLAN ID values: 000 and FFF. For those who can't do binary/hex/decimal conversions in your head, FFF in hex equals 4,095 (since zero is included, that's the expected 4,096 of total possible VLAN values). That's why there are only 4,094 possible VLANs used on most switches: 000 and FFF are reserved.

Anyway, the value 000 means *this frame is dot1Q encoded, but there is no VLAN ID.* Encode the frame with dot1Q, set the VID to 000, and now you've got a frame capable of CoS prioritization! Those RFC guys sure are clever, huh?

If you're not familiar with QoS, there are three phases to the process. They are:

Classification
    Determine what type of packet or frame this is.

Marking
    Mark the packet or frame according to the classification.

Policing
    Adjust the sending of packets according to the applied mark. This is usually some sort of prioritization, which could be done in either software or hardware.

If you've done any QoS on routers, or read the QoS chapter in *Network Warrior*, then you're probably used to using class maps and policy maps. That works great for L3 QoS, but down at L2, things work a little differently. First, there is very little tolerance for delay at L2, especially when talking about Arista switches. Second, we really don't want to do complex classification schemes on the switch. Classification should really be done on the device sourcing the packets, but of course those devices cannot always be trusted. What's more, those devices may only be capable of setting L3 QoS values of IP precedence or DSCP, and the switch really wants to use CoS.

One of the things that can make QoS on switches so confusing is the fact that it can be largely dependent on the hardware within the switch. While Arista's EOS is great in that the same software image works on every Arista device, the fact remains that different Arista switches use different ASICs. As we'll see, different switches have slightly different commands and capabilities when it comes to QoS. The first thing we have to do, regardless of platform, is decide if we *trust* the existing QoS markings received on an interface.

There are three methods of trust on an interface: *trust CoS*, *trust DSCP*, and *untrusted*. OK, so it doesn't make any sense to say that *untrusted* is a method of trust, but bear with me and all will be revealed.

When a packet is received, it may or may not have QoS markings in it. If we don't trust those markings, we set the interface to *untrusted*. If we trust those markings, but only if they're CoS, then we set the interface to *trusted CoS*. Similarly, if we trust the DSCP markings, then we set the interface to *trusted DSCP*. But what happens if we trust one method, and a packet arrives with markings from another, or even no markings at all? In that case, we assign a *default* QoS value (either CoS or DSCP) to the packet. All of this is configurable on each interface, but it is important to understand that all of this trusting and default stuff is for *inbound packets only*.

Once the packets are classified, they are then mapped to a *traffic class*. A traffic class is analogous to the hardware transmit queues (*tx-queues*) on the outbound interfaces. All this talk of DSCP and CoS is great, but when it comes to the hardware, those values don't really matter. What we, the ones with the big brains and opposable thumbs, need to do is somehow tell the switch what traffic gets assigned to what traffic class. This is done by something called *mapping*.

Think of it this way: the QoS/CoS values are merely marks in the packets or frames and, as such, they are logical. The switch is a physical device, and each interface has physical output queues attached to it. We need to configure the switch so that it understands what packets get funneled into which hardware queue.

 These hardware queues are different than the buffers I talked about in Chapter 2. Those buffers, including virtual output queues, are used to prevent intraswitch blocking. These queues are used for prioritization when transmitting packets. The distinction isn't terribly relevant to your daily operation of the switches, but I just want to make sure we're all on the same page.

Since a picture is worth at least two paragraphs worth of words, let me draw some pictures. Figure 17-1 shows a high-level flow of a packet through the QoS process on an Arista switch when it is received on an interface configured to trust CoS markings. The packet comes into an interface, where the switch has been configured to trust the CoS marking. The CoS marking is mapped to a traffic class, which determines what hardware tx-queue should be used on the outbound interface. This is the simplest of the QoS configurations on an Arista switch.

Figure 17-1. QoS from a trusted CoS configured interface

In Figure 17-2, a packet is received on an interface configured to trust DSCP markings. The DSCP markings are mapped to a traffic class, but before the packet is sent, a configurable CoS marking is applied. This step is called *CoS rewrite*, and is explained in detail later in this chapter.

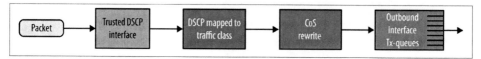

Figure 17-2. QoS from a trusted DSCP configured interface

Figure 17-3 shows a packet's flow through the QoS mechanisms when received on an untrusted interface. In this case, a default CoS or DSCP value (either configured or not) is applied, after which this value is mapped to a traffic class. The packet then has the proper CoS value written to it in the CoS rewrite stage, after which it can be sent out to the proper tx-queue on the outbound interface.

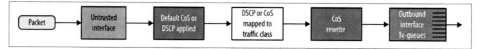

Figure 17-3. QoS from an untrusted interface

Hopefully, these pictures will help to convey what's going on with all these QoS commands. I know it took me a while to get it into my thick skull and once I laid out the process in a visual manner, it all made more sense to me.

Once the packets get to the output interface, even more QoS can be performed. First, the outbound interface can be configured with *shaping*. Shaping is used to rate limit an interface to a data rate lower than the physical interface's speed.

I say lower because I've actually had people ask me if the rate could be higher than the physical interface's speed. The first time that happened, I just stared, speechless, which is a pretty rare condition for me. So let me say categorically that no, you cannot rate limit the speed of an interface to a value higher than the physical speed of the interface.

Lastly, the individual tx-queues can be shaped too. And check this out: at least in EOS version 4.9.4, you can absolutely configure one of the individual tx-queues to a rate higher than the interface's shape rate. Of course, the difference is that the interface's shape rate isn't a physical limitation, and no laws of nature are being broken. If you do configure a tx-queue with a rate higher than the interface's shape rate, the interface's shape rate takes precedence, so the tx-queue will never get enough data to shape close to that rate anyway.

Not only can you shape the tx-queues, but you can also prioritize them. There are a couple of different ways to do this, which I'll show in the configuration section. Speaking of which, let's see how to configure QoS.

Configuring QoS

When a packet is received on an interface, it may have CoS or DSCP markings already in place. There are three options as to how the switch might deal with these markings. When packets are received on an interface, they can either be *trusted* (using CoS or DSCP) or *untrusted*. Trusted means that the packet's CoS or DSCP values are trusted, and those values will be used to assign the packet to a traffic class. Untrusted means that the values found in the CoS or DSCP fields will be ignored, and default CoS, DSCP, will be assigned. These new values will be used to assign the packet to a traffic class.

Configuring Trust

To configure an interface to trust CoS values, use the qos trust cos interface command. Note that this command will not show up in the *running-config* because it is the default state for QoS on interfaces:

```
SW1(config-if-Et1)#qos trust cos
```

To trust DSCP values on an inbound interface, use the qos trust dscp interface command:

```
SW1(config-if-Et1)#qos trust dscp
```

 Only CoS and DSCP are available as options. If you're used to using IP precedence values, you'll need to do the math and convert the IP precedence value to a DSCP value.

To remove either trust, simply negate the command. To place the interface into *untrusted* mode, use the no qos trust command:

```
SW1(config-if-Et1)#no qos trust
```

Configuring Defaults

When an interface is set to untrusted mode, or if no QoS value is found when in trusted mode, the switch will assign a *default* CoS or DSCP value to every packet received on the interface. The value assigned to the packets is determined by the qos cos or qos dscp interface commands. These commands behave differently depending on the ASIC on which the switch is built. Details for each platform are as follows:

FM4000-based switches (7124SX, etc.)
> Default CoS and DSCP values can be set on each interface.

Trident-based switches (7050, etc.)
> Default CoS and DSCP values can be set on each interface.

Petra-based switches (7048T, 7500, etc.)
> Petra-based switches employ multiple ASICs, with each supporting multiple interfaces. Each Petra chip is configurable, which means that default CoS and DSCP values affect groups of interfaces. Individual interfaces cannot be configured with default CoS and DSCP values on these switches.

Let's take a look at how to configure trust on each platform, starting with the FM4000 and Trident-based switches, since they are treated the same way.

FM4000 and Trident-based switches

For FM4000 and Trident-based switches, each interface may be configured with a default CoS or DSCP value. To configure a default CoS value on an interface, use the qos cos *cos-value* interface command, where *cos-value* is a number in the range of 0 through 7, with 0 being the default:

```
SW1(config-if-Et1)#qos cos ?
  <0-7>  Class of Service (CoS) value between 0 and 7
```

Here I'll set the default CoS value on Ethernet1 to 5:

```
SW1(config-if-Et1)#qos cos 5
```

To configure a default DSCP value on an interface, use the qos dscp *dscp-value* command, where *dscp-value* is a number in the range of 0 through 63, with 0 being the default:

```
SW1(config-if-Et1)#qos dscp ?
  <0-63>  DSCP value between 0 and 63
```

Here I'll set the default DSCP value on Ethernet1 to 44:

```
SW1(config-if-Et1)#qos dscp 44
```

Note that both of these commands can be active at once on the interface, regardless of the configured trust mode. Here's the *running-config* for Ethernet4, which I've configured with the same values as before, and with a trust setting of DSCP. Since the interface is trusting DSCP values, the default CoS and DSCP values have no effect unless a packet arrives with no DSCP value, in which case the default DSCP value will be applied:

```
SW1#sho run int e4
interface Ethernet4
   qos trust dscp
   qos cos 5
   qos dscp 44
```

Petra-based switches

Petra-based switches are a little tougher to figure out, because you don't configure the interfaces directly. Instead, you need to configure the ASIC that controls them.

> This may seem confusing because it's so different, but it's actually simpler because there are less options. On a Petra switch, there is no way to assign default DSCP or CoS values. You can only assign a default traffic class. As we'll see in a bit, CoS or DSCP values have to be mapped to a traffic class anyway, so this kind of makes it simpler, in a confusing sort of way. It's like calculus or talking to a pretty girl—once you figure it out, you're golden, but if you try too hard you'll be frustrated forever.

As of July 2012, there are two Petra-based switches in the Arista product catalog: the 7048T 48-port 1 Gbps copper switches, and the 7500 chassis switches. The linecards on the 7500 switches employ Petra ASICs that control eight interfaces each, while the 7048Ts have two Petras split between all the ports.

> As an interesting side note, the 7048T has one Petra that supports the first 32 1 Gbps ports, and another that supports the remaining 16 1 Gbps ports, plus the 4 SFP+ ports.

In order to figure out how many Petra ASICs you have, use the platform petraA Petra? global configuration command:

```
7048T(config)#platform petraA Petra?
Petra0  Petra1
```

On a modular chassis switch, this command will differ due to there being linecards. Here I searched for ASIC names on linecard 5:

```
7508(config)#platform petraA linecard5?
linecard5-Petra-0   linecard5-Petra-1   linecard5-Petra-2
linecard5-Petra-3   linecard5-Petra-4   linecard5-Petra-5
```

To configure a default traffic class of 5 for *linecard5-Petra-1*, use the following command. This will configure ports 9 through 16:

```
7508(config)#platform petraA linecard5-Petra-1 traffic-class 5
```

Alternatively, you can configure an entire module in a 7500 switch with the following variation, which in this example sets the default traffic class to 3 for module 1:

```
7508(config)#platform petraA module 1 traffic-class 3
```

Mapping

The switch needs to translate CoS or DSCP markings into traffic classes so that it knows which hardware queue to use when forwarding the packet. There are actually two types of mappings that can be done: QoS to traffic class, and traffic class to CoS. The first type of mapping is for mapping packets into traffic classes, while the second is for configuring CoS rewrite.

Mapping is configured globally on the switch. There can be multiple map statements, or multiple mappings for a single traffic class can be performed on a single line. The thing to remember is that we're mapping logical QoS mappings from packet fields to hardware queues via traffic classes. Why is this mapping necessary? Well, remember, we can leave well enough alone and just use defaults, but usually we want to prioritize something over something else that wouldn't normally be prioritized in such a way. Additionally, when it comes to DSCP, there are 64 different levels to choose from, but most switches have only seven or eight outbound hardware queues, so the switch needs to know how to translate all those QoS values into the limited number of hardware queues.

To map CoS values to a traffic class, use the qos map cos *cos-value* to traffic-class *traffic-class-value* command. Here, I'll assign packets containing a CoS value of 5 to traffic class 3:

```
SW1(config)#qos map cos 5 to traffic-class 3
```

Multiple CoS values can be mapped using a single statement. Here I'll map packets marked with CoS values of 2, 3, or 6 to traffic class 5:

```
SW1(config)#qos map cos 2 3 6 to traffic-class 5
```

 The values I'm using are arbitrary. I would generally not split multiple noncontiguous CoS values into a single traffic class like this, but it works as an example of performing multiple maps in one statement.

DSCP values can be mapped in exactly the same way; just replace the cos keyword with dscp, again noting that you can list one or multiple DSCP values on a single line. Here I'll map the DSCP values of 12, 23, and 36 to traffic class 3:

```
SW1(config)#qos map dscp 12 23 36 to traffic-class 3
```

CoS is the preferred method of QoS at layer-2, and an Arista switch will perform something called *CoS rewrite* on packets that were received on any interfaces not configured as CoS trusted ports. In other words, if it doesn't have CoS applied, or we didn't trust the CoS, the switch will mark those packets with the appropriate CoS value. But what CoS value is appropriate? It's up to us puny humans to decide, assuming we don't want to use the defaults (which are, again, platform specific).

This is done by mapping again, but this time instead of mapping a QoS value to a traffic class, we'll need to map one or more traffic classes to a CoS value. This makes perfect sense if you think about it. Since we either learned via DSCP or configured a default (trusted CoS ports don't get rewritten, remember), then we need to translate those values to a CoS value to be written. What makes this appear confusing is that we already mapped one QoS value to a traffic class, and now we're mapping a traffic class to another QoS value. It took me days to get this straight, so don't worry if it's a bit dizzying. Try looking at the process flows I did in Figures 17-2 and 17-3 again if you need a visual reference.

In order to map a traffic class to a CoS value for CoS rewrite, use the qos map traffic-class *traffic-class-value* to cos *cos-value* command. As with other qos map commands, multiple traffic classes can be listed on one line. Here I'll assign a CoS value of 3 to any packet in traffic classes 2, 3, or 4:

```
SW1(config)#qos map traffic-class 2 3 4 to cos 3
```

 Wait a minute! You can't assign multiple traffic classes in any other qos map command, but what you can always do is map multiples of the things you're mapping *from* to a single thing you're mapping *to*.

By this point in the packet's life within the switch, it should have a traffic class assigned to it. Either nothing is configured and the defaults are in place, CoS or DSCP values have been read, trusted, and mapped to traffic classes, or the inbound interface was configured as untrusted and all traffic has been marked with a default CoS or DSCP value (and then mapped accordingly).

The defaults regarding traffic classes vary between switch platforms (oh boy, that again!) but that's one of the costs of using merchant silicon, which is one of the things that make these switches so great in the first place. The Arista documentation devotes pages to tables showing these defaults, so I won't bore you with them here. Besides, in the next section, I'll show you how to display all the maps in one place. Just do that on an un-configured switch (which I will also show you), and you'll have most of the defaults for that platform.

Traffic classes can also be mapped to tx-queues. This is a global mapping, so it affects every interface. To do this type of mapping, use the same syntax used when mapping *traffic-classes* to *CoS*, only use `tx-queue` instead of `cos`. Maybe it would be easier if I just showed you what I mean. Here I'm mapping traffic classes 2 and 3 to tx-queue 4:

```
SW1(config)#qos map traffic-class 2 3 to tx-queue 4
```

Interface Shaping

You can limit the data throughput of an interface with the `shape rate` *shape-rate* interface command. Note that shaping is done on egress:

```
SW1(config-if-Et1)#shape rate ?
  <464-10000000>  Shape Rate in Kbps
```

Be careful with this command because unpredictable results may occur if you're not careful. Notice that the command allows a value of up to 10,000,000, which is 10 Gbps. That seems fine given that this is one of those newfangled Arista super switches full of 10 Gbps ports that you've read so much about. The problem is that I've got this interface stuffed with a copper SFP that's configured for 100 Mbps!

```
SW1(config-if-Et1)#sho run int e1
interface Ethernet1
   description [ To R1 ]
   speed sfp-1000baset auto 100full
   no switchport
   ip address 10.0.0.1/30
```

Remember when I said that you couldn't configure shaping for a speed faster than the physical limitations of the interface? Well, it looks like I was wrong…in a way. You cannot configure shaping to a speed faster than the highest physical speed that the interface is capable of, which in this case is 10 Gbps. When I jammed the copper SFP in there, the CLI didn't adjust for that fact, so the limitations are based on the 10 Gbps capability of the port. To keep things logical, I'll shape the interface to half of 100 Mbps:

```
SW1(config-if-Et1)#shape rate 50000
```

 For all of Arista's brilliance in operating system design, they still make us do the math from kbps. I can remember how to determine the volume of a cone, and I can do IP subnetting in my head, but converting from kbps to Mbps or even Gbps makes my teeth itch. Seriously, I have itchy teeth right now.

With the interface throttled to 50 Mbps, I'll now go into the tx-queues and really mess things up.

Shaping tx-queues

Every platform is different, so to find out how many tx-queues there are, use the `tx-queue ?` interface command (or `show qos map`; see "Showing QoS Information" (page 213) for details):

```
SW1(config-if-Et1)#tx-queue ?
  <0-6>  Transmit queue id
```

There are seven queues on this switch (a 7124SX) for each interface. To configure each, use the `tx-queue queue#` interface command. This will put you into tx-queue configuration mode on that interface:

```
SW1(config-if-Et1)#tx-queue 1
SW1(config-if-Et1-txq-1)#
```

Setting a shape rate is done the same way that it was done on the interface, with the `shape rate shape-rate` command:

```
SW1(config-if-Et1-txq-1)#shape rate ?
  <464-10000000>  Shape Rate in Kbps
```

Here, I'll set this tx-queue to a shape rate of 10 Mbps. Excuse me while I go scratch my teeth:

```
SW1(config-if-Et1-txq-1)#shape rate 10000
```

Prioritizing tx-queues

The tx-queues on each interface can be prioritized, too. There are two methods available: *strict-priority* and *round-robin*.

With strict-priority queues, each queue must be exhausted before the next queue can be serviced. In other words, tx-queue 6 will be serviced until empty, then tx-queue 5 will be serviced. Tx-queue 4 will not be serviced until tx-queue 5 is empty, and so on.

The highest numbered tx-queues have the highest priority.

With round-robin queues, the queues are serviced proportionally based on bandwidth statements configured for each tx-queue, or equally if no bandwidth statements are present on the tx-queues for that interface.

Not only that, but you can jazz things up a bit by having both priority and round-robin queues on the same interface. The limitation here is that when you set a tx-queue to be a round-robin queue, all the queues below that queue are automatically configured for round robin as well. You wouldn't want a priority queue in the middle of a group of round-robin queues anyway.

Tx-queues are set up in strict priority by default, and the default tx-queue used (if no custom traffic class tx-queue maps are in place) is tx-queue 0. To see the status of the queues for an interface, use the show qos int *interface-name* command:

```
SW1(config-if-Et1)#sho qos int e1
Ethernet1:
    Trust Mode: UNTRUSTED
    Default COS: 5
    Default DSCP: 44

    Port shaping rate: 500000Kbps

    Tx-Queue   Bandwidth   Shape Rate   Priority
               (percent)     (Kbps)
    -------------------------------------------
        0         N/A        1000000       strict
        1         N/A          10000       strict
        2         N/A        disabled      strict
        3         N/A        disabled      strict
        4         N/A        disabled      strict
        5         N/A        disabled      strict
        6         N/A        disabled      strict
```

We can see the many changes that we've done to this interface already, so let's really stir things up and change the tx-queue priority. First I'll change the priority of tx-queue 3 to round robin with the no priority command:

```
SW1(config-if-Et1)#tx-queue 3
SW1(config-if-Et1-txq-3)#no priority
```

This has the effect of placing not only tx-queue 3 into round-robin mode, but all of the queues beneath it as well. Remember, the queues beneath tx-queue 3 are the ones lower in numerical value, and not the ones visibly lower on the output of the show qos interface command:

```
SW1(config-if-Et1-txq-3)#sho qos int e1 | beg Priority
    Tx-Queue   Bandwidth   Shape Rate   Priority
               (percent)     (Kbps)
    -------------------------------------------
        0          25        1000000    round-robin
        1          25          10000    round-robin
        2          25        disabled   round-robin
        3          25        disabled   round-robin
        4         N/A        disabled      strict
        5         N/A        disabled      strict
        6         N/A        disabled      strict
```

Notice that the four queues in round-robin mode now display a bandwidth percentage as well. With no configured percentage, the switch will evenly distribute all round-robin tx-queues on the interface. This can be altered with the bandwidth percent *percent age* tx-queue command. Here I'll set the bandwidth percentage on tx-queue 3 to 30%:

```
SW1(config-if-Et1-txq-3)#bandwidth percent 30
```

This has an interesting effect on the tx-queues for this interface. Let's take a look:

```
SW1(config-if-Et1-txq-3)#sho qos int e1 | beg Priority
  Tx-Queue   Bandwidth    Shape Rate      Priority
             (percent)      (Kbps)
  -----------------------------------------------------
      0          17         1000000     round-robin
      1          17           10000     round-robin
      2          17        disabled     round-robin
      3          47        disabled     round-robin
      4         N/A        disabled          strict
      5         N/A        disabled          strict
      6         N/A        disabled          strict
```

Whoa! That's not what I configured at all! Here's what happened: there were four tx-queues, each with 25% configured. When I configured one for 30%, the switch realized that the total for all four tx-queues was now 110%, and that's just not cool, man. The switch does some math on its own, making me wonder if it's becoming self-aware again, and decides on a better solution. Here's what the Arista configuration guide for EOS version 4.9.4 has to say on the subject:

```
When the cumulative configured bandwidth is greater than 100%, each
queue's share is adjusted to provide a bandwidth proportional with
the other queues' share.
```

I'll be completely honest with you, and admit that I have no idea what that means. So let's see what happens when we make the number lower. First I'll reset it:

```
SW1(config-if-Et1-txq-3)#no bandwidth percent
```

Then I'll set it to 5%, which is lower than the 25% it defaulted to, and then see how the percentages look:

```
SW1(config-if-Et1-txq-3)#bandwidth percent 5
SW1(config-if-Et1-txq-3)#sho qos int e1 | beg Priority
  Tx-Queue   Bandwidth    Shape Rate      Priority
             (percent)      (Kbps)
  -----------------------------------------------------
      0          23         1000000     round-robin
      1          23           10000     round-robin
      2          23        disabled     round-robin
      3          28        disabled     round-robin
      4         N/A        disabled          strict
      5         N/A        disabled          strict
      6         N/A        disabled          strict
```

What the hell? Let's see what the EOS 4.9.4 manual has to say about lowering the total tx-queue bandwidth percentage below 100%:

> When the cumulative configured bandwidth of all round robin queues is less than 100%, the remaining bandwidth is shared equally by all queues.

You know what? Screw this, I'm going to hardcode them all. I'll make tx-queues 0, 1, 2, and 3 have 30%, 30%, 30%, and 10% of the available bandwidth, respectively:

```
SW1(config-if-Et1)#tx-queue 0
SW1(config-if-Et1-txq-0)#bandwidth percent 30
SW1(config-if-Et1-txq-0)#tx-queue 1
SW1(config-if-Et1-txq-1)#bandwidth percent 30
SW1(config-if-Et1-txq-1)#tx-queue 2
SW1(config-if-Et1-txq-2)#bandwidth percent 30
SW1(config-if-Et1-txq-2)#tx-queue 3
SW1(config-if-Et1-txq-3)#bandwidth percent 10
```

Crossing my fingers and muttering to myself about machines that think they know better than me, I look once more to see the bandwidth percentages for my tx-queues:

```
SW1(config-if-Et1-txq-3)#sho qos int e1 | beg Priority
    Tx-Queue    Bandwidth    Shape Rate     Priority
                (percent)      (Kbps)
    ------------------------------------------------
        0           30        1000000      round-robin
        1           30          10000      round-robin
        2           30        disabled     round-robin
        3           10        disabled     round-robin
        4          N/A        disabled        strict
        5          N/A        disabled        strict
        6          N/A        disabled        strict
```

Halle-*freaking*-lujah! That'll teach that smart-ass switch to think on its own!

 If there's one thing I learned from my CCIE pursuits all those years ago, it's that I never let a networking device make its own decisions. Maybe these automatic percentages are a good thing, but I'm too much of a control freak to allow the switch to decide something like this for me.

Queues can be returned to their default state (strict), unless they are in the midst of a round-robin group. For example, I cannot put tx-queue 2 back to strict priority on my interface. The command will take, but nothing will happen:

```
SW1(config-if-Et1-txq-3)#tx-queue 2
SW1(config-if-Et1-txq-2)#priority strict
SW1(config-if-Et1-txq-2)#sho qos int e1 | beg Priority
    Tx-Queue    Bandwidth    Shape Rate     Priority
                (percent)      (Kbps)
    ------------------------------------------------
```

```
          0           30       1000000   round-robin
          1           30         10000   round-robin
          2           30      disabled   round-robin
          3           10      disabled   round-robin
          4          N/A      disabled        strict
          5          N/A      disabled        strict
          6          N/A      disabled        strict
```

Note that if you only have one tx-queue configured for round robin, thus defaulting all the tx-queues below it (as we've done here), then setting the configured tx-queue back to its default will also reconfigure all the tx-queues beneath it:

```
SW1(config-if-Et1-txq-2)#tx-queue 3
SW1(config-if-Et1-txq-3)#priority strict
SW1(config-if-Et1-txq-3)#sho qos int e1 | beg Priority
   Tx-Queue   Bandwidth    Shape Rate    Priority
             (percent)      (Kbps)
   ---------------------------------------------------
          0          N/A       1000000        strict
          1          N/A         10000        strict
          2          N/A      disabled        strict
          3          N/A      disabled        strict
          4          N/A      disabled        strict
          5          N/A      disabled        strict
          6          N/A      disabled        strict
```

Before I log out and look for a therapist, let me show you how to read some of the exciting output regarding QoS show commands.

Showing QoS Information

Showing QoS information involves only a few commands, but the output can be a little overwhelming until you learn how to read it. Also, this output will vary depending on switch platform, so don't be surprised if you see subtle differences on varying switches. I'll show you the output from all three of the major types, so there shouldn't be any surprises when you look at your own switches. As of July 2012 and EOS version 4.9.3.2, there are two QoS show commands: show qos interface and show qos map.

```
SW1#sho qos ?
  interfaces  Show QoS status for a specific interface
  maps        Show various QoS mappings
```

The show qos interface command shows information about QoS pertaining to a specific interface. The show qos map command shows a pile of information relating to all the map statements we talked about in the last section.

Since the output for both of these commands differs by platform, I'll show them both for each of the three current platform types: Petra (7048T and 7500s), FM4000 (7124SX), and Trident (7050s). The first switch type I'll show is a Petra-based 7048 with all of the QoS values left to their defaults.

Petra-Based Switches

The show qos interface *interface-name* command on a 7048T looks like this for an unconfigured interface:

```
Arista-7048T#sho qos int e1
Ethernet1:
  Trust Mode: COS

  Port shaping rate: disabled

  Tx-Queue   Bandwidth    Shape Rate    Priority
             (percent)     (Kbps)
  ----------------------------------------------
         0      N/A       disabled       strict
         1      N/A       disabled       strict
         2      N/A       disabled       strict
         3      N/A       disabled       strict
         4      N/A       disabled       strict
         5      N/A       disabled       strict
         6      N/A       disabled       strict
```

We can see from this output that the trust mode is CoS (the default), but there is also a bunch of information about port shaping, which I've already covered in excruciating detail. This command will also show detail regarding the trust mode, default CoS and DSCP values, and the port shaping rate, if configured. Here's the output from the interface used in the previous section on my 7124SX:

```
SW1(config-if-Et1)#sho qos int e1
Ethernet1:
  Trust Mode: UNTRUSTED
  Default COS: 5
  Default DSCP: 44

  Port shaping rate: 500000Kbps

  Tx-Queue   Bandwidth    Shape Rate    Priority
             (percent)     (Kbps)
  ----------------------------------------------
         0      N/A        1000000       strict
         1      N/A          10000       strict
         2      N/A       disabled       strict
         3      N/A       disabled       strict
         4      N/A       disabled       strict
         5      N/A       disabled       strict
         6      N/A       disabled       strict
```

The output of the show qos maps command is much more interesting, at least once you've figured out how all that mapping stuff works. Don't worry, I'm going to break this output down since this is the first time we're seeing it. There's a lot of information there, and it's worth understanding it if you're going to use QoS:

```
Arista-7048T#sho qos map
    Number of Traffic Classes supported: 8
    Number of Transmit Queues supported: 7

  Cos-tc map:
    cos:  0  1  2  3  4  5  6  7
    ----------------------------
    tc:   1  0  2  3  4  5  6  7

  Dscp-tc map:
    d1 : d2 0  1  2  3  4  5  6  7  8  9
    ----------------------------------------
     0 :     1  1  1  1  1  1  1  1  0  0
     1 :     0  0  0  0  0  0  2  2  2  2
     2 :     2  2  2  2  3  3  3  3  3  3
     3 :     3  3  4  4  4  4  4  4  4  4
     4 :     5  5  5  5  5  5  5  5  6  6
     5 :     6  6  6  6  6  6  7  7  7  7
     6 :     7  7  7  7

  Tc-cos map:
    tc:   0  1  2  3  4  5  6  7
    ----------------------------
    cos:  1  0  2  3  4  5  6  7

  Tc-queue map:
    tc:       0  1  2  3  4  5  6  7
    --------------------------------
    tx-queue: 0  1  2  3  4  5  6  7
```

The first two lines report on the number of traffic classes and tx-queues:

```
Number of Traffic Classes supported: 8
Number of Transmit Queues supported: 7
```

I think this output is a bug, because the last two lines of the output clearly show eight traffic classes mapped to eight tx-queues. At any rate, not all switch platforms display this information.

 I opened a TAC case with Arista and found that this is indeed a bug on the rev of code I was running. The bug is resolved in EOS version 4.10.

Next is the CoS-to-traffic class map. This output shows the default, which can be a useful thing to know, especially since if you look closely, CoS 0 is mapped to traffic class 1, and CoS 1 is mapped to traffic class 0. This is the default on a Petra-based switch for reasons unknown to me. It's good to know this though, because you might be tempted to spend hours trying to see who mucked up your switch when this is the default on this platform:

```
Cos-tc map:
  cos:  0  1  2  3  4  5  6  7
        ----------------------------
  tc:   1  0  2  3  4  5  6  7
```

Next is the big, scary DSCP-to-transmit queue map. It's not really all that scary, but it does include a boatload of information. The trick in understanding this table is in knowing how to read it. First, here's the table:

```
Dscp-tc map:
  d1 :  d2 0  1  2  3  4  5  6  7  8  9
        ----------------------------------------
  0 :      1  1  1  1  1  1  1  1  0  0
  1 :      0  0  0  0  0  0  2  2  2  2
  2 :      2  2  2  2  3  3  3  3  3  3
  3 :      3  3  4  4  4  4  4  4  4  4
  4 :      5  5  5  5  5  5  5  5  6  6
  5 :      6  6  6  6  6  6  7  7  7  7
  6 :      7  7  7  7
```

In Figure 17-4, I've taken this table and added some helpful labels. The numbers going down the left side of the chart are the first digit of the DSCP value. The numbers across the top of the chart are the second digit of the DSCP value. If you use this method, you'll see that the highest value shown on the chart is 63, which is the largest DSCP value allowed. When you match up the two digits of the DSCP value, they will intersect at a number. That number is the traffic class mapped to that DSCP value.

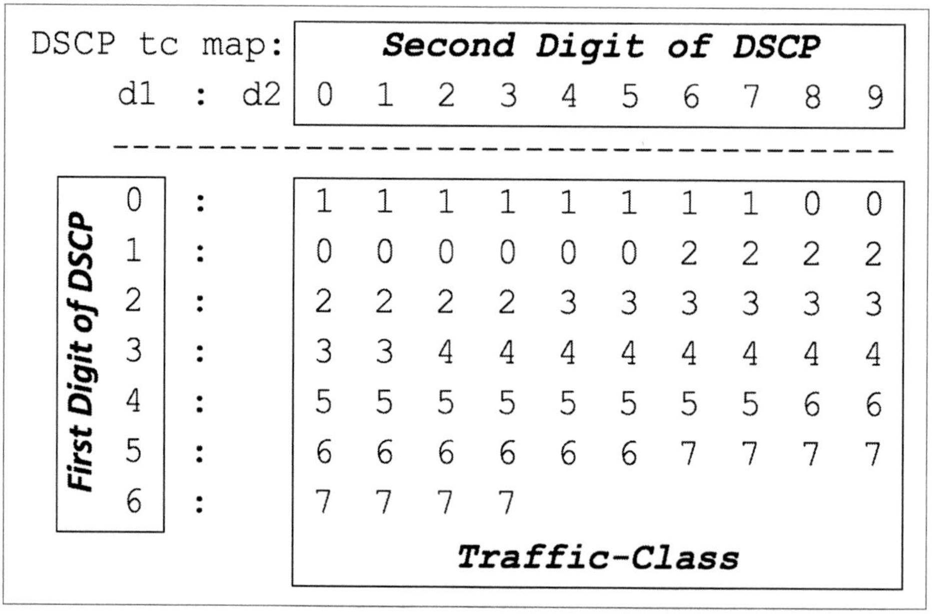

Figure 17-4. Explanation of the DSCP traffic class map on a 7048T

As an exercise, try to find out what traffic class is mapped to DSCP 26. The answer is shown in Figure 17-5.

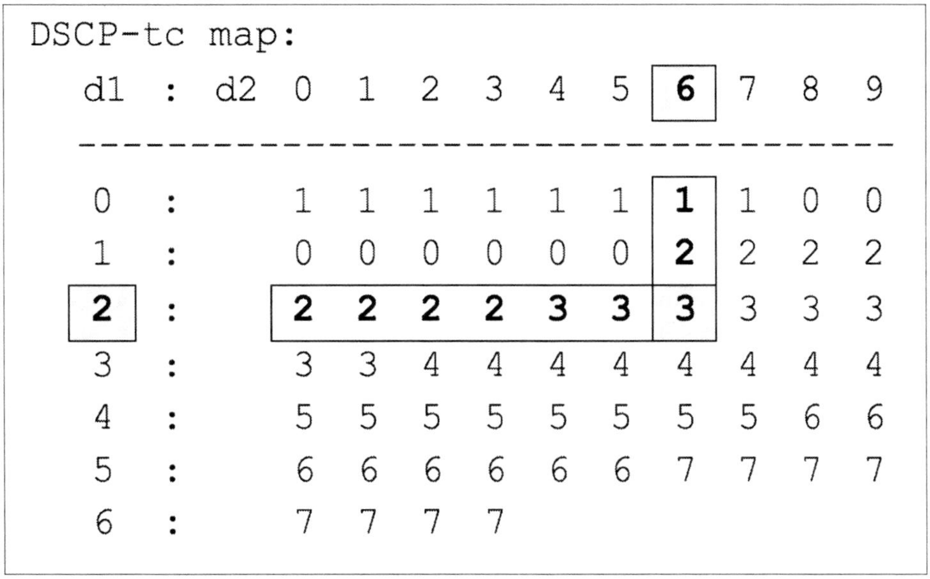

```
DSCP-tc map:
   d1  :  d2  0   1   2   3   4   5  │ 6 │ 7   8   9

   -------------------------------------------------

    0   :       1   1   1   1   1   1 │ 1 │ 1   0   0
    1   :       0   0   0   0   0   0 │ 2 │ 2   2   2
  │ 2 │ :     │ 2   2   2   2   3   3 │ 3 │ 3   3   3
    3   :       3   3   4   4   4   4   4   4   4   4
    4   :       5   5   5   5   5   5   5   5   6   6
    5   :       6   6   6   6   6   6   7   7   7   7
    6   :       7   7   7   7
```

Figure 17-5. Traffic class map for DSCP value 26 on a 7048T

As you can see, traffic class 3 mapped to the DSCP value of 26 on this chart (the default on a 7048T running EOS 4.9.3.2).

Next in the output is the traffic class to CoS mapping used when *CoS rewrite* is active (on all non-CoS-trusted interfaces):

```
Tc-cos map:
   tc:   0  1  2  3  4  5  6  7
         --------------------------
   cos:  1  0  2  3  4  5  6  7
```

This chart also has the seemingly strange 0:1 and 1:0 mapping we saw earlier, which makes sense, because if we used a default CoS value of 1, then it would get mapped to traffic class 0 (based on the previously shown map), but we'd want that to get written as CoS 1 in the packet during the CoS rewrite.

The last section of output from the show qos maps command is the *traffic class to tx-queue* map. This map does not show up on all platforms, but where it does, it seems to be a 1:1 mapping across the range by default. This is the default map from my 7124SX:

```
Tc-queue map:
   tc:        0  1  2  3  4  5  6  7
              ----------------------------
   tx-queue:  0  1  2  3  4  5  6  7
```

This is the map after running the mapping command (shown again) from earlier in the chapter:

```
SW1(config)#qos map traffic-class 2 3 to tx-queue 4
   Tc-queue map:
      tc:        0  1  2  3  4  5  6
      -----------------------------
      tx-queue:  0  1  4  4  4  5  6
```

This output shows that traffic classes 2 and 3 have been mapped to tx-queue 4.

Trident-Based Switches

I'm showing the Trident-based switch next because it's the most boring of them all. Well, that's not a very nice thing to say about one of my favorite Arista products, so I'll let the output speak for itself. First, the output of the show qos interfaces e1 command:

```
Arista-7050#sho qos interfaces e1
Ethernet1:
Trust Mode: COS
Default COS: 0
Default DSCP: 0
```

See what I mean? Boring! But it does include the default CoS and DSCP values, where the Petra-based switch did not, so that's pretty cool. To see how this interacts with the previously described commands, I'll go in and configure this interface to have a trust mode of untrusted, and a default CoS value of 3:

```
Arista-7050(config-if-Et1)#no qos trust
Arista-7050 (config-if-Et1)#qos cos 3
```

Here's how the interface looks after my changes:

```
Arista-7050(config-if-Et1)#sho qos int e1
Ethernet1:
Trust Mode: UNTRUSTED
Default COS: 3
Default DSCP: 0
```

The output of the show qos maps command is also pretty tame when compared with the output from other platforms. The tables show the same information in the same way as seen on the Petra-based switch, there just aren't as many tables. This output shows the default values:

```
Arista-7050#sho qos map
   Number of Traffic Classes supported: 8

   Cos-tc map:
      cos:  0  1  2  3  4  5  6  7
      -----------------------------
      tc:   1  0  2  3  4  5  6  7
```

```
Dscp-tc map:
  d1 :  d2 0  1  2  3  4  5  6  7  8  9
  -------------------------------------
   0 :      0  0  0  0  0  0  0  0  1  1
   1 :      1  1  1  1  1  1  2  2  2  2
   2 :      2  2  2  2  3  3  3  3  3  3
   3 :      3  3  4  4  4  4  4  4  4  4
   4 :      5  5  5  5  5  5  5  5  6  6
   5 :      6  6  6  6  6  6  7  7  7  7
   6 :      7  7  7  7

Tc-cos map:
   tc:   0  1  2  3  4  5  6  7
  ----------------------------
  cos:   1  0  2  3  4  5  6  7
```

FM4000-Based Switches

Now hang onto your hats while we have some real fun. OK, so my idea of fun is sitting in the dark at 3 a.m. writing this, but this output is the most interesting because this output is from the switch I used to make all the crazy QoS changes in my examples earlier in this chapter. As a result, this section will be filled with nondefault values. Seriously, how is that not fun?

First, let me refresh your memory by showing you the current configuration for interface e1 on my 7124SX switch:

```
SW1#sho run int e1
interface Ethernet1
   no qos trust
   qos cos 5
   qos dscp 44
```

That's mildly interesting, so let's see what the output of the show qos interface ethernet1 command looks like with those commands applied to interface e1:

```
SW1#sho qos int e1
Ethernet1:
   Trust Mode: UNTRUSTED
   Default COS: 5
   Default DSCP: 44

   Port shaping rate: disabled

   Tx-Queue  Bandwidth   Shape Rate   Priority
             (percent)    (Kbps)
   -------------------------------------------
          0     N/A      disabled      strict
          1     N/A      disabled      strict
          2     N/A      disabled      strict
```

```
            3        N/A      disabled       strict
            4        N/A      disabled       strict
            5        N/A      disabled       strict
            6        N/A      disabled       strict
```

 Again, higher numbered queues have a higher priority. Although I can appreciate the idea of a higher numbered queue having a higher priority, they're displayed in numerical order, with 0 on the top. This hurts my head, and I've got enough to worry about, what with my math-induced dental irritations.

Once again, we're treated to the trust mode, and the default CoS and DSCP values, both of which have been altered. This switch also seems to support the ability for port shaping, although no such configuration exists to alter these values at this time.

Moving on to the output of the show qos maps command, remember that I made quite a few changes to the QoS maps earlier. Here's a summary of all the changes from the *running-config* of this switch:

```
SW1#sho run | grep map
qos map cos 2 to traffic-class 5
qos map cos 3 to traffic-class 5
qos map cos 5 to traffic-class 3
qos map dscp 12 to traffic-class 3
qos map dscp 23 to traffic-class 3
qos map dscp 36 to traffic-class 3
qos map traffic-class 2 to cos 3
qos map traffic-class 4 to cos 3
```

That's quite a few lines, but remember that I entered many of them as single lines. The command parser split them up in order to make them easier to read. I appreciate that in a command parser, don't you? Here's how all of those changes show up in the output of the show qos maps command. Knowing what you now know about how to read this output, can you verify that all the listed qos map commands are actually active?

```
SW1#sho qos maps
   Number of Traffic Classes supported: 7
   Number of Transmit Queues supported: 7

   Cos-tc map:
     cos:  0  1  2  3  4  5  6  7
     --------------------------
     tc:   1  0  5  5  4  3  5  6

   Dscp-tc map:
     d1 :  d2 0  1  2  3  4  5  6  7  8  9
     -------------------------------------
      0 :      1  1  1  1  1  1  1  1  0  0
      1 :      0  0  3  0  0  0  2  2  2  2
```

```
    2 :     2  2  2  3  3  3  3  3  3  3
    3 :     3  3  4  4  4  4  3  4  4  4
    4 :     4  4  4  4  4  4  4  4  5  5
    5 :     5  5  5  5  5  5  5  5  5  5
    6 :     5  5  5  5

Tc-cos map:
  tc:  0  1  2  3  4  5  6
  -------------------------
  cos: 1  0  3  3  3  6  7

Tc-queue map:
  tc:      0  1  2  3  4  5  6
  -----------------------------
  tx-queue: 0  1  2  3  4  5  6
```

Just to keep me honest, I'll include the output from the same command from a switch without any QoS configured (running the same version of EOS):

```
Arista-7124SX#sho qos maps
  Number of Traffic Classes supported: 7
  Number of Transmit Queues supported: 7

  Cos-tc map:
    cos: 0  1  2  3  4  5  6  7
    ---------------------------
    tc:  1  0  2  3  4  4  5  6

  Dscp-tc map:
    d1 : d2 0  1  2  3  4  5  6  7  8  9
    ------------------------------------
      0 :     1  1  1  1  1  1  1  1  0  0
      1 :     0  0  0  0  0  0  2  2  2  2
      2 :     2  2  2  2  3  3  3  3  3  3
      3 :     3  3  4  4  4  4  4  4  4  4
      4 :     4  4  4  4  4  4  4  4  5  5
      5 :     5  5  5  5  5  5  5  5  5  5
      6 :     5  5  5  5

  Tc-cos map:
    tc:  0  1  2  3  4  5  6
    -------------------------
    cos: 1  0  2  3  4  6  7

  Tc-queue map:
    tc:      0  1  2  3  4  5  6
    -----------------------------
    tx-queue: 0  1  2  3  4  5  6
```

In Conclusion

QoS on a switch isn't really all that difficult. It's just a bit different than what you may be used to. Just remember that QoS markings (whether trusted or added) need to be converted to traffic classes, which correspond to physical transmit queues on outbound interfaces. If the QoS marking isn't a result of *trusted CoS*, then the switch will perform a *CoS rewrite* on the packet, which you should configure as well. There are no queues to manage like there are in higher level QoS methods such as class-based weighted-fair queuing, just trusting, defaults, and mapping. As I like to say, it's easy when you know how, and now you know how!

## CHAPTER 18

Aboot

Aboot is the bootloader for EOS in an Arista switch. The bootloader is a small program that loads automatically (often from nonvolatile ROM on a switch) when the system is powered on. The bootloader's primary job is to load the primary operating system, which is usually stored elsewhere, such as flash memory or disk. If you've ever installed a Linux system, you've likely encountered bootloaders such as GRUB. On Windows NT/ 2000/XP machines, the default bootloader is NTLDR.

> Technically, there are two types of bootloaders: first stage and second stage. The first-stage bootloader usually operates at a very low level and is often responsible for hardware system checks. A PC's BIOS would be considered a first-stage bootloader, while the bootloaders mentioned in this chapter would be second-stage bootloaders.

Before EOS is loaded, the switch loads the Aboot process from ROM. Aboot looks for a file called *boot-config* in *flash:/*, which to be painfully accurate, is actually */mnt/flash*:

```
[admin@Arista flash]$ ls /mnt/flash
EOS-4.7.8.swi  boot-config  fullrecover  schedule      zerotouch-config
EOS-4.8.1.swi  debug        persist      startup-config
```

Aboot reads the contents of this file, determines the image to be loaded, and then loads it. If the *boot-config* file does not exist, Aboot will halt the system and present an Aboot# prompt. In fact, if any of the following should occur, Aboot will halt the system:

- *boot-config* file is corrupt or not found
- Configured EOS image is corrupt or not found
- Control-C is entered from the console while the Aboot process is running

Normally, the system boots as follows (details may differ depending on loaded modules and the version of EOS installed):

```
Aboot 1.9.2-140514.2006.eswierk

Press Control-C now to enter Aboot shell
Booting flash:/EOS-4.8.1.swi
Starting new kernel
Switching rootfs
Welcome to Arista Networks EOS 4.8.1
Mounting filesystems: [ OK ]
Entering non-interactive startup
Starting EOS initialization stage 1: [ OK ]
ip6tables: Applying firewall rules: [ OK ]
iptables: Applying firewall rules: [ OK ]
iptables: Loading additional modules: nf_conntrack_tftp [ OK ]
Starting system logger: [ OK ]
Starting system message bus: [ OK ]
Starting NorCal initialization: [ OK ]
Starting EOS initialization stage 2: [ OK ]
Starting ProcMgr: [ OK ]
Completing EOS initialization: [ OK ]
Starting Power On Self Test (POST): [ OK ]
Starting sshd: [ OK ]
Starting xinetd: [ OK ]
crond: [ OK ]
Model: DCS-7124S
Serial Number: JSH101XXXXX
System RAM: 2043424 kB
Flash Memory size:  1.8G

Arista login:
```

By hitting Control-C on the console when prompted, we interrupt the boot process and drop into the Aboot shell:

```
Aboot 1.9.2-140514.2006.eswierk


Press Control-C now to enter Aboot shell^C
Welcome to Aboot.
Aboot#
```

While in Aboot, the fans in the switch run at high speed. They put out some significant noise in this state, so if you're playing with a switch on your desk at work, prepare for all of your local cube dwellers to hate you. If you work in an open office environment, then I recommend leaving the switch in the office and connecting to it from home with a console server so that the noise won't bother you. That'll teach 'em.

Aboot has no help commands, at least in the versions I've used thus far, so navigating around can be an adventure; although, if you're familiar with Linux, then Aboot shouldn't be too daunting. According to the excellent Arista documentation found online (*http://www.aristanetworks.com/docs/Manuals/ConfigGuide.pdf*), the list of the following commands are commonly used. The documentation also goes on to explain that Busybox (*http://www.busybox.net/downloads/BusyBox.html*) provides many of the commands, which is an open source version of Unix utilities compiled into a single small executable. The thing to remember about Aboot is that it's a tiny Linux. Think of it as such, and you'll do fine. Unless you don't know anything about Linux, in which case, you're screwed. Good thing you bought this book!

ls
> Prints a list of the files in the current working directory

cd
> Changes the current working directory

cp
> Copies a file

more
> Prints the contents of a file one page at a time

vi
> Edits a text file

boot
> Boots a software image (SWI)

swiinfo
> Prints information about an SWI

recover
> Recovers the factory default configuration

reboot
> Reboots the switch

udhcpc
> Configures a network interface automatically via DHCP

ifconfig
> Prints or alters network interface settings

wget
> Downloads a file from an HTTP or FTP server

From within the Aboot prompt, the first thing we'll do is to try and get our bearings. When I'm lost on a Linux box, I issue the `pwd` command to see what directory I'm in. Sure enough, this works just fine in Aboot:

```
Aboot# pwd
/
```

So we're in the root, which means I'm bored. Let's take a look around with the `ls` command:

```
Aboot# ls
MD5SUMS   dev      init    mnt     root    tmp
bin       etc      lib     proc    sys
```

Looks harmless enough. I wonder if more elaborate versions of these commands work?

```
Aboot# ls -al
drwxr-xr-x   11 0        0              0 Apr 15 23:47 .
drwxr-xr-x   11 0        0              0 Apr 15 23:47 ..
-rw-r--r--    1 0        0           1455 May 19  2009 MD5SUMS
drwxr-xr-x    2 0        0              0 May 19  2009 bin
drwxr-xr-x    2 0        0              0 Apr 15 23:47 dev
drwxr-xr-x    2 0        0              0 Apr 15 23:47 etc
-rwxr-xr-x  108 0        0         406600 May 19  2009 init
drwxr-xr-x    2 0        0              0 May 19  2009 lib
drwxr-xr-x    4 0        0              0 Apr 15 23:47 mnt
dr-xr-xr-x   55 0        0              0 Apr 15 23:47 proc
drwx------    2 0        0              0 May 14  2009 root
drwxr-xr-x   11 0        0              0 Apr 15 23:47 sys
drwxrwxrwt    2 0        0              0 Apr 15 23:47 tmp
```

Cool! But this looks like any Unix machine. Where's the good stuff? Since I'm in Aboot, I'd probably want to check, change, or otherwise mangle the *boot-config* file, and I know that resides in *flash:/* from within EOS, but that doesn't seem to exist here. That's because *flash:/* is an EOS construct. The key to mounted file systems in Linux is */mnt*, so let's take a look there:

```
Aboot# cd /mnt
Aboot# ls -al
drwxr-xr-x    4 0        0              0 Apr 15 23:47 .
drwxr-xr-x   11 0        0              0 Apr 15 23:47 ..
drwxrwx---    6 0        88          4096 Jan  1  1970 flash
-rw-rw-rw-    1 0        0             94 Apr 15 23:47 flash-recover.conf
-rw-rw-rw-    1 0        0             94 Apr 15 23:47 flash.conf
drwxrwx---    5 0        88          4096 Jan  1  1970 usb1
-rw-rw-rw-    1 0        0             94 Apr 15 23:47 usb1.conf
```

I tend to repeat this bit about *flash:/* being an EOS construct because I've found that people not familiar with Unix find this a bit confusing. That, and I really like the word *construct*. It makes me feel like I'm in Star Trek when I say it out loud. Try it for yourself and see. *Construct...*

Looks promising! There's a directory within */mnt* named *flash*, so let's see what's in there:

```
Aboot# cd flash
Aboot# pwd
/mnt/flash
Aboot# ls -al
```

```
drwxrwx---    6 0      88         4096 Jan  1 1970 .
drwxr-xr-x    4 0       0            0 Apr 15 23:47 ..
-r-xr-x---    1 0      88    225217184 Apr 15 20:09 .boot-image.swi
drwxrwx---    2 0      88         4096 Dec 22 17:33 .extensions
-rwxrwx---    1 0      88    222153243 Dec 22 11:40 EOS-4.7.8.swi
-rwxrwx---    1 0      88    225217184 Apr 15 12:48 EOS-4.8.1.swi
-rwxrwx---    1 0      88           25 Apr 15 13:31 boot-config
drwxrwx---    2 0      88         4096 Apr 15 16:46 debug
-rwxrwx---    1 0      88            0 May  7 2008 fullrecover
drwxrwx---    2 0      88         4096 Apr 15 16:33 persist
drwxrwx---    3 0      88         4096 Apr 15 13:14 schedule
-rwxrwx---    1 0      88         2693 Apr 15 13:36 startup-config
-rwxrwx---    1 0      88            0 Apr 10 16:20 zerotouch-config
```

Ah-ha! We've found the *flash:/* location from within Aboot. In the future, we can just issue the cd /mnt/flash/ command from within *Aboot* and we'll be right here.

 The file structure in Aboot is pretty much the same is it would be in bash, though any temporary file structures created when EOS boots will be missing.

To see the contents of a file in Linux, we might use the more command. Let's do exactly that in order to see what's contained within the *boot-config* file:

```
Aboot# more boot-config
SWI=flash:/EOS-4.8.1.swi
```

Not very exciting, is it? The single line indicates that the SWI can be found at *flash:/ EOS-4.8.1.swi*. Note that this is configured using EOS reference points (*flash:/*) and not Linux reference points (*/mnt/flash/*). Now let's see what other sorts of trouble we can get ourselves into with this file. As of mid-2012, there are four options that can be configured in the *boot-config* file. They are:

SWI
    Set the location of the SWI

CONSOLESPEED
    Set the speed of the console port

PASSWORD
    Set a password for the Aboot shell

NET commands
    Set various configurations pertaining to simple network connectivity

These commands are placed within the *boot-config* file, with the syntax of `COM MAND=configuration`. This file can be examined from within Aboot or the bash shell using the `more /mnt/flash/boot-config` command, or from within EOS with the `show boot` command:

```
Arista#sho boot
Software image: flash:/EOS-4.8.1.swi
Console speed: (not set)
Aboot password (encrypted): (not set)
```

We've already seen the SWI command in action, but let me just point out that while the obvious method is to point to an image on flash, we can also point to images outside the box. Here are some cool examples from the Arista documentation:

SWI on flash:
```
SWI=flash:EOS.swi
```

SWI on USB1:
```
SWI=usb1:/EOS1.swi
```

SWI on /mnt/flash (same as flash:/):
```
SWI=/mnt/flash/EOS.swi
```

SWI on an HTTP server:
SWI=*http://foo.com/images/EOS.swi*

SWI on an FTP server:
SWI=*http://foo.com/images/EOS.swi*

SWI on a TFTP server:
```
SWI=tftp://foo.com/EOS.swi
```

SWI on an NFS mounted file system:
```
SWI=nfs://foo.com/images/EOS.swi
```

OK, you get the point. Now let's move on to the other *boot-config* commands.

The CONSOLESPEED command is pretty simple. We can apply one of a list of speeds, and that's it. We cannot set stop bits, parity bits, or anything other than speed with this command. Values include common speeds for serial ports, including 1,200; 2,400; 4,800; 9,600; 19,200; and 38,400. Here is an example *boot-config* file with the CONSOLESPEED set to 38,400:

```
Aboot# more boot-config
SWI=flash:/EOS-4.8.1.swi
CONSOLESPEED=38400
```

The CONSOLESPEED setting can also be configured with the EOS `boot console speed` *speed* command:

```
Arista(config)#boot console speed ?
  baud  Console port speed (1200, 2400, 4800, 9600, 19200 or 38400)
```

The PASSWORD command is also pretty simple, but it should not be configured from within Aboot. The PASSWORD command should only be set using the EOS command `boot secret`. With a password in place, you'll need to authenticate in order to access the Aboot shell, and this password cannot be recovered from Aboot, so assign an Aboot password with care.

Let's assign a password to Aboot from within EOS with the `boot secret` command. Here, I'll set the password to *Arista-Rocks!*:

```
Arista(config)#boot secret Arista-Rocks!
```

 I know I keep going back and forth between EOS and Aboot, and that might be confusing. You cannot go back and forth between these modes; I'm just showing how these items would be configured when within each of the modes. Stay with me, and watch the prompts carefully if you get mixed up as to where I am.

Now, viewing the *boot-config* file (this time from bash, not from Aboot), we can see that the file now contains a PASSWORD command, and that the password is encrypted:

```
[admin@Arista flash]$ more boot-config
PASSWORD=$1$hq/7SSPh$32N2lxwePiZAs3st8vUFD1
SWI=flash:/EOS-4.8.1.swi
```

Whether or not the password is easily cracked is not germane to the subject matter of this book, and shame on you for thinking such things!

Upon a reboot, with the PASSWORD command set, we are now prompted for authentication when we enter Control-C at the Aboot message:

```
Restarting system


Aboot 1.9.2-140514.2006.eswierk


Press Control-C now to enter Aboot shell^C
Aboot password:
```

At this point, if we enter the incorrect password three times, we are greeted with this friendly message:

```
Press Control-C now to enter Aboot shell^C
Aboot password:
incorrect password
Aboot password:
incorrect password
```

```
Aboot password:
incorrect password
Type "fullrecover" and press Enter to revert /mnt/flash to factory
Default state, or just press Enter to reboot:
```

If we feel the need to issue the `fullrecover` command, we are warned once again:

```
Type "fullrecover" and press Enter to revert /mnt/flash to factory
Default state, or just press Enter to reboot: fullrecover
All data on /mnt/flash will be erased; type "yes" and press Enter to
proceed, or just press Enter to cancel:
```

While it may not be obvious that "All data on */mnt/flash* will be erased" is a bad thing, consider that the following files exist in */mnt/flash*:

- The SWI files (you know, EOS and stuff!)
- The *boot-config* file
- The *startup-config* file
- The *zerotouch-config* file
- All scheduler logs (unless stored elsewhere)
- Anything you might have put there
- Anything in the */mnt/flash/persist/* folder

In other words, if you perform a *fullrecover* on the switch, your switch will lose everything, and you'll have to start from scratch. Fun! Still, my pain is your gain, so let's go ahead and see what happens:

```
Type "fullrecover" and press Enter to revert /mnt/flash to factory
Default state, or just press Enter to reboot: fullrecover
All data on /mnt/flash will be erased; type "yes" and press Enter
to proceed, or just press Enter to cancel: yes
Erasing /mnt/flash
Writing recovery data to /mnt/flash
EOS-4.4.0.swi
startup-config
boot-config
368403 blocks
Restarting system.
```

Ouch! We went from EOS version 4.8.1 to version 4.4.0 (the version my very old switch originally shipped with). Not only that, but our configuration is gone, the multiple EOS versions are gone from flash, and the switch is now a big unconfigured time sink. Luckily for you, that's my time being sunk, so while you sit back enjoying a cocktail, I'll be here rebuilding the switch.

So what's the moral of the story? Don't issue the fullrecover command unless you really mean it, because it doesn't just delete the *boot-config* file. It deletes everything!

To remove the password from Aboot, use the no boot secret command from within EOS. You could also just remove the PASSWORD= line in the *boot-secret* file from bash:

```
Arista(config)#no boot secret
```

With nothing but the SWI set in *boot-config*, you should get something like the following output when using the show boot command from within EOS:

```
Arista(config)#sho boot
Software image: flash:/EOS-4.8.1.swi
Console speed: (not set)
Aboot password (encrypted): (not set)
```

Moving on, let's take a look at some of the NET commands within the Aboot environment. NET commands include the following:

NETDEV=interface
The interface that the switch will be configured to use for loading configurations or SWI files. This interface can only be an out-of-band management port, not one of the normal Ethernet switch interfaces.

NETAUTO=auto_setting
If using DHCP, then this would be set to dhcp.

NETIP=interface_address
The IP address for the NETDEV interface.

NETMASK=interface_mask
The IP subnet mask for the NETDEV interface.

NETGW=gateway_address
The IP gateway address to allow the NETDEV interface to communicate outside its directly connected IP network.

NETDOMAIN=domain_name
The DNS domain name for the switch.

NETDNS=dns_address
The IP address of a DNS server that can be used to resolve external hostnames.

Note that there is no support for IPv6, and that only dotted decimal notation can be used (no /24 masks, for example). Also, be advised that these commands can only be set from within Aboot or from the bash shell. They cannot be configured from within EOS:

```
Arista(config)#boot ?
  console  Console port settings
  secret   Assign the Aboot password
  system   Software image URL
```

Here's an example of how the *boot-config* file might be configured on a simple network:

```
Aboot# more /mnt/flash/boot-config
SWI=flash:/EOS-4.8.1.swi
NETDEV=mgmt1
NETIP=192.168.1.199
NETMASK=255.255.255.0
NETGW=192.168.1.1
NETDOMAIN=gad.net
NETDNS=192.168.1.201
```

When I first started messing with this file, I naturally placed all new commands where they belonged, then rebooted and dutifully hit Control-C as soon as the message commanded me to. Only, it didn't work! After about 90 tries, I wasn't paying attention and hit Control-C later in the boot process, and that is when my Aboot network configuration worked. Here, I'll show you. First, I'll reboot the switch, and hit Control-C the second I see the message:

```
Aboot# reboot
Requesting system reboo
Restarting system.


Aboot 1.9.2-140514.2006.eswierk


Press Control-C now to enter Aboot shell^C
Welcome to Aboot.
```

Looks great, but all is not well in the world of network attached bootloaders. By using the ifconfig command, I can see that the *mgmt1* interface has no configuration!

```
Aboot# ifconfig mgmt1
mgmt1    Link encap:Ethernet  HWaddr 00:1C:73:08:80:AC
         BROADCAST MULTICAST  MTU:1500  Metric:1
         RX packets:0 errors:0 dropped:0 overruns:0 frame:0
         TX packets:0 errors:0 dropped:0 overruns:0 carrier:0
         collisions:0 txqueuelen:1000
         RX bytes:0 (0.0 B)  TX bytes:0 (0.0 B)
         Interrupt:20 Base address:0x2000
```

I really hate when that happens.

Watch out! Mashing on Control-C too quickly will prevent the network configuration from loading in Aboot!

One of the tech reviewers for this book was one of the system developers, who agreed that "yeah, that's pretty lame," and decided to start the process to try and improve it. He also said that the NET statements were designed to get an image from the network while already in Aboot, and not on reboot the way I was using it. That makes sense, but I'm still a happy keyboard masher, and always will be.

This time, I'll reboot, but count to five after I see the command to hit Control-C:

```
Aboot# reboot
Requesting system reboo
Restarting system.


Aboot 1.9.2-140514.2006.eswierk


Press Control-C now to enter Aboot shell
Booting flash:/EOS-4.8.1.swi^C
Welcome to Aboot.
Aboot#
```

By the way, if you're about to fire up your web browser to report multiple typos in this book, be advised that Aboot actually says, *Requesting system reboo* on the Arista 7124S that I used for some of these chapters. The newer 7124SX models don't seem to do it. Sure I could have fixed each line, but I like to paste things exactly as I see them when I run the examples on my switches. Besides, *requesting system reboo* just makes me giggle when I read it. I know; I'm simple.

Now this time, let's see what ifconfig mgmt1 shows us:

```
Aboot# ifconfig mgmt1
mgmt1     Link encap:Ethernet  HWaddr 00:1C:73:08:80:AC
          inet addr:192.168.1.198  Bcast:192.168.1.255
          Mask:255.255.255.0
          UP BROADCAST RUNNING MULTICAST  MTU:1500  Metric:1
          RX packets:18 errors:0 dropped:0 overruns:0 frame:0
          TX packets:3 errors:0 dropped:0 overruns:0 carrier:0
          collisions:0 txqueuelen:1000
          RX bytes:1456 (1.4 KiB)  TX bytes:268 (268.0 B)
          Interrupt:30 Base address:0x2000
```

For years, I've trained myself to sit and stare at the screen, and to hit Control-C (or F2, or F12, or whatever damn key I've been commanded to engage) the millisecond that the message appeared. We've all missed those messages and had to reboot time and again, which is why this really drove me nuts.

 It's worth noting again that if your NET commands in *boot-config* don't seem to be working, wait a few seconds after the *Press Control-C now to enter Aboot shell* prompt before mashing those keys. There's a good chance that they'll work if you can restrain your key-mashing impulse, if even for a few seconds.

Once we've got our network configured, we can copy files from outside the switch using the wget command. wget is pretty cool. Here, take a look:

```
Aboot# wget
BusyBox v1.13.1 (2009-05-18 21:20:22 EDT) multi-call binary

Usage: wget [-csq] [-O file] [-Y on/off] [-P DIR] [-U agent] url

Retrieve files via HTTP or FTP

Options:
        -s      Spider mode - only check file existence
        -c      Continue retrieval of aborted transfer
        -q      Quiet
        -P      Set directory prefix to DIR
        -O      Save to filename ('-' for stdout)
        -U      Adjust 'User-Agent' field
        -Y      Use proxy ('on' or 'off')
```

Let's grab a copy of EOS version 4.9.3, which I know is sitting on my web server. First, let's see if it's there by using the spider mode option, if for no other reason than it's fun to use something called *spider mode*:

```
Aboot# wget -s http://192.168.1.200/Arista/EOS-4.9.3.swi
Connecting to 192.168.1.200 (192.168.1.200:80)
Aboot#
```

Note that nothing was actually copied; wget just did a check to see if it was there. Kind of like a spider bot crawling a website to populate an online search engine. If we point to a file that doesn't exist, we get an HTTP error 404. Here, I'll try to grab an older version of code that I know is not there:

```
Aboot# wget -s http://192.168.1.200/Arista/EOS-4.8.1.swi
Connecting to 192.168.1.200 (192.168.1.200:80)
wget: server returned error: HTTP/1.1 404 Not Found
```

Enough goofing off! In order to get the file, I'll change directories to */mnt/flash*, since that's where it belongs:

```
Aboot# cd /mnt/flash
```

Now I'll use the same wget command as before, but without any options:

```
Aboot# wget http://192.168.1.200/Arista/EOS-4.9.3.swi
Connecting to 192.168.1.200 (192.168.1.200:80)
EOS-4.9.3.swi          22% |****              | 55408k 00:00:06 ETA
```

For a stripped down version of Linux, the wget command shows a nice status bar that increments as the file progresses. That's actually nicer than what we get in EOS in some circumstances! When the file is done, the status changes and we're dropped back to the Aboot# prompt:

```
EOS-4.9.3.swi         100% |********************|   237M 00:00:00 ETA
Aboot#
```

At this point, with the new version of EOS on board, we can edit the *boot-config* file, put in the new SWI= statement, and reboot the switch, at which point it will load the new version of code. Here's the new *boot-config* file after my vigorous editing:

```
Aboot# more boot-config
NETDEV=mgmt1
NETDNS=192.168.1.201
NETDOMAIN=gad.net
NETGW=192.168.1.1
NETIP=192.168.1.198
NETMASK=255.255.255.0
SWI=flash:/EOS-4.9.3.swi
```

And here's what happens when we boot with said *boot-config* file from Aboot:

```
Aboot# reboot
Requesting system reboo
Restarting system.


Aboot 1.9.2-140514.2006.eswierk


Press Control-C now to enter Aboot shell
Booting flash:/EOS-4.9.3.swi
Starting new kernel
Data in /mnt/flash/EOS-4.9.3.swi differs from previous boot image on
/mnt/flash.
Saving new boot image to /mnt/flash...
[--- output truncated ---]
```

 The NET commands are all wiped from the *boot-config* file once EOS boots, so don't get too attached to them. Technically, the file is reconfigured from the *running-config*, which has no method for writing these entries.

Booting most network devices into their bootloaders is an exercise in frustration, at least for me. I do it so rarely that I struggle to remember the arcane commands, and then invariably look up what I need to do online. Aboot changes all that, since the bootloader environment is just another flavor of Linux. If you find yourself in Aboot, just keep your wits about you and remember to look for the *boot-config* file in */mnt/flash*.

Running through Aboot once or twice is a good practice for anyone who works with Arista switches. I once mucked up a switch so severely that we couldn't get it to cancel or disable ZTP, and it wouldn't let us do any configuration (see Chapter 25 to see what I mean). I was able to boot the switch, drop into Aboot, and issue the `fullrecover` command, which saved the switch, prevented us from bothering TAC (which saved a lot of time), and made me look like a hero. Let's face it, technical writers don't get all the girls because of our breathtaking vocabularies, so any chance to play the hero is welcome, even if this particular heroism was only witnessed by a bunch of IT guys in a cold data center.

## CHAPTER 19

Email

Email on a switch? Hell yes! Arista switches allow emails to be sent from the EOS command line, from bash, from scripts, and from all sorts of interesting places. Once you see this in action, you'll wonder how you ever lived without it. Ever have to copy the output of a show tech from flash, to a TFTP server, and then to your laptop? You'll never need to go through that nonsense again with email configured on your Arista switch. Ever copy and paste from the screen, only to discover that your scrollback buffer wasn't big enough? With email on an Arista switch, just email the output directly to your (or anyone's) inbox. But enough hype, let's dig in and see how it's done.

Arista switches contain an email configuration mode that is accessed with the email command:

```
Arista#conf t
Arista(config)#email
```

Once there, hit the question mark and see what's available:

```
Arista(config-email)#?
  auth       Email account authentication
  comment    Up to 240 characters, comment for this mode
  default    Set a command to its defaults
  exit       Exit from Email configuration mode
  from-user  Send email from this user
  help       Description of the interactive help system
  no         Negate a command or set its defaults
  server     Email relay
  show       Show running system information
  tls        Require TLS
  !          Append to comment
```

In its simplest form, mail on an Arista switch requires configuration for a *from* address and an email server to send through. This is done with the from-user and server commands. Here, I'll configure the from-user to be *Arista1@gad.net*, and the server to be 192.168.1.200. If DNS is configured, I could also use a fully qualified domain name such as *mail.gad.net*:

```
Arista(config-email)#from-user Arista1@gad.net
Arista(config-email)#server 192.168.1.200
```

While within the email configuration mode, the command show active will display what's currently configured for email:

```
Arista(config-email)#show active
email
   from-user Arista1@gad.net
   server 192.168.1.200
```

For more advanced scenarios, email in EOS supports username and password authentication using the cleverly named username and password commands:

```
Arista(config-email)#auth username gad
Arista(config-email)#auth password ILikePie
```

If a password is entered in plain text, as I've done here, the switch will convert it into an encrypted string. Show active will display this encrypted string, as will the configuration:

```
Arista(config-email)#sho active
email
   from-user Arista1@gad.net
   server 192.168.1.200
   auth username gad
   auth password 7 MHTq67ztWA9dQOfAwOWOqQ==
```

 Passwords encrypted within configurations are not very secure. Remember that given this configuration, the username and password will be sent over the network in clear text as well.

If your mail server supports Transport Layer Security (TLS), you can enable that with the TLS command:

```
Arista(config-email)#tls
```

My lab is not set up for TLS, so it won't show up in later command outputs. TLS will solve the problem of passwords being sent in clear text, so it's a recommended solution to use wherever possible.

With my email set up, I'll now flex my new power by sending the output of a command to my inbox. This can be done with any show command by using the pipe (vertical bar) character followed by the word email. Note that this option does not show up if you search for it:

```
Arista#sho run | ?
  LINE      Filter command pipeline
  append    Append redirected output to URL
  begin     Begin with the line that matches
  exclude   Exclude lines that match
  include   Include lines that match
  no-more   Disable pagination for this command
  nz        Include only non-zero counters
  redirect  Redirect output to URL
  tee       Copy output to URL
```

Rest assured, though, that it works. By now it shouldn't surprise you that email is actually a command in bash that's referenced from EOS. To see the possible options, drop to bash and issue the email --help command:

```
Arista#bash

Arista Networks EOS shell

[admin@Arista ~]$ email --help
Usage: email -- send email through the configured SMTP server

Options:
  -h, --help                     show this help message and exit
  -a, --attachment               send content as an attachment
  -d, --debug                    debug interaction with SMTP server
  -r REF, --ref=REF              specify case ref
  -s SUBJECT, --subject=SUBJECT  specify subject
  --sysname=SYSNAME              specify Sysdb sysname
```

Let's get back to EOS and try some of those. First, I'll pipe the output of the show run command to my email with a subject of *Show Run*. I'll specify a subject for the email with the -s flag, and then list the email address of the intended recipient:

```
Arista(config-email)#sho run | email -s "Show Run" gad@gad.net
Arista(config-email)#
```

No output is displayed since it's all been redirected to the email program. A quick jump over to my email client, and there's the email!

```
Date: Tue, 15 May 2012 01:44:07
From: Arista1@gad.net
To: gad@gad.net
Subject: Show Run

! device: Arista (DCS-7124S, EOS-4.9.3)
!
! boot system flash:/EOS-4.9.3.swi
```

```
!
email
   from-user Arista1@gad.net
   server 192.168.1.200
!
queue-monitor length
!
hostname Arista
ip name-server 192.168.1.200
ip name-server 4.2.2.2
[---output truncated---]
```

This time, I'll send the output of the command show interface e24 to my email, but without specifying a subject. Without a subject specified, a generic subject is inserted on my behalf:

```
Arista(config-email)#sho int e24 | email gad@gad.net
```

Here is the resulting email, with the subject line in bold:

```
Date: Tue, 15 May 2012 01:48:18
From: Arista1@gad.net
To: gad@gad.net
Subject: Support email sent from the switch

Ethernet24 is down, line protocol is down (notconnect)
  Hardware is Ethernet, address is 001c.7308.80ae
  No Internet protocol address assigned
  MTU 1500 bytes, BW 1000000 Kbit
  Full-duplex, 1Gb/s, auto negotiation: fail
  Down 9 hours, 1 minutes, 39 seconds
  Last clearing of "show interface" counters never
  5 minutes input rate 0 bps (0.0% with framing), 0 packets/sec
  5 minutes output rate 0 bps (0.0% with framing), 0 packets/sec
     0 packets input, 0 bytes
     Received 0 broadcasts, 0 multicast
     0 runts, 0 giants
     0 input errors, 0 CRC, 0 alignment, 0 symbol
     0 PAUSE input
     0 packets output, 0 bytes
     Sent 0 broadcasts, 0 multicast
     0 output errors, 0 collisions
     0 late collision, 0 deferred
     0 PAUSE output
```

Let's try and do our show interface command, but this time send it as an attachment by using the –a flag. Let's specify a subject this time too:

```
Arista#sho int e24 | email -s "Sho int e24" gad@gad.net -a
```

And here's what I see in Pine (yes, I still use Pine [Alpine, actually] as my email client):

```
Date: Tue, 15 May 2012 01:53:47
From: Arista1@gad.net
```

```
To: gad@gad.net
Subject: Sho int e24
Parts/Attachments:
   1 Shown      2 lines   Text
   2   OK      20 lines   Text
----------------------------------------
see attachment



      [ Part 2, Text/PLAIN 20 lines. ]
      [ Not Shown. Use the "V" command to view or save this part. ]
```

Flummoxed by email failures after you've configured your switch for this feature? You can specify the -d option with email, after which you will be rewarded with pages of debug information reflecting every detailed interaction performed by the email process. Let's take a look:

```
Arista#sho int e24 | email -d gad@gad.net
connect: ('192.168.1.200', 25)
connect: (25, '192.168.1.200')
reply: '220 mail.example.com ESMTP Postfix (Ubuntu)\r\n'
reply: retcode (220); Msg: mail.example.com ESMTP Postfix (Ubuntu)
connect: mail.example.com ESMTP Postfix (Ubuntu)
send: 'ehlo [127.0.0.1]\r\n'
reply: '250-mail.example.com\r\n'
reply: '250-PIPELINING\r\n'
reply: '250-SIZE 30000000\r\n'
reply: '250-VRFY\r\n'
reply: '250-ETRN\r\n'
reply: '250-STARTTLS\r\n'
reply: '250-ENHANCEDSTATUSCODES\r\n'
reply: '250-8BITMIME\r\n'
reply: '250 DSN\r\n'
reply: retcode (250); Msg: mail.example.com
PIPELINING
SIZE 30000000
VRFY
ETRN
STARTTLS
ENHANCEDSTATUSCODES
8BITMIME
DSN
send: 'mail FROM:<Arista1@gad.net> size=1038\r\n'
reply: '250 2.1.0 Ok\r\n'
reply: retcode (250); Msg: 2.1.0 Ok
send: 'rcpt TO:<gad@gad.net>\r\n'
reply: '250 2.1.5 Ok\r\n'
reply: retcode (250); Msg: 2.1.5 Ok
send: 'data\r\n'
reply: '354 End data with <CR><LF>.<CR><LF>\r\n'
reply: retcode (354); Msg: End data with <CR><LF>.<CR><LF>
data: (354, 'End data with <CR><LF>.<CR><LF>')
```

```
send: 'Content-Type: text/plain; charset="us-ascii"\r\nMIME-Version: 1.0\r
    \nContent-Transfer-Encoding: 7bit\r\nTo: gad@gad.net\r\nSubject:
 Support email sent from the switch\r\nMessage-ID:
      <20120515231040.24975.45112.email@Arista>\r\nDate: Tue, 15 May 2012
 19:10:40 -0400\r\nFrom: Arista1@gad.net\r\n\r\nEthernet24 is down,
 line protocol is down (notconnect)\r\n  Hardware is Ethernet, address
  is 001c.7308.80ae\r\n  No Internet protocol address assigned\r\n  MTU
  1500 bytes, BW 1000000 Kbit\r\n  Full-duplex, 1Gb/s, auto
 negotiation: fail\r\n  Down 1 days, 2 hours, 24 minutes, 1
 seconds\r\n  Last clearing of "show interface" counters never\r\n
  5 minutes input rate 0 bps (0.0% with framing), 0 packets/sec\r\n
  5 minutes output rate 0 bps (0.0% with framing), 0 packets/sec\r\n
      0 packets input, 0 bytes\r\n      Received 0 broadcasts, 0
 multicast\r\n      0 runts, 0 giants\r\n      0 input errors, 0 CRC,
  0 alignment, 0 symbol\r\n      0 PAUSE input\r\n      0 packets
 output, 0 bytes\r\n      Sent 0 broadcasts, 0 multicast\r\n        0
 output errors, 0 collisions\r\n      0 late collision, 0 deferred\r\n
      0 PAUSE output\r\n.\r\n'
reply: '250 2.0.0 Ok: queued as D9D1D8EC5B4\r\n'
reply: retcode (250); Msg: 2.0.0 Ok: queued as D9D1D8EC5B4
data: (250, '2.0.0 Ok: queued as D9D1D8EC5B4')
send: 'quit\r\n'
reply: '221 2.0.0 Bye\r\n'
reply: retcode (221); Msg: 2.0.0 Bye
```

In this case, everything went through fine. This output would be invaluable during a
failure. Here, I've misconfigured the server's IP address in my email configuration in
order to generate a failed connection:

```
Arista#sho int e24 | email -d -s "Show Int e24" gad@gad.net
connect: ('192.168.1.203', 25)
connect: (25, '192.168.1.203')
% Failed to send email: [Errno 113] No route to host
```

Here, I've mistakenly sent an email to an address that doesn't exist on my server:

```
Arista#sho int e24 | email -d -s "Show Int e24" cisco@gad.net
connect: ('192.168.1.200', 25)
connect: (25, '192.168.1.200')
reply: '220 mail.example.com ESMTP Postfix (Ubuntu)\r\n'
reply: retcode (220); Msg: mail.example.com ESMTP Postfix (Ubuntu)
connect: mail.example.com ESMTP Postfix (Ubuntu)
send: 'ehlo [127.0.0.1]\r\n'
reply: '250-mail.example.com\r\n'
reply: '250-PIPELINING\r\n'
reply: '250-SIZE 30000000\r\n'
reply: '250-VRFY\r\n'
reply: '250-ETRN\r\n'
reply: '250-STARTTLS\r\n'
reply: '250-ENHANCEDSTATUSCODES\r\n'
reply: '250-8BITMIME\r\n'
reply: '250 DSN\r\n'
reply: retcode (250); Msg: mail.example.com
```

```
PIPELINING
SIZE 30000000
VRFY
ETRN
STARTTLS
ENHANCEDSTATUSCODES
8BITMIME
DSN
send: 'mail FROM:<Arista@gad.net> size=1018\r\n'
reply: '250 2.1.0 Ok\r\n'
reply: retcode (250); Msg: 2.1.0 Ok
send: 'rcpt TO:<cisco@gad.net>\r\n'
reply: '550 5.1.1 <cisco@gad.net>: Recipient address rejected: User
unknown in local recipient table\r\n'
reply: retcode (550); Msg: 5.1.1 <cisco@gad.net>: Recipient address
rejected: User unknown in local recipient table
send: 'rset\r\n'
reply: '250 2.0.0 Ok\r\n'
reply: retcode (250); Msg: 2.0.0 Ok
send: 'quit\r\n'
reply: '221 2.0.0 Bye\r\n'
reply: retcode (221); Msg: 2.0.0 Bye
% None of the addresses were valid: cisco@gad.net: 550 5.1.1
<cisco@gad.net>: Recipient address rejected: User unknown in local
recipient table
```

Since email is actually a bash command, you can use it for redirecting output in bash, too. Here, I've redirected the output of ls -al to my email address:

```
[admin@Arista ~]$ ls -al | email -s "ls -al" gad@gad.net
```

And here's the output from Pine:

```
Date: Tue, 15 May 2012 19:35:01
From: Arista@gad.net
To: gad@gad.net
Subject: ls -al

total 16
drwxr-x--- 3 admin eosadmin 160 May 15 01:34 .
drwxr-xr-x 3 root  root      60 May 15 01:23 ..
-rw------- 1 admin eosadmin 542 May 15 19:10 .bash_history
-rw-r--r-- 1 admin eosadmin  17 May 15 01:23 .bash_logout
-rw-r--r-- 1 admin eosadmin 176 May 15 01:23 .bash_profile
-rw-r--r-- 1 admin eosadmin 124 May 15 01:23 .bashrc
-rw-r--r-- 1 admin eosadmin   0 May 15 01:23 .dircolors
drwxr-xr-x 8 admin eosadmin 160 May 15 01:29 .esmtp_queue
```

If you're like me, you'll find yourself using this feature a lot more than you ever thought you would. But then, I've been told there aren't a lot of people quite like me.

## CHAPTER 20

LANZ

If you've read the chapter on buffers, you know that they can be a benefit or bane, depending on a lot of factors. When buffers in a switch become a problem, it can be very difficult to isolate the problem, since there usually aren't detailed counters that show the buffer contents. When running QoS on routers, there are all kinds of commands to run that will show you the status of your buffers, but those buffers are software constructs that take memory from the system. The buffers I'm referring to here are hardware switch interface buffers. Let's dig in and I'll show you what I mean.

Here's the output from the show interface command on an Arista 7124SX. As you can see, there is no mention of buffers:

```
Arista#sho int e5
Ethernet5 is up, line protocol is up (connected)
  Hardware is Ethernet, address is 001c.7308.80ae
  Internet address is 10.10.10.5/24
  Broadcast address is 255.255.255.255
  Address determined by manual configuration
  MTU 1500 bytes, BW 100000 Kbit
  Full-duplex, 100Mb/s, auto negotiation: on
  Up 1 days, 20 hours, 57 minutes, 59 seconds
  Last clearing of "show interface" counters never
  5 minutes input rate 183 bps (0.0% with framing), 0 packets/sec
  5 minutes output rate 45 bps (0.0% with framing), 0 packets/sec
     828028 packets input, 1130495492 bytes
     Received 6 broadcasts, 8355 multicast
     0 runts, 0 giants
     0 input errors, 0 CRC, 0 alignment, 0 symbol
     0 PAUSE input
     855277 packets output, 1187043452 bytes
     Sent 3 broadcasts, 8729 multicast
     0 output errors, 0 collisions
     0 late collision, 0 deferred
     0 PAUSE output
```

Why is there no mention of buffers? I didn't write the code, but I can guess that the status of the interface buffers changes at the microsecond level, so between the time you start to hit the Enter key, and the time you finish, the status of the buffers likely changed. Any information put into the output of the show interface command would be woefully outdated by the time it gets presented.

That's all well and good, but having lived through microburst events that caused performance problems, I can tell you that I would have given my right arm for useful tools. OK, maybe not my entire right arm, but believe me when I say that the lack of visibility into these buffers is extremely frustrating. I've been through enough of these problems that I can smell them, but being unable to prove them makes it hard to get management to spend money to fix them. If only someone would make a switch that had real troubleshooting tools at the interface buffer level!

Latency analyzer (LANZ) is Arista's solution to this problem. On the 7100 series of Arista switches, the ASICs allow visibility into the interface buffers at a heretofore unheard of reporting granularity of less than one millisecond. For those of you who can't keep the whole micro/nano/pico thing straight, a millisecond is one thousandth of a second. That's right, we can now get reports that show the status of our interface buffers one thousand times per second. Cool, huh? Sounds like too much information to me, but I'm a cranky old nerd. Let's take a look and see how it works.

For my first example, I have a very simple network setup as shown in Figure 20-1. This network is comprised of an Arista switch hooked up to another vendor's switch. The other switch is almost irrelevant for this test; it just happens to be a device I had available for testing.

Figure 20-1. Simple LANZ test lab

I've connected these two switches using copper. To accomplish this on my 10 Gbps SFP-based Arista switch, I'm using a copper SFP. I've lowered the speed of this interface down to 100 Mbps and assigned it an IP address. The speed sfp-1000baset auto 100full command tells the switch to only negotiate up to 100 Mbps full duplex when using the 1000 Base-T SFP I have installed:

```
Arista(config)#interface Ethernet5
Arista(config-if-Et5)#speed sfp-1000baset auto 100full
Arista(config-if-Et5)#no switchport
Arista(config-if-Et5)#ip address 10.10.10.5/24
```

For the sake of completeness, here is the configuration for the g1/0/15 port on the other switch (a Cisco 3750):

```
SW-3750#sho run int g1/0/15
Building configuration...

Current configuration : 103 bytes
!
interface GigabitEthernet1/0/15
 no switchport
 ip address 10.10.10.15 255.255.255.0
 speed 100
end
```

With my link set up, I dropped down to bash to initiate some traffic. This command sends one thousand 15,000-byte ping packets to the IP address 10.10.10.15. Note that I actually ran the ping command shown about 90 times. Since this is Linux, I used the ampersand at the end of each line so that each command ran in the background. This allowed me to run many of them at once, thus generating more traffic than I could with a single command. I call this technique the lazy man's traffic generator. Sure, it's crude, and it's a bit slow to get going, but I didn't have to download anything, install anything, configure anything, or otherwise waste precious time better spent yelling at clouds:

```
Arista#bash

Arista Networks EOS shell

[admin@Arista ~]$ ping -s 15000 -c 1000 10.10.10.15 > /dev/null &
[1] 9054
[admin@Arista ~]$ ping -s 15000 -c 1000 10.10.10.15 > /dev/null &
[2] 9057
[admin@Arista ~]$ ping -s 15000 -c 1000 10.10.10.15 > /dev/null &
[3] 9060
```

While that spins up (it takes a while for all those streams to get up to speed), let's go in and configure LANZ. First, we need to enable the feature globally. This is done with the queue-monitor length command:

```
Arista#queue-monitor length
```

At this point, LANZ is running and will record information when the proper thresholds are met. Next, we'll configure LANZ on the interface connected to the other switch. This is done with a similar command that needs to include two threshold values, the lower threshold and the upper threshold:

```
Arista(config-if-Et5)#queue-monitor length thresholds 2 1
```

This command can be a little baffling until you understand what the thresholds are referencing. The trick is to remember that your thresholds are being allocated in 512-byte segments (on this switch at least). The high threshold is the point at which LANZ will start recording. The low threshold is where LANZ will stop recording after the high threshold has been met.

To see the details of how big your buffer segments are, use the show queue-monitor length status command. This command will also show you the port thresholds for each interface. We can see that the default high threshold is 512 segments, while the default low threshold is 256 segments. We can also see that we've altered the defaults on interface e5:

```
Arista#sho queue-monitor length status
queue-monitor length enabled
Segment size in bytes          :   512
Maximum queue length in segments :  3268
Port thresholds in segments:
 Port High threshold  Low threshold
   Et1          512            256
   Et2          512            256
   Et3          512            256
   Et4          512            256
   Et5            2              1
   Et6          512            256
   Et7          512            256
   Et8          512            256
   Et9          512            256
   Et10         512            256
 [--- output truncated ----]
```

I set the thresholds very low so that we could see what they look like with very little traffic. In fact, I had to set the interface speed so low because these switches are so fast that I couldn't get it to buffer sourcing packets at all from bash on a 10 Gbps interface. Actually, I never tried. I was too lazy to wait and figured that I'd get results more quickly with a slow 100 Mbps interface.

Back to our thresholds. The command I've entered will trigger reporting when two or more buffer segments are utilized, and logging will stop when one or fewer buffer segments are used on interface e5.

Now that my numerous, fat pings have had a chance to get up to speed, let's take a look at the interface and see what sort of trouble I've caused:

```
Arista#sho int e5 | grep rate
   5 minutes input rate 8.06 Mbps (8.2% with framing), 718 packets/sec
   5 minutes output rate 8.70 Mbps (8.8% with framing), 777 packets/sec
```

My multiple background ping processes have generated over 8 Mbps of traffic. Note that if you try this on your own switch (please don't do this in a production environment), it will take a few minutes for the traffic to ramp up to this level.

One of my favorite features of Arista's EOS is the way in which it displays traffic rates with the show interface command. I am so tired of looking at numbers like 8374625374 and trying to figure out if that's megabits, or gigabits, or tens of gigabits. I mean, would it kill them to put in some commas? Also, how cool is it that the output shows us the percent utilization in simple English? This is one of the many things that Arista just gets right.

With some respectable traffic flowing, let's see what LANZ can do for us. To see the status of the buffer on interface e5, use the show queue-monitor length *interface* command:

```
Arista#sho queue-monitor length e5 | more

Report generated at 2012-05-08 23:34:52
Time                      Interface   Queue length
                                      (segments, 1 to 512 bytes)
----------------------------------------------------------------
0:00:00.01414 ago            Et5      18
0:00:00.01480 ago            Et5      35
0:00:00.01546 ago            Et5      22
0:00:00.02987 ago            Et5      6
0:00:00.03060 ago            Et5      22
0:00:00.03370 ago            Et5      3
0:00:00.03436 ago            Et5      19
0:00:00.03513 ago            Et5      4
0:00:00.03537 ago            Et5      21
0:00:00.05032 ago            Et5      4
0:00:00.05098 ago            Et5      22
0:00:00.06885 ago            Et5      16
0:00:00.06955 ago            Et5      35
0:00:00.07025 ago            Et5      52
0:00:00.07156 ago            Et5      22
0:00:00.08607 ago            Et5      19
0:00:00.09646 ago            Et5      6
0:00:00.09713 ago            Et5      22
```

This output shows the timestamp for each measured interval, the interface, and the number of buffer segments used at that point in time. Take a look at the intervals on the left. The delta (difference) between the first two lines (0:00:00.01414 ago and 0:00:00.01480 ago) is 00.00066 seconds. That's 0.66 milliseconds. Not too shabby!

To give a better indication of how granular this data is, have some fun with the limit keyword to this command. On my switch, issuing the sho queue-monitor length e5 limit 1 seconds command yields 243 lines of data. For those of you who like to do math in your head, remember that LANZ is only recording buffer levels when the upper threshold (2) has been met, and has not fallen below the low threshold (1). If the buffers were to remain empty for half of a second, then there would be many fewer lines. Similarly, if I were trying to pump 10 Gbps through my 100 Mbps link, the buffers would likely be higher more consistently:

```
Arista#sho queue-monitor length e5 limit 1 seconds

Report generated at 2012-05-09 00:10:21
Time                            Interface     Queue length
                                              (segments, 1 to 512 bytes)
-----------------------------------------------------------------------
0:00:00.00480 ago               Et5           16
0:00:00.00508 ago               Et5           22
0:00:00.00974 ago               Et5           6
0:00:00.01041 ago               Et5           22
0:00:00.01628 ago               Et5           3

[--- many pages of buffer detail removed ---]

0:00:00.97528 ago               Et5           22
0:00:00.98436 ago               Et5           6
0:00:00.98509 ago               Et5           22
0:00:00.99172 ago               Et5           16
0:00:00.99189 ago               Et5           22
```

The output can also be limited to a set number of samples using the **samples** modifier:

```
Arista#sho queue-monitor length e5 limit 10 samples

Report generated at 2012-05-09 00:12:20
Time                            Interface     Queue length
                                              (segments, 1 to 512 bytes)
-----------------------------------------------------------------------
0:00:00.00063 ago               Et5           6
0:00:00.00148 ago               Et5           22
0:00:00.02014 ago               Et5           6
0:00:00.02081 ago               Et5           22
0:00:00.02239 ago               Et5           6
0:00:00.02306 ago               Et5           22
0:00:00.02466 ago               Et5           6
0:00:00.02532 ago               Et5           22
0:00:00.05041 ago               Et5           6
0:00:00.05107 ago               Et5           22
```

After having some fun with LANZ, I decided to really kick things up a notch. I decided to initiate about 100 more ping commands, this time increasing the count to 10,000:

```
[admin@Arista ~]$ ping -s 15000 -c 10000 10.10.10.15 > /dev/null &
[2] 14382
[admin@Arista ~]$ ping -s 15000 -c 10000 10.10.10.15 > /dev/null &
[3] 14385
[admin@Arista ~]$ ping -s 15000 -c 10000 10.10.10.15 > /dev/null &
[4] 14388
```

Something interesting began to happen after I did this. Take a look at the Arista interface's rate information:

```
Arista#sho int e5 | inc rate
  5 minutes input rate 9.36 Mbps (9.5% with framing), 834 packets/sec
  5 minutes output rate 15.7 Mbps (15.9% with framing), 1400 packets/sec
```

My Arista switch is sending almost 16 Mbps of nasty, huge ping packets, but I'm only receiving just over 9 Mbps of them back. What gives? Curious, I dug in to try and figure it out. LANZ reports that the buffers are filling, but are nowhere near capacity:

```
Arista#sho queue-monitor length e5 limit 10 samples

Report generated at 2012-05-09 00:23:16
Time                        Interface        Queue length
                                             (segments, 1 to
                                             512 bytes)
--------------------------------------------------------------
0:00:00.01379 ago           Et5              13
0:00:00.01449 ago           Et5              31
0:00:00.01531 ago           Et5              21
0:00:00.02071 ago           Et5              10
0:00:00.02142 ago           Et5              27
0:00:00.02211 ago           Et5              44
0:00:00.02605 ago           Et5              19
0:00:00.02675 ago           Et5              37
0:00:00.02745 ago           Et5              22
0:00:00.03823 ago           Et5              1
```

There's nothing unusual there. The entire show interface output doesn't show anything either, other than the fact that I'm sending 1,407 packets per second and only receiving 855 packets per second. So where are all the packets going?

```
Arista#sho int e5
Ethernet5 is up, line protocol is up (connected)
   Hardware is Ethernet, address is 001c.7308.80b3 (bia 001c.7308.80b3)
   MTU 9212 bytes, BW 100000 Kbit
   Full-duplex, 100Mb/s, auto negotiation: on
   Up 1 days, 22 hours, 23 minutes, 17 seconds
   Last clearing of "show interface" counters never
   5 minutes input rate 9.59 Mbps (9.7% with framing), 855 packets/sec
   5 minutes output rate 15.8 Mbps (16.0% with framing), 1407 packets/sec
      3119601 packets input, 4343127595 bytes
      Received 6 broadcasts, 8609 multicast
      0 runts, 0 giants
      0 input errors, 0 CRC, 0 alignment, 0 symbol
      0 PAUSE input
      3723524 packets output, 5200954972 bytes
      Sent 5 broadcasts, 10820 multicast
      0 output errors, 0 collisions
      0 late collision, 0 deferred
      0 PAUSE output
```

I decided to look at the Cisco switch, since the Arista reported that it was sending fine, but not receiving all the replies. I discovered something interesting when I looked at the CPU histograms:

```
SW-3750#sho proc cpu hist
      11111
    99000000999999999999999999999999999999999999999999999999
    99000000999999999999999999999999999999999999999999999999
100 ********************************************************
 90 ********************************************************
 80 ********************************************************
 70 ********************************************************
 60 ********************************************************
 50 ********************************************************
 40 ********************************************************
 30 ********************************************************
 20 ********************************************************
 10 ********************************************************
    0....5....1....1....2....2....3....3....4....4....5....5....
             0    5    0    5    0    5    0    5    0    5
              CPU% per second (last 60 seconds)
```

Whoa! The Cisco 3750 is running hot with a continued CPU utilization of 99% to 100%. Why? Let's look at the processes:

```
SW-3750#sho proc cpu sort
CPU utilization for five secs: 99%/5%; one mins: 99%; five mins: 98%
 PID Runtime(ms) Invoked uSecs   5Sec   1Min   5Min TTY Process
 177    2643245  286049  9240  68.15% 66.85% 65.61%   0 IP Input
 122   32341224 3901110  8290  14.07% 15.28% 15.41%   0 Hulc LED Proces
  55     328746 8866216    37   3.67%  3.09%  3.02%   0 Fifo Error Dete
  90    1616229  190855  8468   1.11%  0.95%  1.00%   0 hpm counter pro
  52      89821 4484423    20   0.63%  0.45%  0.41%   0 RedEarth Tx Man
  86      73310 1659407    44   0.31%  0.23%  0.25%   0 hpm main proces
 130     664725   38654 17196   0.31%  0.35%  0.37%   0 HQM Stack Proce
 123       1361  141810     9   0.15%  0.01%  0.00%   0 HL3U bkgrd proc
  39       1878 3840483     0   0.15%  0.01%  0.00%   0 DownWhenLooped
```

The top process is IP Input, which on a Cisco switch means that many packets are being punted out of Cisco Express Forwarding (CEF) or Fast Switching and are being handled by the processor. This is happening because I'm pinging an IP address on the switch itself with a frightening amount of huge packets. To be fair, this is not a valid test of switch performance because had I sent these packets through the switch, instead of to it, they would have passed through with ease.

Although it may be unfair to point out that the Cisco switch couldn't keep up with my ping onslaught, consider this: the Arista switch not only delivered that onslaught with ease, it also generated it. Not only that, but check out the output from the show proc top command while all these pings were running:

```
top - 20:32:32 up 2 days, 6:04, 1 user, load average: 0.09, 0.04, 0.01
Tasks: 275 total,   1 running, 274 sleeping,   0 stopped,   0 zombie
```

```
Cpu(s): 14.4%us, 2.5%sy, 0.0%ni, 81.0%id, 0.0%wa, 0.2%hi, 2.0%si
Mem:   2043416k total, 1315056k used,  728360k free, 108020k buffers
Swap:        0k total,       0k used,       0k free, 803792k cached

  PID USER   PR NI  VIRT  RES  SHR S %CPU %MEM    TIME+  COMMAND
 1994 root   20  0  187m  42m  19m S  8.0  2.1 242:34.22 PhyAeluros
 1930 root   20  0  179m  34m  14m S  6.3  1.7 193:00.17 Mdio
 1931 root   20  0  596m  55m  21m S  6.3  2.8 178:44.90 FocalPoint
 1581 root   20  0  204m  80m  47m S  3.3  4.0  88:55.00 Sysdb
 8286 root   20  0  174m  29m  13m S  2.3  1.5   1:28.56 FPLanz
 8077 admin  20  0  206m  66m  32m S  1.7  3.3  38:26.16 Cli
 1583 root   20  0  200m  63m  38m S  1.0  3.2  25:30.58 Fru
 1624 root   20  0  172m  26m  10m S  1.0  1.3  24:37.63 AgentMonitor
 1636 root   20  0  183m  31m  10m S  0.7  1.6  17:21.13 Lag+LacpAgen
 1647 root   20  0 98.4m  58m  46m S  0.7  2.9   2:25.30 ribd
 1955 root   20  0  178m  26m 7076 S  0.7  1.3  23:10.17 PhyEthtool
 1580 root   20  0  177m  20m 2388 S  0.3  1.0  13:03.47 ProcMgr-work
 1934 root   20  0  179m  33m  14m S  0.3  1.7  13:35.47 Smbus
 1954 root   20  0  179m  33m  14m S  0.3  1.7   9:21.97 Adt7462Agent
 1959 root   20  0  174m  30m  14m S  0.3  1.5   4:02.52 FanDetector
14042 admin  20  0  2296  616  492 S  1.5  0.0   0:00.29 ping
14296 admin  20  0  2296  620  492 S  1.5  0.0   0:00.21 ping
```

If you're familiar with the Linux top command, then you'll see that not only is the Arista switch barely breathing hard, but ping isn't even one of the top 10 processes! Meanwhile it continues to shovel out so many packets that the 3750 can't keep up with them all:

```
Arista#sho int e5 | inc rate
  5 minutes input rate 9.85 Mbps (10% with framing), 878 packets/sec
  5 minutes output rate 15.9 Mbps (16% with framing), 1416 packets/sec
```

Back to the buffers on the Arista, all those numbers are cool, but I'd sure like to see all that data in a graph. Luckily, the output can be presented in CSV format with the csv keyword on the show queue-monitor length command. Note that with the csv keyword, the oldest samples are displayed first, which is the opposite of what we've seen previously:

```
Arista#sho queue-monitor length csv e5

Report generated at 2012-05-07 02:26:15
2012-05-07 02:06:09.48718,Et5,3
2012-05-07 02:06:09.50783,Et5,22
2012-05-07 02:06:09.50851,Et5,6
2012-05-07 02:06:09.52265,Et5,22
2012-05-07 02:06:09.52334,Et5,6
2012-05-07 02:06:09.54107,Et5,22
2012-05-07 02:06:09.54176,Et5,6
2012-05-07 02:06:09.57933,Et5,22
2012-05-07 02:06:09.58000,Et5,6
2012-05-07 02:06:09.58795,Et5,43
[--- output truncated ---]
```

I suggest that if you use this command, you either pipe it to more or redirect it to file. I suggest this because using the csv keyword will report the last 100,000 *over-threshold events*, which is a lot of data to watch on the console. To redirect the output to a file, use the >> operator just like you would in Linux:

```
Arista#sho queue-monitor length csv >> file:/home/admin/CSV-GAD.txt
```

A quick look into bash reveals that my file is now in the directory specified:

```
Arista#bash

Arista Networks EOS shell

[admin@Arista ~]$ ls -lh
total 3.2M
-rw-rw-rw- 1 admin eosadmin 3.2M May  8 21:29 CSV-GAD.txt
```

 If you want this file to survive a reboot, you'll need to place it somewhere on */mnt/flash/*.

That's a 3.2 MB *.txt* file. Aren't you glad I didn't paste the whole thing into this book? Taking a look at the first few lines, we can see that it looks similar to the previous output:

```
[admin@Arista ~]$ head CSV-GAD.txt

Report generated at 2012-05-09 01:29:14
2012-05-09 01:22:47.60513,Et5,4
2012-05-09 01:22:47.61294,Et5,22
2012-05-09 01:22:47.61405,Et5,25
2012-05-09 01:22:47.61474,Et5,7
2012-05-09 01:22:47.62090,Et5,22
2012-05-09 01:22:47.62110,Et5,18
2012-05-09 01:22:47.62594,Et5,22
2012-05-09 01:22:47.62603,Et5,19
```

Using a small chunk of this data, I copied it, imported it into Excel, and created the quick and dirty chart in Figure 20-2. While this is a rudimentary example of what can be done, it shows what CSV can be used for.

Creating Excel charts from data gathered at the CLI is fun, but it is limited in its usefulness. If your network is massively congested, the last 100,000 samples might be a small amount of time. Remember that this file may contain the buffer information for every interface on the switch and, as we've seen, in a congested network these entries add up quickly. What would be more useful would be the ability to stream all this data elsewhere. Luckily, the folks at Arista had this in mind when they built this feature.

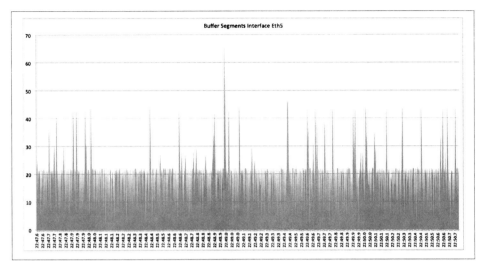

Figure 20-2. Excel chart from LANZ CSV-formatted data

As you've seen, LANZ can output a lot of data in a short amount of time. Because of this, the people at Arista decided that typical logging solutions like Syslog couldn't keep up with the data flow. Instead, LANZ is streamed using something called *Google Protocol Buffers* (GPB). Configuration of a GPB client is beyond the scope of this book, but setting up LANZ to send to such a client is not.

To enable LANZ streaming, enter queue monitor streaming mode with the `queue-monitor streaming` command:

```
Arista(config)#queue-monitor streaming
```

There's really not much else that needs to be done, and not much else that can be done. Here are all the options for this mode:

```
Arista(config-qm-streaming)#?
  comment          Up to 240 characters, comment for this mode
  default          Set a command to its defaults
  exit             Exit from Queue-monitor streaming configuration mode
  help             Description of the interactive help system
  max-connections  Set maximum number of client connections
  no               Negate a command or set its defaults
  show             Show running system information
  shutdown         Disable queue-monitor streaming
  !                Append to comment
```

In a nutshell, by enabling this mode, a server runs on the switch that listens on port 50001. GPB clients connect to the switch, after which LANZ streaming publishes buffer events to the client. You can limit the number of clients that can connect at any given time with the `max-connections` command (the default is 100):

```
Arista(config-qm-streaming)#max-connections 10
```

Finally, to enable LANZ streaming, issue the `no shutdown` command from within the mode, and then exit:

```
Arista(config-qm-streaming)#no shutdown
Arista(config-qm-streaming)#exit
Arista(config)#
```

At this point, the LANZ streaming server is active. You can see if the streaming service is listening by using the bash `netstat` command to see if the switch is listening on port 50001. Here's the output with LANZ streaming configured and active:

```
Arista(config)#bash netstat -na | grep 50001
tcp        0      0 0.0.0.0:50001           0.0.0.0:*               LISTEN
```

Now, I'll shut the service off and issue the same command:

```
Arista(config-qm-streaming)#shut
Arista(config-qm-streaming)#bash netstat -na | grep 50001
'netstat -na | grep 50001' returned error code:1
```

Though this test is not fool-proof, it will show if the switch is listening on port 50001. Unless you've configured another service to listen on that port, the test should work as advertised. Of course, you can always use the `show active` command from within the queue monitor streaming configuration mode, too:

```
Arista(config-qm-streaming)#sho active
queue-monitor streaming
   no shutdown
```

Personally, I like to see what Unix thinks.

Though LANZ is only available on the 7100 series of Arista switches, a new feature called LANZ Lite will be available on the 7058 and 7500 series switches at the end of 2012. It was not available at the time of this writing. LANZ Lite will not have the same microsecond granularity as LANZ, but it will offer visibility into buffer utilization, which is still a massive improvement over other vendors who don't offer anything.

Lastly, LANZ is a licensed feature, so make sure your license fees are paid up before you reap its benefits.

sFlow

sFlow is an open source sampling tool that provides constant traffic flow information on all enabled interfaces simultaneously. sFlow data is sent from the switch by a process called an *agent* in sFlow parlance. The sFlow data is sent to a *collector* that usually formats the data into cool-looking charts and graphs while recording and reporting trends for use in diagnostics, troubleshooting, and analysis. sFlow is defined in RFC 3176, and because it's an open source tool, there are many agents and collectors out there, some of which are free, and some of which cost tens of thousands of dollars. If you're thinking that this all sounds like Cisco's NetFlow, you're right, but sFlow is open source, while NetFlow is Cisco proprietary.

The agent within the switch samples packets from the data flows, and then forwards the headers of those sampled packets to the collector at regular intervals. The sampling is just that, a sample packet from the data flows and not a copy of every packet. The number of packets sampled from the total packets seen is called the *sample rate*, which can be configured with the default being about 1 in every 65,000 packets. These packets are stored and then sent to the collector at a configurable interval called the *polling interval*. The default polling interval is two seconds.

Not all packets or flow types are sampled. Packets that are sampled include frames sent to the interfaces or CPU of the switch, routed packets (with certain exceptions), flooded packets, and multicast packets. The following packet types are not sampled by sFlow:

- LACP frames
- LLDP frames
- STP BPDUs
- IGMP packets
- Ethernet PAUSE frames

- PIM_HELLO packets
- Frames that have CRC errors
- Packets dropped by ACLs
- Packets dropped due to VLAN violations
- Routed packets with IP options or MTU violations

Configuring sFlow

In order to see sFlow in action, you'll need a collector. If you're just messing with one in a lab, any of them will do. For his chapter, I downloaded *sFlow Trend*, which is a free tool that can be found at *http://www.immon.com*. Of the four or so that I tried, this was the easiest to set up and get working, and it's actually free (not just a time-limited demo). As I like to say, free is better than not free.

I set up my lab with the following IP addresses:

- Arista switch: 192.168.1.188
- sFlow collector: 192.168.1.100

The first step in configuring sFlow on the switch is to tell the switch where the collector is located. This is done with the `sflow destination` *ip-address port#* global configuration command. The port number is optional, and defaults to 6343. Since I'm fine with that port, I'll just include the IP address:

```
SW1(config)#sflow destination 192.168.1.188
```

Next, I'll configure the agent source. This can be either an IP address or an interface (but not both). To configure a source IP address, use the `sflow source` *ip-address* command. To specify a source interface instead, use the `sflow source-interface` *interface-name* command. I'll be using the `source interface` options and specifying the `Management1` interface:

```
SW1(config)#sflow source-interface Management1
```

To get sFlow running, we'll need to use the `sflow run` command:

```
SW1(config)#sflow run
```

At this point, the collector should be receiving sFlow packets from the switch. There are two more items that can be configured globally, but you probably won't mess with them unless you need to. The first is the `sflow polling-interval` *seconds* command. The polling interval is how often the switch sends its collection data to the collector. The default value is two seconds and can be configured for anywhere from 1 to 3,600 seconds. This can be useful if your collector becomes overwhelmed when hundreds of devices are sending sFlow data to it. Here I'll set my switch to a polling interval of five seconds:

```
SW1(config)#sflow polling-interval 5
```

The next option that can be configured is the sample rate. By default, the switch samples (on average) one out of every 65,526 packets. If you'd like to lighten the load on the switch and provide less granular data to the collector, you can raise that number so that it samples less often. Or, you could lower the value to get more granular data. The values that you can use are anywhere in the range of 16,384 to 16,777,216. Here I'll set the sample rate to 1 in every 16,384 packets:

```
SW1(config)#sflow sample 16384
```

If you really want to throw caution to the wind, you can set it to any value you'd like by including the dangerous keyword, followed by the value of your choosing (well, from 1 to 4,294,967,295 anyway). I'm feeling especially dangerous today, so I'll set my sample to a very dangerous level of 1 in 100 packets:

```
SW1(config)#sflow sample dangerous 100
```

 Configuring sFlow with such a low value is, in fact, dangerous, especially in a production environment. sFlow is a process that runs on the switch, and if the sample rate is set too low, that process can monopolize system resources. I can play with any value I want because my network consists of a few routers and an Arista switch with a collector attached. I could say something like, "Don't try this at home!", but in this case, home is about the only place that I would recommend you try this.

Though sFlow is enabled globally, it can be disabled on individual interfaces. To do so, issue the `no sflow enable` command in interface configuration mode. Here, I've disabled sFlow on interface Ethernet10:

```
SW1(config)#int e10
SW1(config-if-Et10)#no sflow enable
```

To re-enable sFlow on the interface, use the `sflow enable` command (which is the default):

```
SW1(config-if-Et10)#sflow enable
```

Showing sFlow Information

To see what interfaces have sFlow enabled, use the `show sflow interfaces` command:

```
SW1#sho sflow interfaces
sFlow Interface (s):
-------------------
Ethernet1 - running
Ethernet2 - running
Ethernet3 - running
Ethernet10 - running
Ethernet11 - running
```

Note that only active interfaces are shown, and if you've disabled sFlow on an interface with the `no sflow enable` command, it will not show up in the list.

After letting my switch send sFlow data for about an hour, I issued the `show sflow` command, which produced the following output:

```
SW1#sho sflow
sFlow Configuration
-------------------
Destination(s):
  192.168.1.100:6343
Source IP: 192.168.1.188 from Management1
Sample Rate: 100
Polling Interval (sec): 5.0

Status
------
Running: Yes
Polling On: Yes
Sampling On: Yes ( default )
Send Datagrams: Yes
Hardware Sample Rate: 128

Statistics
----------
Total Packets: 1548560
Number of Samples: 1891
Sample Pool: 1290496
Hardware Trigger: 1891
Number of Datagrams: 8770
```

The first paragraph of output shows all of the configuration changes we made, including the destination, the UDP port in use (port 6343 is the default), the sampling rate, and the polling interval. The rest of the output shows status and statistics, which can be useful when troubleshooting to make sure that the switch is actually sending packets.

There is also a `show sflow detail` command, which shows exactly two more lines of information, both of which I've highlighted in bold:

```
SW1#sho sflow detail
sFlow Configuration
-------------------
Destination(s):
  192.168.1.100:6343
Source IP: 192.168.1.188 from Management1
Sample Rate: 100
Polling Interval (sec): 2.0 ( default )

Status
------
Running: Yes
Polling On: Yes
```

```
Sampling On: Yes ( default )
Send Datagrams: Yes
Hardware Sample Rate: 128
Hardware Sampling On: Yes

Statistics
----------
Total Packets: 1555303
Number of Samples: 1893
Sample Pool: 1290752
Hardware Trigger: 1893
Number of Datagrams: 13198
Number of Samples Discarded: 0
```

With sFlow configured, I proceeded to generate some traffic in order to see how my collector was working. Figure 21-1 is the sFlowTrend dashboard that shows the top interfaces by utilization and total frames.

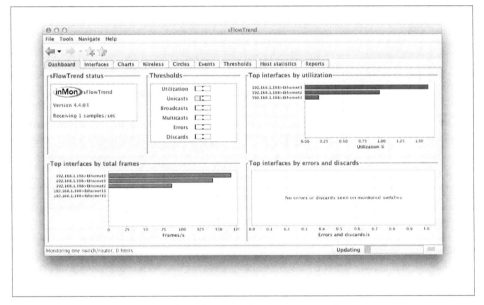

Figure 21-1. sFlowTrend's dashboard screen showing my switch stats

Figure 21-2 shows the counters chart from sFlowTrend for interface Ethernet1. In a production environment, there would also be very interesting charts and graphs showing communication pairs, top talkers, and a variety of other useful stats. Sadly, my underground lair only has a small number of hosts, and the resulting graphs were too embarrassing to include.

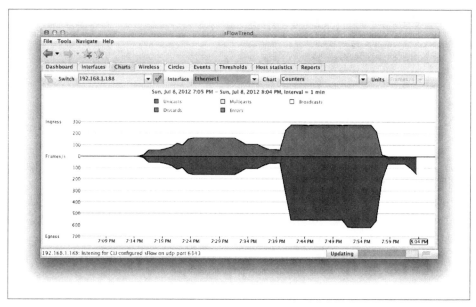

Figure 21-2. sFlowTrend's Ethernet interface counters graph

sFlow is a powerful tool that allows third-party tools to display useful data about the traffic moving through your switches. In the future, sFlow may play an important roll in concepts like Software Defined Networking (SDN) when used in conjunction with other open protocols such as OpenFlow. Knowing how to get the sFlow data to a collector will allow you to get better visibility into the traffic patterns that exist on your network today.

## CHAPTER 22

VM Tracer

Working in a large scale multitenant data center can mean a network with hundreds or even thousands of virtual machines. VLANs may be added, moved, or deleted 50 times a day in such an environment. Those VLANs need to be added and removed from edge switches by networking personnel who need to work closely with the VM teams. In my experience, this is often a time consuming task because of the high number of clients in a large multitenant environment. The Virtual Machine (VM) guys get annoyed when they have to wait for network changes, and the network team gets annoyed having to do boring work like adding and removing VLANs from trunk ports all day.

Enter VM Tracer. VM Tracer can be given a range of VLANs with which it can add, change, and remove without human interaction. The range of VLANs is communicated to the VM teams, and when they bring up a new VM, they choose one from the pool. When they configure the VLAN on the virtual switch, VM Tracer senses this change. It then adds the VLAN to the Arista switch, provisions the network port connected to the VM for the new VLAN, and the network team didn't have to lift a finger. If the VM team decides to later remove the VLAN, the switch will automatically remove it from the server's trunk port, and remove it if it is no longer used elsewhere on the switch.

 To be completely accurate, VM Tracer doesn't *sense* anything. VM Tracer takes advantage of the application programing interface (API) provided by VMware in order to communicate with vSphere. The VM Tracer features are simply making use of this API in order to interact with vSphere in clever and useful ways.

If the thought of letting the server guys make changes to your VLANs without your guidance gives you chills, read on and you'll see how it can be contained, as well as some limitations of how this all works.

VM Tracer, in its simplest form, just reports which VMs are attached to which ports on your Arista switches. It does this through two methods: direct communication with vSphere, and through CDP. If you're looking cross-eyed at the page because I mentioned CDP in an Arista book, I felt the same way when I learned about it, but rest assured, the Cisco Discovery Protocol is alive and well and living in your Arista switch. Hell, I didn't believe it either until I saw it with my own eyes. Don't worry, I'll make you a believer, too.

Though you can't go so far as to issue a `show cdp neighbor` command, Arista used CDP because, at the time, VMware did not support LLDP. In the latest revs of VMware, LLDP is supported, and future Arista code will utilize either CDP or LLDP depending on the attached device. As of mid-2012, though, CDP is the only game in town for VM Tracer.

In order to show how VM Tracer works, I've set up a lab, as shown in Figure 22-1. The lab contains two VMware servers, marked as A and B. There are four switches between them. Switches 1 and 2 are Arista 7124s configured as an MLAG pair. Switches 3 and 4 are Arista 7050s, and are also configured as an MLAG pair. Though I could have built the lab much simpler with only one switch on either side, this scenario more closely mimics VMware server connectivity in a data center.

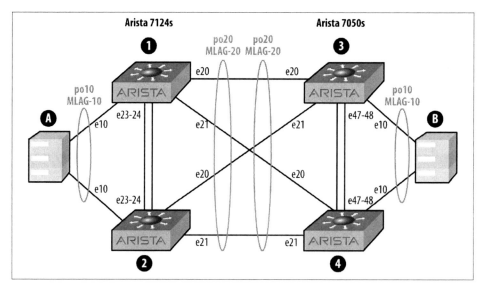

Figure 22-1. Simple VM Tracer lab

Server A has a VM on it named VM-A, while server B has a VM on it named VM-B. Sure, I could have named them Siegfried and Roy or something, but I guess I just wasn't feeling the magic that day.

Two VLANs were manually configured on all four switches. VLAN 99 was set up strictly for communication with vSphere, and VLAN 49 was set up so that we could ping from VM to VM. Additionally, VLAN 1 is the default (and is always there), and VLAN 4094 is in use on the MLAG peer-link between each switch pair.

Here's the output from the show vlan command from each switch to prove that I have nothing up my sleeve:

SW1

```
SW1#sho vlan
VLAN  Name                              Status     Ports
----- --------------------------------- ---------  --------------------
1     default                           active     Po1, Po10, Po20
49    VLAN0049                          active     Po1, Po10, Po20
99    VLAN0099                          active     Cpu, Po1, Po10, Po20
4094  VLAN4094                          active     Cpu, Po1
```

SW2

```
SW2#sho vlan
VLAN  Name                              Status     Ports
----- --------------------------------- ---------  --------------------
1     default                           active     Po1, Po10, Po20
49    VLAN0049                          active     Po1, Po10, Po20
99    VLAN0099                          active     Cpu, Po1, Po10, Po20
4094  VLAN4094                          active     Cpu, Po1
```

SW3

```
SW3#sho vlan
VLAN  Name                              Status     Ports
----- --------------------------------- ---------  --------------------
1     default                           active     Et1, Po1, Po10, Po20
49    VLAN0049                          active     Et1, Po1, Po10, Po20
99    VLAN0099                          active     Cpu, Et1, Po1, Po10,
                                                   Po20
4094  VLAN4094                          active     Cpu, Po1
```

SW4

```
SW4#sho vlan
VLAN  Name                              Status     Ports
----- --------------------------------- ---------  --------------------
1     default                           active     PEt1, Po1, Po10, Po20
49    VLAN0049                          active     PEt1, Po1, Po10, Po20
99    VLAN0099                          active     Cpu, PEt1, Po1, Po10,
                                                   Po20
4094  VLAN4094                          active     Cpu, Po1
```

SW3 shows interface e1 as active because e1 is connected to a switch with a laptop plugged in to it to manage the VMs. SW4 shows an interface Pet1, which is the MLAG peer's (SW3) e1 port. As you can see, each of the four switches has only these four VLANs configured.

The trunk between the switched (port-channel 20 on both sides) is configured to trunk all VLANs (none are pruned). All switches are configured the same way:

```
SW3#sho run int po 20
interface Port-Channel20
   switchport mode trunk
   mlag 20
```

The first step in configuring VM Tracer is to enter VM Tracer configuration mode. In order to do this, you must specify a session name. The session name should make sense to you, and it should somehow relate to the vSphere being queried. Since we have only one, I'll call this session *Lab*:

```
SW3(config)#vmtracer session Lab
SW3(config-vmtracer-Lab)#
```

If you're so inclined, you can add a comment to the session with the comment command. Enter the command, and then hit Return, after which you'll be allowed to type multiple lines. When done, type EOF alone on a line to return to the session:

```
SW1(config-vmtracer-Lab)#comment
Enter TEXT message. Type 'EOF' on its own line to end.
GAD's VMware vSphere Lab session
EOF
SW1(config-vmtracer-Lab)#
```

In order to communicate with vSphere, we need to specify the URL for the vSphere Software Development Kit (SDK) with the url command, which is usually formed as https://[ip-address/DNS-name]/sdk. In my lab, the vSphere is located at 10.10.10.5, so the url command is written as follows:

```
SW1(config-vmtracer-Lab)#url https://10.10.10.5/sdk
```

A username and password are required for access to the VMware SDK. Since I'm using a demo version of VMware, the defaults work fine:

```
SW1(config-vmtracer-Lab)#username root
SW1(config-vmtracer-Lab)#password vmware
```

The switch will convert the password to an encrypted form that looks like this in the config:

```
password 7 y5BlQXAUxQWJ+MkzwWsatg==
```

Note that the configuration for your VM Tracer session does not take effect until you exit the VM Tracer configuration mode:

```
SW1(config-vmtracer-Lab)#exit
SW1(config)#
```

At this point, you'll be tempted to start looking at what VM Tracer sees, but there's still one more step we need to take. In order for VM Tracer to correlate what it learns from vSphere, it needs to be able to communicate with the servers directly using CDP. This is accomplished with the vmtracer vmware-esx interface command:

```
SW1(config)#int po 10
SW1(config-if-Po10)#vmtracer vmware-esx
```

 The vmtracer vmware-esx command *must* go on the port-channel interface if your ESX host is attached via port-channel. Attaching this command to the physical interface may seem like the right thing to do, but it won't work. The command will be accepted, and if you're like me, you'll spend hours trying to figure out why it doesn't work. Save yourself the aggravation, and just put it on the port-channel.

After everything is configured, you may be frustrated to see output that doesn't seem to show any data. Initial communication with vSphere can take a minute, so be patient. VM Tracer is correlating everything it learns from vSphere with everything it's learned from CDP, so give it a chance to do its thing. CDP updates are only sent every 60 seconds by default.

The command to see the VMs attached to interfaces configured with the vmtracer vmware-esx command is show vmtracer interface. If you're impatient and didn't wait long enough (or if it's truly not working), this is what you'll see:

```
SW1#sho vmtracer int

Port-Channel10 :
 Ethernet10 : --/--/--
 PeerEthernet10 : --/--/--
    VM Name                   VM Adapter        VLAN   Status   State
```

Once VM Tracer gets its act together, you'll be rewarded with more useful information. For my money, this is the most useful tool in the VM Tracer arsenal. Later on in this chapter, we'll be using it a lot:

```
SW1#sho vmtracer int

Port-Channel10 :
 Ethernet10 : 10.10.10.21/lab-dvSwitch/dvUplink1
 PeerEthernet10 : --/--/--
    VM Name                   VM Adapter        VLAN   Status   State
    VM-A                      Network adapter 2 49     Up/Up    --
```

To see information about your configured VM Tracer session, use the show vmtracer session command:

```
SW1#sho vmtracer sess
Session                        Lab
vCenter URL                    https://10.10.10.5/sdk
```

```
username                           root
autovlan                           enabled
allowed-vlans                      1-4094
sessionState                       Connected
```

Notice that the autovlan setting is on, and the allowed-vlans is shown as 1–4094. This is the default, and it's actually pretty dangerous. I'll explain why in a minute, but for now, let's take a look at some other show commands used with VM Tracer.

A very useful tool when trying to figure out why VM Tracer is not working is the show vmtracer session *session-name* detail command. With it you can see the last time messages were sent and received, the last state change, and a host of other useful information:

```
SW1#sho vmtracer sess Lab detail
Session                            Lab
vCenter URL                        https://10.10.10.5/sdk
username                           root
autovlan                           enabled
allowed-vlans                      1-4094
sessionState                       Connected
lastStateChange                    0:16:29 ago
lastMsgSent                        queryNetworkMsg
timeOfLastMsg                      0:00:00 ago
resonseTimeForLastMsg              0.000116485991839
numSuccessfulMsg                   66
lastSuccessfulMsg                  queryNetworkMsg
lastSuccessfulMsgTime              0:00:00 ago
numFailedMsg                       0
lastFailedMsg                      none
lastFailedMsgTime                  never
lastErrorCode
```

The show vmtracer all command will show the known information from every switch known to vSphere, including virtual switches on the ESX hosts. This command can spit out a lot of information, to the point that I don't use it much in a busy environment. In this example, all four switches have been configured with VM Tracer. As a result, I see them all when executing the command on SW1. This is with two VMs on two ESX hosts with only four switches. Imagine the output from 200 ESX hosts and 50 switches!

```
SW1#sho vmtracer all

Switch : SW1(0.0.0.0)
Ethernet10 : 10.10.10.21/lab-dvSwitch/dvUplink1
    VM Name                VM Adapter          VLAN   Status    State
    VM-A                   Network adapter 2   49     Up/--     --

Switch : SW2(0.0.0.0)
Ethernet10 : 10.10.10.21/lab-dvSwitch/dvUplink2
    VM Name                VM Adapter          VLAN   Status    State
    VM-A                   Network adapter 2   49     Up/--     --
```

```
Switch : SW3(0.0.0.0)
Ethernet10 : 10.10.10.22/lab-dvSwitch/dvUplink1
    VM Name                 VM Adapter          VLAN   Status    State
    VM-B                    Network adapter 2   49     Up/--     --

Switch : SW4(0.0.0.0)
Ethernet10 : 10.10.10.22/lab-dvSwitch/dvUplink2
    VM Name                 VM Adapter          VLAN   Status    State
    VM-B                    Network adapter 2   49     Up/--     --

Switch : testb.local(0.0.0.0)
vmnic2     : 10.10.10.22/vSwitch0/vmnic0
    VM Name                 VM Adapter          VLAN   Status    State
    VM-A                    Network adapter 3   99     Up/--     --
    vCenterApp              Network adapter 1   99     Up/--     --
    VMKernel                vmk0                99     Up/--     --
    VMKernel                vmk0                99     Up/--     --
```

So that's all pretty cool, but let's see how VM Tracer can enable the ESX hosts to make changes to VLANs on the switches. First, let's take a look again at the VLANs on SW4:

```
SW4#sho vlan
VLAN  Name                          Status     Ports
----- ----------------------------- ---------  ----------------------------
1     default                       active     PEt1, Po1, Po10, Po20
49    VLAN0049                      active     PEt1, Po1, Po10, Po20
99    VLAN0099                      active     Cpu, PEt1, Po1, Po10, Po20
4094  VLAN4094                      active     Cpu, Po1
```

Given the current configuration, we don't need to do anything else on the switches. After adding VLANs 32 and 34 to VM-B and attaching them to the virtual switch, SW4 now shows this:

```
SW4#sho vlan
VLAN  Name                          Status     Ports
----- ----------------------------- ---------  ----------------------------
1     default                       active     PEt1, Po1, Po10, Po20
32*   VLAN0032                      active     PEt1, Po1, Po10, Po20
34*   VLAN0034                      active     PEt1, Po1, Po10, Po20
49    VLAN0049                      active     PEt1, Po1, Po10, Po20
99    VLAN0099                      active     Cpu, PEt1, Po1, Po10,
                                               Po20
4094  VLAN4094                      active     Cpu, Po1

* indicates a Dynamic VLAN
```

The switch has dynamically added VLANs 32 and 34, based on what it learned through CDP and vSphere. That's pretty darn cool, but the first thing to understand is that this only happened on the switches directly attached to the ESX host. That means that for VM-B, the VLANs were only added on SW3 and SW4. Sure enough, here's the VLAN table from SW1, where there is no sign of VLANs 32 and 34:

```
SW1#sho vlan
VLAN  Name                                Status    Ports
----- ----------------------------------- --------- --------------------
1     default                             active    Po1, Po20
49    VLAN0049                            active    Po1, Po20
99    VLAN0099                            active    Cpu, Po1, Po20
4094  VLAN4094                            active    Cpu, Po1
```

In order to get VLANs 32 and 34 dynamically created on SW1, we need to add the VLANs and configure them on VM-A. Once this is done, SW1 sees the VLANs and all is well:

```
SW1#sho vlan
VLAN  Name                                Status    Ports
----- ----------------------------------- --------- --------------------
1     default                             active    Po1, Po10, Po20
32*   VLAN0032                            active    Po1, Po10, Po20
34*   VLAN0034                            active    Po1, Po10, Po20
49    VLAN0049                            active    Po1, Po10, Po20
99    VLAN0099                            active    Cpu, Po1, Po10, Po20
4094  VLAN4094                            active    Cpu, Po1

* indicates a Dynamic VLAN
```

There is another point to consider here, and that is the fact that VM Tracer will not add or prune VLANs from interswitch trunks; it only adds or prunes them from trunks attached to ESX hosts configured with the vmtracer vmware-esx command. The reason my example allows end-to-end connectivity is because the link between the two sides (port-channel 20) is set to trunk all VLANs.

Make sure that when you allow VM Tracer to configure VLANs dynamically, that the VLANs it is allowed to create are allowed on any and all trunks connecting the switches together. VM Tracer does not add or prune VLANs from inter-switch trunks!

Going back to the show vmtracer interface command, we can see what VLANs are connected to what VMs on what interface. Here, we can see that interface Po10 (and interface e10 within that port-channel) are seeing that VM-B is using VLANs 32, 34, and 49:

```
SW4#sho vmtracer interface

Port-Channel10 :
 Ethernet10 : 10.10.10.22/lab-dvSwitch/dvUplink2
 PeerEthernet10 : --/--/--
    VM Name                 VM Adapter         VLAN    Status    State
```

```
VM-B               Network adapter 2   49    Up/Up      --
VM-B               Network adapter 3   32    Up/Up      --
VM-B               Network adapter 1   34    Up/Up      --
VMKernel                       vmk1    34    Up/Down    --
```

Next, I've removed VLAN 32 from the ESX VMs connected to SW4. Within seconds of making the change, VM Tracer removes the VLAN:

```
SW4#sho vlan
VLAN  Name                             Status    Ports
----- -------------------------------- --------- -------------------------------
1     default                          active    PEt1, Po1, Po10, Po20
34*   VLAN0034                         active    PEt1, Po1, Po10, Po20
49    VLAN0049                         active    PEt1, Po1, Po10, Po20
99    VLAN0099                         active    Cpu, PEt1, Po1, Po10,
                                                 Po20
4094  VLAN4094                         active    Cpu, Po1

* indicates a Dynamic VLAN
```

This change is also reflected in the output of the show vmtracer interface command on SW4:

```
SW4#sho vmtracer interface

Port-Channel10 :
  Ethernet10 : 10.10.10.22/lab-dvSwitch/dvUplink2
  PeerEthernet10 : --/--/--
    VM Name            VM Adapter          VLAN  Status     State
    VM-B               Network adapter 2   49    Up/Up      --
    VM-B               Network adapter 1   34    Up/Up      --
    VMKernel           vmk1                34    Up/Down    --
```

If allowing VM Tracer to stomp all over your VLANs sounds like a bad idea, I'm with you. Luckily, we can limit the number of VLANs for which VM Tracer is allowed to change. This is done with the allowed-vlan command from within vmtracer mode. You can list VLANs, add or remove them to and/or from an existing range, or remove them all entirely. I'm not sure why you'd want to enable auto-vlan while not giving it any VLANs to use, but I do like options:

```
SW1(config-vmtracer-Lab)#allowed-vlan ?
  WORD    VLAN IDs of the allowed VLANs for the session
  add     Add VLANs to the current list
  all     All VLANs
  except  All VLANs except the following
  none    No VLANs
  remove  Remove VLANs from the current list
```

Configuring this is sort of like configuring trunks allowed on an interface. Let me warn you though, since it's a little bit more dangerous if you're not paying attention.

In our little lab, we've configured VM Tracer such that it has created two VLANs on our switches: VLANs 32 and 34. Here's the VLAN table from SW1 as a reminder:

```
SW1(config-if-Po20)#sho vlan
VLAN  Name                            Status     Ports
----- ------------------------------- ---------- ------------------------------
1     default                         active     PPo10, Po1, Po10, Po20
32*   VLAN0032                        active     PPo10, Po1, Po10, Po20
34*   VLAN0034                        active     PPo10, Po1, Po10, Po20
49    VLAN0049                        active     PPo10, Po1, Po10, Po20
99    VLAN0099                        active     Cpu, PPo10, Po1, Po10,
                                                 Po20
4094  VLAN4094                        active     Cpu, Po1
```

Now let's say that after getting all this working, that I realize my mistake and decide to limit the VLANs that VM Tracer is allowed to create or delete. I'm all about big, even numbers, so I'm going to limit VM Tracer to the range of VLANs inclusive of 100 through 110:

```
SW1(config-vmtracer-Lab)#allowed-vlan 100-110
```

Being a paranoid freak, I immediately check to see if anything bad happened:

```
SW1(config-vmtracer-Lab)#sho vlan
VLAN  Name                            Status     Ports
----- ------------------------------- ---------- ----------------------
1     default                         active     PPo10, Po1, Po10, Po20
32*   VLAN0032                        active     PPo10, Po1, Po10, Po20
34*   VLAN0034                        active     PPo10, Po1, Po10, Po20
49    VLAN0049                        active     PPo10, Po1, Po10, Po20
99    VLAN0099                        active     Cpu, PPo10, Po1, Po10,
                                                 Po20
4094  VLAN4094                        active     Cpu, Po1


* indicates a Dynamic VLAN
```

Looks like I'm in the clear! Now I'll just exit and go on my way:

```
SW1(config-vmtracer-Lab)#exit
```

And here's where my stupidity will save your job. Changes to your VM Tracer session are only applied when you exit the mode. Look at the VLAN table now!

```
SW1(config)#sho vlan
VLAN  Name                            Status     Ports
----- ------------------------------- ---------- ----------------------
1     default                         active     PPo10, Po1, Po10, Po20
49    VLAN0049                        active     PPo10, Po1, Po10, Po20
99    VLAN0099                        active     Cpu, PPo10, Po1, Po10,
                                                 Po20
4094  VLAN4094                        active     Cpu, Po1
```

The two VLANs that were created by VM Tracer are gone because they're no longer within the range of allowed VLANs. Quickly, before the boss notices or all the status screens go red, I'll pop back in and add both of my previously learned VLANs, 32 and 34, to the allowed VLAN range:

```
SW1(config-vmtracer-Lab)#allowed-vlan add 32,34
```

Now let's see if they're back:

```
SW1(config-vmtracer-Lab)#sho vlan
VLAN Name                             Status    Ports
---- -------------------------------- --------- ---------------------
1    default                          active    PPo10, Po1, Po10, Po20
49   VLAN0049                         active    PPo10, Po1, Po10, Po20
99   VLAN0099                         active    Cpu, PPo10, Po1, Po10, Po20
4094 VLAN4094                         active    Cpu, Po1
```

Dammit! Burned again! I need to exit from VM Tracer session mode before my changes will be committed:

```
SW1(config-vmtracer-Lab)#exit
SW1(config)#sho vlan
VLAN Name                             Status    Ports
---- -------------------------------- --------- -------------------------------
1    default                          active    PPo10, Po1, Po10, Po20
32*  VLAN0032                         active    PPo10, Po1, Po10, Po20
34*  VLAN0034                         active    PPo10, Po1, Po10, Po20
49   VLAN0049                         active    PPo10, Po1, Po10, Po20
99   VLAN0099                         active    Cpu, PPo10, Po1, Po10,
                                                Po20
4094 VLAN4094                         active    Cpu, Po1

* indicates a Dynamic VLAN
```

I swear, every time I configure VM Tracer, I fall into this trap. Beware of limiting VLANs after they've been dynamically allocated by VM Tracer, and remember that you must exit VM Tracer session mode before your changes take effect.

CDP Weirdness

When I first put the lab together, I noticed some very strange behavior in both VM Tracer and the VMs themselves. The weirdness caught me off guard, as weirdness often does, but what made me scratch my head was the way in which CDP was behaving.

I always thought that CDP was a link local protocol. In other words, I thought that it was only transmitted from device to device, and was not forwarded through switches. I was wrong.

CDP uses the layer-2 (link layer) broadcast address of 01:00:0c:cc:cc:cc ("c" for Cisco!) to send packets. The least significant digit in the first octet (the first 01 in the address) indicates that this is a multicast packet. Here's output from tcpdump showing a CDP packet being sent by an Arista switch. The CDP packet is in bold.

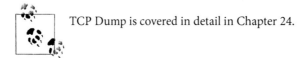

TCP Dump is covered in detail in Chapter 24.

```
[admin@Arista ~]$ tcpdump -i et10
tcpdump: WARNING: et10: no IPv4 address assigned
tcpdump: verbose output suppressed, use -v or -vv for full protocol decode
listening on et10, link-type EN10MB (Ethernet), capture size 65535 bytes

16:29:01.839138 00:1c:73:17:4a:98 (oui Arista Networks) >
01:80:c2:00:00:0e (oui Unknown), ethertype LLDP (0x88cc),
length 175: LLDP, name SW4, length 161

16:29:19.923062 00:1c:73:17:4a:98 (oui Arista Networks) >
01:00:0c:cc:cc:cc (oui Unknown), 802.3, length 81: LLC,
dsap SNAP (0xaa) Individual, ssap SNAP (0xaa) Command,
ctrl 0x03: oui Cisco (0x00000c), pid CDP (0x2000): CDPv2,
ttl: 90s, Device-ID '00:1c:73:17:4a:8e', length 59

16:29:22.711267 2c:27:d7:4a:18:4c (oui Unknown) >
01:80:c2:00:00:0e (oui Unknown), ethertype LLDP (0x88cc), length 148:
[--- output truncated ---]
```

Multicast packets are flooded to all ports in a switch by default, but Cisco devices never forward CDP packets. Since CDP was a proprietary protocol, Cisco bent the rules a bit to have the protocol work the way they desired. As a result, Cisco devices *eat* CDP packets that they receive after processing them.

Details on the operation of CDP can be found in the Cisco document entitled *Cisco Discovery Protocol Configuration Guide*, which is available for your Googling pleasure.

Arista is a very pro open-standards company, and as a result, they follow the rules of multicast to the letter. That means that CDP packets received on one interface will be flooded to all other interfaces on an Arista switch. While that may not seem like a big deal, I've seen it cause some confusing complications in a mixed vendor environment.

In my lab, I've added a single link to a Cisco Nexus switch hanging off of SW4, as shown in Figure 22-2. This Nexus switch is doing nothing, it's just attached to the lab network, and it's not participating in any way other than by injecting CDP packets.

Because CDP is being forwarded by the Arista switches, VMware sees the Nexus switch as being directly attached. This is shown in the vSphere screen capture shown in Figure 22-3. Even though VM-B is directly connected to the Arista switches SW3 and SW4, VMware thinks that it's attached to the Nexus switch NX-SW2.

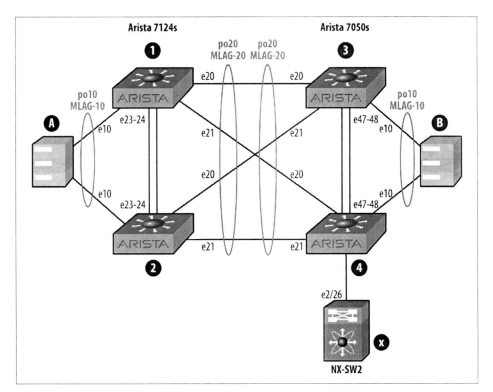

Figure 22-2. VM Tracer lab with Cisco switch added

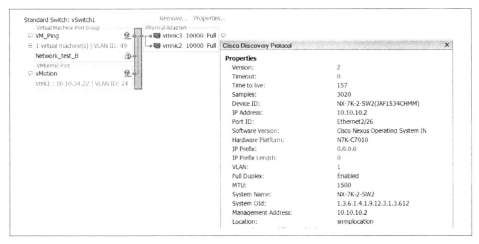

Figure 22-3. VMware seeing the Nexus switch through the Arista switch

This is a problem because it's confusing, but it get's worse. Since VMware is confused, it sends incorrect information to VM Tracer as well. With this topology, the output of show vmtracer all now shows a mess of incorrect and confusing information about VMs on both ESX hosts being attached to the single interface on the Cisco Nexus switch:

```
SW4#sho vmtracer all

Switch : NX-SW2(10.10.10.2)
Ethernet2/26 : 10.10.10.22/vSwitch0/vmnic0
    VM Name                 VM Adapter              VLAN    Status      State
    VM-A                    Network adapter 3       99      Up/--       --
    vCenterApp              Network adapter 1       99      Up/--       --
    VMKernel                vmk0                    99      Up/--       --
    VMKernel                vmk0                    99      Up/--       --
    VM-B                    Network adapter 2       49      Up/--       --
    VM-A                    Network adapter 2       49      Up/--       --
    VM-B                    Network adapter 3       32      Up/--       --
    VM-A                    Network adapter 4       32      Up/--       --
    VMKernel                vmk1                    34      Up/--       --
    VM-B                    Network adapter 1       34      Up/--       --
    VMKernel                vmk1                    34      Up/--       --
    VM-A                    Network adapter 1       34      Up/--       --
[--- output truncated ---]
```

Since CDP packets are sent every 60 seconds, I've seen this type of environment cause VMware and VM Tracer to flip flop between accurate information and incorrect information. It seems that VMware believes the last CDP packet it receives. Believe me when I say that this can be very frustrating when you're trying to make sense of it all.

The simplest way to prevent this from happening is to disable CDP on the Cisco device on the interface attached to the Arista switches. Here, I've disabled CDP on the Cisco interface attached to SW4:

```
NX-SW2(config)# int e2/26
NX-SW2(config-if)# no cdp enable
```

Within a minute or so, VMware and VM Tracer settle down and the output of show vmtracer all looks much more like the actual topology of the network:

```
SW4#sho vmtracer all

Switch : SW1(0.0.0.0)
Ethernet10 : 10.10.10.21/lab-dvSwitch/dvUplink1
    VM Name         VM Adapter          VLAN    Status      State
    VM-A            Network adapter 2   49      Up/--       --
    VM-A            Network adapter 4   32      Up/--       --
    VMKernel        vmk1                34      Up/--       --
    VM-A            Network adapter 1   34      Up/--       --

Switch : SW2(0.0.0.0)
Ethernet10 : 10.10.10.21/lab-dvSwitch/dvUplink2
```

```
VM Name          VM Adapter          VLAN   Status   State
VM-A             Network adapter 2   49     Up/--    --
VM-A             Network adapter 4   32     Up/--    --
VMKernel         vmk1                34     Up/--    --
VM-A             Network adapter 1   34     Up/--    --

Switch : SW3(0.0.0.0)
Ethernet10 : 10.10.10.22/lab-dvSwitch/dvUplink1
VM Name          VM Adapter          VLAN   Status   State
VM-B             Network adapter 2   49     Up/--    --
VM-B             Network adapter 3   32     Up/--    --
VM-B             Network adapter 1   34     Up/--    --
VMKernel         vmk1                34     Up/--    --

Switch : SW4(0.0.0.0)
Ethernet10 : 10.10.10.22/lab-dvSwitch/dvUplink2
VM Name          VM Adapter          VLAN   Status   State
VM-B             Network adapter 2   49     Up/--    --
VM-B             Network adapter 3   32     Up/--    --
VM-B             Network adapter 1   34     Up/--    --
VMKernel         vmk1                34     Up/--    --
```

As a general rule, disable CDP on your Cisco device interfaces that attach to Arista switches. Not only do we not need to see the CDP packets, but they can also cause havoc with features like VM Tracer since they will be flooded out every switch port. Enable LLDP on your Cisco devices if you'd like to see neighbors. See Chapter 8 for details on how to do this.

VM Tracer can be a very powerful tool if it fits your needs. I know many a network manager that refused to enable the *autovlan* feature because they don't like VLANs being configured without human oversight. And I know many others that love it for the same reason. I, for one, love having the option.

## CHAPTER 23

Scheduler

I was working in a data center, building out an Arista network, when I decided that I wanted to automate a command that should run every five minutes. Knowing that these super cool Arista switches run Linux, I dropped into bash and proceeded to muck around with *cron*. I couldn't get it to work, got frustrated, and called my Arista sales engineer who asked, "Why not just use schedule?"

Schedule is a feature introduced in EOS 4.8 that allows the regular scheduling of commands. The cool part of this feature is that it's completely configured from CLI. Let's take a look at this powerful tool.

The schedule command is the root of just about everything we're going to do in this chapter. It's simple to use, and the question mark along with tab completion will get you most of what you want to know about its function:

```
Arista(config)#schedule ?
  WORD  Scheduled job name
```

To create a scheduled job, you must first specify a name for the job. Since I'm the writer, I'll use the name GAD for my job:

```
Arista(config)#schedule GAD ?
  interval  Set interval for CLI command execution
```

The interval is the amount of time in minutes to wait between each iteration of the job. If you want the job to run every five minutes, the interval would be five. In version 4.9.3, acceptable values range from 1 to 1,440:

```
Arista(config)#schedule GAD interval ?
  <1-1440>  Interval in minutes for CLI command execution
```

The next thing I need to specify is the maximum number of logfiles that will be retained. Every time my job runs, it will create output. That output is saved to a logfile that we'll see in a bit. If the job runs every minute, for the next year, the job would produce a half-million log entries. Chances are, I'd only want to see the last 100 or so, so I'll specify `max-log-files 100`, after which the switch will only save the last 100 log entries. The range of acceptable values is inclusive from 1 to 10,000:

```
Arista(config)#schedule GAD interval 5 max-log-files ?
  <1-10000>  Number of logfiles to be stored
```

Finally, we must include the word `command`, followed by the command to be run:

```
Arista(config)#schedule GAD interval 5 max-log-files 100 command
sho int e24
Arista(config)#
```

Note that the parser does not check the validity of the commands entered with the `schedule` command. The command `schedule mistake int 1 max 10 command ILikeCake` will be accepted without complaint, but the job will never run, and you'll never see an error message, or get any cake. If you see *No log files are stored in flash* when you show the job, check to see if your command is entered correctly. There is no indication as to whether the cake is a lie, so don't bother asking.

With the job now entered, nothing obvious happens. That's pretty anticlimactic, but rest assured that good things are happening (assuming you entered a valid command). To see what jobs have been scheduled on the switch, use the `show schedule summary` command. Note that the word summary must be spelled in its entirety, lest it be confused with the name of a scheduled job:

```
Arista#sho schedule summary
Name            Last    Interval  Max     Log file location
                time    (mins)    log
                                  files
--------------- ------  --------- ------- ------------------------------
gad             18:14   5         100     flash:/schedule/gad
tech-support    18:07   60        100     flash:/schedule/tech-support
```

Schedules may be entered with capital letters, but the parser will convert them to all lowercase. For a writer who expects to see his initials in all caps, this is frustrating, but generally harmless.

To see the specifics of a scheduled job, use the `show schedule` *job-name* command. This will show the command scheduled, the details of the schedule limitations as configured, and information regarding the logfiles generated as a result of this job. As we can see in this example, my job has run three times:

```
Arista(config)#sho schedule gad
CLI command "sho int e24" is scheduled, interval is 5 minutes
```

```
Maximum of 100 log files will be stored
3 log files currently stored in flash:/schedule/gad

Start time              Size              Filename
--------------------    ----------------  ---------------------------
May 16 2012 18:14       403.0 bytes       gad_2012-05-16.1814.log.gz
May 16 2012 17:49       608.0 bytes       gad_2012-05-16.1749.log.gz
May 16 2012 17:49       608.0 bytes       gad_2012-05-16.1749.log.gz
```

Remember how I said that getting my initials converted to lowercase was mostly harmless? Here's why I used the word, "mostly." If I decide to delete my job, I would do so with the no schedule *job-name* command; only, when I use my initials in all caps, like I do by habit, the command is taken but nothing happens:

```
Arista(config)#no schedule GAD
Arista(config)#
```

When I use show schedule summary to make sure my job is gone, it's still there!

```
Arista(config)#sho schedule summary
Name            Last   Interval  Max   Log file location
                time   (mins)    log
                                 files
--------------  ------ --------- ------- ---------------------------
gad             18:14      5     100   flash:/schedule/gad
tech-support    18:07     60     100   flash:/schedule/tech-support
```

I have to delete it using all lowercase letters. I hate having to conform, but I've chosen to let these types of battles go at the recommendation of my therapist:

```
Arista(config)#no schedule gad
Arista(config)#
Arista(config)#sho schedule summary
Name            Last   Interval  Max   Log file location
                time   (mins)    log
                                 files
--------------  ------ --------- ------- ---------------------------
tech-support    18:07     60     100   flash:/schedule/tech-support
```

 When you delete a scheduled job, the logfiles remain. Since these logfiles are on flash, they persist after a reboot.

By the way, if you're the type who needs to try and create a job entitled *summary* because summary is a reserved word, let me save you the trouble and show you what happens. First, I'll create the job:

```
Arista(config)#schedule summary int 5 max 1 command sho int e1
```

The switch takes this command without complaint. The problem is, there is no way for me to see the detail of my job! When I issue the show schedule summary command, I get a summary list of all jobs:

```
Arista(config)#sho schedule summary
Name            Last    Interval  Max     Log file location
                time    (mins)    log
                                  files

--------------- ------  --------- ------- ----------------------------
summary         18:17      5      100     flash:/schedule/summary
tech-support    18:07      60     100     flash:/schedule/tech-support
```

Luckily, I can delete it with ease.

```
Arista(config)#no schedule summary
```

You may have noticed that there is a job in each example named *tech-support*. This job is installed by Arista, and runs on all switches by default. Though it can be removed, there's generally no reason to do so. I'm sure you're as curious as I was to see what this job is doing, so let's take a look, because it's an excellent example of how schedule can be used.

First, let's use the show schedule tech-support command:

```
Arista(config)#sho schedule tech-support
CLI command "show tech-support" is scheduled, interval is 60 minutes
Maximum of 100 log files will be stored
100 log files currently stored in flash:/schedule/tech-support

Start time             Size      Filename
-------------------    --------- ------------------------------------------
May 16 2012 18:07      17.9 KB   tech-support_2012-05-16.1807.log.gz
May 16 2012 16:50      17.7 KB   tech-support_2012-05-16.1650.log.gz
May 16 2012 15:50      17.7 KB   tech-support_2012-05-16.1550.log.gz
May 16 2012 14:50      17.8 KB   tech-support_2012-05-16.1450.log.gz
May 16 2012 13:50      17.7 KB   tech-support_2012-05-16.1350.log.gz
[--- output truncated ---]
```

As we can see in the second line, this scheduled job performs a show tech-support command once every hour. Take a look at the output of the third line down (in bold). It says that there are 100 logfiles currently stored in *flash:/schedule/tech-support*. It then goes on to list them. So how can we see what's in these logfiles? With bash, of course.

To see the logfiles, drop into bash and change directories to the */mnt/flash/schedule* directory:

```
Arista#bash

Arista Networks EOS shell

[admin@Arista flash]$ cd /mnt/flash/schedule
[admin@Arista schedule]$
```

Within this directory, you'll find a directory for every schedule job that's ever run:

```
[admin@Arista schedule]$ ls -al
total 36
drwxrwx--- 6 root eosadmin  4096 May 16 18:18 .
drwxrwx--- 6 root eosadmin  4096 Dec 31  1969 ..
drwxrwx--- 2 root eosadmin  4096 May 16 18:25 gad
drwxrwx--- 2 root eosadmin  4096 May 16 12:14 gad2
drwxrwx--- 2 root eosadmin  4096 May 16 18:28 summary
drwxrwx--- 2 root eosadmin 16384 May 16 18:07 tech-support
```

We can see that there's a directory for my gad job, another for gad2, one for our summary test, and one for the tech-support job. Changing into the tech-support directory will let us see the logs for the tech-support job:

```
[admin@Arista tech-support]$ ls
tech-support_2012-05-12.1954.log.gz
tech-support_2012-05-14.1850.log.gz
tech-support_2012-05-12.2009.log.gz
tech-support_2012-05-14.1904.log.gz
tech-support_2012-05-12.2050.log.gz
tech-support_2012-05-14.1950.log.gz
tech-support_2012-05-12.2150.log.gz
tech-support_2012-05-14.2034.log.gz
tech-support_2012-05-12.2250.log.gz
tech-support_2012-05-14.2050.log.gz
tech-support_2012-05-12.2350.log.gz
[--- output truncated ---]
```

Since the tech-support job is configured to keep the last 100 log entries, there are 100 files in this directory, each with the date and timestamp in the filename. The files are all in the *gzip* format. To view them, use the zcat Linux command from bash. You can also use gunzip, but that will expand the file on disk, which is a waste of space when we just want to look at the contents for no other reason than to see what's there:

```
[admin@Arista tech-support]$ zcat tech-support_2012-05-12.1954.log.gz

------------ show version detail ------------

Arista DCS-7124S-F
Hardware version:     06.02
Deviations:           D0000213, D0000203
Serial number:        JSH10170315
System MAC address:   001c.7308.80ae

Software image version: 4.8.1
Architecture:           i386
Internal build version: 4.8.1-495947.2011eric481Showstopper
Internal build ID:      b15379fb-13e9-4255-819f-e55dde3c3471

Uptime:               5 minutes
Total memory:         2043424 kB
```

```
Free memory:              896408 kB

Installed software packages:
[--- output truncated ---]
```

The switch has done a show tech-support command every hour since the switch booted. There are 100 files in this directory, which represents the state of the switch in hourly intervals for the past 100 hours. That's 4.166 days for the mathematically challenged. Had a problem yesterday and want to see the status of the switch? It was saved in these files. Think that's cool and would like to see it save the last 1,000 hours? Just go in and resubmit the tech-support job the way you'd like.

Schedule is cool and all, but what if you want to run more than one command? Not only can the schedule command run CLI commands, but it can run bash commands through the use of the bash CLI command. Here I've created a script in */mnt/flash* called GAD. I used all caps because it makes me feel like I've won my earlier battle and to show that caps can be used as a reference in the command, even if they can't be used in the schedule job name.

The file looks like this:

```
[admin@Arista flash]$ cat GAD
#!/usr/bin/Cli

sho ver | grep version | email -s "Show Version" gad@gad.net
sho int e24 | email -s "Show int e24" gad@gad.net
```

> See Chapter 19 for details on configuring and using the email command.

Next, back in EOS, I'll create the schedule that calls this script:

```
Arista(config)#schedule dog int 1 max 10 command bash /mnt/flash/GAD
```

And now, every minute, I get two emails showing the requested output. Trust me when I say that this gets old quickly:

```
+ N 2665 May 16  7:16pm Arista@gad.net    (943) Show Version
+ N 2666 May 16  7:16pm Arista@gad.net    (2K) Show int e24
+ N 2667 May 16  7:17pm Arista@gad.net    (943) Show Version
+ N 2668 May 16  7:17pm Arista@gad.net    (2K) Show int e24
+ N 2669 May 16  7:18pm Arista@gad.net    (943) Show Version
+ N 2670 May 16  7:18pm Arista@gad.net    (2K) Show int e24
```

Imagine that you're having a problem, and you'd like to see what the running processes are on your switch every five minutes. Maybe you're convinced that you've got a runaway process on your switch and you want to see for yourself. The Linux command ps-ef r will show the running processes:

```
[admin@Arista ~]$ ps -ef r
UID          PID  PPID  C STIME TTY       STAT    TIME CMD
root        1454  1453  3 18:02 ?         R       2:42 Sysdb
root        1827  1453  6 18:03 ?         R       4:54 Mdio
admin       4058  3923 13 19:24 pts/2     R+      0:00 ps -ef r
```

I can schedule a job to email me that information every five minutes. The schedule command I would use would look like this:

```
Arista(config)#schedule proc interval 5 max-log-files 1 command bash
ps -ef r | email -s "Running Procs" gad@gad.net
```

There in my email, every five minutes, is a list of the running processes on my switch:

```
Date: Wed, 16 May 2012 19:27:35
From: Arista@gad.net
To: gad@gad.net
Subject: Running Procs

UID          PID  PPID  C STIME TTY       STAT    TIME CMD
root        4143  4142 14 19:27 ?         R       0:00 ps -ef r
root        4144  4142 15 19:27 ?         R       0:00 python /usr/bin/
 email -s Running Procs gad@gad.net
```

## CHAPTER 24

TCP Dump

TCP dump is an open source packet capture and analyzer tool that's been around since the late 1980s. TCP dump is useful because it allows pretty powerful packet capture sessions from the command line. Even better, you can use it from either bash or CLI. Let's take a look. First I'll show you how it works from within bash, and then I'll show you what it's like from within EOS.

> TCP dump will only capture packets destined to or sourced from the CPU. It will not capture data plane traffic because the CPU couldn't possibly keep up with it all. There are ways to combine *tcpdump* with *sflow* to capture some data plane traffic, but you'll have to wait for the second edition to see that.

Unix

If you've got Unix experience and already know how to use TCP dump, you might feel more at home using it from bash. To do so, just drop into bash and have at it:

```
Arista#bash

Arista Networks EOS shell

[admin@Arista ~]$ tcpdump -help
tcpdump version 4.2.1
libpcap version 1.1.1
Usage: tcpdump [-aAbdDefhHIKlLnNOpqRStuUvxX] [ -B size ] [ -c count ]
                [ -C file_size ] [ -E algo:secret ] [ -F file ]
                [ -G seconds ]
```

```
[ -i interface ] [ -M secret ]
[ -r file ] [ -s snaplen ] [ -T type ] [ -w file ]
[ -W filecount ] [ -y datalinktype ] [ -z command ]
[ -Z user ] [ -@ file_index ] [ expression ]
```

 In early editions of EOS, tcpdump needed to be run from root. Arista has since modified it to automatically run sudo tcpdump whenever tcpdump is entered.

In its simplest form, TCP dump will display packet information for an interface specified with the -i flag. The thing to remember is that TCP dump is a Unix command and, as such, is looking for Unix interface names, not EOS interface names. This gets me every time I use it. I can be stubbornly stupid sometimes, or so my wife tells me:

```
[admin@Arista ~]$ tcpdump -i e10
tcpdump: e10: No such device exists
(SIOCGIFHWADDR: No such device)
```

Oops—that's not right!

```
[admin@Arista ~]$ tcpdump -i Ethernet10
tcpdump: Ethernet10: No such device exists
(SIOCGIFHWADDR: No such device)
```

Dammit! I swear I go through this every time I try to use TCP dump on an Arista switch, thus proving my wife right, which only enrages me more. An easy way to see the interface names from within the bash shell is with the ifconfig command. Supplying the -s flag will provide a summary list of the interfaces with a bunch of counters. Note that this command puts out a lot of information that extended beyond the end of the page, so I've truncated the last two columns. We don't need them for this exercise anyway since we're only looking for a list of interface names:

```
[admin@Arista ~]$ ifconfig -s
Iface   MTU Met   RX-OK RX-ERR RX-DRP RX-OVR   TX-OK TX-ERR TX-DRP
cpu    9216  0      0      0      0      0       0      0      0
et1    9212  0      0      0      0      0       0      0      0
et2    9212  0      0      0      0      0       0      0      0
et3    9212  0      0      0      0      0       0      0      0
et4    9212  0      0      0      0      0       0      0      0
et5    9212  0      0      0      0      0       0      0      0
et6    9212  0      0      0      0      0       0      0      0
et7    9212  0      0      0      0      0       0      0      0
et8    9212  0      0      0      0      0       0      0      0
et9    9212  0      0      0      0      0       0      0      0
et10   1500  0    1889      0      0      0    1889      0
et11   1500  0    1889      0      0      0    1889      0
[--- output truncated ---]
```

Ah yes! The interfaces are named such that interface *Ethernet10* in EOS is called *et10* in bash. And remember, you cannot abbreviate interface names in Unix like you can in EOS.

 Technically, the interface names are the *CLI shortnames*, in all lowercase. On modular systems, or systems with QSFP+ interfaces, the slashes in the interface names are replaced with underscores.

Let's try TCP dump again using the proper name format:

```
[admin@Arista ~]$ tcpdump -i et10
tcpdump: WARNING: et10: no IPv4 address assigned
tcpdump: verbose output suppressed, use -v or -vv for full protocol
decode listening on et10, link-type EN10MB (Ethernet), capture size
65535 bytes
18:24:06.850603 00:1c:73:08:80:b9 (oui Arista Networks) >
01:80:c2:00:00:0e (oui Unknown), ethertype LLDP (0x88cc), length 172:
LLDP, name Arista, length 158
18:24:06.850647 00:1c:73:08:80:b8 (oui Arista Networks) >
01:80:c2:00:00:0e (oui Unknown), ethertype LLDP (0x88cc), length 172:
LLDP, name Arista, length 158
18:30:06.879720 00:1c:73:08:80:b8 (oui Arista Networks) >
01:80:c2:00:00:0e (oui Unknown), ethertype LLDP (0x88cc), length 172:
LLDP, name Arista, length 158
[--- output truncated ---]
```

Cool, but boring. Let's take a look at the management interface:

```
[admin@Arista ~]$ tcpdump -i ma1
tcpdump: verbose output suppressed, use -v or -vv for full protocol
decode
listening on ma1, link-type EN10MB (Ethernet), capture size 65535
bytes
18:35:43.154885 00:1c:b0:84:cf:99 (oui Unknown) > 01:80:c2:00:00:00
(oui Unknown), 802.3, length 119: LLC, dsap STP (0x42) Individual,
ssap STP (0x42) Command, ctrl 0x03: STP 802.1s, Rapid STP, CIST Flags
[Learn, Forward, Agreement]
18:35:44.321707 00:1c:b0:84:cf:99 (oui Unknown) > 01:00:0c:cc:cc:cc
(oui Unknown), 802.3, length 60: LLC, dsap SNAP (0xaa) Individual,
ssap SNAP (0xaa) Command, ctrl 0x03: oui Cisco (0x00000c), pid DTP
(0x2004): DTPv1, length 38
18:35:44.321797 00:1c:b0:84:cf:99 (oui Unknown) > 01:00:0c:00:00:00
(oui Unknown), 802.3, length 90: LLC, dsap SNAP (0xaa) Individual,
ssap SNAP (0xaa) Command, ctrl 0x03: oui Cisco (0x00000c), pid Unknown
(0x0003): 00:1c:b0:84:cf:99 (oui Unknown) 01:00:0c:cc:cc:cc (oui
Unknown) 66:
        0x0000: 0029 aaaa 0300 000c 2004 0100 0100 0c47  .)............G
        0x0010: 4144 2d4c 6162 0000 0200 0504 0003 0005  AD-Lab.........
        0x0020: 4000 0400 0a00 1cb0 84cf 990f 0000 0040  @..............@
        0x0030: 0c89 2fce                                 ../.
```

```
18:35:45.182923 00:1c:b0:84:cf:99 (oui Unknown) > 01:80:c2:00:00:00
(oui Unknown), 802.3, length 119: LLC, dsap STP (0x42) Individual,
ssap STP (0x42) Command, ctrl 0x03: STP 802.1s, Rapid STP, CIST Flags
[Learn, Forward, Agreement]
[--- output truncated ---]
```

Wow, that sure does dump a lot of information, and this switch isn't even doing anything!
Let's generate some background ping packets and see what happens:

```
[admin@Arista ~]$ ping -c 10000 192.168.1.1 > /dev/null  &
[1] 16081

[admin@Arista ~]$ tcpdump -i ma1
tcpdump: verbose output suppressed, use -v or -vv for full protocol decode
listening on ma1, link-type EN10MB (Ethernet), capture size 65535 bytes
18:38:39.968712 00:1c:73:08:80:ac (oui Arista Networks) >
00:14:6a:a2:d4:38 (oui Unknown), ethertype IPv4 (0x0800), length 98:
192.168.1.170 > pix.gad.net: ICMP echo request, id 16081, seq 31, length 64
18:38:39.969643 00:1c:73:08:80:ac (oui Arista Networks) >
00:02:55:b7:da:9d (oui Unknown), ethertype IPv4 (0x0800), length 84:
    192.168.1.170.34858 > cozy.gad.net.domain: 23521+ PTR?
1.1.168.192.in-addr.arpa. (42)
18:38:39.970000 00:02:55:b7:da:9d (oui Unknown) > 00:1c:73:08:80:ac
(oui Arista Networks), ethertype IPv4 (0x0800), length 137:
cozy.gad.net.domain > 192.168.1.170.34858: 23521* 1/1/0 PTR
pix.gad.net. (95)
[--- output truncated ---]
```

Of course, I can pipe the output to other commands because I'm a Unix guru (hardly).
Here, I've filtered the output with grep so that I only see packets containing the string
"STP". Use Control-C to break out of TCP dump:

```
[admin@Arista ~]$ tcpdump -i ma1 | grep STP
tcpdump: verbose output suppressed, use -v or -vv for full protocol decode
listening on ma1, link-type EN10MB (Ethernet), capture size 65535 bytes
18:41:22.737781 00:1c:b0:84:cf:99 (oui Unknown) > 01:80:c2:00:00:00
(oui Unknown), 802.3, length 119: LLC, dsap STP (0x42) Individual,
ssap STP (0x42) Command, ctrl 0x03: STP 802.1s, Rapid STP, CIST Flags
 [Learn, Forward, Agreement]
18:41:24.780377 00:1c:b0:84:cf:99 (oui Unknown) > 01:80:c2:00:00:00
(oui Unknown), 802.3, length 119: LLC, dsap STP (0x42) Individual,
ssap STP (0x42) Command, ctrl 0x03: STP 802.1s, Rapid STP, CIST Flags
[Learn, Forward, Agreement]
18:41:26.805998 00:1c:b0:84:cf:99 (oui Unknown) > 01:80:c2:00:00:00
(oui Unknown), 802.3, length 119: LLC, dsap STP (0x42) Individual,
ssap STP (0x42) Command, ctrl 0x03: STP 802.1s, Rapid STP, CIST Flags
[Learn, Forward, Agreement]
18:41:28.846644 00:1c:b0:84:cf:99 (oui Unknown) > 01:80:c2:00:00:00
(oui Unknown), 802.3, length 119: LLC, dsap STP (0x42) Individual,
ssap STP (0x42) Command, ctrl 0x03: STP 802.1s, Rapid STP, CIST Flags
[Learn, Forward, Agreement]
```

```
^C
62 packets captured
62 packets received by filter
0 packets dropped by kernel
```

Since TCP dump often creates a lot of output, it's usually best to dump it to a file for later enjoyment. With typical Unix style, I'll just redirect the output to the file, *STP.capture* in the */mnt/flash/* directory. Use Control-C to exit the capture:

```
[admin@Arista flash]$ tcpdump -i ma1 > /mnt/flash/GAD.capture
tcpdump: verbose output suppressed, use -v or -vv for full protocol
decode
listening on ma1, link-type EN10MB (Ethernet), capture size 65535
bytes
^C
38 packets captured
38 packets received by filter
0 packets dropped by kernel
```

Really, though, it's better to let TCP dump handle the file creation itself using the –w flag:

```
[admin@Arista ~]$ tcpdump -w /mnt/flash/GAD.capture -i ma1
tcpdump: listening on ma1, link-type EN10MB (Ethernet), capture size
65535 bytes
^C
18 packets captured
18 packets received by filter
0 packets dropped by kernel
```

The file can now be viewed as you might view any text file:

```
[admin@Arista flash]$ more /mnt/flash/GAD.capture
18:50:12.820928 00:1c:73:08:80:ac (oui Arista Networks) >
00:14:6a:a2:d4:38 (oui Unknown), ethertype IPv4 (0x0800), length 98:
192.168.1.170 > pix.gad.net: ICMP
 echo request, id 16081, seq 723, length 64
18:50:12.821879 00:1c:73:08:80:ac (oui Arista Networks) >
00:02:55:b7:da:9d (oui Unknown), ethertype IPv4 (0x0800),
    length 84: 192.168.1.170.41131 > cozy.gad.net.domain: 20193+ PTR?
1.1.168.192.in-addr.arpa. (42)
18:50:12.822085 00:14:6a:a2:d4:38 (oui Unknown) >
00:1c:73:08:80:ac (oui Arista Networks), ethertype IPv4 (0x0800),
length 98: pix.gad.net > 192.168.1.170: ICMP
 echo reply, id 16081, seq 723, length 64
```

Now that we're dumping output to a file, we could even grab more information from each packet. To do so, use the –v option.

I'm not going to go any deeper into the Unix side of TCP dump right now because this isn't a Unix book. Let's take a look at how these features are implemented in EOS.

EOS

TCP dump from within EOS is pretty similar, but we don't have to use all those Unix-looking flags like -i. Instead, we just use keywords. Here's a list from using the ? character with tcpdump:

```
Arista#tcpdump ?
  file            Set the output file
  filecount       Specify the number of output files
  filter          Set the filtering expression
  interface       Select an interface to monitor
  max-file-size   Specify the maximum size of output file
  packet-count    Limit number of packets to capture
  session         Define the name of a session
  size            Set the maximum number of bytes to dump per packet
  <cr>
```

I will warn you that although TCP dump is friendlier in EOS, it's just a pretty façade. The nice keywords just map to Unix flags, so you still can't use EOS interface names. Here, I've specified an invalid Unix interface name that happens to be a valid EOS interface abbreviation. Note the last two lines that show what bash command my EOS command translated to:

```
Arista#tcpdump int e10
tcpdump: e10: No such device exists
(SIOCGIFHWADDR: No such device)
Starting tcpdump process with command:
" tcpdump -i e10 "
```

Since I have to use Unix-formatted interface names, I'll try again with what I learned from the output of ifconfig -s from earlier in this chapter. Control-C still breaks out of TCP dump in EOS:

```
Arista#tcpdump int et10
tcpdump: WARNING: et10: no IPv4 address assigned
tcpdump: verbose output suppressed, use -v or -vv for full protocol
decode listening on et10, link-type EN10MB (Ethernet), capture size
65535 bytes
19:14:37.058073 00:1c:73:08:80:b9 (oui Arista Networks) >
01:80:c2:00:00:0e (oui Unknown), ethertype LLDP (0x88cc), length 172:
LLDP, name Arista, length 158
19:14:37.058116 00:1c:73:08:80:b8 (oui Arista Networks) >
01:80:c2:00:00:0e (oui Unknown), ethertype LLDP (0x88cc), length 172:
LLDP, name Arista, length 158
^C
2 packets captured
2 packets received by filter
0 packets dropped by kernel
Starting tcpdump process with command:
" tcpdump -i et10 "
```

Though the help from within EOS doesn't show this, you can still specify some (but not all) Unix command-line flags as you would from within bash:

```
Arista#tcpdump -i et10
tcpdump: WARNING: et10: no IPv4 address assigned
tcpdump: verbose output suppressed, use -v or -vv for full protocol
decode
listening on et10, link-type EN10MB (Ethernet), capture size 65535
bytes
19:16:07.065892 00:1c:73:08:80:b9 (oui Arista Networks) >
01:80:c2:00:00:0e (oui Unknown), ethertype LLDP (0x88cc), length 172:
LLDP, name Arista, length 158
19:16:07.065975 00:1c:73:08:80:b8 (oui Arista Networks) >
01:80:c2:00:00:0e (oui Unknown), ethertype LLDP (0x88cc), length 172:
LLDP, name Arista, length 158
^C
2 packets captured
2 packets received by filter
0 packets dropped by kernel
Starting tcpdump process with command:
" tcpdump -i et10 "
```

Because tcpdump in EOS maps to tcpdump in bash, there can be some weirdness when specifying file locations. From EOS, I might want to send the output to *flash:EOS.capture*, which is a perfectly acceptable location. Unfortunately, when the command gets translated to its Unix format, it doesn't translate the idea of the *flash:* drive from EOS. As a result, the output gets dumped to a file named, literally, *flash:EOS.capture* in my home directory. Let's take a look. Here, I'll tell TCP dump to capture from the *management1* interface and dump it to *flash:EOS.capture*:

```
Arista#tcpdump int ma1 file flash:EOS.capture
tcpdump: listening on ma1, link-type EN10MB (Ethernet), capture size
65535 bytes
^C
21 packets captured
21 packets received by filter
0 packets dropped by kernel
Starting tcpdump process with command:
" tcpdump -w flash:EOS.capture -i ma1 "
```

Look at the command shown on the last line. Looks OK from an EOS perspective, but from bash, this doesn't mean "put the file named *EOS.capture* on the *flash:* drive." It means "put the file named *flash:EOS.capture* in the current directory." Sure enough, looking in the *flash:* location from within EOS shows no such file (though the *GAD.capture* file from earlier is there):

```
Arista#dir
Directory of flash:/

        -rwx   248665992        May 23 02:16  EOS-4.9.3.swi
        -rwx        2230        May 23 19:24  GAD.capture
```

```
        -rwx        7792             May 23 18:48   STP.capture
        -rwx         137             May 23 02:32   boot-config
        drwx        4096             May 23 02:34   debug
        drwx        4096             May 23 02:33   persist
        drwx        4096             May 16 19:27   schedule
        -rwx        1415             May 23 02:13   startup-config
        -rwx           0             May 14 16:46   zerotouch-config

    1862512640 bytes total (8810496 bytes free)
```

If I drop down into bash and look in the default directory (my user home directory), I see the file:

```
Arista#bash

Arista Networks EOS shell

[admin@SW4 ~]$ pwd
/home/admin
[admin@Arista ~]$ ls -l
total 4
-rw-rw-rw- 1 admin eosadmin 2422 May 23 19:18 flash:EOS.capture
```

This behavior is exactly what TCP dump would do in Unix if I specified the command shown previously that used the flag -w followed by *flash:EOS.capture*, since Unix has no concept of a *flash:* device.

 The moral of the story is to always use Unix file paths with TCP dump, even from within EOS.

Using a Unix-style file path solves this problem handily:

```
Arista#tcpdump int ma1 file /mnt/flash/EOS.capture
tcpdump: listening on ma1, link-type EN10MB (Ethernet), capture size
65535 bytes
^C
26 packets captured
26 packets received by filter
0 packets dropped by kernel
Starting tcpdump process with command:
" tcpdump -w /mnt/flash/EOS.capture -i ma1 "
```

Now a dir command from EOS shows my file in *flash:*

```
Arista#dir
Directory of flash:/

        -rwx   248665992             May 23 02:16   EOS-4.9.3.swi
        -rwx        3013             May 23 19:32   EOS.capture
        -rwx        2230             May 23 19:24   GAD.capture
        -rwx        7792             May 23 18:48   STP.capture
```

```
-rwx          137        May 23 02:32  boot-config
drwx         4096        May 23 02:34  debug
drwx         4096        May 23 02:33  persist
drwx         4096        May 16 19:27  schedule
-rwx         1415        May 23 02:13  startup-config
-rwx            0        May 14 16:46  zerotouch-config

1862512640 bytes total (8806400 bytes free)
```

 TCP dump files can be very large, and a lot of testing can litter directories with these files. Please get in the habit of removing TCP dump output files that you no longer need. There's a finite amount of *flash*, and it fills a lot more quickly than most people realize.

Of course, you can also capture the packets traversing VLAN interfaces. Here, I'll capture packets on the MALG interface (VLAN 4094):

```
Arista#tcpdump int vlan4094
tcpdump: verbose output suppressed, use -v or -vv for full protocol decode
listening on vlan4094, link-type EN10MB (Ethernet), capture size 65535 bytes
22:44:27.554755 00:1c:73:17:4a:8e (oui Arista Networks) >
00:1c:73:17:5d:a2 (oui Arista Networks), ethertype IPv4 (0x0800),
length 97: 10.0.0.2.4432 > 10.0.0.1.4432: UDP, length 55
22:44:27.554784 00:1c:73:17:4a:8e (oui Arista Networks) >
00:1c:73:17:5d:a2 (oui Arista Networks), ethertype IPv4 (0x0800),
length 99: 10.0.0.2.4432 > 10.0.0.1.34467: Flags [P.], seq
3108183801:3108183834, ack 4279832075, win 89, options [nop,nop,TS val
42882629 ecr 38856952], length 33
22:44:27.554889 00:1c:73:17:5d:a2 (oui Arista Networks) >
00:1c:73:17:4a:8e (oui Arista Networks), ethertype IPv4 (0x0800),
length 66: 10.0.0.1.34467 > 10.0.0.2.4432: Flags [.], ack 33, win 501,
options [nop,nop,TS val 38857453 ecr 42882629], length 0
[--- output truncated ---]
```

TCP dump is capable of some really cool filtering, none of which is obvious from the limited help output I showed at the beginning of the chapter. There are also some cool flags that you can specify from the Unix prompt. To enable either of these, use the `filter` keyword in EOS. For example, the `-X` flag in Unix will display the packets in excruciating detail, including the bytes in hexadecimal and ASCII. Additionally, the `-c` flag can be used to limit the capture to a finite number of packets. Here, from Unix, I'll capture only two packets and display the hex and ASCII contents of the packets:

```
[admin@SW4 ~]$ tcpdump -i vlan4094 -Xc 2
tcpdump: verbose output suppressed, use -v or -vv for full protocol decode
listening on vlan4094, link-type EN10MB (Ethernet), capture size 65535 bytes
23:08:16.490465 00:1c:73:17:4a:8e (oui Arista Networks) >
00:1c:73:17:5d:a2 (oui Arista Networks), ethertype IPv4 (0x0800),
length 185: 10.0.0.2.4432 > 10.0.0.1.4432: UDP, length 143
    0x0000: 4500 00ab 0000 4000 ff11 673f 0a00 0002  E.....@...g?....
```

```
    0x0010:  0a00 0001 1150 1150 0097 57b8 0223 b88e   .....P.P..W..#..
    0x0020:  f391 0002 0180 c200 0000 001c 7317 5da3   ............s.].
    0x0030:  0079 4242 0300 0003 027c 1000 64a0 e744   .yBB.....|..d..D
    0x0040:  5bc2 0000 07cf 8000 021c 7317 4a8e 80c9   [.........s.J...
    0x0050:  0100 1400 0200 0f00 0000 5000 0000 0000   ..........P.....
    0x0060:  0000 0000 0000 0000 0000 0000 0000 0000   ................
    0x0070:  0000 0000 0000 0000 0000 0000 0000 4fee   ..............O.
    0x0080:   b818 370b cfd9 b376 9ec3 b10b 23ae 0000   ..7....v....#...
    0x0090:   0000 8000 021c 7317 4a8e 137c 2001 021c   ......s.J..|....
    0x00a0:   7313 35ec 0000 07cf 8080 13               s.5........
23:08:16.505841 00:1c:73:17:5d:a2 (oui Arista Networks) >
00:1c:73:17:4a:8e (oui Arista Networks), ethertype IPv4 (0x0800),
length 185: 10.0.0.1.4432 > 10.0.0.2.4432: UDP, length 143
    0x0000:   4500 00ab 0000 4000 ff11 673f 0a00 0001   E.....@...g?....
    0x0010:   0a00 0002 1150 1150 0097 dbaa 0223 b88e   .....P.P.....#..
    0x0020:   f391 00cf 0180 c200 0000 001c 7313 4cf4   ............s.L.
    0x0030:   0079 4242 0300 0003 0278 1000 64a0 e744   .yBB.....x..d..D
    0x0040:   5bc2 0000 07cf 8000 021c 7317 4a8e 8067   [.........s.J...g
    0x0050:   0200 1400 0200 0f00 0000 5000 0000 0000   ..........P.....
    0x0060:   0000 0000 0000 0000 0000 0000 0000 0000   ................
    0x0070:   0000 0000 0000 0000 0000 0000 0000 4fee   ..............O.
    0x0080:   b818 370b cfd9 b376 9ec3 b10b 23ae 0000   ..7....v....#...
    0x0090:   07cf 8000 021c 7313 35ec 127c 2001 021c   ......s.5..|....
    0x00a0:   7313 35ec 0000 0000 2080 14               s.5........
2 packets captured
2 packets received by filter
0 packets dropped by kernel
```

I know I said I wasn't going to go into the details of TCP dump before, but I'm showing you these options in order to explain how to include them in the EOS version of TCP dump. In a nutshell, anything you want to add to the command line that doesn't fit elsewhere should go after the filter keyword. Thus, from EOS, the previous command would look like this:

```
SW4#tcpdump int vlan4094 filter -Xc 2
tcpdump: verbose output suppressed, use -v or -vv for full protocol
decode
listening on vlan4094, link-type EN10MB (Ethernet), capture size
65535 bytes
23:09:10.490487 00:1c:73:17:4a:8e (oui Arista Networks) >
00:1c:73:17:5d:a2 (oui Arista Networks), ethertype IPv4 (0x0800),
length 185: 10.0.0.2.4432 > 10.0.0.1.4432: UDP, length 143
    0x0000:   4500 00ab 0000 4000 ff11 673f 0a00 0002   E.....@...g?....
    0x0010:   0a00 0001 1150 1150 0097 57b8 0223 b88e   .....P.P..W..#..
    0x0020:   f391 0002 0180 c200 0000 001c 7317 5da3   ............s.].
    0x0030:   0079 4242 0300 0003 027c 1000 64a0 e744   .yBB.....|..d..D
    0x0040:   5bc2 0000 07cf 8000 021c 7317 4a8e 80c9   [.........s.J...
    0x0050:   0100 1400 0200 0f00 0000 5000 0000 0000   ..........P.....
    0x0060:   0000 0000 0000 0000 0000 0000 0000 0000   ................
    0x0070:   0000 0000 0000 0000 0000 0000 0000 4fee   ..............O.
    0x0080:   b818 370b cfd9 b376 9ec3 b10b 23ae 0000   ..7....v....#...
    0x0090:   0000 8000 021c 7317 4a8e 137c 2001 021c   ......s.J..|....
```

```
       0x00a0:  7313 35ec 0000 07cf 8080 13              s.5........
23:09:10.506855 00:1c:73:17:5d:a2 (oui Arista Networks) >
00:1c:73:17:4a:8e (oui Arista Networks), ethertype IPv4 (0x0800),
length 185: 10.0.0.1.4432 > 10.0.0.2.4432: UDP, length 143
       0x0000:  4500 00ab 0000 4000 ff11 673f 0a00 0001  E.....@...g?....
       0x0010:  0a00 0002 1150 1150 0097 dbaa 0223 b88e  .....P.P.....#..
       0x0020:  f391 00cf 0180 c200 0000 001c 7313 4cf4  ............s.L.
       0x0030:  0079 4242 0300 0003 0278 1000 64a0 e744  .yBB.....x..d..D
       0x0040:  5bc2 0000 07cf 8000 021c 7317 4a8e 8067  [........s.J..g
       0x0050:  0200 1400 0200 0f00 0000 5000 0000 0000  ..........P.....
       0x0060:  0000 0000 0000 0000 0000 0000 0000 0000  ................
       0x0070:  0000 0000 0000 0000 0000 0000 0000 4fee  ..............O.
       0x0080:  b818 370b cfd9 b376 9ec3 b10b 23ae 0000  ..7....v....#...
       0x0090:  07cf 8000 021c 7313 35ec 127c 2001 021c  ......s.5..|....
       0x00a0:  7313 35ec 0000 0000 2080 14              s.5........
2 packets captured
2 packets received by filter
0 packets dropped by kernel
Starting tcpdump process with command:
" tcpdump -i vlan4094 -Xc 2 "
```

To wrap up, here is a nice list of TCP dump flags to play with. Enjoy.

-c number

> Limit capture to the specified number of packets

-n

> Don't resolve hostnames

-vnn

> Don't resolve hostnames or port names

-s number

> Limit the capture to the number of bytes specified

-S

> Print absolute sequence numbers

-x

> Show hex content of packets

-X

> Show hex and ASCII content of packets

-xx

> Same as -x, but include the Ethernet header

I encourage you to read up more on TCP dump. Once you master its use, it can be a very powerful tool, especially on an Arista switch.

## CHAPTER 25

Zero-Touch Provisioning

When a fixed configuration Arista switch boots, and no *startup-config* is found, the switch will default to Zero-Touch Provisioning (ZTP) mode (on EOS v3.7 and higher). Your first reaction to ZTP may be that it's a pain in the ass, but I assure you it's not, and I hope that by the end of this chapter, you'll agree. In fact, it's a seriously cool feature that can be used to great effect.

Have you ever installed a new switch out of the box? Chances are you mounted it and sat in the data center with a console cable, or you sat with it on your desk while your workmates plotted against you because of all the fan noise. Or consider the idea of remote installations. I've had many clients who have bought remote "smart" hands service, only to discover that those remote hands weren't so smart after all. ZTP is designed to provide the ability to eliminate both situations, all through the use of standards-based Dynamic Host Configuration Protocol (DHCP).

 Late in the production of this book, I received word that ZTP would be coming to chassis-based switches sometime soon after EOS v4.10, due to popular demand.

The reason I say that it can be a pain, is because when a new switch is powered up, and steps to use ZTP have not been taken, configuring the switch is next to impossible. Here's the first indication that you're in for a long day if you've no idea how Arista switches behave. When you hit Enter at the login prompt of a new switch, you're greeted with the following warning:

```
localhost login:

No startup-config was found.
```

```
The device is in Zero Touch Provisioning mode and is attempting to
download the startup-config from a remote system. The device will not
be fully functional until either a valid startup-config is downloaded
from a remote system or Zero Touch Provisioning is cancelled.

To cancel Zero Touch Provisioning, login as admin and type
'zerotouch cancel' at the CLI. Alternatively, to disable Zero Touch
Provisioning permanently, type 'zerotouch disable' at the CLI.
Note: The device will reload when these commands are issued.
```

Now, if you're a high-level know-it-all network guy like me, you glossed over that because there were too many words. Allow me to point out the important bits in bold:

```
The device will not be fully functional until either a valid
startup-config is downloaded from a remote system or Zero Touch
Provisioning is cancelled.
```

Yeah, that looks important…especially the part about the device not being fully functional. Still didn't read? Allow me to demonstrate. Ignoring all dire warnings of impotent switches, I've logged in and started configuring. First, the hostname; it will need to be something special:

```
localhost#conf t
localhost(config)#hostname Arista
Arista(config)#
```

Cool! Now that my switch has a clever hostname, I'll save the configuration, because 30 years of bad habits are hard to undo:

```
Arista(config)#wri
```

Life is good, so I take a well-deserved break for my hourly dose of caffeine and sugar, after which I come back and hit Return. Again, 30 years of bad habits force me to perform actions beyond my control, so without thinking I mash the Return key a couple of times:

```
Arista(config)#
localhost(config)#
localhost(config)#
```

What the hell? I configured the switch, even saved the config, and the switch reverted to a generic hostname on its own! Stupid new switches that…wait a minute. What was that error message I saw earlier? Wasn't there something about canceling something? Here's the part:

```
To cancel Zero Touch Provisioning, login as admin and type
'zerotouch cancel' at the CLI. Alternatively, to disable Zero Touch
Provisioning permanently, type 'zerotouch disable' at the CLI.
Note: The device will reload when these commands are issued.
```

This little comedy of errors I just walked you through is almost a word-for-word account of my first interaction with an Arista switch. Because I'm a man, and a high-level networking know-it-all, I found no reason to read the documentation, let alone the warning message. Let's cut to the chase, and I'll show you what's really going on.

When an Arista switch boots for the first time, ZTP is enabled. The switch sees that there is no *startup-config*, so it configures all interfaces with the no switchport command, then sends out DHCP queries on any Ethernet and Management interfaces. If you're patient (I'm not), and take the time to read the messages (I didn't), you'll see exactly what's going on. Here's a sample from a switch in such a state:

```
Apr 10 23:17:19 localhost ZeroTouch: %ZTP-5-DHCP_QUERY: Sending DHCP
request on [ Ethernet10, Ethernet11, Ethernet24 ]
Apr 10 23:18:19 localhost ZeroTouch: %ZTP-5-DHCP_QUERY_FAIL: Failed
to get a valid DHCP response
Apr 10 23:18:19 localhost ZeroTouch: %ZTP-5-RETRY: Retrying Zero Touch
Provisioning from the begining (attempt 2)
```

The switch found three connected interfaces (E10, E11, and E24), and sent DHCP queries out to all of them. Sadly, there were no responses, so it kept trying. If you leave it in this state, it will try forever. If you configure the switch, the configuration will be trashed, as ZTP tries again and again to find a config, or at least an IP address.

At this point, there are four things you can do:

- Cancel ZTP
- Disable ZTP
- Actually boot using ZTP to our advantage
- Give up, quit your job, move to Texas, and grow sugar beets

I suppose we could also turn off the switch and hit the bar for some cocktails, but let's keep this discussion focused on ZTP and examine each choice.

Cancelling ZTP

Cancelling ZTP is pretty simple. Just log in, enter configuration mode, and issue the zerotouch cancel command:

```
localhost#conf t

localhost(config)#zerotouch cancel
Apr 10 23:19:26 localhost ZeroTouch: %ZTP-5-CANCEL: Cancelling Zero
Touch Provisioning
localhost(config)#Apr 10 23:19:26 localhost ZeroTouch: %ZTP-5-RELOAD:
Rebooting the system

Broadcast messagStopping sshd: [ OK ]
watchdog is not running
SysRq : Remount R/O
Restarting system
```

Notice that there is no "Are you sure?" prompt. If you issue this command, the switch *will* reload. That's not such a bad thing, since anything we tried to configure got wiped out anyway. Besides, those ZTP messages get old quickly.

When the switch reboots, you'll be able to configure it as you would expect. Here's the rub: if you cancel ZTP, it's still there, it's just not bothering you this time. In fact, the configuration will still have the login banner programmed with the ZTP warning message.

If, with ZTP cancelled, you erase the *startup-config* and reboot, you will again be treated to ZTP's never ending messages and attempts at finding a DHCP server:

```
May 14 05:44:59 localhost ZeroTouch: %ZTP-5-INIT: No startup-config
found, starting Zero Touch Provisioning
May 14 05:45:34 localhost ZeroTouch: %ZTP-5-DHCP_QUERY: Sending DHCP
request on  [ Ethernet10, Ethernet11, Ethernet24 ]
```

Let's say that for some reason, no matter what, you don't want to see ZTP's ugly face again. In order for that to happen, ZTP must be completely disabled.

Disabling ZTP

To completely disable ZTP, log in as admin and issue the `zerotouch disable` command. The switch will immediately reboot (again, without warning or confirmation), only this time, ZTP is terminated with extreme prejudice as evidenced by the following messages;

```
localhost#zerotouch disable
May 14 05:47:42 localhost ZeroTouch: %ZTP-5-CANCEL: Cancelling Zero Touch Provisioning
May 14 05:47:42 localhost ZeroTouch: %ZTP-5-RELOAD: Rebooting the system
May 14 05:47:43 localhost ProcMgr-worker: %PROCMGR-6-WORKER_WARMSTART:
ProcMgr worker warm start. (PID=1446)
May 14 05:47:43 localhost ProcMgr-worker:
%PROCMGR-6-TERMINATE_RUNNING_PROCESS: Terminating
deconfigured/reconfigured process 'ZeroTouch' (PID=1506)
May 14 05:47:44 localhost ProcMgr-worker:
%PROCMGR-6-PROCESS_TERMINATED: 'ZeroTouch' (PID=1506) has terminated.
May 14 05:47:44 localhost ProcMgr-worker:
%PROCMGR-6-PROCESS_NOTRESTARTING: Letting 'ZeroTouch' (PID=1506)
exit - NOT restarting it.
```

Now, the system boots once more, and there isn't even a trace of ZTP:

```
The system is going down for reboot NOW!
Stopping sshd: [  OK  ]
watchdog is not running
[  253.549272] SysRq : Remount R/O
Restarting system


Aboot 1.9.2-140514.2006.eswierk
```

```
Press Control-C now to enter Aboot shell
Booting flash:/EOS-4.9.3.swi
Starting new kernel
Switching rootfs
Welcome to Arista Networks EOS 4.9.3
Mounting filesystems: [ OK ]
Starting udev: [ OK ]
Setting hostname localhost: [ OK ]
Entering non-interactive startup
Starting EOS initialization stage 1: [ OK ]
ip6tables: Applying firewall rules: [ OK ]
iptables: Applying firewall rules: [ OK ]
iptables: Loading additional modules: nf_conntrack_tftp [ OK ]
Starting system logger: [ OK ]
Starting NorCal initialization: [ OK ]
Retrigger failed udev events[ OK ]
Starting EOS initialization stage 2: [ OK ]
Starting ProcMgr: [ OK ]
Completing EOS initialization: [ OK ]
Starting Power On Self Test (POST): [ OK ]
Starting sshd: [ OK ]
Starting xinetd: [ OK ]
Starting crond: [ OK ]
Model: DCS-7124S
Serial Number: JSH10170315
System RAM: 2043416 kB
Flash Memory size:  1.8G

localhost login:
```

At this point you can reboot the switch to your heart's content, and ZTP will not come
back. If you'd like to bring ZTP back, you can't even do it from **exec** mode:

```
localhost#zerotouch ?
  cancel              Cancel ZeroTouch and reload the switch
  disable             Disable ZeroTouch and reload the switch
  script-exec-timeout Change timeout for the downloaded script to
                      finish execution
```

In fact, you can't even do it in config mode, though there's an option for enable, which
gives us a clue as to what we need to do:

```
localhost#conf t
localhost(config)#zerotouch enable
% Configuration ignored: ZeroTouch can not be enabled interactively.
To enable ZeroTouch, delete startup-config and reload the switch.
```

Sadly, that doesn't work either, at least in EOS version 4.9.3. ZTP is dead. Unless you
accept the fact that nothing is impossible with an Arista switch! Check out what's on the
flash: drive:

```
localhost#dir
Directory of flash:/

        -rwx    188621783         Apr 16 02:32  EOS-4.4.0.swi
        -rwx    221921815         Apr 16 02:38  EOS-4.7.7.swi
        -rwx    222153243         Apr 16 02:39  EOS-4.7.8.swi
        -rwx    225217184         Apr 16 02:38  EOS-4.8.1.swi
        -rwx    245827739         Apr 16 08:19  EOS-4.9.1.swi
        -rwx    248665992         May 12 12:36  EOS-4.9.3.swi
        -rwx          137         May 12 13:44  boot-config
        drwx         4096         May 14 06:00  debug
        drwx         4096         May 14 06:00  persist
        drwx         4096         Apr 15 19:47  schedule
        -rwx            0         May 14 19:31  startup-config
        -rwx           13         May 14 06:10  zerotouch-config
```

Hmm. Let's dig into that file and see what we find, shall we?

```
localhost#bash

Arista Networks EOS shell

[admin@localhost ~]$ cd /mnt/flash
[admin@localhost flash]$ more zerotouch-config
DISABLE=True
```

Ha! I bet if we change that to false, that we'll get ZTP back. Let's try it and see. I've gone in and flexed my nerdy *vi* skills, and changed the file to show DISABLE=False:

```
[admin@localhost flash]$ more zerotouch-config
DISABLE=False
```

Now I'll clear the *startup-config* with write erase and reboot to see what happens:

```
[admin@localhost flash]$ exit
logout
localhost#
localhost#write erase
localhost#reload
System configuration has been modified. Save? [yes/no/cancel/diff]:no
Proceed with reload? [confirm]
Broadcast message from root@localhost
        (unknown) at 19:40 ...

The system is going down for reboot NOW!
[--- lots of output truncated ---]
May 14 19:42:54 localhost ZeroTouch: %ZTP-5-INIT: No startup-config
found, starting Zero Touch Provisioning
```

This was actually pretty cool for me when I first figured it out. Though I could find no mention of how to do this in the documentation, with my experience using Arista switches, I reasoned that there had to be a configuration file somewhere, and that Arista would never permanently disable a feature. Following that logic, I found the configuration file, changed it, and was rewarded with the expected results.

 You can also reset ZTP by issuing the `fullrecover` command in Aboot. Be careful though, as this will wipe out *everything* on your switch. See Chapter 18 for more information on Aboot.

Booting with ZTP

Hopefully you've considered the possibility of booting with ZTP, because as we're about to see, it's pretty darn cool. As with all things Arista, it's well thought out and powerful.

The first thing we need to know is that while ZTP can load a configuration from the network, it can also run scripts. Before we get to that, let's take a look at what needs to happen in order for an Arista switch to boot using ZTP.

When a switch boots in ZTP mode, it configures all the Ethernet and Management interfaces with the `no switchport` command in order to allow DHCP to be run on those interfaces. DHCP is capable of much more than just providing an IP address, and ZTP takes advantage of this fact. In order to see how, let's first take a look at how to configure a DHCP server in order to use ZTP.

I've set up a lab where I have an Ubuntu Linux server, an existing network, and a new Arista switch. I'm using *dhcpd* on the Linux server to serve DHCP. The examples used in this section will reflect the configuration required for *dhcpd*, though the concepts should be universal for any DHCP server that supports them. The lab network is shown in Figure 25-1.

To start with, I've configured the regular DHCP parameters as follows to fit with my network:

```
option subnet-mask 255.255.255.0;
option broadcast-address 192.168.1.255;

option routers 192.168.1.1;
option domain-name-servers 192.168.1.200, 192.168.1.205;
option domain-name "gad.net";

subnet 192.168.1.0 netmask 255.255.255.0 {
range 192.168.1.160 192.168.1.167;
```

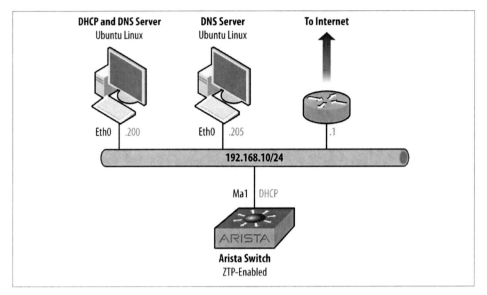

Figure 25-1. ZTP-enabled switch lab network

Given this configuration, dynamically allocated IP addresses will be served from the pool 192.168.1.160–167. Now I'll configure a specific IP address outside of that range for my Arista switch. First, I'll need to know the MAC address for the management 1 interface on my switch. To get that, I'll use the show interface ma1 command:

```
localhost#sho int management 1
Management1 is up, line protocol is up (connected)
  Hardware is Ethernet, address is 001c.7308.80ac (bia 001c.7308.80ac)
  Description: [ Management Link ]
  MTU 1500 bytes, BW 1000000 Kbit
  Full-duplex, 1Gb/s, auto negotiation: on
  Up 17 minutes, 58 seconds
  Last clearing of "show interface" counters never
  5 minutes input rate 748 bps (0.0% with framing), 1 packets/sec
  5 minutes output rate 52 bps (0.0% with framing), 0 packets/sec
     814 packets input, 103190 bytes
     Received 201 broadcasts, 608 multicast
     0 runts, 0 giants
     0 input errors, 0 CRC, 0 alignment, 0 symbol
     0 PAUSE input
     47 packets output, 8296 bytes
     Sent 0 broadcasts, 0 multicast
     0 output errors, 0 collisions
     0 late collision, 0 deferred
     0 PAUSE output
```

With the MAC address in hand, I can now configure my DHCP server for this switch:

```
host Arista1 {
  option dhcp-client-identifier 00:1c:73:08:80:ae;
  fixed-address 192.168.1.170;
  option bootfile-name "http://www2.gad.net/Arista/Arista1-ZTP";
  }
```

This configuration will deliver the IP address 192.168.1.170 to the device that requests an IP address from the MAC address shown. Note that I had to change the format of the MAC address since it is shown differently on the switch than the way the DHCP configuration file requires it. Lastly, the option bootfile-name line shows an HTTP URL. The switch, upon receiving and activating the IP address, will go to this URL and download the bootfile. Here's where this gets fun.

This file can be either a *startup-config*, in which case the switch will apply the configuration and reboot, or it can be a script. ZTP will decide based on the first line of the file found at the bootfile-name address. If the first line includes the path to a shell, the shell will be loaded and the file will be considered a shell script. If not, the file will be considered a *startup-config* file, and treated accordingly.

Let's look at an example that might apply for the real world. Here's how I've configured my *Arista1-ZTP* file on the webserver:

```
[root@cozy Arista]$ more Arista1-ZTP
#!/usr/bin/Cli -p2
enable
copy http://www2.gad.net/Arista/Arista1-startup flash:startup-config
copy http://www2.gad.net/Arista/EOS-4.9.3.swi flash:
config
boot system flash:EOS-4.9.3.swi
```

This file will perform the following actions on the switch, in order, after ZTP loads it:

- Load the CLI process
- Enter EOS CLI enable mode
- Copy the *startup-config* from the webserver to *flash:*
- Copy the desired revision of EOS from the web server to *flash:*
- Enter EOS CLI configuration mode
- Set the *boot-config* to boot from the new EOS version just downloaded

Once the script has completed, the switch will reload. Let's take a look at the switch as it boots with the ZTP configuration loaded on the DHCP server.

Here, my switch is running EOS version 4.8.1:

```
Arista#sho ver
Arista DCS-7124S-F
Hardware version:    06.02
Serial number:       JSH10170315
```

```
System MAC address:  001c.7308.80ae

Software image version: 4.8.1
Architecture:           i386
Internal build version: 4.8.1-495947.2011eric481Showstopper
Internal build ID:      b15379fb-13e9-4255-819f-e55dde3c3471

Uptime:                 1 day, 19 hours and 38 minutes
Total memory:           2043424 kB
Free memory:            785968 kB
```

And the existing boot configuration is pointing to 4.8.1 as well:

```
Arista#sho boot
Software image: flash:/EOS-4.8.1.swi
Console speed: (not set)
Aboot password (encrypted): (not set)
```

Now I'll erase the *startup-config* with the write erase command:

```
Arista#write erase
```

I'll prove there's nothing there:

```
Arista#sho start
Arista#
```

And reload:

```
Arista#reload
System configuration has been modified. Save? [yes/no/cancel/diff]:no
Proceed with reload? [confirm]
```

Now let's watch the ZTP messages as the switch boots. I've only included the relevant message here to save space:

```
May 12 20:28:45 localhost ZeroTouch:
%ZTP-5-DHCP_QUERY: Sending DHCP request on  [ Ethernet10, Ethernet11,
 Management1 ]
May 12 20:28:48 localhost ZeroTouch: %ZTP-5-DHCP_SUCCESS: DHCP
response received on Management1  [ Ip Address: 192.168.1.170/24;
Nameserver: 192.168.1.200; Nameserver: 192.168.1.205; Domain: gad.net;
 Gateway: 192.168.1.1; Boot File:
 http://www2.gad.net/Arista/Arista1-ZTP ]
May 12 20:28:53 localhost ZeroTouch: %ZTP-5-CONFIG_DOWNLOAD:
Attempting to download the startup-config from
http://www2.gad.net/Arista/Arista1-ZTP
May 12 20:28:54 localhost ZeroTouch: %ZTP-5-CONFIG_DOWNLOAD_SUCCESS:
Successfully downloaded config script from
http://www2.gad.net/Arista/Arista1-ZTP
May 12 20:28:54 localhost ZeroTouch: %ZTP-5-EXEC_SCRIPT:
Executing the downloaded config script
```

At this point the switch has downloaded the Arista ZTP file, applied what it found there, and reloaded. Note that this message may seem to hang for a bit if you're watching it and the switch is downloading new code:

```
May 12 20:29:18 localhost ZeroTouch: %ZTP-5-EXEC_SCRIPT_SUCCESS:
Successfully executed the downloaded config script
May 12 20:29:18 localhost ZeroTouch: %ZTP-5-RELOAD: Rebooting the system
Stopping sshd: [  OK  ]
watchdog is not running
[  148.565460] SysRq : Remount R/O
Restarting system


Aboot 1.9.2-140514.2006.eswierk


Press Control-C now to enter Aboot shell
Booting flash:/EOS-4.9.3.swi
Starting new kernel
Data in /mnt/flash/EOS-4.9.3.swi differs from previous boot image
 on /mnt/flash.
Saving new boot image to /mnt/flash...
Switching rootfs
Welcome to Arista Networks EOS 4.9.3
Mounting filesystems: [  OK  ]
Starting udev: [  OK  ]
Setting hostname localhost: [  OK  ]
Entering non-interactive startup
Starting EOS initialization stage 1: [  OK  ]
ip6tables: Applying firewall rules: [  OK  ]
iptables: Applying firewall rules: [  OK  ]
iptables: Loading additional modules: nf_conntrack_tftp [  OK  ]
Starting system logger: [  OK  ]
Starting NorCal initialization: [  OK  ]
Retrigger failed udev events[  OK  ]
Starting EOS initialization stage 2: [  OK  ]
Starting ProcMgr: [  OK  ]
Completing EOS initialization:
Starting Power On Self Test (POST): [  OK  ]
Starting sshd: [  OK  ]
Starting xinetd: [  OK  ]
Starting crond: [  OK  ]
Model: DCS-7124S
Serial Number: JSH10170315
System RAM: 2043416 kB
Flash Memory size:  1.8G


Arista login:
```

So without direct interaction, the switch booted, ran our script, loaded the new configuration, downloaded new code, rebooted, and applied the new code. Did you notice that the switch suddenly has a hostname (Arista)? That's due to the configuration being loaded from the URL listed in the *Arista1-ZTP* file.

Imagine a scenario where you're installing 50 new Arista switches. This procedure could put a base configuration on them all while also loading the right version of code. That's my kind of time-saving feature!

Not only that, but some customers have developed scripts that auto-archive the configs on all their switches every day (which is always a good idea), and then update the ZTP files accordingly. When a switch fails, ZTP on the replacement switch references the proper files that have been scripted to contain the config of the switch being replaced. Think about the time saved during an outage when the switch configures itself after a replacement.

event-handler

event-handler is a feature in Arista switches that allows bash scripts to be executed when certain system events occur. As of EOS version 4.9.3, the triggers are pretty limited, but I have a feeling that they will be expanded upon in the future.

 This chapter is written based on the feature set found in EOS version 4.9.3. Future versions may support additional features.

So what's the benefit of such a feature? Let's say that you've got a system that's been spontaneously rebooting at odd times, and your executive management is too cheap to buy network management software. You could configure an *event handler* to email you (or the system guys, or whomever you'd like) any time the switch's interface to that server goes down.

Description

Event-handler allows the creation of a *trigger*, and an *action*. The trigger in my server example would be the interface on the switch going up or down. The action would be the email being sent. Additionally, a *delay* can be set so that a configured amount of time must pass after the trigger before the action is taken.

Two types of triggers are allowed. They are:

onBoot
> Triggered when the system boots. Note that this trigger also activates when exiting from event-handler configuration mode.

onIntf
> Triggered on certain interface-specific events.

I've been told that additional triggers likely to arrive soon include *on-startup-config*, which will be triggered any time the *startup-config* is written, and *on-vm*, which will be triggered any time a VM discovered with VMTracer) is moved. A version keyword is also likely that will let you test for the correct version of EOS.

Additionally, I've been told that the CamelCase (medial capitals for the pedantic) format of the trigger names will likely change. For example, onBoot will probably change to *on-boot*.

The *onBoot* trigger has no other options, while the *onInt* trigger allows the following more specific trigger types:

ip
> Triggered on changes to the interface's IP address assignment.

operstatus
> Changes to the interface's operational status (up, down, etc.).

If both the *ip* and *operstatus* triggers are specified, then the trigger will be activated when either of them occur. In other words, specifying them both equals the pseudo-code `ip OR operstatus`, and not `ip AND operstatus`.

To add even more power to this feature, the following variables are passed to bash when an *onInf*-triggered action is performed:

$INTF
> The interface name of the interface specified in the trigger.

$OPERSTATE
> The current (after the triggered event) operation status of the interface specified in the trigger.

$IP-PRIMARY
> The current (after the triggered event) primary IP address of the interface specified in the trigger. Note that secondary IP addresses are not included.

No variables are passed when an *onBoot*-triggered action is performed.

OnBoot effectively replaces the use of the *rc.eos* file mentioned in Chapter 11, and is usually a cleaner option since *onBoot* happens later in the boot process.

Actions are bash commands of any type. If you'd like your action to perform more than one command, then write a script in bash, then reference the script in the action.

Configuration

Configuring event handlers is a pretty simple affair. The most difficult part would be writing any scripts that you'd like to call. Let's take a look and see some real examples.

To configure an event handler, enter the event-handler configuration mode with the `event-handler` *event-name* command. The event name is anything you'd like it to be, but I urge you to make the name obvious and related to the event trigger in some way. Here, I'll configure a simple `event-handler` called `Int-e10-updown`:

```
Arista(config)#event-handler Int-e10-updown
Arista(config-handler-Int-e10-updown)#
```

This drops me into event-handler configuration mode. From here, I can do a bunch of stuff (I love the word *stuff*, don't you?) as evidenced by the following:

```
Arista(config-handler-Int-e10-updown)#?
  action    Define event-handler action
  comment   Up to 240 characters, comment for this mode
  default   Set a command to its defaults
  delay     Configure event-handler delay
  exit      Exit from Event handler configuration mode
  help      Description of the interactive help system
  no        Negate a command or set its defaults
  show      Show running system information
  trigger   Configure event trigger condition
  !         Append to comment
```

Adding comments to parts of the configuration is a wonderful Arista feature that I encourage you to make use of. Let's add a comment to our event by entering the command `comment` alone on a line. This will drop you into comment mode, where you can type a whole bunch of stuff (yeah! more stuff!) across multiple lines. Enter EOF alone on a line to exit this mode:

```
Arista(config-handler-Int-e10-updown)#comment
Enter TEXT message. Type 'EOF' on its own line to end.
Trigger for Int-e10 status change
Added May 27, 2012 by GAD
EOF
Arista(config-handler-Int-e10-updown)#
```

Now let's define the trigger. I'd like my action to take place any time the interface's status changes, so I'll use `trigger onIntf` *interface-name* `operstatus`:

```
Arista(config-handler-Int-e10-updown)#trigger onIntf e10 operstatus
```

With my trigger set, now I need to configure the action to be performed on the trigger being, well, triggered. This is done with the `action bash` *bash-command* command. The command I'm going to use is `email -s "Int $INTF is now $OPERSTATE"`. This will send an email with the subject line of *Int Ethernet10 is now linkdown* when the interface goes down, and *Int Ethernet10 is now linkup* when it comes up:

```
Arista(config-handler-Int-e10-updown)#action bash email -s "Int $INTF
is now $OPERSTATE"
```

In order for this example to work, email must be configured. See Chapter 19 for instructions on how to accomplish this. Kudos if you've read that chapter and can see what's wrong already.

Just for fun, I'll include a delay of 5 seconds:

```
Arista(config-handler-Int-e10-updown)#delay 5
```

While still in event-handler configuration mode, the event is not yet active. To enable it, exit the mode:

```
Arista(config-handler-Int-e10-updown)#exit
Arista(config)#
```

My configured event-handler looks like this in the *running-config*:

```
event-handler Int-e10-updown
   ! Trigger for Int-e10 status change
   ! Added May 27, 2012 by GAD
   trigger onIntf Ethernet10 operstatus
   action bash email -s "Int $INTF is now $OPERSTATE"
   delay 5
```

That's all great, but let's see what happens when the event is actually triggered. After walking up and pulling the cable from interface e10, the following lines appeared in the switch's log:

```
Arista#sho log last 5 min
May 27 17:18:03 Arista Cli: %SYS-5-CONFIG_I: Configured from console
by admin on con0 (0.0.0.0)
May 27 17:20:17 Arista Fru: %FRU-6-TRANSCEIVER_REMOVED: The
transceiver for interface Ethernet10 has been removed
May 27 17:20:17 Arista Ebra: %LINEPROTO-5-UPDOWN: Line protocol on
Interface Ethernet10, changed state to down
May 27 17:20:17 Arista Ebra: %LINEPROTO-5-UPDOWN: Line protocol on
Interface Ethernet11, changed state to down
May 27 17:20:22 Arista SuperServer: %SYS-6-EVENT_TRIGGERED:
Event-handler Int-e10-updown was activated
May 27 17:20:22 Arista SuperServer: %SYS-5-EVENT_ACTION_FAILED:
Event-handler action Int-e10-updown did not complete with exit
code 0. Action returned with exit code 2.
```

Well, that doesn't look good!

Looking at the config, I'm sure many of you saw my earlier mistake, but I did it on purpose (seriously!) to show that incorrect commands will be freely accepted by the command.

Let's take a look at the event-handler with the show event-handler command to see where I messed up:

```
Arista#sho event-handler
Event-handler Int-e10-updown
Trigger: onIntf Ethernet10 on operstatus delay 5 seconds
Action: email -s "Int $INTF is now $OPERSTATE"
Last Trigger Activation Time: 4 minutes 29 seconds ago
Total Trigger Activations: 1
Last Action Time: 4 minutes 24 seconds ago
Total Actions: 1
```

This shows some cool information regarding my configured event, including how long ago it was triggered and how many times it's been triggered. What we're looking for, however, is why it doesn't work. That answer is in the action command string. The email command I referenced requires a destination email address to work, but I didn't give it one. To fix that, I'll go back into event-handler configuration mode and re-enter the action command:

```
Arista(config)#event-handler Int-e10-updown
Arista(config-handler-Int-e10-updown)#action bash email -s "Int $INTF
is now $OPERSTATE" gad@gad.net
Arista(config-handler-Int-e10-updown)#exit
```

Now, I'll go plug in my cable into interface e10 and see what happens:

```
Arista#sho log last 5 min
May 27 17:33:26 Arista Fru: %FRU-6-TRANSCEIVER_INSERTED: A transceiver
for interface Ethernet10 has been inserted. manufacturer: Arista
Networks model: CAB-SFP-SFP-5M part number CAB-SFP-SFP-5M rev 0002
serial number XPV104130681
May 27 17:33:30 Arista Ebra: %LINEPROTO-5-UPDOWN: Line protocol on
Interface Ethernet11, changed state to up
May 27 17:33:30 Arista Ebra: %LINEPROTO-5-UPDOWN: Line protocol on
Interface Ethernet10, changed state to up
May 27 17:33:32 Arista Lldp: %LLDP-5-NEIGHBOR_NEW: LLDP neighbor with
chassisId 001c.7308.80ae and portId "Ethernet11" added on interface
Ethernet10
May 27 17:33:32 Arista Lldp: %LLDP-5-NEIGHBOR_NEW: LLDP neighbor with
chassisId 001c.7308.80ae and portId "Ethernet10" added on interface
Ethernet11
May 27 17:33:35 Arista SuperServer: %SYS-6-EVENT_TRIGGERED:
Event-handler Int-e10-updown was activated
```

Sure enough, five seconds after insertion, I received the following email:

```
Date: Sun, 27 May 2012 17:33:39
From: Arista@gad.net
To: gad@gad.net
Subject: Int Ethernet10 is now linkup
```

All in all, setting up and using an event-handler is pretty simple, yet this can be a pretty powerful tool. My hope is that Arista adds more and more trigger events, because the thought of the switch sending an email every time *vmtracer* automatically configures a dynamic VLAN is pretty appealing to me. I anticipate that event-handler will be significantly expanded in the future, and I look forward to writing about all the wonderful developments in the second edition of *Arista Warrior*.

## CHAPTER 27

Event Monitor

The Event Monitor on an Arista switch is a slick little tool that, according to the documentation, "writes system event records to local files for access by *sqlite* database commands." While a technically accurate description, allow me to expand on that a bit.

Event monitor is a process that records certain common events on the switch. As of EOS version 4.9.3.2, the events recorded include changes to the MAC address table (what MAC is mapped to what port), changes to the IP routing table, and changes to the ARP table (MAC address to IP address mapping).

 Generally, EOS releases are named in the A.B.C format. When I wrote this chapter, the latest revision was 4.9.3.2, which included an urgent patch serious enough to warrant a minor release. The revision was quickly replaced by 4.9.4, but the newer release did not effect any of the chapters where I used 4.9.3.2.

OK, I'll admit that still sounds boring, but let's dig into this tool and see what it does, and how it might be useful.

Using Event Monitor

The home base for using Event Monitor from EOS is the show event-monitor command. As of EOS v.4.9.3.2, there are only four options:

```
Arista#sho event-monitor ?
  arp     Monitor ARP table events
  mac     Monitor MAC table events
  route   Monitor routing events
  sqlite  enter a sqlite statment
```

There are three tables that we can view, and one very cool option named `sqlite`. The `sqlite` option lets us send sqlite commands from EOS to the sqlite database, which, as we'll see, is pretty darn useful.

> *Sqlite* is a software library that, according to the sqlite website, "implements a self-contained, serverless, zero-configuration, transactional SQL database engine." In other words, it's a very simple, scaled down version of SQL that also happens to be in the public domain. For more information on sqlite, see the project web page (*http://www.sqlite.org/*). Though you may have not heard of sqlite before, if you've ever used an Apple Mac running OS X, an iPhone, or an iPad, then you've used a product that incorporates sqlite. If you don't like Apple products, then look no further than the Firefox browser, the Thunderbird email client, the Google Chrome browser, or the Android phone operating system for other examples of the widespread use of sqlite.

Actually, to be painfully accurate, there is only one database, and each of the type of events being recorded is in a table within that database. Let's take a look at each one of these tables.

ARP

Normally, ARP changes are not logged on a switch. Even if they were, scrolling through pages of log entries is not my idea of fun, so the idea of storing these events in a database is a bit appealing to me. It's been a long time since I was a database guy, so let's see how rusty I am. The way to retrieve the ARP events from the database is with the `show event-monitor arp` command.

> Many of the code excerpts in this chapter are wrapped in unnatural looking ways to fit within the confines of the printed page. Since much of the output from these commands is actually Unix output piped through the EOS CLI, the format and width may look the way you might expect from a traditional switch operating system.

```
Arista#sho event-monitor arp
2012-05-23 02:34:12|192.168.1.200|Management1|00:02:55:b7:da:9d|0|added|3
2012-05-23 02:34:12|192.168.1.200|Management1|||removed|4
2012-05-23 06:38:49|192.168.1.1|Management1|00:14:6a:a2:d4:38|0|added|26
2012-05-23 18:11:27|192.168.1.200|Management1|00:02:55:b7:da:9d|0|added|27
```

My main problem with this tool is that the output is, shall we say, ugly. Well, it's ugly from my "all user interfaces should be elegant and beautiful" point of view. From my "it's SQL, and that's what SQL output looks like" point of view, it's beautiful. I know, I'm a complicated person.

Don't get me wrong, this is very useful information, but I have no idea what some of the values are. For example, I see some fields with zeros in them, and some with no values, and I have no idea what that last field in every line represents.

To help figure out what this stuff is, I'll take advantage of a nifty sqlite command that shows me the command used to create the table. This command is called .schema, and can be accessed by using the sqlite keyword. I'll cover the usage of the sqlite keyword a bit later in this chapter, but for now, bear with me and know that I'm sending the sqlite command .schema arp from EOS with the following command:

```
Arista#sho event-monitor sqlite .schema arp
CREATE TABLE arp( time text, prefix text, intf text, ethAddr text,
static integer, delta text,counter integer UNIQUE );
```

This output tells me that there was a table created named *arp* that contains the following fields, listed in order. I've also added what they mean for any nonprogrammer types out there:

Time (text string)
> The time in which this log entry was added.

Prefix (text string)
> The IP address related to the ARP entry.

Interface (text string)
> What interface the ARP event occurred on.

Ethernet Address (text string)
> The MAC address tied to the IP address (prefix).

Static (integer)
> Value is *0* if ARP entry was dynamically learned, and *1* if statically assigned.

Delta (text string)
> Typical entries are *added* and *removed*.

Counter (unique integer)
> Every time an entry is made, it is assigned a counter value as a unique identifier for this record.

Let's see this table in action. First, here is the list of existing ARP entries:

```
Arista(config)#sho arp
Address          Age (min)  Hardware Addr   Interface
192.168.1.1             0   0014.6aa2.d438  Management1
192.168.1.200           0   0002.55b7.da9d  Management1
```

Now I'll add a static ARP entry to my switch by mapping the IP address 192.168.1.2 to the MAC address learned for 192.168.1.1:

```
Arista(config)#arp 192.168.1.2 0014.6aa2.d438 arpa
```

Let's see what the Event Monitor database shows now that I've added the static ARP:

```
Arista(config)#sho event-monitor arp
2012-05-23 02:34:12|192.168.1.200|Management1|00:02:55:b7:da:9d|0|
added|3
2012-05-23 02:34:12|192.168.1.200|Management1|||removed|4
2012-05-23 06:38:49|192.168.1.1|Management1|00:14:6a:a2:d4:38|0|
added|26
2012-05-23 18:11:27|192.168.1.200|Management1|00:02:55:b7:da:9d|0|
added|27
2012-05-25 16:05:37|192.168.1.2|Management1|00:14:6a:a2:d4:38|1|
added|108
% Writing 1 Arp, 0 Route, 1 Mac events to the database
```

Take a look at the line in bold, and let's apply what we know. At 4:05 p.m. on May 25th, 2012, a static ARP was added that mapped the IP address 192.168.1.2 to the MAC address 00:14:6a:a2:d4:38. The ARP entry became active on interface Management1.

Now I'll go in and delete the static ARP entry:

```
Arista(config)#no arp 192.168.1.2 0014.6aa2.d438 arpa
```

And here's the output from the show event-monitor arp command after the change:

```
Arista(config)#sho event-monitor arp
2012-05-23 02:34:12|192.168.1.200|Management1|00:02:55:b7:da:9d|0|added|3
2012-05-23 02:34:12|192.168.1.200|Management1|||removed|4
2012-05-23 06:38:49|192.168.1.1|Management1|00:14:6a:a2:d4:38|0|added|26
2012-05-23 18:11:27|192.168.1.200|Management1|00:02:55:b7:da:9d|0|added|27
2012-05-25 16:05:37|192.168.1.2|Management1|00:14:6a:a2:d4:38|1|added|108
2012-05-25 16:06:56|192.168.1.2|Management1|||removed|109
% Writing 1 Arp, 0 Route, 0 Mac events to the database
```

Reading the line in bold, we can see that at 4:06 p.m. on May 25th, 2012, the ARP entry for the IP address 192.168.1.2 was removed. The ARP entry was previously active on interface Management1.

Remember that ARP entries are only made on the switch when the switch communicates directly using IP, or if the ARP table is manually manipulated. If you have no IP addresses active on your switch, this table will be empty. For example, if you manage your switches solely though console servers, and don't even use the Management interface, you may not need to have IP addresses active on your switch at all. In this case, there would be no ARP activity to record.

MAC

MAC changes are logged any time a MAC address is learned, added, or deleted. This can happen a lot on a busy switch, but it might not happen much at all on a smaller, stable network. This can be a pretty useful tool, and I'll show you how, so let's start by taking a look at the table the same way we did for the ARP table. First, let's look at the schema with the .schema mac sqlite command:

```
Arista#sho event-monitor sqlite .schema mac
CREATE TABLE mac( time text, fid integer, ethAddr text, intf text,
type text, delta text, counter integer UNIQUE);
% Writing 0 Arp, 0 Route, 2 Mac events to the database
```

Here's the breakdown of the fields:

Time (text string)
: The time in which this log entry was added.

FID (integer)
: FID stands for Filter ID. Switches keep an internal database of VLANs, and Arista switches assign internal VLANs to certain ports. This number will likely be unimportant to you, since the interface on which the MAC address was learned is also present.

Ethernet Address (MAC) (text string)
: The MAC address related to this event.

Interface (text string)
: The interface on which this MAC event occurred.

Type (text string)
: How did the entry change? A typical value would be *learnedDynamicMac*. When a MAC address is removed from the table, this field is null. If you statically add a MAC address with the mac address-table static command, this field will read *configuredStaticMac*.

Delta (text string)
: How did the entry change? Typical entries are *added* and *removed*.

Counter (unique integer)
: Every time an entry is made, it is assigned a counter value as a unique identifier for this record.

So let's look at an example of how I like to use this feature. Generic Bob comes up to you at 4:30 p.m. on a Friday and says, "Hey, the network sucks."

"What is it this time, Bob?" you ask, trying really hard not to roll your eyes since you read that chapter in *Network Warrior* about how not to be *that guy*.

"My system doesn't work, and it used to. Nothing changed, and I don't feel like thinking, so it has to be the network."

After a heavy sigh, you stop the important work you were doing and focus on Generic Bob's dilemma. "Where are you connected, Bob?"

"How should I know? You're the network guru, and it's your crappy network, so you figure it out."

Repressing the thoughts that are better left to mystery writers and psychopaths, you ask, "Well, do you know your IP address?"

"No, I think it's dynamic or something. Will this take long?"

"Look Bob, I need either the IP address or the MAC address to find your system. Get me either of those, or even better, both, and I'll see what I can find, OK?"

Generic Bob storms off to do his generic thing while you pull up your résumé. Just as you start to include all your Arista switch experience, Bob comes back and thrusts a piece of paper at your face. "Here's your *Mick* address."

You smile the false, hopeless smile of the damned, gently take the paper, and log in to your Arista switch. Generic Bob's coffee-stained paper has 3c:07:54:43:88:d4 scribbled on it in what appears to be red crayon, or maybe lipstick.

With event-monitor, you have a record of every MAC event for quite some time. Using the match-mac keyword, you pull up the event-monitor mac table including only events regarding the MAC address you care about:

```
Arista#sho event-monitor mac match-mac 3c:07:54:43:88:d4
2012-11-03 09:18:08|1006|3c:07:54:43:88:d4|Ethernet24|
learnedDynamicMac|added|549
2012-05-26 16:19:51|1|3c:07:54:43:88:d4|Ethernet6|learnedDynamicMac|
added|553
```

Looking at this data, you can see that Generic Bob's MAC address was first learned on January 11th, 2012, and this switch saw it on interface e24. Since you know that e24 is an uplink to another switch, you know that Bob's system was originally on another switch.

But the next line shows that the MAC address was learned today (hey, it was today when I wrote it), at 4:19 p.m. on the switch's local interface, e6. That seems odd, so you look at the *running-config* for e6 on this switch:

```
Arista#sho run int e6
interface Ethernet6
   description [ Unused ]
   switchport access vlan 999
```

Since you've configured the switch with a dead VLAN (999) that you put on all unused ports, you're sure that Generic Bob glommed a free interface on a different switch than the one to which he was assigned. With a couple of short commands, you've shown that Generic Bob was lying because someone had clearly moved his system from one switch to another, and that's why it stopped working. You can't blame the guy for thinking the new Arista switches would give him better performance, but plugging into network ports without prior authorization should not be tolerated.

I'll leave it to your imagination as to how you might deal with Generic Bob now that you have the tools to prove him wrong. Just try not to be *that guy*…much. I'd probably just smile and tell him to put his system back into the network port where it belonged, and then make sure his access to the data center was revoked, but not until I was done adding Event Monitor to my resume.

 This story is a complete fabrication. I've never met anyone named Bob who wrote a Mick address in red crayon. I did know someone who wrote her address in lipstick once, but that's a story for another book. OK, that's actually a fabrication too.

Route

If you've got your switches configured for IP routing, the show `event-monitor route` command can be a great tool to see historical information regarding route changes. As with the others, let's take a look at the schema, and then work up an example to see it in action:

```
Arista#sho event-monitor sqlite .schema route
CREATE TABLE route( time text, prefix text, protocol text, metric integer,
    preference integer, delta text,counter integer UNIQUE );
```

Here's the breakdown of the fields from the route table:

Time (text string)
 The time in which this log entry was added.

Prefix (text string)
 The IP prefix, including the Classless Internet Domain Routing (CIDR) mask related to the route entry.

Protocol (text string)
 I would imagine that this should read the protocol from which the prefix was learned or removed, but I've only ever seen this field read *invalid* when a route is added, or null when a route is removed.

Metric (integer)
 Again, I would assume this field should contain the metric for the route, but I've never been able to make it say anything other than *0* when adding a route, and null when removing a route.

Preference (integer)

This field should include the administrative distance for the route, but in my testing, this field reports a *1* regardless of route type learned.

Delta (text string)

How did the entry change? Typical entries are *added* and *removed*.

Counter (unique integer)

Every time an entry is made, it is assigned a counter value as a unique identifier for this record.

 I submitted my observation regarding the odd behaviors in this table to Arista TAC and received notification that this is a bug (ID #30146), which is scheduled to be resolved in the next major release of EOS. As of August 2012, Arista has not decided on whether that version will be called v4.11 or v5.0.

Let's start with a simple example. Here, I'll add a static route to the switch:

```
Arista(config)#ip route 20.20.20.0/24 192.168.1.1
```

Using the match-ip *ip-prefix* option, here's what shows up in the Event Monitor:

```
Arista(config)#sho event-monitor route match-ip 20.20.20.0/24
2012-05-27 00:54:40|20.20.20.0/24|invalid|0|1|added|1310
```

Now I'll delete that route:

```
Arista(config)#no ip route 20.20.20.0/24 192.168.1.1
```

And an appropriate remove message shows up in the Event Monitor:

```
Arista(config)#sho event-monitor route match-ip 20.20.20.0/24
2012-05-27 00:54:40|20.20.20.0/24|invalid|0|1|added|1310
2012-05-27 00:56:29|20.20.20.0/24||||removed|1312
```

When the switch learns routes through other means, the results are pretty much the same, but since I went through the trouble to prove that to myself, I figure it's only fair to share.

First, I'll show what the routing table looks like:

```
Arista#sho ip route | begin Gateway
Gateway of last resort:
 S    0.0.0.0/0 [1/0] via 192.168.1.1

 C    30.30.30.0/24 is directly connected, Loopback0
 C    192.168.1.0/24 is directly connected, Vlan901
```

Next, I'll add a simple OSPF configuration:

```
Arista(config)#router ospf 100
Arista(config-router-ospf)#network 192.168.1.0/24 area 0
Arista(config-router-ospf)#redistribute connected
```

Make sure we have a working neighbor (I'm not showing the neighbor's configuration because it's not an Arista switch, and really, who wants to see that?):

```
Arista(config-router-ospf)#sho ip ospf neighbor
Neighbor ID     Pri   State          Dead Time   Address        Interface
70.91.46.85       1   FULL/DR        00:00:34    192.168.1.1    Vlan901
```

So now that OSPF is up and working, let's see what routes we've learned from our neighbor:

```
Arista#sho ip route | begin Gateway
Gateway of last resort:
 S        0.0.0.0/0 [1/0] via 192.168.1.1

 C        30.30.30.0/24 is directly connected, Loopback0
 O E2     192.168.0.0/24 [110/10] via 192.168.1.1
 C        192.168.1.0/24 is directly connected, Vlan901
 O E2     192.168.2.0/24 [110/10] via 192.168.1.1
```

Now that we've got two OSPF routes learned, each of which has a metric of 10, let's take a look at Event Monitor. Before I do that, I'm going to clear out the buffer using the event-monitor clear command, because there's too much output to wade through, and I'm tired of filtering the output:

```
Arista(config)#event-monitor clear
Clearing buffer and forever logs
```

Since I cleared the buffer with the event-monitor clear command, the counters at the end of the lines have restarted. Notice also that the OSPF routes shown previously show a metric of 10, but the route entries in the Event Monitor show protocol values of *invalid*, and metric values of *0*:

```
Arista(config-router-ospf)#sho event-monitor route
2012-05-27 01:35:07|192.168.0.0/24|invalid|0|1|added|7
2012-05-27 01:35:07|192.168.2.0/24|invalid|0|1|added|8
% Writing 0 Arp, 4 Route, 4 Mac events to the database
```

Now let's see what happens when I remove OSPF from the switch. First, I'll remove the protocol from active duty:

```
Arista(config)#no router ospf 100
```

Then take a quick look to make sure all my OSPF routes are gone:

```
Arista(config)#sho ip route | beg Gateway
Gateway of last resort:
 S        0.0.0.0/0 [1/0] via 192.168.1.1
```

```
S      20.20.20.0/24 [155/0] via 192.168.1.1
C      30.30.30.0/24 is directly connected, Loopback0
C      192.168.1.0/24 is directly connected, Vlan901
```

And finally, a look into the Event Monitor to see how it responded:

```
Arista(config)#sho event-monitor route
2012-05-27 01:35:07|192.168.0.0/24|invalid|0|1|added|7
2012-05-27 01:35:07|192.168.2.0/24|invalid|0|1|added|8
2012-05-27 01:39:02|192.168.0.0/24||||removed|11
2012-05-27 01:39:02|192.168.2.0/24||||removed|12
% Writing 0 Arp, 2 Route, 2 Mac events to the database
```

As you can see, it reacts pretty much the same way as when I added and removed static routes. Convinced that I could get the protocol field to show something other than invalid, I fired up a similar test using BGP. Again, I'm only showing the Arista side of things because this isn't a lesson on routing, but rather a view into the workings of Event Monitor.

 Again, this behavior is a result of bug ID #30146, which is scheduled to be resolved in EOS version 5.0.0. Though I would love to have waited for 5.0.0 to come out before finishing this book, I ran out of time, so I had no choice but to report how it works at the time of writing (mid-2012). Besides, updating this chapter goes right into my "reasons O'Reilly should approve the 2nd edition" file for later use.

Here's my quick and dirty BGP config, just to show that the protocol, metric, and preferences never change:

```
Arista(config)#router bgp 100
Arista(config-router-bgp)#neighbor 192.168.1.1 remote-as 100
```

And here's the newly learned BGP route sitting snug in the routing table:

```
Arista(config-router-bgp)#sho ip route | begin Gateway
Gateway of last resort:
 S      0.0.0.0/0 [1/0] via 192.168.1.1

 S      20.20.20.0/24 [155/0] via 192.168.1.1
 C      30.30.30.0/24 is directly connected, Loopback0
 C      192.168.1.0/24 is directly connected, Vlan901
 B I    192.168.2.0/24 [200/0] via 192.168.1.1
```

And here's the new route as seen in event-monitor:

```
Arista#sho event-monitor route
2012-05-27 02:00:51|192.168.2.0/24|invalid|0|1|added|18
```

Now I'll remove BGP from the switch:

```
Arista(config)#no router bgp 100
```

And show that the BGP route is gone:

```
Arista(config)#sho ip route | beg Gateway
Gateway of last resort:
 S      0.0.0.0/0 [1/0] via 192.168.1.1

 S      20.20.20.0/24 [155/0] via 192.168.1.1
 C      30.30.30.0/24 is directly connected, Loopback0
 C      192.168.1.0/24 is directly connected, Vlan901
```

And here's the final output from event-monitor:

```
Arista(config)#sho event-monitor route
2012-05-27 02:00:51|192.168.2.0/24|invalid|0|1|added|18
2012-05-27 02:01:44|192.168.2.0/24||||removed|19
```

Advanced Usage

Event monitor uses sqlite, as I've already stated, but using the CLI commands really doesn't allow the full use of sqlite if you've got SQL skills. Luckily, there are a few ways to get to the good stuff.

First, you can issue sqlite commands through the show event-monitor sqlite *sqlite-command* command as you've already seen. Let's get a list of all the databases, so we'll need to list the tables. The sqlite command, .tables, does just that. So, let's add that to our command:

```
Arista#sho event-monitor sqlite .tables
arp     mac     route
```

That makes sense, since the only things we can use Event Monitor for (as of EOS 4.9.3.2) is ARP, MAC, and route changes. Being nosy, I decided that I wanted to know where the database was actually stored.

Here's a great example of why I love Arista products. Instead of bugging the guys at Arista for information about the default database location, I dug in and tried to figure it out on my own. Because everything is open and not some custom application, a little bit of online research revealed tips and tricks for using sqlite. The sqlite command, .databases, will show the location of the database files in use. By using the sqlite keyword and appending this command, I easily found what I wanted:

```
Arista#sho event-monitor sqlite .databases
seq  name           file
---  -------------  -------------------------------------------------------------
0    main           /tmp/eventMon.db
```

You can also get some helpful commands by issuing the `sho event-monitor sqlite .help` command in CLI.

You can do almost anything you'd like this way, though I've had trouble trying to stack sqlite commands though the CLI with this method. Thankfully, there's a way around this. By issuing the `event-monitor interact` command from CLI, you'll drop into sqlite's own command-line interface:

```
Arista#event-monitor interact
SQLite version 3.6.23.1
Enter ".help" for instructions
Enter SQL statements terminated with a ";"
sqlite>
```

From here, you can do anything you could do as if you ran the `sqlite` command from the bash prompt. I'd suggest spending a bit of time learning simple sqlite commands before you play with this, but remember these two key points: every command must be terminated with a semicolon, and use `.quit` or Control-D to exit. Here's the command to list all the entries in the route table:

```
sqlite> select * from route;
2012-05-27 02:00:51|192.168.2.0/24|invalid|0|1|added|18
2012-05-27 02:01:44|192.168.2.0/24||||removed|19
sqlite>^D
Arista#
```

Of course, if you feel the need to access the program from bash, you may do so with the `sqlite3` command (on EOS v4.9.3.2). First I'll drop into bash:

```
Arista#bash

Arista Networks EOS shell

[GAD@Arista ~]$
```

And from there, I'll issue the `sqlite3` command:

```
[GAD@Arista ~]$ sqlite3
SQLite version 3.6.23.1
Enter ".help" for instructions
Enter SQL statements terminated with a ";"
```

And now I can issue my commands:

```
sqlite> select * from route;
Error: no such table: route
```

Whoops! When I dropped to bash, I lost the friendly CLI frontend to sqlite. From bash, I need to specify the database to use when starting sqlite (unless I'm going to create a new one from scratch). Remember back a bit when I showed where the database was? Now's the time to use that information:

```
[GAD@Arista ~]$ sqlite3 /tmp/eventMon.db
SQLite version 3.6.23.1
Enter ".help" for instructions
Enter SQL statements terminated with a ";"
```

Now we can select from our tables just like we did before:

```
sqlite> select * from route;
2012-05-27 02:00:51|192.168.2.0/24|invalid|0|1|added|18
2012-05-27 02:01:44|192.168.2.0/24||||removed|19
```

And remember that Control-D or .quit gets you out:

```
sqlite>.quit
[GAD@Arista ~]$
```

Configuring Event Monitor

The database for Event Monitor is found in the /tmp directory. This directory does not survive a reboot, so all of the Event Monitor entries will be lost every time the switch reboots. If you'd like to keep a (sort of) permanent log of these events, then you'll need to give Event Monitor a location to store its logs in the /mnt/flash directory. This can be done with the event-monitor backup path file-path command:

```
Arista(config)#event-monitor backup path em.log
```

Specifying a filename without a path will result in the file being placed in flash:

```
Arista(config)#dir
Directory of flash:/

        -rwx    245827739         Apr 16 04:19   EOS-4.9.1.swi
        -rwx    248665992         May 23 02:16   EOS-4.9.3.swi
        -rwx          137         May 23 02:32   boot-config
        drwx         4096         May 27 12:05   debug
        -rwx       336964         May 27 12:08   em.log.0
        drwx         4096         May 27 12:04   persist
        drwx         4096         May 16 19:27   schedule
        -rwx         1868         May 27 12:03   startup-config
        -rwx            0         May 14 16:46   zerotouch-config

    1862512640 bytes total (256790528 bytes free)
```

If you specify what you think is a full Unix path, such as /home/admin/em.log, you will not get the expected results, as this will translate to flash:/home/admin/em.log:

```
Arista(config)#event-monitor backup path /home/admin/em.log
Arista(config)#dir
```

```
Directory of flash:/

    -rwx     245827739        Apr 16 04:19   EOS-4.9.1.swi
    -rwx     248665992        May 23 02:16   EOS-4.9.3.swi
    -rwx           137        May 23 02:32   boot-config
    drwx          4096        May 27 12:05   debug
    drwx          4096        May 27 12:08   home
    drwx          4096        May 27 12:04   persist
    drwx          4096        May 16 19:27   schedule
    -rwx          1868        May 27 12:03   startup-config
    -rwx             0        May 14 16:46   zerotouch-config
```

You can specify a Unix path. The command provides two options when asked:

```
Arista(config)#event-monitor backup path ?
  file:   forever log URL
  flash:  forever log URL
```

The idea of a forever log sounds oddly romantic, like rescuing a dog from the pound and bringing him to his forever home, but what this *file versus flash* choice is offering is the choice between a Unix path (*file:*) or a CLI path (*flash:*). By not specifying either, the parser will assume *flash:*. That's why our previous command, using */home/admin* created a directory in *flash:*. To actually put the file in */home/admin* (which would be dumb, since */home* will not survive a reboot either), use the following command, incorporating *file:* at the beginning of the path:

```
Arista(config)#event-monitor backup path file:/home/admin/em.log
```

That will put the database file where you want it:

```
Arista#bash ls /home/admin
em.log.0
```

 The EOS device, *file:*, is a pseudodevice that lets you access the Linux file system from within CLI. You can use it anywhere you would use another device name, such as `copy flash:GAD.txt file:/tmp`.

You may have noticed that my files all have a *.0* appended to them, although I did not specify that. Event monitor will write 500 events to the file, after which it will create a new file, appended with a *.1*. The logs are circular, so when the last log (default *.200*) is reached, the *.0* file is deleted, and new data will be written there. That's why I wrote earlier that these files were *sort of* permanent. To configure how many logfiles you would like to retain, use the `event-monitor backup max-size` *number* command:

```
Arista(config)#event-monitor backup max-size ?
  <1-200>  maximum number of stored backup logs
```

I'll specify 10 logfiles, for no other reason than I like the number 10:

```
Arista(config)#event-monitor backup max-size 10
```

To disable Event Monitor completely, use the `no event-monitor all` configuration command:

```
Arista(config)#no event-monitor all
```

To enable only one of the Event Monitor functions, use the `event-monitor` command, followed by the function (`mac`, `arp`, or `route`) that you'd like to enable. You can also disable single functions by negating these commands:

```
Arista(config)#event-monitor route
```

To enable them all again, use the `all` keyword:

```
Arista(config)#event-monitor all
```

Finally, you can configure a max buffer size for Event Monitor. The Arista manuals show the buffer size in Kb (kilobits), which I kind of think is a mistake, but if it's not, one kilobit = 128 bytes.

The buffer size can be configured from 6 to 50 units in size. If backup logs are configured, they are written to when the buffer becomes full:

```
Arista(config)#event-monitor buffer max-size ?
<6-50>  maximum size of the primary event monitor log
```

For most environments, leaving the Event Monitor as is and enabled probably makes the most sense. I see no reason to disable it, and even though you might use it rarely, it can be an invaluable tool when you do need it.

## CHAPTER 28

Extending EOS

EOS is the Extensible Operating System, so let's have some fun and extend it! OK, so my idea of fun is installing extensions into a networking switch. What can I say? I'm living the dream.

Extensions are nothing more than RPMs. For those not familiar with Linux, RPM stands for *RPM Package Manager*. If that makes you twitch because your fifth grade teacher wouldn't let you use the word being defined within the definition, you're not alone. RPM originally stood for *Red Hat Package Manager*, which is far less likely to offend fifth-grade teacher sensibilities. The reason for the change is that RPMs are used in many more operating systems these days, even if the recursive name gives me hives.

 There are more ways to extend EOS than using RPMs. I'll give a couple of examples at the end of this chapter.

RPMs are *packages* that usually contain compiled code. Using an RPM is just like downloading a program from the Internet that needs to be unpacked and installed. On a Windows machine, you might download an Installer, while on a Mac you might download a DMG image that contains a PKG package file. The idea is the same. RPMs are just the way Linux handles packages. Since EOS is running on Linux, it's only natural to use RPMs to add extensions.

So what sort of extensions can be added? If you were a skilled programmer, I'd say that you could add anything you wanted! If you're like me, looking for existing packages, then it will depend what's out there. A quick place to look for existing extensions is on Arista's EOS Extensions web page, located on their EOS Central site (*https://eos.arista networks.com/wiki/index.php/EOS_Extensibility:Extensions_And_Scripts_Library*).

Looking there, I discovered something I'd love to add: the manual for CLI commands. For this chapter, I'm going to download it, install it, and see how it all works, so let's get started.

First, I needed to download the package. The EOS Central page linked to another website that had the download links all coded in Flash, so I downloaded it and moved it to my server. That way, I could show you one of the cool features in EOS—the ability to copy files from a web page right to the switch.

In order to do this next step, your switch will need access to the Internet. Naturally, it will also need an IP address and a default gateway, but it will also need a DNS server or a configured ip host in order to resolve the hostnames. Since I had my web server inside my private network, I used the ip host solution:

```
Arista(config)#ip host www.gad.net 192.168.1.222
```

With my hostname set, and the file located on my server, I could copy directly from the web server to my switch. In order to accomplish this, I did what most of us do and looked at what my options were with the ? character at the command prompt:

```
Arista#copy ?
  boot-extensions       Copy boot extensions configuration
  extension:            Source file path
  file:                 Source file path
  flash:                Source file path
  ftp:                  Source file path
  http:                 Source file path
  https:                Source file path
  installed-extensions  Copy installed extensions status
  running-config        Copy from current system configuration
  scp:                  Source file path
  sftp:                 Source file path
  startup-config        Copy from startup configuration
  system:               Source file path
  tftp:                 Source file path
```

As you can see, there are a lot of options. I'll be using http: for this example, but note that you can copy from secure websites (https:), secure copy (scp:), and a bunch of other cool options. I'll include the entire URL and then include the destination extension:

```
Arista#copy http://www.gad.net/RPM/manCli.noarch.rpm extension:
```

If the file is small, as this one is, you may see a message flash so quickly that you can't see it. Don't worry too much about it; it's more important for huge files or for files being transferred over slow connections. If you're really wondering (as I was) what it says, here's a snapshot while downloading a generic huge file:

```
Arista#copy http://www.gad.net/RPM/HugeFile.zip extension:
'RPM/HugeFile.zip' at 5235283 (3%) [Receiving data]
```

To see what's in your *extension:* drive, you can use the `dir extension:` command from EOS:

```
Arista#dir extension:
Directory of extension:/

     -rwx      257062           May 9 19:43  manCli.noarch.rpm
```

A much better command to use is the `show extensions` command.

```
Arista#show extensions
Name                               Version/Release           Status RPMs
---------------------------------- ------------------------- ------ ----
manCli.noarch.rpm                  3.3/3                     A, NI    1

A: available | NA: not available | I: installed | NI: not installed |
F: forced
```

This command shows some great information about the extensions, including the version, if it's available, and if it's installed or not.

 If you're using a chassis-based switch like the Arista 7500s, you'll need to copy extensions on all supervisors.

So now that we've got our RPM, let's get that sucker installed. To do so, simply use the `extension` command, followed by the name of the extension. You can use the ? character to get a list of available extensions:

```
Arista#extension manCli.noarch.rpm
% manCli Extension installation is complete

If this extension modifies the behavior of the Cli, any running Cli
sessions will need to be reset in order for the Cli modifications to
take effect.
```

Success! The last message is important if your extension has modified anything at the EOS command line, in which case you'll need to log out and back in to see the effects.

With our extension successfully installed, let's check the status again with the `show extensions` command:

```
Arista#sho extensions
Name                               Version/Release           Status RPMs
---------------------------------- ------------------------- ------ ----
manCli.noarch.rpm                  3.3/3                     A, I     1

A: available | NA: not available | I: installed | NI: not installed |
F: forced
```

The flag under the Status column now shows an I (installed), whereas before we installed it, it showed an NI (not installed).

So what does this extension get us anyway? This extension basically installed the entire Arista User Manual into the switch. The manual is accessed using the man command:

```
Arista#man ?
% Unrecognized command
```

Whoops! Remember that warning that said I needed to reset the CLI? I never logged out, so let me do that and try again:

```
Arista#exit

Arista login: GAD
Password:
Last login: Wed May  9 20:40:58 on ttyS0
Arista>en
Arista#man ?
  grep    Search for documents containing a pattern
  topics  List topics
  update  Update system documentation from Arista Networks or
          alternate URL
```

To see the chapters, use the man topics ? command:

```
Arista#man topics ?
  Chapter_10_Access_Control/  Chapter_10_Access_Control sections
  Chapter_11_VRRP_and_VARP/   Chapter_11_VRRP_and_VARP sections
  Chapter_12_STP/             Chapter_12_STP sections
  Chapter_13_OSPF/            Chapter_13_OSPF sections
  Chapter_14_BGP/             Chapter_14_BGP sections
  Chapter_15_RIP/             Chapter_15_RIP sections
  Chapter_16_Multicast/       Chapter_16_Multicast sections
[--- output truncated ---]
```

To find a topic, use the grep command, followed by the subject in which you are interested:

```
Arista#man grep extensions

References to the pattern "extensions" were found in the following
sections:

Section                         Topic

Chapter_12_Spanning_Tree_Protocol 12.3_Configuring_a_Spanning_Tree
Chapter_3_Command-Line_Interface  3.7_Command-Line_Interface_Commands
Chapter_3_Command-Line_Interface  3.5_Other_Command-Line_Interfaces
Chapter_1_Product_Overview        1.1_Supported_Features
```

I'm going to go with `1.1_Supported_Features`, so let's see how to get more information. When it comes to this RPM, tab completion is your friend. Here, I've used a mixture of tab completion and the ? character to figure out how to view the manual for the section of interest:

```
Arista#man topics Chapter_1_
Arista#man topics Chapter_1_Product_Overview/
Arista#man topics Chapter_1_Product_Overview/1.
Arista#man topics Chapter_1_Product_Overview/1.?
Chapter_1_Product_Overview/1.1_Supported_Features
Chapter_1_Product_Overview/1.2_Feature_Availability_on_Switch_Platform
```

A-ha! I'll choose the first one, `1.1_Supported_Features`:

```
Arista#man topics Chapter_1_Product_Overview/1.1_Supported_Features
1.1 Supported Features
1.1.1 Management and Security Utilities
The following features configure, maintain, and secure the switch
and its network connections:
Extensible Operating System (EOS): EOS is the interface between the
switch and the software that controls the switch and manages the
network. Refer to Section 3.1: Accessing the EOS CLI.
[--- output truncated ---]
```

 Remember, the Arista team may not have written extensions you download, so they may not work the way you might expect, and they may not follow established user interface guidelines.

Installed extensions will not survive a reboot by default. To make them permanent, you'll need to issue the `copy installed-extensions boot-extensions` command:

```
Arista#copy installed-extensions boot-extensions
```

To make sure your extensions will survive a reboot, use the `show boot-extensions` command:

```
Arista#sho boot-extensions
manCli.noarch.rpm
```

If you'd like to remove an installed extension, simply negate the extension command, followed by the extension name:

```
Arista#no extension manCli.noarch.rpm
% manCli Extension removal is complete
```

After removing an extension, the rule about resetting the CLI still applies, although it's not reinforced with a warning. Here, I run the same command I used to show the chapter, but now I get an error because the extension has been removed:

```
Arista#man topics Chapter_1_Product_Overview/1.1_Supported_Features
/mnt/flash/persist/docs/Chapter_1_Product_Overview/1.1_Supported_
Features: No such file or directory
```

This is because when I removed the extension, the RPM management process removed all the chapters from the flash drive. Since I haven't reset my CLI, the man command still works, but it has none of its files to display. I can fix this by exiting CLI and logging in again:

```
Arista#exit

Arista login: GAD
Password:
Last login: Wed May  9 20:43:20 on ttyS0

Arista>en
Arista#
Arista#man topics Chapter_1_Product_Overview/1.1_Supported_Features
% Invalid input
```

Now the man command is no longer supported.

As an interesting aside, this process once more illustrates how the CLI is nothing more than a process in Linux. When I logged out, the process was terminated, and when I logged in, a new one was spawned.

Though my extension has been deactivated, the RPM is still sitting in the *extensions:* drive as evidenced by the show extensions command:

```
Arista#sho extensions
Name                          Version/Release           Status RPMs
----------------------------- ------------------------- ------ ----
manCli.noarch.rpm             3.3/3                     A, NI   1

A: available | NA: not available | I: installed | NI: not installed |
F: forced
```

To remove it from the switch, simply delete it from the *extensions:* drive:

```
Arista#del extension:manCli.noarch.rpm
```

That's removed it completely—it no longer shows up in the output of show extensions:

```
Arista#sho extensions
No extensions are available
```

If you made your extension bootable, it will try to come back the next time you reload, unless you remove it from the boot extensions:

```
SW1#sho extensions
Name                          Version/Release           Status RPMs
----------------------------- ------------------------- ------ ----
CloudVision-1.1.0_4.8.swix    1.1.0/496645.EOS481.7     A, NI   1
CloudVision.swix              1.1.0/496645.EOS481.7     A, NI   1
```

```
manCli.noarch.rpm                    Error: extension is not available

A: available | NA: not available | I: installed | NI: not installed |
F: forced
```

On EOS version 4.9.3.2, there is seemingly no way to get rid of the boot extension entry for a deleted extension. There is no del boot-extensions command available, and I could find no other way to delete it from within the CLI. Luckily, this is EOS, and there's always another way. The list of items in boot extension is simply a list of extension names found in Flash. Here's the contents of the boot extensions file from bash:

```
[admin@SW1 ~]$ more /mnt/flash/boot-extensions
manCli.noarch.rpm
```

To delete one line, use *vi* from bash and delete the line. If you just delete the file, you'll get an error when trying to view it:

```
SW1(config)#sho boot-extensions
% Error displaying flash:/boot-extensions (No such file or directory)
```

You can always fix that by copying installed extensions (which is just another file) to boot extensions, after which the show boot-extensions command will stop throwing an error:

```
SW1(config)#copy installed-extensions boot-extensions
SW1(config)#sho boot-extensions
```

 A Request for Enhancement has been introduced (#37263) to resolve the issue of not being able to remove boot extensions.

There are many other cool extensions out there as well. Mark Berly of Arista wrote a fabulous Python script that will automatically add interface descriptions based on the information discovered by LLDP. Another one of his scripts monitors and records the power output of the optical SFP transceivers. Neither of these scripts use the extensions feature as outlined previously, but they are both extensions to EOS. Both of these extensions are available in the EOS Central repository, located at *https://eos.aristanet works.com* (registration required).

## CHAPTER 29

CloudVision

CloudVision is a framework that will allow a pile of cool management features in the future. For now, it gives you the ability to instant message (IM) commands to your switch, after which the switch sends its response (if any) back to you with another IM.

When I tell people that they can IM commands to their Arista switches without having to log in to them, I get mixed reactions ranging from nerdy appreciation for a cool feature that they never even considered a possibility, to outright horror that such a thing might exist. Personally, I think it's one of the coolest features I've ever seen, but it's rare that I recommend its use. That said, in the right environment, it could be an amazing tool that can make your life much easier. Let's take a look and see how such a powerful feature could be put to good use.

Description

CloudVision is an extension to EOS (as of version 4.9.3.2) that allows the switch to participate in XMPP-based near real-time messaging. XMPP is a protocol commonly used for open source client/server chat, and is defined in RFC 3920, entitled *Extensible Messaging and Presence Protocol (XMPP)*. The RFC has this to say about XMPP:

```
While XMPP provides a generalized, extensible framework for exchanging
XML data, it is used mainly for the purpose of building instant
messaging and presence applications that meet the requirements of RFC
2779 (Instant Messaging / Presence Protocol Requirements).
```

One or more XMPP servers are required for CloudVision to work. Arista recommends the *ejabberd* server, and that seems to be the standard, but any server/client system that supports XMPP can be used. I do recommend that if you use this feature, you ensure that only clients within your secured environment can access your switch. My reasons for this recommendation should become fairly obvious as you see how CloudVision works.

I'll not cover the details of configuring and running an XMPP server in this book, opting instead to use the publicly available jabber.org server. Please note that I do not recommend this for production use in any way, shape, or form. Your XMPP server should be secured and inside your firewall, accessible from the outside only through VPN or other similarly secure means.

That's worth a bigger warning. When using this feature, make sure that you only use private, secure XMPP servers. The reasons for that should be fairly obvious, but let me be blunt. With the current iteration of CloudVision, if you use a public XMPP server, anyone who knows the username assigned to your switch can access your switch from anywhere in the world without so much as a password.

I will also warn you that the temptation will be great to use a public server, or to allow outside access to your XMPP server. Don't. Why do I warn about the possibility of temptation? Because CloudVision is a seriously cool feature. I mean *seriously* cool! Let's take a look and you can decide for yourself.

Configuring and Using CloudVision

The current Arista web page (*https://eos.aristanetworks.com/2011/08/management-over-xmpp/*) describes CloudVision, and on that page is a list of downloads, separated by EOS version. You can also download the extensions from the support download page (*http://www.aristanetworks.com/support/download/*), which requires a valid login.

I've been told that CloudVision will likely be integrated into EOS by the end of 2012, so look forward to this chapter looking very different in the second edition of *Arista Warrior*!

There are different versions of this extension, so make sure you download the correct one for your version of EOS. For this chapter, I'll be using EOS version 4.8.1 and Cloud-Vision version 1.1.0_4.8. Though EOS version 4.9.3.2 is the latest EOS available, a matching CloudVision has not yet been released, and the 4.8 version of CloudVision does not work with EOS 4.9.3.2. Believe me, I tried.

This changed a bit at the absolute last minute in the production of this book. As a result, part of this chapter contains commands from EOS 4.9 and CloudVision version 1.2.3_4.9.

The first step is to get CloudVision onto the switch. To simplify matters, I've loaded it on my local server. Using the copy command, I'll copy it to the *extension:* drive:

```
Arista#copy http://www.gad.net/A/CloudVision-1.1.0_4.8.swix extension:
```

I'll use the show extensions command, just to make sure it's really there:

```
Arista#sho extensions
Name                            Version/Release           Status RPMs
------------------------------- ------------------------- ------ ----
CloudVision-1.1.0_4.8.swix      1.1.0/496645.EOS481.7     A, NI    1

A: available | NA: not available | I: installed | NI: not installed |
F: forced
```

Comfortable that the file got transferred properly, I'll install it using the extension *extension-name* command:

```
Arista#extension CloudVision-1.1.0_4.8.swix
If this extension modifies the behavior of the Cli, any running Cli
sessions will need to be reset in order for the Cli modifications to
take effect.
```

Indeed, we do need to exit and restart CLI, since this extension will add commands to the CLI:

```
Arista#exit

Arista login: admin
Last login: Thu May 31 14:33:03 on ttyS0
Arista>en
Arista#
```

Remember, if you want your installed extensions to survive a reboot, you'll need to copy the installed extension status to the boot extensions configuration:

```
Arista#copy installed-extensions boot-extensions
```

A quick look to make sure that this was really done is always a good idea for neurotic admins like me:

```
Arista#sho boot-extensions
CloudVision-1.1.0_4.8.swix
```

 If you don't configure the extension to be installed at boot, all of your XMPP configuration will disappear after booting. I forget to do this every time, and I sit there scratching my head trying to figure out what's wrong. Don't forget to make your extensions load at boot!

With the extension loaded, we can get down to the business of configuring XMPP. All XMPP commands for CloudVision are entered after issuing the `management xmpp` command, which only become available after exiting and restarting the CLI (you only need to do this once). This will put you into `mgmt-xmpp` configuration mode. Note that no commands issued in this mode are active until you exit from the mode:

```
Arista(config)#management xmpp
```

The first thing that the switch needs to know is where the XMPP server is. I've configured my switch with a username and password on the publicly available jabber.org server, so that's what I'll configure with the `server` command:

```
Arista(config-mgmt-xmpp)#server jabber.org
```

If you're using a private jabber server (and you really should), then you'll need to know the configured server name. Next, I have to tell the switch what username and password it will use to connect to the server. Every switch configured with CloudVision will need to have its own username and password. Not surprisingly, this step is configured using the `username` *username* `password` *password* command. Usernames with XMPP look like email addresses in that they use the format *username@domain*:

```
Arista(config-mgmt-xmpp)#username GAD-Arista@jabber.org password PIE!
```

As of May 2012, there is no ability to encrypt the password, and it even tells you that in a sort of passive-aggressive way if you ask for help on the command:

```
Arista(config-mgmt-xmpp)#username GAD-Arista@jabber.org password ?
  LINE  The UNENCRYPTED (cleartext) XMPP password
```

One of the cooler abilities of this feature is that switches can belong to groups. The groups don't need to be preconfigured anywhere. When you start a group with the matching name (most XMPP clients allow this), the switch will automatically join. Don't worry, I'll show that in action in a bit. What you need to know is that the group name is just like a username, but it must include `conference` before the domain, separated by a period. Here, I've configured the switch for the group called *gad-7124s@conference.jabber.org*:

```
Arista(config-mgmt-xmpp)#switch-group gad-7124s@conference.jabber.org
```

 Private XMPP servers might be configured to use a word other than conference, but conference is the default.

Finally, you can issue `shut` and `no shut` commands just like you would an interface, and you'll need to issue the `no shut` command to make it work (I forget this easily 90% of the time). I've seen this feature get a bit confused, causing the switch to say that it's connected, but not appearing in my contact list. When that happens, going into `management xmpp` and doing a `shut` and `no shut` on the switch fixes it right up (after you exit the mode):

```
Arista(config-mgmt-xmpp)#no shut
```

To make it all take effect, exit this configuration mode:

```
Arista(config-mgmt-xmpp)#exit
```

And we're done! Once I hit `exit`, I can add the switch to my contact list. I added an alias so that the switch just appears as *Arista* in my client. The info screen for my switch's contact can be seen in Figure 29-1. I'm using a Mac, and the IM client I'm using is Adium, which supports XMPP. I've got a user configured for myself named *GADify@jabber.org* on the *jabber.org* server.

 As you might have noticed, I can be a little nutty about capitalizing my initials, even for things like XMPP usernames. Case is irrelevant in XMPP addresses, just as it is in email addresses.

![Arista's Info screen showing gad-arista@jabber.org with Alias Arista, resource 748bd1bf13f15908, priority 0, status Available: Arista Networks DCS-7124S, family name gad-arista, contacts Arista, full name Arista]

Figure 29-1. Info screen for my Arista switch's XMPP username

And now, my Arista switch appears in my contact list next to all my other close friends, as you can see in Figure 29-2. If you have your client set to approve new contacts, you'll have to go through the approval process.

Figure 29-2. Arista switch added to my contact list

At this point, I can send the switch commands right from my IM client. Let's try something simple, like the show version command. The output from my short IM session is shown in Figure 29-3.

When I saw this feature for the first time, I started to question things. First off, notice that I was not challenged for a password, or a username, or anything. I issued a show command from my IM client, and the switch responded with the output. Let's try another. How about show interface ethernet10? The output is shown in Figure 29-4.

But that was just a show command. What about enable commands? In Figure 29-5, I try to issue the following commands, in order: en, conf t, and int e10. From the command line, this would have the following effect:

```
Arista>en
Arista#conf t
Arista(config)#int e10
Arista(config-if-Et10)#
```

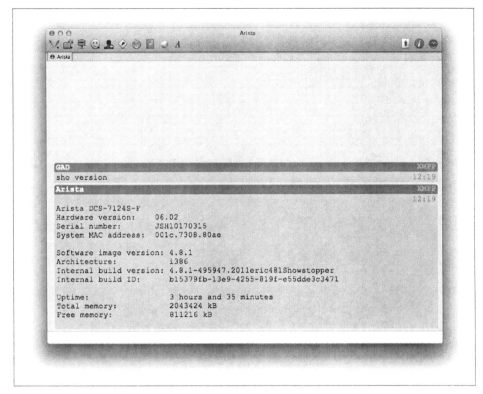

Figure 29-3. Show version, as seen on my IM client

Sending en results in the message, *Sorry, I didn't understand what you wrote. Type 'help' for a list of things you can ask me.* The command conf t seemed to have no effect at all, and int e10 resulted in an *Unknown command 'int e10'* error. So it would appear that we couldn't configure the switch through XMPP. That doesn't seem very useful now, does it?

I then thought about how I might write CloudVision, and came to the conclusion that I wouldn't want to leave the switch in configuration mode after sending an IM. I thought that if I were to write it, I might make the client only accept multiple commands from a single IM, which would allow me to paste chunks of configuration in at once, but not interactively. So I decided to send the following config snippet to my switch in a single IM to see how it would behave:

```
Conf t
 int e10
 description [ GAD e10 ]
 switchport mode trunk
 no shut
```

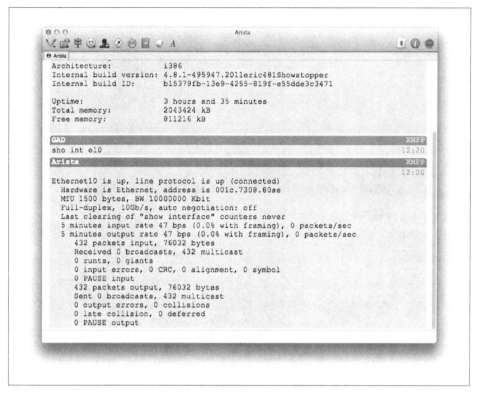

```
                                    Arista
                                                          ↑ ⓘ ⊗
θ Arista
  Architecture:              i386
  Internal build version:   4.8.1-495947.2011eric481Showstopper
  Internal build ID:        b15379fb-13e9-4255-819f-e55dde3c3471

  Uptime:                   3 hours and 35 minutes
  Total memory:             2043424 kB
  Free memory:              811216 kB

  GAD                                                           XMPP
  sho int e10                                                   12:20
  Arista                                                        XMPP
                                                                12:20
  Ethernet10 is up, line protocol is up (connected)
    Hardware is Ethernet, address is 001c.7308.80ae
    MTU 1500 bytes, BW 10000000 Kbit
    Full-duplex, 10Gb/s, auto negotiation: off
    Last clearing of "show interface" counters never
    5 minutes input rate 47 bps (0.0% with framing), 0 packets/sec
    5 minutes output rate 47 bps (0.0% with framing), 0 packets/sec
      432 packets input, 76032 bytes
      Received 0 broadcasts, 432 multicast
      0 runts, 0 giants
      0 input errors, 0 CRC, 0 alignment, 0 symbol
      0 PAUSE input
      432 packets output, 76032 bytes
      Sent 0 broadcasts, 432 multicast
      0 output errors, 0 collisions
      0 late collision, 0 deferred
      0 PAUSE output
```

Figure 29-4. Output of the show interface e10 command in my IM client

In Figure 29-6, I send the command `sho run int e10` in order to show the original condition of the interface's configuration, then I paste the entire chunk from the previous post, all in one IM. I then issue the `show run int e10` command again to show that the commands were accepted. As you can see, it worked like a charm.

In order to enter configuration mode and change the config, you'll need to enter all of the configuration commands into a single IM.

So what else can we do? Well, the switch told us to type "help" for a list before, so let's go ahead and do that. This results in the response, *Here are some of the things I can help you with: - I can run any enable mode cli command.* That's mostly true, provided you paste the commands together in one IM, as I showed previously.

Figure 29-5. Trying to enter enable and configuration modes through XMPP

As a fun aside, here's a bit of nerdtastic coding I found: I decided to see if I could issue the exit command, and when I tried, I got the response, *I'm sorry gadify@jabber.org, I'm afraid I can't do that* shown in Figure 29-7. Either the original developers had a sense of humor along with a love for classic science fiction, or my switch has become self-aware. I'm hoping for the former, because I really don't have the time to fight off another robot invasion.

What else can we do in enable mode? How about reloading the switch? This doesn't seem to work, even when pasting reload and yes in a single IM. While we can't reboot with the interactive reload command, EOS allows you to reboot without interaction using the reload now command, which works just fine through CloudVision. You can see the results of me doing this to my switch in Figure 29-8. Note that there is no warning, and no indication that the switch actually did reload, aside from the fact that I lost connection to the switch for a short time while it reloaded. Even the show reload cause command was vague:

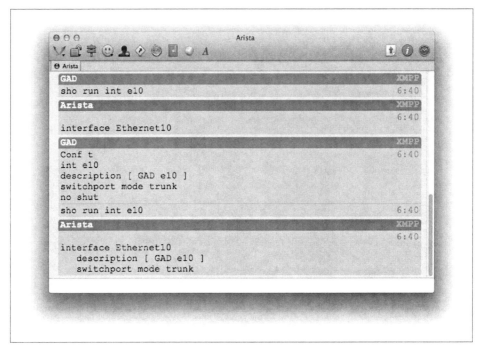

Figure 29-6. Config pasted all in one chunk

```
Arista#sho reload cause
Reload Cause 1:
------------------
Reload requested by the user.

Recommended Action:
------------------
No action necessary.

Debugging Information:
----------------------
None available.
```

This does lead me to one of my main concerns with the CloudVision feature: I could not find any log of the fact that the system was reloaded though XMPP, nor any indication of what user initiated the request.

I spoke with Arista about this, and they agreed that it would be a great idea, so although I complain about it in this chapter, I'm sure that most of my annoyances will be resolved in future code.

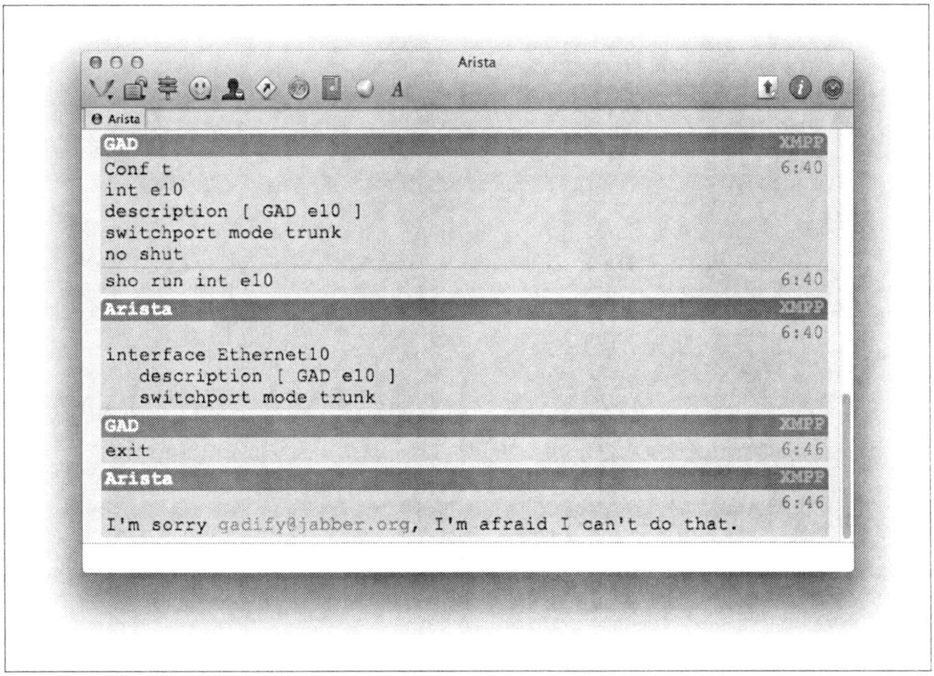

Figure 29-7. My switch seems to have become self-aware

Using EOS version 4.8.1 and CloudVision 1.1.0_4.8 (the latest version available as of May 2012), I could find no accountability whatsoever for CloudVision commands. This alone would make me not want to use this feature in a production environment.

In my experience, one of the ways that disgruntled or otherwise troublesome employees cause trouble is through devices with little or no user accountability. In the case of CloudVision, I'd have to rely on the IM client logs, which are easily cleared or modified. I would like to see the XMPP user configuration somehow tied to Authentication, Authorization, and Accounting (AAA), and logs recorded that show all XMPP user activity.

To be fair, most (if not all) XMPP servers can log IMs being sent, and most clients do so by default, so the messages sent by users to the switch are likely logged somewhere. I'd really like to see it logged in the switch though, since as a network guy, I may not have easy access to the XMPP server.

```
 ● ● ●                                    Arista
 ⅄ 🗔 🖳 😊 ⚑ ◈ ◎ 🖼 ⤾ 𝐴                                    ⬆ ⓘ ⊛
 ⊖ Arista
       - I can run any enable mode cli command
 GAD                                                                      XMPP
 sho run int e10                                                          2:58
 Arista                                                                   XMPP
                                                                         2:58
 interface Ethernet10
   no switchport
 GAD                                                                      XMPP
 sho run int e24                                                          2:58
 Arista                                                                   XMPP
                                                                         2:58
 interface Ethernet24
   switchport access vlan 901
   ip address 192.168.2.188/24
 GAD                                                                      XMPP
 reload                                                                   3:00
 Arista                                                                   XMPP
                                                                         3:00
 Proceed with reload? [confirm]
 GAD                                                                      XMPP
 yes                                                                      3:02
 Arista                                                                   XMPP
                                                                         3:02
 Unknown command 'yes'
 GAD                                                                      XMPP
 reload now                                                               3:07
```

Figure 29-8. Results of issuing the reload now command through CloudVision

The marketing material for CloudVision says that it is "authenticated, encrypted, and fully logged." (For details, assuming it hasn't changed, see *http://www.aristanetworks.com/products/eos/cloudvision*). When I asked the developer that worked on CloudVision about this, he said that meant that the XMPP server did all the logging.

Groups

CloudVision can be configured to allow the switch to join group chats. This is one of the most powerful and useful features of CloudVision, for reasons that should become apparent shortly.

In order to allow the switch to join a group chat, enter the command `switch-group` *group-name* in the `management xmpp` block. The group name is in the format of *group name@conference.domain*. If you're a "just gloss over the details now and wonder why it doesn't work later" type (like I am), the word *conference* must precede the domain, separated by a period. Since my switch is an Arista 7124, I'll add it to a group called *gad-7124s@conference.jabber.org*:

```
Arista(config)#management xmpp
Arista(config-mgmt-xmpp)#switch-group gad-7124s@conference.jabber.org
```

The switch can belong to more than one group. I'll add another called *gad-all*:

```
Arista(config-mgmt-xmpp)#switch-group gad-all@conference.jabber.org
```

You can add multiple groups with one command by separating them with a space. For example, the same two groups could be added as follows:

```
Arista(config-mgmt-xmpp)#switch-group gad-7124s@conference.jabber.org
gad-all@conference.jabber.org
```

The switch will separate each group out into its own command in the *running-config*:

```
management xmpp
   no shutdown
   server jabber.org
   username GAD-Arista@jabber.org password PIE!
   switch-group gad-7124s@conference.jabber.org
   switch-group gad-all@conference.jabber.org
```

I have two other switches, located in my secret underground lair, also configured with XMPP. These two switches are Arista 7050s and have been named SW10 and SW11, and have been configured as follows in XMPP. Here's SW10:

```
management xmpp
   no shutdown
   server jabber.org
   username GAD-Arista10@jabber.org password Arista
   switch-group GAD-7050s@conference.jabber.org
   switch-group GAD-all@conference.jabber.org
```

And here's SW11:

```
management xmpp
   no shutdown
   server jabber.org
   username GAD-Arista11@jabber.org password Arista
   switch-group GAD-7050s@conference.jabber.org
   switch-group GAD-all@conference.jabber.org
```

Of course, I could IM to any of them directly, but that's only the beginning of the fun. Since they're all in the switch group *gad-all*, I'll open a new group chat in my XMPP client using that as the room name, as shown in Figure 29-9.

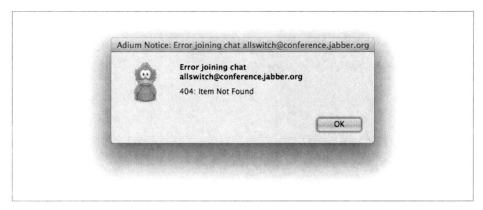

Figure 29-9. Group chat invite for all my switches

I've seen issues with XMPP and popular clients like Trillian and iChat where once the group is closed, trying to get back into it reports an error, as shown in Figure 29-10.

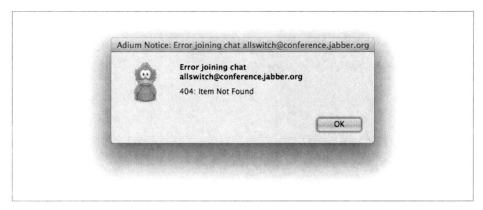

Figure 29-10. A 404 error when trying to rejoin previous group chat on jabber.org with Adium

If you see this, it may clear itself after a time when the server times out the old room name. To prevent a 404 error from happening, when you first make the group chat with your XMPP client, make the room persistent. This option should be available in your client when you create the group. The error shown previously shows a different group name because I copied it from my experiments before I knew what was wrong.

Note that when I joined the group chat, I did not invite my switches. As soon as the room becomes available, they joined the group. If for some reason they don't appear in your group chat, invite them. If they still don't join, check your configuration. A simple misspelling in the group name is usually the cause. To show how the group behaves, I'll send the command show version | grep Arista to the group, which should report the model number. The results are seen in Figure 29-11.

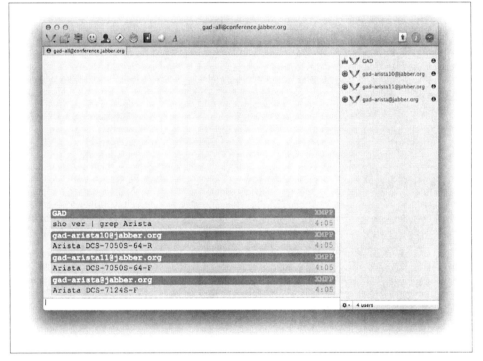

Figure 29-11. Getting model numbers from the group

Every switch in the group received the command, processed it, and sent the results back to the group chat. This is a very cool feature, no doubt, but the group is not secured in any way. In Figure 29-12, someone who is definitely not me has attached to the group and is able to not only see everything I do, but can also send commands to the group.

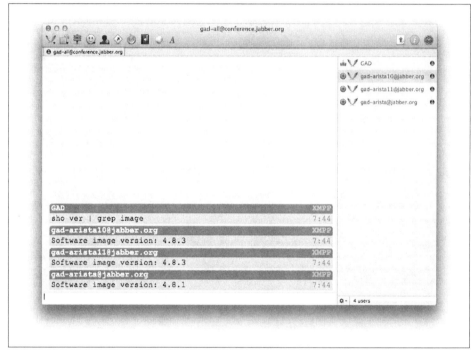

Figure 29-12. Some filthy lurker watching my group chat

Figure 29-13. Getting the EOS version with CloudVision

Most XMPP servers allow chat groups to be created with passwords, but as of EOS version 4.8.5, there is no option to specify a password on the `switch-group` command. This is another reason I'm not a fan of using CloudVision in a production environment, and definitely not with a public XMPP server. Though there may be ways to secure this on a private XMPP server, there is not from the switch.

Enough about the shortcomings, let's do something cool. Let's use the *gad-all* group to determine the versions of EOS installed on each switch. In Figure 29-13, I've sent the command `sho version | grep image` to retrieve the installed version of EOS on all of the switches in my group.

They're all a bit out of date, so let's copy some newer code to the switches. With one IM, I can initiate a copy on all three switches, as shown in Figure 29-14.

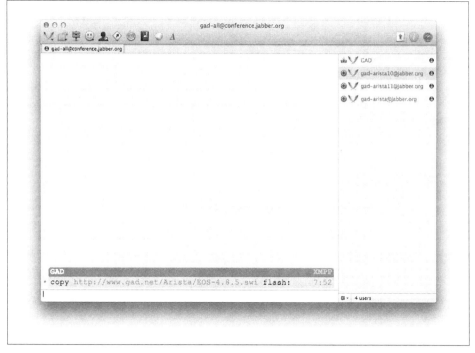

Figure 29-14. Initiating an http copy on all three switches at once

Though EOS version 4.9.3.2 is the latest as of June 2012, I needed to keep to the latest 4.8.x code because there was not yet a CloudVision released for version 4.9.3.

Note that when using XMPP, you won't get any status messages that you would see from the command line. For example, if I were to initiate the same copy from the command line of one of my switches, I would see this:

```
Arista(config)#copy http://192.168.1.200/Arista/EOS-4.8.5.swi flash:
Arista/EOS-4.8.5.swi' at 45684057 (19%) 20.90M/s eta:8s [Receiving data]
```

This type of continuously updating status is not practical over XMPP, so instead, we get no response at all, not even a message indicating that the file has been successfully copied. There's no reason to blame CloudVision about this though, since all it does is act as a portal to EOS. To see if the file is done, execute the `dir` command, either locally on the switch or through CloudVision. If you see your file with an odd extension like *.X85GBp*, then the file is still in transit. When it's done, this extension will disappear:

```
SW11#dir EOS-4.8.5*
Directory of flash:/EOS-4.8.5*

      -rwx     62428337              Jun 9 23:02   EOS-4.8.5.swi.X85GBp

1778040832 bytes total (1004822528 bytes free)
```

When using CloudVision remotely, as I am for the examples in this chapter, I've noticed that the switches have a tendency to become unavailable during large file transfers like this. That may be due to the way I've designed my lab (using a public XMPP server), or may have something to do with the way XMPP presence works. Either way, I've found that as soon as the file transfer is complete, the switches become available again. Just to be sure, I'll send the `dir EOS-4.8*` command to them. The results are shown in Figure 29-15.

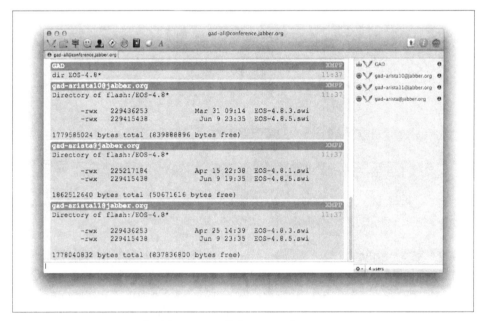

Figure 29-15. Directory of EOS-4.8* on all three switches

With the file safely stored on all three switches, let's upgrade them all. The steps for this, as shown in Chapter 7, are to set the boot statement, then reload. Setting the boot statement requires entering config mode, so we'll need to paste the commands together. Here's what I plan to send:

```
conf t
  boot system flash:EOS-4.8.5.swi
  wri
```

My experience shows that these commands won't produce a response in my IM client, so I'll add a final command, show boot, to see if they worked. If all looks well, I'll reboot the switches with the reboot now command. The results of these commands are shown in Figure 29-16.

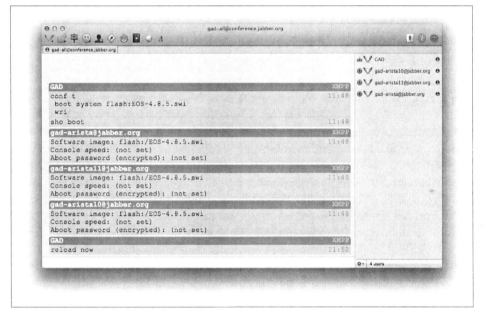

Figure 29-16. Setting the boot variable and reloading through CloudVision

Again, the results of the reload now command are not visible through CloudVision, so you'll have to take my word for it that all three switches rebooted.

Once the switches came back online, I issued the show version | inc image command one more time to see if the upgrade worked. As you can see in Figure 29-17, it worked perfectly. I love it when technology makes me efficient! Efficiency means more time for important things like lunch.

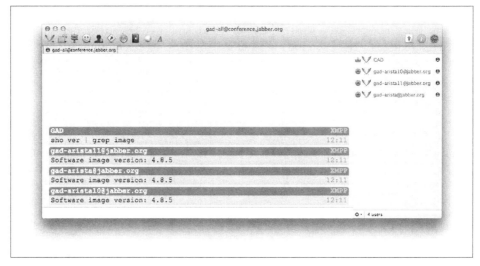

Figure 29-17. Versions on all three switches after upgrading through CloudVision

Upgrading all three switches at once is pretty cool, but let's think a step further. Imagine that you have 100 switches installed in a data center, in 50 MLAG pairs. With MLAG ISSU, you could upgrade them all without incurring an outage (assuming everything was properly dual homed). Of course properly using MLAG ISSU means that only one switch in the pair can be upgraded at a time. Imagine that all of the switches had Cloud-Vision installed, and the switches were in three switch groups: left, right, and all. By sending upgrade commands like we did in this chapter to only the left switches, you could upgrade 150 switches without leaving your desk, without causing an outage, and without spending more than about three minutes of your time. After waiting five more minutes to let the MLAG peers sync, you could then upgrade the other half of your switches. Assuming that you previously loaded the code onto your switches, the entire time needed to upgrade 300 switches, including the wait for MLAG, would be about 11 minutes. That's the kind of increase in productivity that makes CloudVision exciting.

You could group switches in any way you can imagine. By switch type (7124, 7050, 7500, etc.), by function (spline, leaf, core, distribution, etc.), by location, by floor, or by any other grouping you can conjure up.

Monitoring CloudVision

CloudVision is still in its infancy as of mid-2012, but there are a couple of tools that can be used to see the status of XMPP on the switch. The first is show xmpp status, which shows the status of the switch's user, and of the switch's connectivity to the configured XMPP server.

```
Arista#sho xmpp status
XMPP Server: jabber.org port 5222
Client username: GAD-Arista@jabber.org
Connection status: connected
```

I've mentioned that I've seen CloudVision get in a funky state. Here's an example of what that looks like, and how a shut/no shut fixes it right up:

```
SW11#sho xmpp status
XMPP Server: jabber.org port 5222
Client username: GAD-Arista11@jabber.org
Connection status: not connected
```

As you can see, the status shows that it's not connected. There might have been a server problem, or a connection problem. For whatever reason, the link to the server is not active. I'll go in and shut/no shut the XMPP session:

```
SW11#conf t
SW11(config)#management xmpp
SW11(config-mgmt-xmpp)#shut
SW11(config-mgmt-xmpp)#no shut
SW11(config-mgmt-xmpp)#exit
SW11(config)#exit
```

At this point, I'll check the status again:

```
SW11#sho xmpp status
XMPP Server: jabber.org port 5222
Client username: GAD-Arista11@jabber.org
Connection status: connected
```

And there you go. Everything is back to normal.

Another useful command is show xmpp neighbors. This command will show a list of XMPP users that are able to IM to the switch. Note that I could only get this to work on EOS 4.9.4 or later using CloudVision version 1.2.3_4.9 or later:

```
Arista#sho xmpp neighbors
Neighbor                     State            Last Seen Login Time
---------------------------- ---------------- ------------------------
gad-arista10@jabber.org      present          0:00:13 ago
gad-arista11@jabber.org      present          0:00:13 ago
gadify@jabber.org            present          0:00:13 ago


Neighbor                     Status Message
---------------------------- -------------------------------------
gad-arista10@jabber.org      Arista Networks DCS-7050S-64
gad-arista11@jabber.org      Arista Networks DCS-7050S-64

gadify@jabber.org
```

With the newer version of code, I can send XMPP messages between switches with the xmpp send command. I'll send the show version command to the switch, highlighted in bold previously. The switch I'm sending from is a 7124S. The switch I'm sending to (*gad-arista11@jabber.org*) is a 7050S-64:

```
Arista#xmpp send gad-arista11@jabber.org command show ver | inc Arista
message from user: gad-arista11@jabber.org
- - - - - - - - - - - - - - - - - - - - - - - - - - - - - - - - - - - - - - - - -

Arista DCS-7050S-64-F
```

That's pretty slick! Imagine the cool things you can do combining this with event manager, email, and any number of other features.

 If you've upgraded to 4.9.4 or 4.10 and are using a management VRF, this will break CloudVision version 1.2.3 since the DNS servers must be moved to the management VRF.

This version of CloudVision also introduces the ability to send XMPP messages through a bash command named XmppCli. To run the same command I showed previously, I'll use the bash command XmppCli gad-arista11@jabber.org -c 'show ver | inc Arista'. The command I want to send must be surrounded by single or double quotes and preceded by the -c flag:

```
[admin@Arista ~]$ XmppCli gad-arista11@jabber.org -c 'show ver | inc Arista'
response from: gad-arista11@jabber.org
- - - - - - - - - - - - - - - - - - - - - - - - - - - - - - - - - - - - - - - - -

Arista DCS-7050S-64-F
```

The ability to run XMPP commands from bash means that you can now script control of multiple switches from other switches. Or you can send emails when a switch goes down since you can monitor it from another switch. The possibilities are almost endless.

Packets are encrypted when using CloudVision, which I'm very glad to see since the *running-config* can be sent. Figure 29-18 shows a Wireshark screenshot of the packets resulting from my sending the show int e10 command to a switch through CloudVision. The packet shown is part of the actual returned text. As you can see in the ASCII section of the dump (bottom pane), the text is unreadable. In other words, neither the commands sent, nor the replies sent are in clear text.

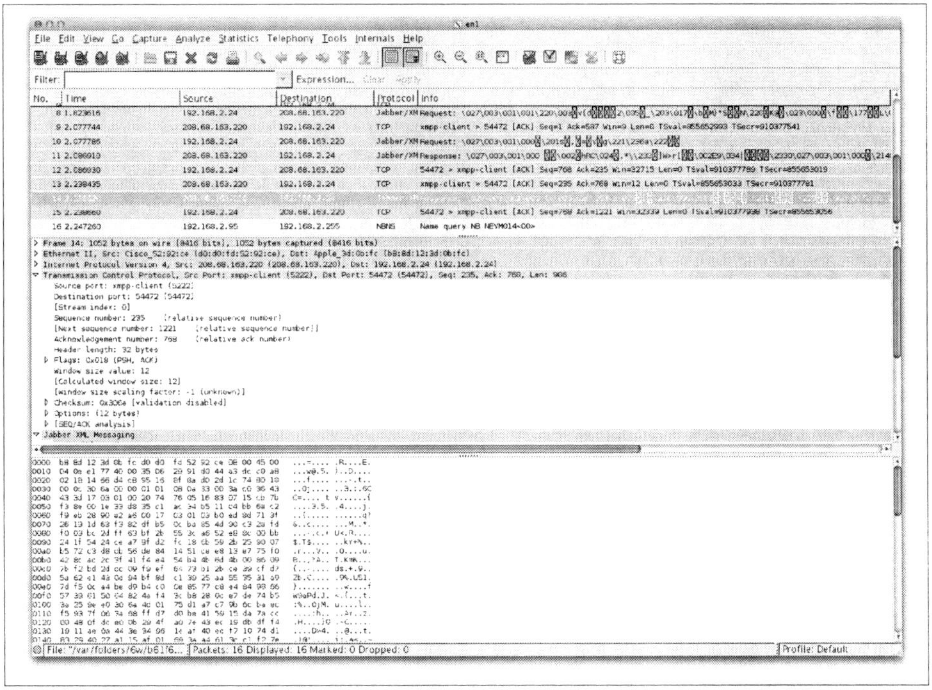

Figure 29-18. Wireshark capture of the results from the command `show int e10` *being sent through CloudVision*

Though I whine a bit about my perceived shortcomings regarding CloudVision, I think these issues will be resolved in future releases. I think that in its current state, Cloud-Vision is great for an environment where you have absolute control over the XMPP server, and where only a small subset of trusted people have the ability to make use of it. It would especially work well in a lab, or in a tightly secured environment.

I see some seriously cool applications in this feature's future. How about an Event Monitor trigger that sends an IM when a certain message is logged? Or when a certain user logs in? Or when the CPU goes over 70%? Or when a port's utilization goes over 70%? I think you get the idea. I'll be watching this feature closely, because I think it has the potential to be a game changer.

## CHAPTER 30

Troubleshooting

There are some pretty useful diagnostic tools on Arista switches, some of which we've already covered, such as TCP dump. Sometimes we need to know more detail about what the switch is doing, and that's where performance monitoring comes into play.

Performance Monitoring

A great tool on Linux systems is the top command. The top command produces output that auto-updates every few seconds (the default is three seconds on Arista switches). This command can be called from CLI with the show process top command, or from bash with the command top. Here's a sample output from a live 7048T that's been running for just over a month. This is a very healthy switch with nothing unusual going on. Depending on the switch platform you're using, the processes near the top may change:

```
7024T#Sho proc top
top - 19:46:03 up 32 days,4:14, 1 user, load average: 0.29, 0.22, 0.19
Tasks: 162 total,   2 running, 160 sleeping,   0 stopped,   0 zombie
Cpu(s): 47.1%us, 2.5%sy, 0.0%ni, 50.2%id, 0.0%wa, 0.0%hi, 0.2%si, 0%st
Mem:   4037980k total, 1443148k used, 2594832k free,  117576k buffers
Swap:        0k total,       0k used,       0k free,  844912k cached

  PID USER    PR  NI  VIRT  RES  SHR S %CPU %MEM    TIME+  COMMAND
 1849 root    20   0  218m  46m  22m S 43.0  1.2 19755:41 PhyBcm54980
 1739 root    20   0  209m  37m  15m S 30.5  1.0 14112:41 Mdio
 1916 root    20   0  270m  91m  43m S 14.9  2.3  7823:18 SandSlice
 1401 root    20   0  243m 101m  62m S  3.0  2.6  1359:33 Sysdb
 1403 root    20   0  229m  72m  43m S  1.3  1.8 672:25.87 Fru
 1744 root    20   0  210m  37m  15m S  1.0  1.0 371:52.86 Smbus
 1451 root    20   0  202m  29m  11m S  0.7  0.7 380:23.24 AgentMonitor
 1465 root    20   0  203m  36m  17m R  0.7  0.9 276:59.80 LedPolicyAgen
 1899 root    20   0  203m  34m  16m S  0.7  0.9 180:23.69 Pmbus
17614 admin   20   0  235m  69m  35m S  0.7  1.8   0:05.84 Cli
   10 root    20   0     0    0    0 S  0.3  0.0  23:38.43 events/1
```

```
1400 root  20   0  207m  23m 2444 S  0.3  0.6 176:34.42 ProcMgr-worke
1440 root  20   0  202m  28m  10m S  0.3  0.7   4:44.08 PowerManager
1447 root  20   0  208m  33m  10m S  0.3  0.8 143:47.67 Thermostat
1754 root  20   0  205m  35m  17m S  0.3  0.9   9:05.20 Ebra
1804 root  20   0  202m  31m  13m S  0.3  0.8  22:55.86 Max6697
1815 root  20   0  219m  55m  31m S  0.3  1.4  17:40.86 SandAgent
1851 root  20   0  214m  44m  20m S  0.3  1.1  95:50.18 PhyAeluros
```

As much as I'd love to show you what a troubled switch might look like, try as I might,
I could not get one to end up in a distressed state. Here's an example where I beat the
crap out of a 7124SX switch with traffic loads, then set sFlow to sample every packet
(dangerous!), and to then send its payload to the collector with an interval of one second.
Even then I couldn't get the sFlow process higher in the list than the main switch processes, and the switch was still reporting 80% idle:

```
top - 06:05:44 up 10:06,  2 users,  load average: 0.07, 0.03, 0.01
Tasks: 221 total,   1 running, 220 sleeping,   0 stopped,   0 zombie
Cpu(s): 16.3%us, 2.2%sy, 0.0%ni, 80.8%id, 0.0%wa, 0.3%hi, 0.5%si, 0%st
Mem:   2043416k total, 1365224k used,  678192k free,  113984k buffers
Swap:        0k total,       0k used,       0k free,  829808k cached

  PID USER   PR  NI  VIRT  RES  SHR S %CPU %MEM    TIME+  COMMAND
 1859 root   20   0  191m  43m  19m S  7.0  2.2  43:32.03 PhyAeluros
 1748 root   20   0  183m  35m  14m S  5.6  1.8  34:45.07 Mdio
 1750 root   20   0  599m  56m  22m S  5.6  2.8  33:43.66 FocalPoint
 1439 root   20   0  208m  83m  49m S  4.0  4.2  20:43.42 Sysdb
 4373 root   20   0  188m  35m  19m S  4.0  1.8   2:39.92 Sflow
```

While I was messing with the switch in seriously unnatural ways, I managed to get the
CLI process to hit the top of the list, but it didn't last for long. You may actually see
something similar if you happen to catch the output while simultaneously issuing the
show running-config command:

```
top - 06:05:02 up 10:05,  2 users,  load average: 0.14, 0.03, 0.01
Tasks: 223 total,   1 running, 222 sleeping,   0 stopped,   0 zombie
Cpu(s): 56.3%us, 2.5%sy, 0.0%ni, 40.4%id, 0.0%wa, 0.2%hi, 0.7%si, 0%st
Mem:   2043416k total, 1396700k used,  646716k free,  113984k buffers
Swap:        0k total,       0k used,       0k free,  829844k cached

   PID USER   PR  NI  VIRT   RES  SHR S %CPU %MEM    TIME+  COMMAND
 17637 root   20   0  199m  116m  88m S 71.0  5.9   0:09.23 Cli
  1439 root   20   0  208m   83m  49m S 11.9  4.2  20:41.18 Sysdb
  1859 root   20   0  191m   43m  19m S  7.3  2.2  43:28.72 PhyAeluros
  1750 root   20   0  599m   56m  22m S  6.0  2.8  33:41.14 FocalPoint
  1748 root   20   0  183m   35m  14m S  5.3  1.8  34:42.38 Mdio
  4373 root   20   0  188m   35m  19m S  4.6  1.8   2:38.16 Sflow
```

There are a variety of ways to sort this output, but the default is by CPU utilization. For
99% of what you'd use this tool for, that's fine. The %CPU column is what determines the
process's place on the list, but remember that processes on a Linux system can bounce
up and down on this list in milliseconds, and you will likely see just that as you watch.

I recommend doing some further reading on the top command online, but there are a couple of things to always look at when you use it. First, the very first line shows three numbers after the words load average:. These numbers will vary from switch to switch, and they're not necessarily an indication of anything unless you know what they are normally. In other words, a 7050 switch in one environment might run with a load average of (for example) 0.90%, while another might run at an average of 1.5%. There are so many things that contribute to these numbers that they're not terribly useful, unless you know what they are on average when the switch is running normally. That said, if you see a number like 15.99%, there's probably something bad happening.

The next bold line in the output shows this:

```
Cpu(s): 56.3%us, 2.5%sy, 0.0%ni, 40.4%id, 0.0%wa, 0.2%hi, 0.7%si, 0%st
```

This is a very important line, though again, it's only for the snapshot of time when the last top iteration ran. In other words, it's not historical; it's a snapshot. The numbers from left to right indicate the following values:

56.3%us
> The CPU spent 56.3% of its time on user processes (agents on an Arista switch).

2.5%sy
> The CPU spent 2.5% of its time on system processes (kernel, etc.).

0.0%ni
> The CPU spent 0% of its time on user processes that have been *niced* (this is a Unix thing that you really don't need to worry about). Unless you've really messed around in bash, this should probably always be 0.

40.4%id
> The CPU is spending 40.4% of its time completely idle. The bigger this number is, the happier the switch is.

0.0%wa
> The CPU spent 0% of its time waiting for I/O to complete.

0.2%hi
> The CPU spent 0.2% of its time servicing hardware interrupts.

0.7%si
> The CPU spent 0.7% of its time servicing software interrupts.

0.0%st
> The CPU spent 0% of its time stolen by a hypervisor.

On a healthy switch, *idle* should be high, while *system* and *user* should be low. On a busier switch, *user* may spike up and down as processes vie for the CPU's attention. Remember, though, that this is just control plane stuff like OSPF, BGP, and STP. Packets are forwarded by ASIC, and not the CPU. Still, high CPU should be monitored, and you should contact Arista support if your CPU stays unreasonably high.

Tracing Agents (Debugging)

Debugging processes is significantly different in EOS than it is in IOS. The amount of debug information available in EOS is staggering, but figuring out where to look can be a bit overwhelming if you're used to using certain IOS debug commands. Once you get the hang of how it works in EOS, though, you'll be amazed at the power.

First, EOS does not have a debug command, so don't bother looking for it. If you're at all like me, that warning has come many chapters too late, and you've already discovered that all your favorite debug commands don't work. Fear not; I'll show you the way.

In EOS, the concept of debugging is replaced with the concept of *tracing*. Almost any process (EOS agents) can be traced with—you guessed it—the trace command. You can't just go typing trace ospf packets, though, so step away from the keyboard and keep reading.

Tracing in EOS can produce an overwhelming amount of data, so by default, the output of your traces do not go to the console or to your Secure Shell (SSH) sessions. Because of the large amount of data, output must first be directed to a file. I'll show you how to view the output to the screen via a couple of methods, but let's take a look at how to get a trace started first.

 Be careful when using trace. Like debug in IOS, it can consume system resources. Unlike debug in IOS, it will not take priority over other processes, nor will it stop everything else to deliver its output to the console. (Seriously, who thought that was a good idea?)

Using OSPF as an example, it quickly becomes obvious that you don't trace *protocols* in EOS, but rather *agents*. To find out the name of the agent you want to trace, issue the show trace ? command:

```
SW1(config)#sho trace ?
  Aaa               Aaa agent
  Acl               Acl agent
  Adt7462           Adt7462 agent
  AgentMonitor      AgentMonitor agent
  Arp               Arp agent
  Cdp               Cdp agent
  Dcbx              Dcbx agent
```

```
DhcpRelay              DhcpRelay agent
Ebra                   Ebra agent

[ -- lots of output removed in the interest of brevity --]

Psmi20                 Psmi20 agent
Qos                    Qos agent
Rib                    Rib agent
Scd                    Scd agent
Scd-system             Scd-system agent
Sflow                  Sflow agent
Smbus                  Smbus agent
Snmp                   Snmp agent
Stp                    Stp agent
StpTopology            StpTopology agent
SuperServer            SuperServer agent
Sysdb                  Sysdb agent
Thermostat             Thermostat agent
TopoAgent              TopoAgent agent
Ucd9012                Ucd9012 agent
Ucd9012-system         Ucd9012-system agent
VisualizationAgent     VisualizationAgent agent
VmAgent                VmAgent agent
VmTracerSess           VmTracerSess agent
Vrm64                  Vrm64 agent
WORD                   Agent name
Xcvr                   Xcvr agent
ZeroTouch              ZeroTouch agent
```

Now we have a list of agents that can be traced. One of the frustrating things about this process is that it may not always be obvious what you're looking for. For example, in this list, there are no agents named *Ospf*, *Bgp*, or *Rip*, and the agents that are listed don't have very useful descriptions. If you know a bit about routing, you may recognize the idea of a *Routing Information Base (RIB)*, and there's a process for that, so let's see where that leads us. To find out details about what you can trace within an agent, use the show trace *agent-name* command. I'll do this for the Rib process:

```
SW1(config)#sho trace Rib
Global trace settings for agent Rib
-----------------------------------------------
Tracing sent to flash:/Rib.txt

date:         enabled
time:         enabled
PID:              enabled
facility name: enabled  (width 20)
trace level:  enabled
filename:         disabled (width 20)
line number:  disabled
function name: disabled (width 20)
object name:      disabled (width 20)
```

```
Trace facility settings for agent Rib is
---------------------------------------------
Activity              enabled   ...........
AdjacencyHelper       enabled   ...........
Agent                 enabled   ...........

[-- Lots of stuff removed ]

Rib::Adv              enabled   ...........
Rib::Bgp              enabled   ...........
Rib::Bgp::Keepalive   enabled   ...........
Rib::Bgp::Normal      enabled   ...........
Rib::Bgp::Notification enabled  ............
Rib::Bgp::Open        enabled   ...........
Rib::Bgp::Policy      enabled   ...........
Rib::Bgp::Route       enabled   ...........
Rib::Bgp::State       enabled   ...........
Rib::Bgp::Task        enabled   ...........
Rib::Bgp::Timer       enabled   ...........
Rib::Bgp::Update      enabled   ...........
Rib::DebugMessages    enabled   ...........

[-- Lots more stuff removed --]

Rib::Ospf             enabled   ...........
Rib::Ospf200::Db      enabled   ...........
Rib::Ospf200::Dd      enabled   ...........
Rib::Ospf200::Debug   enabled   ...........
Rib::Ospf200::DrElect enabled   ............
Rib::Ospf200::Flood   enabled   ...........
Rib::Ospf200::Hello   enabled   ...........
Rib::Ospf200::Lsa     enabled   ...........
Rib::Ospf200::Lsr     enabled   ...........
Rib::Ospf200::Lsu     enabled   ...........
Rib::Ospf200::Spf     enabled   ...........
Rib::Ospf200::State   enabled   ...........
Rib::Parse            enabled   ...........
Rib::Policy           enabled   ...........
Rib::Rip              enabled   ...........
Rib::Rip::Normal      enabled   ...........
Rib::Rip::Other       enabled   ...........
Rib::Rip::Policy      enabled   ...........
Rib::Rip::Request     enabled   ...........
Rib::Rip::Response    enabled   ...............
Rib::Rip::Route       enabled   ...........
Rib::Rip::State       enabled   ...........
Rib::Rip::Task        enabled   ...........
Rib::Rip::Timer       enabled   ...........
Rib::Route            enabled   ...........
Rib::State            enabled   ...........
Rib::Task             enabled   ...........
Rib::Timer            enabled   ...........
```

```
Rib::Tracing            enabled  ...........
Rib::Vrrp               enabled  ...........
Rib::Vrrp::Advertisement enabled  ............
Rib::Vrrp::State        enabled  ...........
Rib::Vrrp::Timer        enabled  ...........

[-- Wow, there's a lot of stuff (removed) --]

Trie                    enabled  ...........
TypeMap                 enabled  ...........
Watchdog                enabled  ...........
```

We found it! We're so clever. Now that we know the name of the agent (Rib), we can start to specify trace commands. The first step should always be to point the output to a file. You can put the file anywhere, but Arista recommends that it be stored on *flash:* since that location usually has the most space, and it can survive a reboot. To do so, use the trace *agent-name* filename *filename* command:

```
SW1(config)#trace Rib filename flash:Rib.txt
```

 Notice how the agent names all start with capital letters? That's not a requirement on the command line for specifying the agent name. I'm just obsessive. If you specify a filename with a capital letter like I have, then that filename will need to be consistent when referencing it later.

Now there are two paths you can take. You can either trace it all (generally a bad idea), or you can restrict what you want to see. Since we're looking to trace OSPF, we'll need to include only the items with OSPF in the name, which I've taken the liberty of highlighting in bold. To include only these entries, use the trace *agent-name* enable *trace-facility-name levels* command. Let me show you how to figure all that out. First, we know the agent name (Rib), so let's start there:

```
SW1(config)#trace rib enable ?
  WORD  Trace facility name
```

The *trace facility name* is one or more entries from that long list we got from using the show trace rib command. Look at the leftmost lines in bold from that output. They all start with Rib::Ospf. To include them all, we can use a wildcard and specify Rib::Ospf* as follows.

 This is one more place where capitalization matters. If you specify rib::ospf* (no caps), it won't work. You need to specify exactly what's listed from the output of show trace *agent-name,* including proper case and the right number of colons.

That leaves one more item to determine: *levels*.

```
SW1(config)#trace rib enable Rib::Ospf* ?
  all     Enable tracing at all levels
  levels  Enable tracing at one or more levels
```

This one is easy, just use `all`. Sure, you can drill down even further if you'd like, and to do so, specify the word `levels` with a question mark to see what the possibilities are:

```
SW1(config)#trace rib enable Rib::Ospf* levels ?
  0         Enable tracing at level 0
  1         Enable tracing at level 1
  2         Enable tracing at level 2
  3         Enable tracing at level 3
  4         Enable tracing at level 4
  5         Enable tracing at level 5
  6         Enable tracing at level 6
  7         Enable tracing at level 7
  8         Enable tracing at level 8
  9         Enable tracing at level 9
  coverage  Enable tracing at level coverage
  function  Enable tracing at level function
```

Like I said, just use `all`. (But feel free to mess with each setting to your heart's content. It's not like I can stop you!)

```
SW1(config)#trace rib enable Rib::Ospf* all
```

Note that this will alter the output of the show trace Rib command to include references to what is being traced:

```
SW1(config)#sho trace Rib
Global trace settings for agent Rib
---------------------------------------------
Tracing sent to stderr

date:         enabled
time:         enabled
PID:             enabled
facility name: enabled  (width 20)
trace level:  enabled
filename:        disabled (width 20)
line number:  disabled
function name: disabled (width 20)
object name:   disabled (width 20)

Trace facility settings for agent Rib is Rib::Ospf200::Flood/
    *cf,Rib::Ospf200::Lsr/*cf,Rib::Ospf200::Spf/*cf,
Rib::Ospf200::Hello/*cf,Rib::Ospf200::Db/*cf,Rib::Ospf200::DrElect/*cf,
Rib::Ospf200::Lsu/*cf,Rib::Ospf200::Lsa/*cf,Rib::Ospf200::Dd/*cf,
Rib::Ospf/*cf,Rib::Ospf200::Debug/*cf,Rib::Ospf200::State/*cf
---------------------------------------------
Activity                 enabled  ...........
AdjacencyHelper          enabled  ...........
```

```
Agent              enabled  ............

[--- output removed because there's a whole lot of it ---]

Rib::Kernel::Timer  enabled  ............
Rib::Mio            enabled  ............
Rib::Normal         enabled  ............
Rib::Ospf           enabled  0123456789cf
Rib::Ospf200::Db    enabled  0123456789cf
Rib::Ospf200::Dd    enabled  0123456789cf
Rib::Ospf200::Debug enabled  0123456789cf
Rib::Ospf200::DrElect enabled  0123456789cf
Rib::Ospf200::Flood enabled  0123456789cf
Rib::Ospf200::Hello enabled  0123456789cf
Rib::Ospf200::Lsa   enabled  0123456789cf
Rib::Ospf200::Lsr   enabled  0123456789cf
Rib::Ospf200::Lsu   enabled  0123456789cf
Rib::Ospf200::Spf   enabled  0123456789cf
Rib::Ospf200::State enabled  0123456789cf
Rib::Parse          enabled  ............
Rib::Policy         enabled  ............
Rib::Rip            enabled  ............
```

The numbers in the right side of the Rib::Ospf entries indicate the logging levels. Since we chose all for the logging level, they're all included. Had we chosen only level 9, for example, then only the 9 would be shown for those entries.

At this point, the trace is active, and provided there is something going on with the agent you've chosen, the file will start to fill up:

```
SW1(config)#dir Rib*
Directory of flash:/Rib*

      -rwx    7449653         Jul 10 23:34  Rib.txt

1862512640 bytes total (17235968 bytes free)
```

As a quick aside, the trace rib enable Rib::Ospf* all command will be expanded in the *running-config* to something that looks like this, which is also shown in the output of show trace Rib:

```
trace Rib setting Rib::Ospf200::Flood/*cf,Rib::Ospf200::Lsr/*cf,Rib::Ospf200::Spf/
*cf,Rib::Ospf200::Hello/*cf,Rib::Ospf200::Db/*cf,Rib::Ospf200::DrElect/
*cf,Rib::Ospf200::Lsu/*cf,Rib::Ospf200::Lsa/*cf,Rib::Ospf200::Dd/*cf,Rib::Ospf/
*cf,Rib::Ospf200::Debug/*cf,Rib::Ospf200::State/*cf
```

Don't worry about that. It's just all of the items you included by using the asterisk wildcard on one line, separated by commas.

A file that's quietly filling with trace output isn't very useful by itself, so let's see what's in it. First, you can monitor the output directly with the `trace monitor` *agent-name* command. Use Control-C to break out of this output. This is NOT like using the terminal monitor command in IOS; when you issue the `trace monitor` *agent-name* command, you cannot use the CLI until you break the output.

```
SW1(config)#trace monitor Rib
RibOspf::ospf_interface_poll_cb(task*, U16, mio_value_tag_array_t*,
    mio_value_tag_array_t*, int, int)
2012-07-10 23:38:11.459797  1515 Rib::Ospf
    7 int RibOspf::ospf_neighbor_poll_cb(task*, U16,
    mio_value_tag_array_t*, mio_value_tag_array_t*, int, int)
2012-07-10 23:38:11 OSPF RECV: 20.0.0.2 -> 224.0.0.5: Version 2, Type
Hello (1), Length 48 ret 0
2012-07-10 23:38:11   Router ID 2.2.2.2, Area 0.0.0.0, Authentication <None> (0)
2012-07-10 23:38:11   Authentication data: 00000000 00000000
2012-07-10 23:38:11   Mask 255.255.255.252, Options <E L> (12),
Priority 1, Neighbours 1
2012-07-10 23:38:11   Intervals: Hello 10s, Dead Router 40s,
Designated Router 20.0.0.2, Backup 20.0.0.1
2012-07-10 23:38:11   Neighbours: 1.1.1.1
2012-07-10 23:38:11 OSPF STATE: NGB 2.2.2.2 (20.0.0.2) EVENT Hello
Recv, current state: Full
2012-07-10 23:38:11 OSPF STATE: NGB 2.2.2.2 (20.0.0.2) EVENT 2 Ways,
current state: Full
2012-07-10 23:38:11 OSPF SEND: 20.0.0.1 -> 224.0.0.5: Version 2, Type
Hello (1), Length 48 ret 48
2012-07-10 23:38:11   Router ID 1.1.1.1, Area 0.0.0.0, Authentication <None> (0)
2012-07-10 23:38:11   Authentication data: 00000000 00000000
2012-07-10 23:38:11   Mask 255.255.255.252, Options <E> (2),
Priority 1, Neighbours 1
2012-07-10 23:38:11   Intervals: Hello 10s, Dead Router 40s,
Designated Router 20.0.0.2, Backup 20.0.0.1
2012-07-10 23:38:11   Neighbours: 2.2.2.2^C
SW1(config)#
```

The method I prefer to use is more Unix-centric. First, drop into bash:

```
SW1#bash

Arista Networks EOS shell

[admin@SW1 ~]$
```

Using the `tail` *filename* command will show you the last few lines of a file. For a constantly updating file like this one, the `tail -f` *filename* command will continuously update until broken (again, with Control-C):

```
[admin@SW1 ~]$ tail -f /mnt/flash/Rib.txt
2012-07-10 23:45:53.034569  1515 Rib::Ospf
    7 int RibOspf::ospf_interface_poll_cb(task*, U16,
    mio_value_tag_array_t*, mio_value_tag_array_t*, int, int)
2012-07-10 23:45:53.034688  1515 Rib::Ospf
```

```
    7 int RibOspf::ospf_neighbor_poll_cb(task*, U16,
    mio_value_tag_array_t*, mio_value_tag_array_t*, int, int)
2012-07-10 23:45:53.034738  1515 Rib::Ospf
    7 int RibOspf::ospf_neighbor_poll_cb(task*, U16,
    mio_value_tag_array_t*, mio_value_tag_array_t*, int, int)
2012-07-10 23:45:53.034988  1515 Rib::Ospf              7
ospf_border_poll_cb recv type MIO_DGET_OSPF_BORDER_ROUTERS count 2
2012-07-10 23:45:53.036390  1515 Rib::Ospf              7
Border router response instance seen is:
    entity('/ar/Sysdb/routing/ospf/status.instanceStatus/200')
2012-07-10 23:45:53.036445  1515 Rib::Ospf              7
ospf_border_poll_cb recv type MIO_DGET_OSPF_BORDER_ROUTERS count 3
2012-07-10 23:45:53.036505  1515 Rib::Ospf              0
Recv border router entry: 2.2.2.2 area: 0.0.0.0 is asbr: 1 is abr: 0^C
[admin@SW1 ~]$
```

I like this method because I can pipe using grep (which doesn't work with trace from the CLI):

```
[admin@SW1 ~]$ tail -f /mnt/flash/Rib.txt  | grep entry
2012-07-10 23:48:09.194027  1515 Rib::Ospf              0 Recv border
 router entry: 2.2.2.2 area: 0.0.0.0 is asbr: 1 is abr: 0
2012-07-10 23:48:10.195789  1515 Rib::Ospf              0 Recv border
 router entry: 2.2.2.2 area: 0.0.0.0 is asbr: 1 is abr: 0
2012-07-10 23:48:11.197117  1515 Rib::Ospf              0 Recv border
 router entry: 2.2.2.2 area: 0.0.0.0 is asbr: 1 is abr: 0
2012-07-10 23:48:12.197292  1515 Rib::Ospf              0 Recv border
 router entry: 2.2.2.2 area: 0.0.0.0 is asbr: 1 is abr: 0
2012-07-10 23:48:13.198982  1515 Rib::Ospf              0 Recv border
 router entry: 2.2.2.2 area: 0.0.0.0 is asbr: 1 is abr: 0
2012-07-10 23:48:14.199694  1515 Rib::Ospf              0 Recv border
 router entry: 2.2.2.2 area: 0.0.0.0 is asbr: 1 is abr: 0
^C
[admin@SW1 ~]$
```

Useful Examples

Instead of digging through all the agents, I figured that I'd show some of the more useful traces here. Remember that you'll need to set up a file for agent one if you use more than one.

BGP

```
    trace Rib enable Rib::Bgp* all
```

OSPF

```
    trace Rib enable Rib::Ospf* all
```

RIP

```
    trace Rib enable Rib::Rip* all
```

VRRP

```
    trace Rib enable Rib::Vrrp* all
```

LACP

```
trace Lag enable Lacp* all
```

STP

```
trace Stp enable Stp* all
```

```
trace Stp enable Errdisable* all
```

Turn It Off!

Traces stay running even when you're not looking at them, and they will run, forever consuming disk space, unless you shut them off. Here's a directory listing from my switch where I left a few traces running for only an hour!

```
SW1(config)#dir *.txt
Directory of flash:/*.txt

      -rwx    122612063          Jul 7 03:50  RIB-Debug.txt
      -rwx    152724544          Jul 11 00:22  Rib.txt
      -rwx    189626048          Jul 11 00:22  STP.txt

1862512640 bytes total (0 bytes free)
```

That's 45 megabytes of file space chewed up by something that I don't need. Let's not forget that those traces are still running, which means they're wasting system resources.

 Though I did run out of disk space, that's more likely due to the fact that this is my test lab switch, which has 12 different versions of EOS on the *flash:* drive, each of which is about 200 MB.

Unfortunately, at least as of EOS version 4.9.3.2, I know of no way to disable all traces at once like you can with the `un all` command in IOS. To disable tracing, use the `no trace` *agent-name* `enable * all` command. This works regardless of what other trace facility names you may have chosen, such as `Rib::Ospf`.

Remember that you may have multiple traces running, too. Here's an example of the mess I've made on my switch:

```
SW1(config)#sho run | inc trace
trace Sysdb setting SysdbSwitchover/*cf,SysdbIntf/*cf,SysdbPlugin::SysdbEthIntf/
*cf,Sysdb/*cf,SysdbPlugin::SysdbAcl/*cf,SysdbEthIntf/*cf,SysdbPlugin::SysdbMlag/
*cf,SysdbEbra/*cf,SysdbPlugin::DhcpRelayHelper/*cf,SysdbPlugin::SysdbFru/
*cf,Activity/*cf,SysdbPlugin::SysdbEthPortId/*cf,SysdbErrdisable/
*cf,SysdbPlugin::FocalPoint/*cf,SysdbMgmtActive/*cf,SysdbPlugin::Snmp/
*cf,SysdbEbraAgent/*cf,SysdbFocalPoint/*cf,SysdbPlugin::ExtensionMgr/
*cf,SysdbLauncher/*cf
trace Sysdb filename flash:/Sysdb.txt
trace Rib setting Rib::Vrrp::State/*cf,Rib::Ospf200::Flood/
```

```
*cf,Rib::Ospf200::Lsr/*cf,Rib::Ospf200::Spf/*cf,Rib::Ospf200::Hello/
*cf,Rib::Vrrp/*cf,Rib::Ospf200::Db/*cf,Rib::Vrrp::Advertisement/
*cf,Rib::Ospf200::DrElect/*cf,Rib::Ospf200::Lsu/*cf,Rib::Ospf200::Lsa/
*cf,Rib::Ospf200::Dd/*cf,Rib::Ospf/*cf,Rib::Ospf200::Debug/
*cf,Rib::Vrrp::Timer/*cf,Rib::Ospf200::State/*cf
trace Rib filename flash:/Rib.txt
trace Stp filename flash:/STP.txt
```

To clean all that up, I'll issue the following commands:

```
SW1(config)#no trace Sysdb enable * all
SW1(config)#no trace Rib enable * all
```

Don't forget that although you've stopped the traces, the files still reside on disk. If you want to save them elsewhere, you can copy them off using a variety of protocols such as FTP, SCP, TFTP, and more. Here's a list:

```
SW1(config)#copy flash:Rib.txt ?
  boot-extensions  Copy to boot extensions configuration
  extension:       Destination file path
  file:            Destination file path
  flash:           Destination file path
  ftp:             Destination file path
  http:            Destination file path
  https:           Destination file path
  running-config   Update (merge with) current system configuration
  scp:             Destination file path
  sftp:            Destination file path
  startup-config   Copy to startup configuration
  system:          Destination file path
  tftp:            Destination file path
```

Usually, I've gotten what I've needed from them, so I just delete them instead:

```
SW1(config)#del Rib.txt
SW1(config)#del Sysdb.txt
```

With the traces disabled, leaving the filename entries cluttering the config doesn't make any sense, so as a final step, we can clean those up too:

```
SW1(config)#no trace Rib filename flash:/Rib.txt
SW1(config)#no trace Stp filename flash:/Sysdb.txt
```

Tracing can seem a bit overwhelming if you're used to IOS and the well-known debug commands, but I think if you spend some time getting used to this format, you'll quickly discover that it's more powerful than debug, and certainly more flexible. The fact that it won't lock up the switch pushing logs to the console is a nice bonus, too.

Arista Support

Arista Support is a fantastic resource, and my experience with them has been far superior to that other company that has nothing to do with crystallized cottonseed oil. They've helped me when I've discovered bugs, they've helped me diagnose configuration problems, and on the rare occasion when we had a switch go bad under warranty, they shipped us a new one in no time. Once you're registered with Arista Support as a valid customer, opening a TAC case is as simple as calling them, or if the issue isn't critical, you can email them as well. And with your valid and registered email address, you can download documentation, EOS revisions, white papers, and a host of other useful documents from *http://www.aristanetworks.com*.

There is also a fabulous online forum and repository of knowledge at the EOS Central website (*https://eos.aristanetworks.com/*). At this site you can post a question to the forum and you might be surprised to find one of the company founders answering it. There is also a development blog and some tech tips that are well worth a look.

Of course you can always email me too, but I'm a cranky, old, recalcitrant nerd who doesn't have a lot of free time, so you'd probably do better emailing Arista. That is, of course, unless you want to tell someone how much you like this book, in which case I'm probably the better choice.

## CHAPTER 31

Aristacisms

This chapter is an appendix of sorts, but it's not really, because some of the content comprises items that I felt should be included in the book, but weren't long enough to warrant their own chapter, while other items are just Arista-specific terms or nuances that I felt should be included but didn't fit in any other chapter. This chapter is like the trash bin in my brain. I took a lot of notes for topics to put in this book, and this is the stuff that's left over or didn't make it into other chapters.

It is with great pleasure that a writer makes up his own words, and since I've been writing for a year and this is the last chapter, I'm a little punchy. I do hereby dub the items in this chapter, *Aristacisms*.

Marketing Glossary

When first learning about any new product or vendor, getting to know the lingo can be a challenge. Arista doesn't have many of these terms, probably because they are very pro open source. There are a few that I've stumbled over, so I made a short list and they ended up here.

Advanced Event Management (AEM)

According to the press release on the topic, AEM is a "suite of new capabilities in Arista's Extensible Operating System, the world's most advanced network operating system, that enables increased and unprecedented levels of network automation while improving overall system uptime." Man, if that doesn't get the marketing guys excited, I don't know what would! But what does all that really mean?

AEM includes the following features, referenced together as a group: event-handler, Event Monitor, the ability to use bash (Linux tools), and the CLI Scheduler. To be fair, these tools grouped together are a huge part of what makes Arista switches so amazing, so I can't fault the marketing team for trying to make some noise about them.

Spine and Leaf Switches

Much of the Arista documentation talks about spine switches and leaf switches. In its simplest deployment, a spine switch is a core device, and a leaf switch is an access device. The spine and leaf design paradigm is more or less a collapsed core network design, and although I'd love to pick on the marketing guys for making up new terms needlessly, the reality is that the old terms don't necessarily make sense any more.

Many data centers don't have distribution layers anymore, instead opting for a wider design with multiple interlinked "cores," with all of the access switches connecting directly to them. Since there's no real "center" to a network like this, it doesn't make sense to call them core switches. When and if new networking protocols like TRILL take off, the spine and leaf paradigm will become a lot more commonplace.

Arista-Specific Configuration Items

Although EOS is a decidedly open source platform, there are some things that are configured differently on an Arista switch than on other vendor's switches. This is my repository for such items that don't warrant their own chapters.

There is no duplex statement in EOS

I learned this the hard way when I tried to import 20 or so Cisco switch configs into my client's shiny new Arista switches. Many of the ports had hardcoded speed and duplex settings (which I quickly scolded them for; read Chapter 3 [Autonegotiation] in *Network Warrior*, if you don't know why). Every one of these entries failed when I pasted them into EOS. Here's what happened when I tried:

```
SW1(config-if-Et5)#Speed 1000
% Invalid input
SW1(config-if-Et5)#Duplex full
% Invalid input
```

Flummoxed, I scrambled around quickly within EOS until I discovered that the speed command is supported (duplex is not), but it works in a very different fashion than that which I was used to.

On a 7048T (48-port copper 1 Gbs) switch, the following options are available for the interface speed command:

```
Arista-7048T(config-if-Et2)#speed ?
  auto          Enable autoneg for speed, duplex, and flowcontrol
  forced        Disable autoneg and force speed/duplex/flowcontrol
  sfp-1000baset Configure autoneg and speed/duplex on 1000BASE-T SFP
```

Since the servers were hardcoded (grr), and I wasn't using copper SFPs, I needed to use the `forced` keyword. Using the `forced` keyword results in the following additional options:

```
Arista-7048T(config-if-Et2)#speed forced ?
  10000full  Disable autoneg and force 10 Gbps/full duplex operation
  1000full   Disable autoneg and force 1 Gbps/full duplex operation
  1000half   Disable autoneg and force 1 Gbps/half duplex operation
  100full    Disable autoneg and force 100 Mbps/full duplex operation
  100gfull   Disable autoneg and force 100 Gbps/full duplex operation
  100half    Disable autoneg and force 100 Mbps/half duplex operation
  10full     Disable autoneg and force 10 Mbps/full duplex operation
  10half     Disable autoneg and force 10 Mbps/half duplex operation
  40gfull    Disable autoneg and force 40 Gbps/full duplex operation
```

Resisting the urge to configure the port for 40 Gbps/full duplex, I used the following command to result in a hardcoded 1,000 Gbps/full duplex interface:

```
Arista-7048T(config-if-Et2)#speed forced 1000full
```

While much of the configuration can be cut and pasted from a Cisco IOS switch into EOS, beware of speed and duplex when they're hardcoded. Better yet, convince the server guys to stop hardcoding gigabit interfaces.

Watch out for those comments!

One of my favorite features of EOS is the ability to put comments in the configuration. As you've no doubt seen by now, when a comment is allowed, I'll jam one in there. Blame my obsessive nature and my college professor who insisted on well-commented code while I was programming COBOL on punch cards in 1984. Ooh, '80s flashback time!

Anyway, another case of pasting configs from an IOS device bit me in the ass when, after a few days, I got a call about one of the ports on the new Arista switches not working. After digging in, one of the guys on the team discovered this configured on the port:

```
interface Ethernet25
!
interface Ethernet26
   !
   ! interface Ethernet28
   description Server11
   switchport access vlan 11
   spanning-tree portfast
   !
```

```
interface Ethernet27
!
interface Ethernet28
!
```

Anything look wrong there to you?

This is the relevant snippet of what was actually pasted:

```
interface Ethernet26
   description Server10
   switchport access vlan 10
   spanning-tree portfast
!
interface Ethernet28
   description Server11
   switchport access vlan 11
   spanning-tree portfast
!
```

When I pasted the configuration, I did so with a console cable, and apparently I pasted too much, which caused the serial port buffer to overrun. That caused a glitch, which caused a carriage return to be missed, which caused the line containing the command `interface Ethernet28` to be considered part of the comment line before it. Because interfaces can include comments, it just took that line as a comment on the previously configured interface (I had removed all empty interfaces to make the cut/paste job go more quickly). As a result, this is what the command parser saw, which resulted in the configuration shown previously:

```
interface Ethernet26
   description Server10
   switchport access vlan 10
   spanning-tree portfast
   !
   !interface Ethernet28
   description Server11
   switchport access vlan 11
   spanning-tree portfast
```

When pasting configs from one switch into another, verify what you've pasted. If possible, don't use a console cable. And whatever you do, watch out for those comments!

The cool thing that I learned from all this was that I could put comments into interface configurations, so now I can annoy my clients with interface descriptions *and* comments!

Some routing protocols are shut down by default

I covered this in the routing chapter, but it's worth another mention. When you configure a simple RIP configuration, before you spend hours trying to figure out why it doesn't work, issue the show active command. You'll promptly discover that RIP is in a shutdown state by default:

```
SW1(config-router-rip)#sho active
router rip
   ! - RIPv2 link to R1
   network 10.0.0.1/32
   shutdown
```

Clearly, even the switch thinks you should use something else, but if you're hell-bent on using RIP, negating the shutdown command will bring up RIP:

```
SW1(config-router-rip)#no shut
```

Trunk groups

Trunk groups are mentioned in the MLAG chapter (Chapter 12), but they're worth another mention since they're pretty darn cool. Here's what the EOS 4.9.4 configuration guide has to say about them:

```
A trunk group is the set of physical interfaces that comprise the
trunk and the collection of VLANs whose traffic is carried on the
trunk. The traffic of a VLAN that belongs to one or more trunk groups
is carried only on ports that are members of trunk groups to which
the VLAN belongs.
```

I just love paragraphs like that in official documentation. They drive people to buy O'Reilly books.

A trunk group is a named group of VLANs with an added twist. Let's look at the potential for such a tool. We've already see it in use for the MLAG peer, but let's try some other ways to use it. Here I'll configure the range of VLANs 100 through 105, and then include them all in the trunk group *Leelu*:

```
SW1(config)#vlan 100-105
SW1(config-vlan-100-105)#trunk group Leelu
```

Now I'll go to interface e10, configure it as a trunk, and apply the trunk group *Servers* to that interface:

```
SW1(config-vlan-100-105)#int e10
SW1(config-if-Et10)#switchport mode trunk
SW1(config-if-Et10)#switchport trunk group Leelu
```

Now, the output of show vlan shows that all of these VLANs are active on the trunk port e10:

```
SW1(config-if-Et10)#sho vlan
VLAN  Name                                 Status    Ports
----- ------------------------------------ --------- --------------------------------
1     default                              active    Et10
100   VLAN0100                             active    Et10
101   VLAN0101                             active    Et10
102   VLAN0102                             active    Et10
103   VLAN0103                             active    Et10
104   VLAN0104                             active    Et10
105   VLAN0105                             active    Et10
200   VLAN0200                             active    Et10
```

While the ability to group VLANs like that is pretty cool, there's more to it than that. When a VLAN is added to a trunk group, trunk ports *must* include that trunk group in order to pass that VLAN! Let me show you what I mean. I'll configure the same VLANs to be allowed on a trunk port configured on e11, only this time I'll use the traditional method of limiting and allowing VLANs on a trunk port by using the `switchport trunk allowed vlan` command:

```
SW1(config-if-Et10)#int e11
SW1(config-if-Et11)#switchport mode trunk
SW1(config-if-Et11)#switchport trunk allowed vlan 100-105
```

From experience, VLANs 100 through 105 should now be included on the e11 trunks, but the output of the show vlan command tells a different story:

```
SW1(config-if-Et11)#sho vlan
VLAN  Name                                 Status    Ports
----- ------------------------------------ --------- --------------------------------
1     default                              active    Et10
100   VLAN0100                             active    Et10
101   VLAN0101                             active    Et10
102   VLAN0102                             active    Et10
103   VLAN0103                             active    Et10
104   VLAN0104                          ·  active    Et10
105   VLAN0105                             active    Et10
200   VLAN0200                             active    Et10
```

To make matters worse, if you're not careful, you'll convince yourself that it should be working by looking at the output of the show interface trunk command:

```
SW1(config-if-Et11)#sho int trunk
Port            Mode            Status          Native vlan
Et5             trunk           trunking        1
Et6             trunk           trunking        1
Et10            trunk           trunking        1
Et11            trunk           trunking        1

Port            Vlans allowed
Et5             All
Et6             All
Et10            All
Et11            100-105
```

```
Port              Vlans allowed and active in management domain
Et5               None
Et6               None
Et10              1,100-105,200
Et11              None


Port              Vlans in spanning tree forwarding state
Et5               None
Et6               None
Et10              1,100-105,200
Et11              None
```

Take a look at the lines in bold in the previous output. It clearly says that VLANs 100 through 105 *are* allowed! The key is that they're not *allowed and active in the management domain* (next paragraph in the output). This is due to the fact that these VLANs are configured in a trunk group.

 You may be tempted to use the trunk group command as sort of a macro for a list of VLANs, and you can, but if you do that, the VLANs will only be included in a trunk if you use the trunk group. You can no longer include even one of the referenced VLANs in a trunk without using the trunk group. Think of this feature more as a way of securing VLANs from use as opposed to a way to make configurations simpler.

The good news is that VLANs can belong to more than one trunk group! That means that if we wanted to include only VLAN 101 on interface e11, we could do so by adding a new trunk group to VLAN 101, and then applying that trunk group to the interface. Let's try that.

First, I'll remove the trunk allowed stuff that wasn't working anyway:

```
SW1(config-if-Et11)#no switchport trunk allowed vlan 100-105
```

Now, I'll go to VLAN 101 and add a new trunk group. Remember, this VLAN is already part of trunk group *Servers*:

```
SW1(config-if-Et11)#vlan 101
SW1(config-vlan-101)#trunk group Multipass
```

At this point, VLAN 101 belongs to two trunk groups, *Leelu* and *Multipass*:

```
SW1(config-vlan-101)#int e11
SW1(config-if-Et11)#switchport trunk group Multipass
```

Now the output of show vlan is more to my liking:

```
SW1(config-vlan-101)#sho vlan
VLAN  Name                            Status    Ports
----- ------------------------------- --------- --------------------
1     default                         active    Et10, Et11
```

```
100    VLAN0100                        active    Et10
101    VLAN0101                        active    Et10, Et11
102    VLAN0102                        active    Et10
103    VLAN0103                        active    Et10
104    VLAN0104                        active    Et10
105    VLAN0105                        active    Et10
```

You can also show what VLANs belong to what trunk groups with the show vlan trunk group command:

```
SW1#sho vlan trunk group
VLAN    Trunk Groups
----    ------------------------------------------------------------
1
100     Leelu
101     Leelu, Multipass
102     Leelu
103     Leelu
104     Leelu
105     Leelu
```

Management VRF

EOS Version 4.10 supports a Virtual Routing and Forwarding (VRF) instance for management. VRFs are essentially multiple copies of the routing table that allow the same IP space to exist more than once in a single switch. Sadly, the way this feature has so far been implemented only allows the management VRF to be used on an SVI, and not on the physical management interface. Still, it's a very cool feature if you do your management in-band on SVIs.

There can be only one additional nondefault VRF configured at this time (EOS v4.10). I'll configure one called *management*.

First, the VRF needs to be defined using the vrf definition *vrf-name* command mode:

```
Arista(config)#vrf definition management
```

The only thing that needs to be done here is to define a *route distinguisher*. VRFs in EOS work through something called *network namespaces* in Linux. This is a very cool feature that is beyond the scope of this book, so since there can only be one nondefault VRF anyway, I'll just use the one included in the Arista EOS 4.10 documentation and not worry about the details. If you'd like to read up on how this really works, check out its page on the Arista website (*https://eos.aristanetworks.com/2011/06/linux-namespaces-at-arista/*). The route distinguisher is comprised of two numbers separated by a colon:

```
Arista(config-vrf-management)#rd ?
  <admin>:<local assignment>  Route Distinguisher

Arista(config-vrf-management)#rd 101:1
```

Now that the VRF is defined, we can apply it to an interface. I'll be using VLAN 901's SVI. First, here's the existing configuration from when I had the SVI set up for management without a VRF:

```
Arista(config)#sho run int vlan 901
interface Vlan901
   ip address 192.168.1.188/24
```

Now I'll go ahead and assign the VRF to the interface:

```
Arista(config)#int vlan 901
Arista(config-if-Vl901)#vrf forwarding management
Interface Vlan901 IP address 192.168.1.188 removed due to enabling
VRF management
```

That's sort of a drag, but necessary I assume. No matter, I'll just reapply the IP address and all is well. Be prepared for this, because it will always remove the IP address if there's one assigned:

```
Arista(config-if-Vl901)#ip address 192.168.1.188/24
```

With that done, I need to add a default route for the new VRF. Routing is not permitted in the nondefault VRF, so all I can add is a static route, which is fine for management:

```
Arista(config)#ip route vrf management 0/0 192.168.1.1
```

To show how it all works, here's the default routing table with the default route in bold:

```
Arista(config)#sho ip route | beg Gateway
Gateway of last resort:
 S      0.0.0.0/0 [1/0] via 20.0.0.2

 C      20.0.0.0/30 is directly connected, Ethernet2
 C      50.50.50.0/24 is directly connected, Vlan101
```

Here's the routing table for the management VRF I created, with the different default route (and the warning about routing) in bold:

```
Arista(config)#sho ip route vrf management | beg Gateway
Gateway of last resort:
 S      0.0.0.0/0 [1/0] via 192.168.1.1

 C      192.168.1.0/24 is directly connected, Vlan901

! IP routing not enabled
```

With the VRF in place, I can ping using the vrf *vrf-name* keywords inserted directly after the ping command. I prefer the Cisco method that puts the VRF keyword at the end, because I constantly make this mistake, and just adding another keyword at the end is easier than inserting it into the middle of a command. But, after a few times of making the mistake, I've learned to adapt:

```
Arista(config)#ping vrf management 192.168.1.1
PING 192.168.1.1 (192.168.1.1) 72(100) bytes of data.
```

```
80 bytes from 192.168.1.1: icmp_req=1 ttl=255 time=4.79 ms
80 bytes from 192.168.1.1: icmp_req=2 ttl=255 time=1.06 ms
80 bytes from 192.168.1.1: icmp_req=3 ttl=255 time=1.29 ms
80 bytes from 192.168.1.1: icmp_req=4 ttl=255 time=1.34 ms
80 bytes from 192.168.1.1: icmp_req=5 ttl=255 time=1.50 ms

--- 192.168.1.1 ping statistics ---
5 packets transmitted, 5 received, 0% packet loss, time 17ms
rtt min/avg/max/mdev = 1.069/2.001/4.791/1.402 ms, ipg/ewma 4.254/3.357 ms
```

When adding a VRF, the behavior of some common services changes a bit. For the most part, this involves the limitation that they can only reside in one VRF. Not surprisingly, these services are all related to management of the switch. Examples include SNMP, Syslog, TACACS+, NTP, and DNS, all of which should be configured to work within the management VRF.

 Though future versions of EOS will likely support multiple VRFs, for now only one nondefault VRF is supported, and it's really designed for in-band management. Hence the limitations, which really aren't that big of a deal.

Configuring these services is simply a matter of adding the vrf *vrf-name* to the command, again, right after the command itself (not at the end). If you've previously configured these services, then you will be greeted with a message similar to the following when configuring them for the new VRF:

```
Arista(config)#ip name-server vrf management 192.168.1.200
% Nameservers are supported in only one VRF at a time.
   Please unconfigure nameservers from Main VRF before continuing.
```

Once you remove the other name servers, the VRF-enabled version no longer gives a warning:

```
Arista(config)#no ip name-server 192.168.1.200
Arista(config)#no ip name-server 192.168.1.205
Arista(config)#ip name-server vrf management 192.168.1.200
Arista(config)#
```

And now management is separate from the rest of the switch. This is cool because I could reuse the network assigned to management in the default VRF without penalty. In other words, I could also apply the same IP address to another interface. This is a great solution for switches that might reside in a customer's network but need to be managed from within the data center's management scheme.

And Finally...

Because you wouldn't believe me unless I showed you myself, here is the version I'm running first:

```
SW1#sho ver | inc image
Software image version: 4.9.4
```

For your Arista CLI enjoyment:

```
SW1#sho donkeys
Farm utilization for 5 seconds: 0%/0%; 1 minute: 0%; 5 minutes: 0%
 DID S  Ty       DC Runtime(ms) Rides Poops       Hay DKY Donkeyname
   1 M  sp 602F3AF0        0  1627     0 2600/3000   0 Eeyore
   2 F  we 60C5BE00        4   136    29 5572/6000   0 Tingaleo
   3 F  st 602D90F8     1676   837  2002 5740/6000   0 Daisy
   4 M  we 602D08F8        0     1     0 5568/6000   0 Wonky Don
   5 F  we 602DF0E8        0     1     0 5592/6000   0 Dakota
   6 M  st 60251E38        0     2     0 5560/6000   0 Superdonkey
   7 M  we 600D4940        0     2     0 5568/6000   0 Cookie Dough
   8 F  we 6034B718        0     1     0 2584/3000   0 Sandy
   9 F  we 603FA3C8        0     1     0 5612/6000   0 Kekie
  10 M  we 603FA1A0        0  8124     0 5488/6000   0 Shrek
  11 M  we 603FA220        0     9     0 4884/6000   0 BillyJoe-Bob
  12 U  we 60406818      124  2003    61 5300/6000   0 Smokey
  13 M  we 60581638        0     1     0 5760/6000   0 Snickers
  14 M  we 605E3D00        0     2     0 5564/6000   0 D.K.
  15 M  we 605FC6B8        0     2   011568/12000    0 Hee-Haw
```

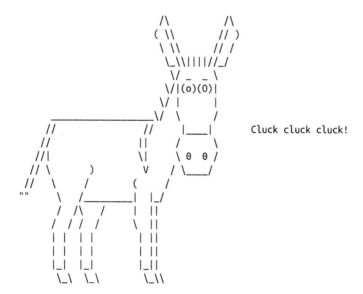

It works on every version I've tried it on, as does show chickens. Try that on a Cisco switch!

Index

Symbols

We'd like to hear your suggestions for improving our indexes. Send email to index@oreilly.com.

About the Author

Gary A. Donahue is a working consultant who has been in the computer industry for 28 years. Gary has worked as a programmer, mainframe administrator, Technical Assistance Center engineer, network administrator, network designer, and consultant. Gary has worked as the Director of Network Infrastructure for a national consulting company and is the president of his own New Jersey consulting company: GAD Technologies.

Colophon

The animal on the cover of *Arista Warrior* is the African Harrier-Hawk (*Polyboroides typus*). It lives in sub-Saharan Africa and sometimes moves seasonally to West Africa. It prefers forest and woodland environments that have some water nearby, and tends to build its home out of sticks in a large gap in trees or in rocky crevices.

The African Harrier-Hawk is a medium-sized bird of prey that grows up to 65 cm in length and has a wingspan of 160 cm. As a young bird, its body color is brown, but as they mature, they become light grey. Other notable physical characteristics of this bird are that the tips of its wings are black with a white stripe in the middle and its belly has thin black and white stripes. It's an effective hunter not only because of its size, but also because of its double-jointed legs, which it uses to take hold of its prey and to climb. It tends to eat small mammals, the eggs of small birds, chicks, reptiles, frogs, and sometimes oil palm fruit.

Typically a silent bird, an adult African Harrier-Hawk has a weak call. It whistles *su-eeeee-ooo* or *suee-suee*, and when near its nest it gives off a high-voiced *wheep-wheep-wheep*. The young in the nest, on the other hand, tend to give off a rapid *ki-ki-ki-ki-ki* sound.

The cover image is from *Wood's Animate Creation*. The cover font is Adobe ITC Garamond. The text font is Minion Pro by Robert Slimbach; the heading font is Myriad Pro by Robert Slimbach and Carol Twombly; and the code font is UbuntuMono by Dalton Maag.

Have it your way.

CPSIA information can be obtained at www.ICGtesting.com
Printed in the USA
BVOW060809101012

302488BV00001B/3/P